What people are saying about
The Balancing Act...

"The authors have achieved a most intriguing and thoughtful work. I could see myself as I read the book—the pulls and trade-offs in my own life and career. The book provided a stimulating and valuable insight into the balancing act that is fundamental to successful leadership."

—James J. Meenan
President and CEO, AT&T Canada, Toronto, Ontario

"The material in this book has been painstakingly prepared and is very well presented. The Praxis Group's sense of humour is evident throughout this work, which makes for easy reading while in no way diluting the important and clearly stated messages it delivers. This is not the 'same old' leadership theory, but rather practical ideas which the Praxis folks have gathered over many years from successful people. These ideas are presented along with the considerable insights of the authors. This is stuff that really works. Over my forty-year career, I have read countless books on leadership, interpersonal communications and managing change. While some good came from that effort, nothing I have previously read comes close to providing the practical help that can be gleaned from *The Balancing Act*."

—Robert H. Whitehead, FCII
Board of Directors, F.H.P. Financial Corporation, Fountain Valley, CA

"*The Balancing Act* is an interesting, thoughtful, and practical approach to a leader's most difficult challenge—how to effectively deal with the complex and competing demands of employees, shareholders, customers, and families. It helps answer the questions to life's difficult 'balancing act.'"

—Nolan D. Archibald
Chairman of the Board, President, and Chief Executive Officer
The Black &Decker Corporation, Towson, MA

"Excellent.... Any business leader who studies and successfully applies these theories and skills will gain a competitive advantage."

—Gerald A. Hines
Chief Operating Officer, AT&T Universal Card Services, Jacksonville, FL

"*The Balancing Act* differs from so many other contemporary management books by providing leaders with practical, applicable advice on improving the culture and leadership effectiveness in their organizations. It is a wonderfully refreshing and useful guide for leaders who are tired of quick fixes and simplistic solutions to complex and competing management problems."

—*Scott Campbell*
Publisher and President, The Columbian, *Vancouver, WA*

"*The Balancing Act* captures years of experience by the authors, drawing on real-life situations with frontline personnel and management of major corporations to give an excellent road map for meeting the challenges of today's changing workforce. Theory and practical applications are combined to provide easy understanding of the concepts presented in this book."

—*Phil Dean*
Manager of Engineering, OG&E Electric Services, Oklahoma City, OK

"Quantum leaps and organizational excellence come only when leadership recognizes the factors which influence motivation and strives to improve these elements rather than employee behavior. If you are ready to connect the dots between your company's culture and the quality of your product, invest in this book."

—*Robert Schrader*
General Manager, Ritz-Carlton Hotel, Kansas City, MO

"*The Balancing Act* is a 'must have' resource for leaders who realize that healthy organizations withstand the strength of competitors more effectively. It is filled with valuable, thought-provoking, and simple-to-implement theories and strategies that can maximize organizational vitality and link organizational health to the achievement of competitive differentiation and success."

—*Linda M. Pittenger*
Director, AT&T Business Communications Services, Bedminster, NJ

"Our company reorganized two years ago and we wanted to move into our new marketplace fast. Praxis worked with us from the beginning. We chose them for their innovative, proactive approach to leadership. We are in a business that requires us to customize products for specialty customers. The Praxis approach customized the concepts and ideas to fit our company. *The Balancing Act* works, and I highly recommend it to companies that are looking to embrace constant change and make it an advantage."

—*Courtney C. Smith*
President and Chief Executive Officer, Coregis Group Insurance, Chicago, IL

"I found the material to be refreshing—no simplistic solutions. Rather, it takes the complex topic of leadership and provides clear, practical guidance—all conveyed with a good mix of humor and memorable examples. It reminded me a lot of [Praxis] consulting and training sessions—useful and enjoyable."

—Roger F. Davis
Vice President, AT&T International Finance, Morristown, NJ

"Changing to and maintaining the appropriate culture for an organization can be a difficult and extremely frustrating experience. Finally, a book has arrived that gives leaders and managers a simple but effective tool to help understand culture and the fundamental processes of how to change it. I enjoyed every page, and was extremely pleased with the multitude of teachings and principles. Unlike so many other business books, *The Balancing Act* is not a weekend reader that, once read, will be put on the bookshelf and forgotten. It is truly a GUIDE to mastering change to keep handy for continuous study."

—David W. Rich
Vice President of Human Resources, Browning Arms, Morgan, UT

"[This] book is that rare combination of management theory, anecdotal information, wit, techniques, and examples that is easy to read and makes one eager to start applying the ideas and suggestions. There were times— an example being the discussion of the culture assessment—when I wished I could jump out of my chair and begin applying the information immediately. This will be an excellent reference when I teach my class in environmental management at Denver University this winter."

—Mark N. Silverman
Manager, U.S. Department of Energy–Rocky Flats Field Office, Golden, CO

"I am most impressed by the practicality of the concepts in *The Balancing Act*. It gave me new insights and angles to help improve our bottom line. The Six-Cell Balancing Tool and the formula for Outcome Vitality are extremely useful."

—Michael J. McConville
Corporate Quality Manager
The Shell Company of Australia, Ltd., Melbourne, Victoria

"The text is crisp, insightful, informative, and easy to follow. Rather than viewing the reader as one desiring a cookie-cutter approach, the authors give credit to the reader's ability to digest complex concepts."

—Caryn B. Siebert
General Counsel, Coregis Group Insurance Companies, Chicago, IL

"*The Balancing Act* is an impressive book. It is very timely for today's ever-changing business environment. As the healthcare market continues to change, we are going to find a complex environment where the winners will be those who can BALANCE THE FUTURE. [*The Balancing Act*] certainly provides a road map in that direction. I want to provide all of our Board of Directors with a signed copy."

—*Rod Skaggs, II*
Vice President of Sales, Smith & Nephew United, Inc., Largo, FL

"This book gets at the hard part of leadership—doing it! The thinking is unique, the concepts are fresh, and the book is entertaining and insightful. It passes the ultimate test—it is useful. It you want to read something really innovative in the field of leadership, this is it!"

—*William L. Marré*
CEO Coach/Consultant and Cofounder of the Covey Leadership Center
The William Marré Company, Provo, UT

"[This] book is written in a wonderfully accessible manner for corporate leaders and practitioners under time pressures. I especially appreciate how the book is an example for professionals in walking the talk—that is, how theory intersects with practice. [Praxis'] language discussing the *why* (theory) works well with suggestions regarding the *how* (practice) in a way that is meaningful for me. I found myself overusing my yellow underliner not unlike a college student preparing for his or her exam."

—*Gary Adkins*
Executive Consultant, AT&T Network Services Division, Long Beach, CA

"It's great to have a book written by authors who have 'walked the walk' and who can 'talk the talk.' Having worked with this team, I can say that these ideas *work*."

—*Stephen W. Prough*
President and CEO, Downey Savings & Loan, Newport Beach, CA

"I have been a student of Praxis (specifically, Ron McMillan) for six years or so. His teachings and style of teaching have clearly accelerated my learnings around leadership and organizational effectiveness. I have read a draft overview of *The Balancing Act* and enthusiastically await its publication. I'm certain that I will read it several times, refer to it frequently, and attempt to exercise its learnings daily...for the remainder of my life."

—*Ed Dell*
Financial Vice President, AT&T, Morristown, NJ

THE BALANCING ACT

Mastering the Competing Demands of Leadership

Kerry Patterson

Joseph Grenny

Ron McMillan

Al Switzler

The Praxis Leadership Series

THOMSON EXECUTIVE PRESS
A Division of South-Western College Publishing

Sponsoring Editor: James L. Sitlington
Developmental Editors: Mary Pommert (CEP) and Susan Carson
Production Editor: Holly Terry
Production House: Desktop Editorial Services
Cover and Internal Design: Joseph M. Devine
Marketing Manager: Stephen E. Momper

Copyright 1996
by THOMSON EXECUTIVE PRESS
Cincinnati, Ohio

I(T)P
International Thomson Publishing
Thomson Executive Press, a division of South-Western College Publishing,
is an ITP company. The trademark ITP is used under license.

Library of Congress Cataloging-in-Publication Data:

The balancing act : mastering the competing demands of leadership / Kerry
    Patterson . . . [et al.]
        p. cm. -- (The Praxis leadership series)
    Includes index.
    ISBN 0-538-86139-8
    1. Leadership. I. Patterson, Kerry. II. Series.
HD57.7.B35 1996
658.4'092--dc20

95-40920
CIP

    2   3   4   5   MT   0   9   8   7   6
Printed in the United States of America

Cover Illustration: *The Balancing Act*, James Christensen, copyright 1995
by Greenwich Workshop, 1 Greenwich Place, Shelton, CT 06484.
For information on this and other limited-edition fine art prints, posters,
and books by James Christensen, please call 1-800-243-4246.

Table of Contents

SECTION FOUR

SECTION FIVE

SECTION SIX

Preface

If you're the type who doesn't read introductory material of any kind . . .

If you're one of those individuals who considers reading introductions a sign of weakness, jump ahead to something that captures your interest—you're going to, anyway. Set aside the preface for one of those days when your flight to Cleveland is delayed on the tarmac, you've already read everything in the pocket in front of you (including the barf bag), and the woman in 4C won't sell you her *USA Today*.

If you're the type who prefers an introduction, you probably have a number of questions, such as:

- Where did you get this stuff?
- Another book on leadership?
- What is this book about?
- What makes this book different?

Where Did You Get This Stuff?

Before we rolled up our sleeves and began to study people at work, we developed a careful methodology for learning what separated effective from ineffective leaders. One of the starting points happened over 15 years ago when one of the authors ascended through the dank stairwell leading from his research cubicle tucked away in the basement of Stanford's business school to visit Al Rush, a colleague who occupied one of the more senior doctoral student offices aboveground.

Captain, My Captain

Al's story is an interesting one. Five years earlier, as a young lieutenant serving under Admiral Zumwalt (of navy fame), Al had been ordered
to prepare a class to help newly appointed captains run a successful
command. Some challenge. Asking a lieutenant to lecture a group of
captains is like asking a choirboy to call the pope to repentance. Besides, what did Al know about being a successful captain? He was still
trying to figure out how to be a successful lieutenant.

Although Al wasn't very senior in the navy, he came up with a clever
methodology for studying captains at work. Al surmised that the only
way to really learn about captains was to spend time observing them on
the job. He knew if he simply interviewed them, he'd be regaled with a
string of semifictitious success stories and learn little of what they
actually did. He also predicted that simply observing captains might,
if anything, be overwhelming. Watching leaders at work would provide
such a morass of data, it might be impossible to divine which of the tens
of thousands of behaviors he observed led to success and which led to
failure.

Who Are Ewe?

At this point Al came up with a creative solution. He asked the navy to
supply him with two pools of captains—one with high and one with low
fitness reports. If the names were mixed and he could sort the "sheep"
from the "goats" after spending time talking to, observing, and otherwise hanging around them and their staffs, it would have to be based
on something he saw in their behavior. This "something" he could share
with those interested in knowing what made good captains "good."

And then Al came up with another superb idea. Nobody really wanted
to learn how to separate "sheep" from "goats." Horror stories of what
not to do abounded. But what if he was supplied with a list that contained 10 of the *best* captains in the entire navy mixed with 10 who
received *good* marks? Comparing the top 1 percent with the top 10 percent would force him to distinguish what made the "best" the "best"
rather than what made the "best" better than "good" or "mediocre." If
he could discern the "best" from the "good," he'd have a fascinating
story to tell.

Could he separate the "best" from the "good"? When Al first proposed his methodology, many of his colleagues doubted whether there
would be readily observable differences between individuals who were
so similar in performance. Sure, if you stand the brilliant next to the

bedraggled, even a raw recruit could point out the disparity, but stand a hotshot next to a high performer, and they might look like twins.

A Tough Test

Al faced a challenge similar to the Gileadites who (in the throes of battle with their enemies the Ephraimites some 3,000 years earlier) found that their foes were so similar in dress, language, and stature that it was almost impossible to tell them from their own soldiers. After the Gileadites had defeated the Ephraimites and taken control of the passes leading to the Ephraimites' homeland, the Ephraimites (who were apparently more creative in defeat than effective in battle) suddenly claimed to be Gileadites as they tried to get past the Gileadite guards. After all, who could tell them apart without a passport?

Eventually someone pointed out that the Gileadites pronounced the word *shibboleth* (meaning corn) with an *sh* sound, whereas the now invisible Ephraimites "could not frame to pronounce it right" (Judges 12:6). (Apparently, when the Ephraimites went on a picnic, they asked for "sibboleth," not "*sh*ibboleth," on the cob.) It didn't take a chariot scientist to come up with a solution. So each soldier was asked to pronounce the word *shibboleth*, and the 42,000 Ephraimites who uttered "sibboleth" were killed. (And we think "Jeopardy" is tough.)

Over the years, the word *shibboleth* has come to mean a quick test that distinguishes one group or individual from another. That's precisely what Al was attempting to find—only he was searching for shibboleths that could be used to separate the good from the brilliant captains.

Subtle, But Not Invisible

Al's proposed methodology worked. He discovered that it typically only took a few hours of intensive observations and interviews to discern what separated the "best" from the "good." Much to the surprise of the skeptics, he was able to predict to which pool each captain belonged. Al learned that the "best" went about their business in ways that were distinctive. They chose different words, delivered them with a different style, and behaved in other ways that differentiated them from their colleagues. The differences were almost always subtle, but they existed nevertheless.

When Al eventually developed the captain's course, not only did he have detailed advice to offer, but as word spread of his methodology, he had the captains' undivided attention. Lieutenant or not, he had discovered valuable senior-officer shibboleths. His inventive design inspired our research methodology, and to this day it remains our primary tool for identifying leadership skills.

Sharing Leadership Excellence

Although we haven't always had the luxury of entering companies and conducting *formal* research, our team continually examines people at work by standing the "best" next to the "good" and probing for differences. *The Balancing Act* presents our findings. It lays out the results of both formal research and informal observations. It holds a magnifying glass to people at work and probes into their subtle acts of effective leadership. It sits in a kitchen corner and pokes into the nonverbal behaviors of parents as they struggle to negotiate study habits with their teenagers. It bores into boardrooms and peeks at the interpersonal strategies of chief executives as they attempt to persuade midlevel managers to reorder their priorities.

To date we've probed, poked, and peeked into hundreds of corporations, volunteer organizations, and government agencies. We've roamed in facilities ranging from sweltering, fire-belching foundries that Dante could well have been describing in his "Inferno" to the pristine, Orwellian "clean rooms" found on high-tech campuses. In each location, we collected shibboleths, recorded them on both paper and videotape, and demonstrated them in workshops, classes, and training sessions. With each iteration of research and its subsequent round of criticism, we've honed our findings.

The Balancing Act recounts what we've learned. It shares shibboleths taught to us by leaders who, in spite of competing demands, turbulent times, and the unrelenting cry for change, have managed to keep their balance. We dedicate this book to the well-balanced leaders, from shop-floor stewards to corporate presidents, who have taught us so much.

Another Book on Leadership?

Leadership theory has been taught to death. Early philosophers launched into the field millennia ago, and there's been a steady stream of offerings ever since. And yet, in all of the forays into the world of leadership, little has been said about what leaders are supposed to do on a Thursday afternoon. The reason for the lack of practical advice is quite simple. Few have carefully examined what effective leaders actually do, and, more importantly, few have studied what highly skilled professionals do that makes them different from their less-effective colleagues. One glance into the topics of popular leadership texts reveals a simple truism. Contemporary authors write about what leaders *should* achieve rather than *how* to achieve it.

This book breaks out of that mold by sharing the hands-on skills of effective leadership *and* the theories behind them. True to the series's title (*praxis* means "the practical application of theory"), we carefully blend the best of theory with how each set of ideas plays itself out in day-to-day life. The book distills our years of working in real situations with leaders across dozens of industries, while simultaneously teaching leadership theory. The result of this dual effort is a compilation of writings that shares the best of leadership theories, values, and actions.

What Is This Book About?

In a nutshell, this book is a guide for:

- Keeping Your Balance
- Surviving Turbulence
- Changing Culture
- Supporting the Thinking Leader
- Dealing with Today's Tough People-Problems

A Guide for Keeping Your Balance

As this book's subtitle suggests, our desire is to help leaders master the competing demands of leadership. The emphasis is on complexities. This is not another single-issue book. We are not going to tell you to "just take care of customers" or to "throw all of your efforts into reengineering." Instead, our goal is to help leaders balance the complex and competing demands of employees, shareowners, customers, families, government agencies, communities—and anybody else who wants a piece of their hide. It's written to individuals who feel like the overworked character James Christensen so cleverly portrayed on the dust jacket of this book.

After more than two decades of working with leaders, we've gained a deep appreciation for the pressures they face every day. Many scholars and critics prefer to cast stones at those who head organizations, departments, and teams. Employees have been taking shots for years, so why not join the club? We take a different approach. Our goal is to help leaders deal with the unprecedented task of serving stakeholders who are becoming frighteningly demanding within an environment that is becoming increasingly competitive. This crunch has led many to a lifestyle that is not only pressure filled but remarkably imbalanced. In addition to the fact that organizations continue to fail at an alarming rate, careers are becoming all-consuming; peace of mind is often a luxury; and families and personal lives are taking a real hit.

Many leaders, after taking a long, hard look at today's daunting complexities, have opted for a conservative approach. They've chosen, usually with great anxiety, to focus on a single variable rather than on many. Typically they've devoted their attention to financial results— even if their decisions have had a negative impact on employees or even customers. After all, they've reasoned, better to keep one ball in the air than drop them all.

You can't work side by side with leaders who are routinely attacked for being too focused on the bottom line without realizing that *motive* is rarely an issue. Leaders *want* to serve everyone. In fact, when faced with tough choices, most look like parents trying to save their own children after a boat capsizes. They desperately scramble to keep everyone afloat. Nobody revels in rescuing one soul while another drifts away or sinks. Leaders don't take joy in satisfying *investors* by alienating their *employees* any more than they take pleasure in serving *customers* by despoiling the *community*.

Unfortunately, motive alone isn't enough.

We write this book to those courageous leaders who *want* to do it all but don't always know *how* to do what it takes. The good news is that there's a great deal of knowledge available to help leaders successfully manage competing demands. We try to share some of that knowledge. We start by looking at ways to diagnose imbalances in order to catch them early on—*before* they get out of hand. We explore ways to develop continuous and easy-to-gather measures. Ultimately (and this part takes up the bulk of this book), we share methods for designing and implementing evenhanded change efforts. The emphasis is on designing and delivering interventions that develop whole solutions to deep-seated problems rather than ones that momentarily satisfy one stakeholder while other stakeholders are left unattended and are eventually sucked into the whirling eddy of neglect.

A Guide for Surviving Turbulence

This book is for leaders who are not only continually trying to balance competing demands but who have to do so within a whirling, spinning environment. It's for those of you who liken your job to tuning up a car while it continues to race along the freeway at 65 miles per hour. You have to change things, but you don't have the luxury of pulling your car over to the side of the road, bringing it to a halt, and working at your leisure. You're in a race, for crying out loud. Customers want your products and services, and they want them now. If you hope to change things, you're going to have to do it on the run.

As we explore typical forms of imbalance (such as too much individualism or inadequate attention to costs), we'll suggest methods for dealing with hot issues without having to turn the entire organization on its ear. By focusing on hands-on skills rather than massive, pipe-dream results, we'll help leaders take away usable chunks they can fit into their already jammed schedules.

A Guide for Changing Culture

The Balancing Act is written to those of you who are interested in doing more than simply chipping away at the surface. It's for leaders who want to change the ways they're currently going about doing business—at the core. For example, it's for people who want to know how to shift to teams. Not just what it takes to dub semihostile groups with the label *team*, but what it really takes to encourage living human beings to embrace the principles and practices of teamwork.

We've divided the culture-change process into six sections.

- In section 1 we'll explore a culture's most important characteristic—its vitality. We'll carefully examine what differentiates vital from average and nearly dead organizations. We'll develop our primary tool for understanding culture—the heart, hands, and mind of the individual decision maker.

- In section 2 we'll explore how to take stock. It starts by exploring techniques for spinning a dream. What culture do you want and why? Next, it examines how to get a handle on your current culture. Just how far away are you from your dream? It handles culture analyses in two steps: (1) how to conduct an in-depth cultural assessment, followed by (2) a powerful tool for keeping your finger on your company's pulse.

- Having explained how to assess your current state, we'll next develop a powerful model for understanding and influencing behavior. Section 3 focuses on the individual, and we'll examine ways to deal with the gaps you find between your dreams and what people are actually doing.

- In section 4 we'll look at problems that stem from the hackneyed, yet rarely understood, concept of social pressure. After exploring how social forces influence behavior, we'll look at methods for capturing opinion leaders' strength, what it takes to manage symbolic action, and how to make the best use of recognition and praise.
- In section 5 we'll shift to an organization's formal systems. The emphasis will be on steps leaders can take to align their systems with their vision and to use their nonhuman factors to influence change.
- Finally, in section 6 we'll look at what leaders can do to breathe life into the theories and practices we can only describe. The focus will be on "next steps."

A Guide for Supporting the Thinking Leader

To teach the wide-ranging skills required to master the complex and competing demands of leadership, *The Balancing Act* extends beyond topics typically taught in business schools. It shares the best practices offered in anthropology, psychology, organizational theory, and drama—to name but a few disciplines. We'll work hard to make complex subjects and theories clear, not simple.

We won't develop five quick steps to help leaders swim with sharks, manage with Attila, win through intimidation, or dress for success. Instead, we'll offer complex, yet practical, theories to leaders who would rather spend time diving deep into what it really takes to bring about change than water-ski across the surface of shallow, but short-lived, solutions.

A Guide for Dealing with Today's Tough People-Problems

Throughout the book, we'll deal with imbalances that have taken years to develop. We'll explore options and solutions for challenges that leaders face every day. For example, employees are demanding to be empowered, but you're not quite sure how empowerment differs from abdication of responsibility. You've seen organizations that have tried to move decision making lower in the organization only to create false expectations.

You're trying to create a learning environment. You'd love to see information, both good and bad news, move rapidly through the organization. However, you're suspicious that people just tell you what they think you want to hear. You're trying to become more customer oriented, but you aren't sure everyone really buys in to the vision. Your engineers, accountants, skilled tradespeople, and other professionals have seen customer initiatives in other organizations and are skeptical. They didn't go through years of training so they could one day kiss up to *anyone*.

You'd like to see your company become more team-oriented but don't want to lose the strength of individual initiative and creativity. You've heard expressions such as "There's no *I* in *team*" and worry about swinging the pendulum from too much emphasis on the individual to too much emphasis on groups. The people you work with don't trust each other. Cynicism fills the air like a stench rising off the carcasses of failed change efforts. You don't expect individuals to cast their eyes upon you and other leaders with the same look typically reserved for Mother Teresa, but they shouldn't call you self-serving pencil-necks either.

What Makes This Book Different?

Praxis — The Practical Application of Theory

We care a great deal about theory—enough so that we've incorporated concepts, notions, models, and algorithms from the best there is and created a fair number of our own. Of course, we stand on the shoulders of giants when it comes to theory. We owe a great debt to scholars such as Albert Bandura, Everett Rogers, and Solomon Asch.[1] We respect their work and give them credit for their monumental contribution to organizational theory.

What makes us a bit different from your average academic is that we're equally passionate about practical applications. Since we spend almost all of our waking consulting hours working with leaders, we're interested in how the theories inform leaders to act on a Thursday afternoon.

Everything we cover in this book has been tested by leaders. We didn't prepare to write by cloistering ourselves in an ivory tower and dreaming up mind-stretching, but risky, ideas. Instead, virtually everything we share has been tested for over 20 years by leaders in dozens of organizations. We thank them for jointly learning with us.

By combining the brilliant work of academics like Albert Bandura of Stanford University with the practical knowledge of Patrice Lincoln (a frontline supervisor working a production line in a steel plant), we make every effort to come up with ideas that pass the test of *praxis*—the practical application of theory.

Balance

Leaders are often portrayed as heartless number crunchers who are driven by the bottom line, or as humanitarians who wouldn't know a bottom line if it bit them. Skilled leaders don't make such simplistic mistakes. They balance their interest in the bottom line with a deep appreciation for people. They realize that careers built on the backs of people are narrow and unfulfilling. They also understand that they're not in the business of designing workplaces that feel more like country clubs than work settings.

We'll go to great pains throughout this book to link our recommendations (even ones that sound quite people oriented) to the bottom line. We won't ask leaders to step off solid platforms supported by hard numbers into the cotton-candy world of happy thoughts and posters that ask, "Have you hugged your employees today?" Instead, we'll explore how people can be brought together in a shared effort to satisfy customers, shareowners, themselves, and others.

Oh yes, and we'll try to have fun along the way. We've made every effort to include engaging stories and exercises to help lighten the load—and for good reason. We've chosen not to reduce complex human interactions into simple rote steps. We've avoided the temptation to compress intriguing, and often subtle, interactions into a handful of fortune-cookie concepts. We've even fought the urge to spout words (maybe even syllables) to live by. Instead, we've hunkered down and wrestled with theories of some heft. And while we were duking it out with cognitive psychologists, anthropologists, and philosophers, we found a way to laugh along the way. After all, if you haven't stared Freud in the face and had a good chuckle, you haven't really lived.

Acknowledgments

*We dedicate this book to the hundreds of leaders in
all levels of organizations who, over the last 20 years,
have helped us come to appreciate the complexities
of life in the trenches and the enormous results
that can be achieved by those who can perform
the balancing act.*

The list of people, theorists, clients, employees, friends, and family members to whom we owe thanks is large.

Special thanks to the leaders and human resources professionals at AT&T; Ford Motor Company; HealthTrust, Inc.; Saturn Corporation; Coregis Insurance Group; AT&T Universal Card Services; and OG&E Electric Services. Not only have they worked side by side with us on comprehensive and challenging change processes, they have become cherished friends.

To our families we express love and appreciation. We've received enormous support—as can be inferred from the many names included here—Louise, Christine, Rebecca, Taylor, Scott, Celia, Aislinn, Cara, Seth, Samuel, Hyrum, Becky, Amber, Megan, Chase, Hayley, Bryn, Linda, Meridith, Lindsey, Kelley, and Todd.

To our staff and colleagues at Praxis, much thanks. We're particularly grateful to those who have helped test our ideas through consulting, training, teaching, and research—Larry Myler, Mark Atkinson, Quinn McKay, John Stoker, Glade Tuckett, Dave Tippetts, Rick Olsen, Juan Riboldi, Paul Forsythe, Daryl Guiver, and Michael Thompson.

Also to Jim Sitlington at Thomson Executive Press and his associates, Mary Pommert at Custom Editorial Publications, Susan Carson, Joe Devine, Holly Terry, and Cheryl Thornes, thank you.

A special thanks to a magical artist, James Christensen, for the wonderful, all-too-true character found on the dust jacket.

To Mel Broberg, Lyle Fletcher, Peggy Olsen, Kevin Sheehan, and Amber Schmidt, who spent more time poring over this document than is legal in most states—you're the best.

So many have helped us over the years that we add a final large, admittedly blanket, thanks to our many colleagues, friends, teachers, and associates.

About the Authors

Kerry Patterson began his research into the challenges of developing and maintaining healthy organizations during his doctoral work at Stanford University. He left Stanford to teach in the Graduate School of Management at Brigham Young University. He cofounded Interact Performance Systems, where he worked for 10 years as the Vice President of Research and Development. He has delivered culture-change interventions at Ford Motor Company, Intermountain Health Care, and Allstate, among others. His award-winning, video-based training initiatives in problem solving, conflict resolution, teamwork, performance management, and ethics have been used successfully by hundreds of companies throughout the Fortune 500. He is a prolific writer and has coauthored articles and training programs on interpersonal skills, culture change, teamwork, and dialogue.

Joseph Grenny holds a degree in International Relations from Brigham Young University. He was president of California Computer Corporation for six years and an executive for Covey Leadership Center for six years. In his dozen-plus years of organization development consulting, he has taught thousands of leaders in state and federal governments and in hundreds of midsize to Fortune 10 corporations. He works closely with senior executives to design and implement long-term change efforts. He has authored and coauthored numerous articles in the areas of personal and organizational effectiveness. He has designed and delivered major culture-change initiatives for the State of California, AT&T, IBM, and corporations facing deregulation and reorganization.

Ron McMillan holds advanced degrees in sociology and organizational behavior. He cofounded Covey Leadership Center and was Vice President of Research and Development there for seven years. He researched, codesigned, and codelivered a comprehensive leadership development program which, to date, has benefitted over 40,000 executives and managers at AT&T. Clients include Browning Arms, Saturn Division of GM, the U.S. Army Corps of Engineers, Hewlett-Packard, Intel, Procter & Gamble, Westinghouse, the U.S. Air Force, Aetna, Disney, and many other organizations. For the past 19 years he has taught and consulted around topics including team development, personal vitality, corporate culture, quality improvement, and paradigm shifting. He has worked with a broad variety of groups, ranging from union and first-level managers to CEOs and corporate executives.

Al Switzler is on the faculty of several programs at the Executive Development Center, University of Michigan. He taught in the Graduate School of Management at Brigham Young University where he received the first "Innovation in Teaching" award and was selected as MBA Professor of the Year. He has taught at Auburn University and the University of Kentucky, receiving awards for outstanding teaching at each. He has served as president of two consulting firms, as Vice President of Marketing for an information firm, and as Director of Training and Management Development for a health-care organization with over 11,000 employees. Over 250 public and private organizations have profited from his broad knowledge of leadership, teamwork, quality, communication, management, marketing, motivation, and personal achievement. Clients include Westcorp, Ford Motor Company worldwide, the U.S. Department of Energy, and OG&E Electric Services.

Each of the authors is a cofounder and partner in The Praxis Group. Their high-energy, humorous, and personable teaching styles and their wide range of business expertise make them highly sought after as consultants and designers and as keynote, conference, and executive-retreat-speakers and facilitators.

About Praxis

praxis\prak-sis\n, [from the Greek, doing, action]: *the practical application of theory to improve personal and organizational effectiveness*

Praxis is a full-service organizational development firm that specializes in management and culture-change consulting, research and development, diagnostic and measurement tools and services, and the training of personal, interpersonal, and organizational skills. Consisting of both The Praxis Group and The Praxis Institute, the firm creates and delivers a full line of products and services that touch every aspect of an organization's development needs. The Praxis Diagnostic Center provides worldwide, full-service custom and standard survey work. The Praxis survey software and training package, Corporate*Pulse*™, allows organizations to bring survey design, administration, and reporting in-house at great savings.

As its name suggests, Praxis applies multidisciplinary theory and practical experience to complex organizational challenges to achieve its mission of helping organizations improve their individual, team, and organizational vitality. Praxis partners with corporate and organizational leaders in diagnosing, designing, implementing, and measuring positive change. More than 300 Fortune 500 companies and numerous organizations large and small have successfully used products and services produced by Praxis professionals.

The Praxis library of dynamic, off-the-shelf training initiatives, including *The Path of Dialogue*, *Advanced Dialogue*, *Personal Vitality*, *Leading Effective Meetings*, *The Foundations of Effective Teamwork* (Quality Process), *Managing Performance*, and *Culture Assessment*. Praxis also provides lightly to highly customizable training modules on a variety of management and interpersonal skill topics. Praxis products and services are represented by a network of trained and certified Praxis Associates located throughout the United

States and in many other countries. The Praxis Leadership Week and the Praxis University provide outstanding learning retreat opportunities to attendees from around the world.

The Praxis Group and The Praxis Institute
55 North University Avenue, Suite 225
Provo, Utah 84601
(801) 373-2233
(801) 373-8884 Fax
e-mail: praxgrp@ix.netcom.com

Finding a Balance

Section 1 lays the groundwork for *The Balancing Act*. It explores what leaders must do to successfully run the gauntlet of today's ever-increasing competition—without losing a limb in the process. It examines the *what* of leadership—what needs to be accomplished, measured, and influenced. In section 1 you'll discover the principles of balance, influence, and praxis.

Balance: The Primary Work of a Leader

After reading chapter 1, you'll know what it takes to create and maintain a vital, balanced, forward-moving organization. You'll understand what we refer to as the Death-to-Vitality Continuum and be able to put your finger on where your company stands and in which direction it's headed. You'll know what vital organizational cultures look like, what they need, and what surprising differences separate robust companies from unhealthy ones. Most important, you'll know where to spend your time so you can create long-term security for yourself and your people.

Influence: The Central Core of Vitality

Chapter 2 dives deep into why your employees, customers, investors, and other stakeholders do what they do. It examines why people give or withhold the resources you need to solve critical business problems. It equips you with an analytical tool for diagnosing root causes and for developing successful action strategies. With the theoretical underpinnings carefully laid out in chapter 2, you'll have access to the future's greatest competitive advantage. **You'll be able to predict and measure your organization's *future* performance instead of merely laboring over measures of *past* performance.**

Praxis: The Practical Application of Theory

Chapter 2 finishes this introductory section with a six-part tool for conducting a balanced diagnosis of your organization's needs and for developing, designing, and delivering plans for balanced action. It explores what leaders should think, feel, and do to guarantee a vital future. With this tool you'll be able to understand what's really going on in your organization and what steps you can take to bring about lasting change. With engaging stories, quotes, and facts, thorough analyses, hands-on applications, and a generous sprinkle of humor, you'll actually enjoy learning how to be a vital, positive force in your company's future.

C H A P T E R   1

Introducing the Balancing Act

balance—noun—a state of equilibrium; a harmonious or satisfying arrangement of parts or elements

The whimsical character found on the dust jacket of this book represents every leader we've ever known. They're all desperately trying to keep a precarious balance. Of course, leaders don't exactly struggle with broccoli, alarm clocks, and cake, but the challenge is the same. They must find a way to keep the competing demands of a host of stakeholders in balance. It isn't easy. No sooner do leaders handle an irate workforce than customers put the squeeze on for better features. No sooner are customers put to rest than owners demand increased profits. To get a feel for this never-ending balancing act, we begin with an early childhood experience of one of the authors. Here's his story.

That's What I Do for a Living!

About once a year on the old "Ed Sullivan Show," typically wedged between Topo Gigio and the Red Army Chorus, a fellow would balance spinning plates on the end of thin, long, flexible rods. After shattering a couple of plates just for show, he would then place one on the end of a pointed rod and spin it until it sat atop the wooden stick like a hovering, porcelain Frisbee. Just getting *one* to spin at the end of a rod was impressive. Then came another rod and plate, and he started over again. The frenetic fellow would keep adding plates until the first one would be spinning so slowly that it seemed only moments away from crashing to the floor. "Look out!" viewers would yell from their living room couches, "It's going to fall." Off he would dash to the first plate, giving it a gentle flick or two until it was spinning anew. The showman continued this routine until he finally had most of the stage filled with spinning plates. It was a breathtaking show of balance.

One June evening in 1953, as I sat in my Red Ryder pajamas watching the fellow for the first time, my mother took the time to teach an object lesson. "Do you see those plates?" she asked. (See them? I was riveted to them!) "They're sort of like the universe—everything spinning, everything hanging in a careful balance. That's how the stars and planets are—and atoms too. Everything, from the earth you stand on to the material making up the eyes in your head, hangs precariously in a vacuum, held aloft in a tenuous equilibrium—more or less like those plates."

The whole idea gave me the willies. Surely this near-impossible balance couldn't last. It was one thing to watch a plate crash to the stage, but what if the cosmic balance were disrupted? What if someone sneezed and activated a cataclysmic and irreversible chain of events? One weird *achoo!* and the known universe might collapse in on itself until all matter was compressed into a single black hole the size, shape, and color of my Uncle Vic's bowling ball. In the new high-gravity environment, 10 trillion Empire State buildings would fit on the head of a pin, and nobody would ever be able to slam-dunk a basketball again.

As I grew older, still thinking about a near-infinite number of spinning, revolving orbs, I couldn't help but wonder why it is that everything important except humans spins around something. It seemed incongruous that those of us who are made of spinning particles (and who live on the surface of a whirling sphere) don't orbit around each other in a human version of the balancing act. Humans, I concluded, were the exception to nature's rule. At least, that's what I thought when I was a kid.

The Human Parallel

I was abruptly taken back one day to my childhood memories of watching the person we had come to call "the plate guy." I recalled that as my mom was metaphorically linking the spinning plates to the universe, my father had dolefully chimed in with, "That's what I do for a living."

Obviously he didn't spin plates, so I dismissed his comment as a joke—
although he was hardly smiling at the time.

I probably never would have thought of the matter again were it not
for a heated argument I found myself pulled into some 20 years later.
While I was trying to settle a quarrel between six angry employees, two
rather aggressive suppliers, and a committee person who had biceps
the size of whole roast turkeys, Dad's comment came to mind. In a burst
of insight, I understood what he had meant. He'd been a frontline supervisor in a production facility at the time he muttered his remarks.
Dad, I thought to myself as I frantically tried to satisfy three competing groups of angry people, *You were right. A leader's job is a balancing act.*

Ironically, most leaders miss this point. They never comprehend that
the central task of leadership involves bringing competing forces into
equilibrium. Most are so caught up in the immediate task of shipping
300 units out the door (or trying to hit a certain profit target) that they
don't take the time to step back and look at what their job is really about.
Leadership is *not* about production (e.g., scheduling parts shipments
on every tick of the clock). It's about bringing people together and creating a common bond. It's about bringing together diverse groups of
people, each with a different set of expectations and list of demands,
and arriving at a state of equilibrium. More specifically, leadership is
an act of balancing competing *wills*.

Juggling *wills*—now *there's* a challenge that makes the plate act seem
almost simple in comparison.

After all the arguments about profits, shipping schedules, and quality
measures settle to a quiet hush, the insightful leader realizes that
leadership is not about managing *things*. It's about balancing intan-
gible, highly ethereal, and mostly ephemeral constructs known as *wills*.

Why Worry about Wills?

Over the past few years, the thoughts and dreams of employees have
been given a great deal of attention. This focus on what people think
and care about started not long ago when John Kotter and James Heskett
produced some groundbreaking research by studying 207 companies—
trying to determine what led to success.[1] When the smoke cleared from
their intense study, they found that success in the marketplace could
be predicted by using a single variable.

In the high-performing companies, if you were to stop the average employee and ask, "What's really important around here?" you'd get an answer such as "Our customers, our margins, our community, *and* our people." Performance-enhancing cultures expressed value for multiple stakeholders—owners, customers, and employees. In the low-performing companies, one stakeholder was emphasized at the expense of the others. Usually the single focus was on the owner.

STAKEHOLDER BALANCE

stakeholder—noun—one who has an interest in an enterprise

Imagine. Success was predicted not by intellectual prowess, financial strength, or even technical expertise. Instead, it was based on employees' willingness and ability to manage multiple stakeholders. If the guy who ran the forklift out back thought in terms of *and* instead of *or*, the company was much more likely to be successful.

Our own research over the past two decades has turned up the same result. Healthy organizations are led by leaders who understand that their future is tied up in four distinct *stakeholder* groups. Unless each stakeholder is satisfied with the *net value* of the relationship, it's all over. That is, in the exchange of resources, the value each stakeholder relinquishes must be matched or exceeded by the value each receives in return. If not, they walk. Here's how it works.

- **Customers.** Those buying the product must be satisfied that the money they're giving up is more than matched by the features and benefits of the product or service (i.e., what they get is worth what they paid for it).
- **Employees.** Those completing the work must be satisfied that their pay and benefits, sense of camaraderie, personal satisfaction, recognition, and so on adequately compensate the effort they're required to expend (i.e., the sacrifices they make are worth the total value received).
- **Investors.** Those loaning the money to get the venture started or keep it growing must be comfortable that the value the money might bring them in other expenditures is matched or exceeded by the benefits of a particular investment (i.e., the financial returns are worth the risk).

- **Others.** Local communities, government agencies, suppliers, and anybody who can shout, "Death to corporate scum!" must be satisfied that what they get out of the arrangement more than makes up for any sacrifices in air and water quality, landscape beauty, traffic patterns, and health (i.e., the contribution to the community is worth the various costs).

It Gets Worse

If satisfying four different stakeholders isn't enough, consider the fact that none of the groups is independent of the rest. Actually, they're more or less pitted against one another. Typically, they fight over fixed resources—which wouldn't be so bad if *all* resources weren't fixed. Quite simply, if a dollar is given to one stakeholder, it has to be taken from another. This, as you might suspect, doesn't happen without a great deal of bickering.

Consider what takes place when a company earns an extraordinary profit. Investors want an increased dividend, bosses want bonuses, employees request a raise, communities cry for a piece of the action, and customers demand either a price cut or a rebate. A leader's job is to balance these competing demands. When company profits take a turn for the worse, the balancing act is that much more difficult.

Here's what it all comes down to. When a leader is through working his or her magic, all stakeholders must sit back, weigh in their own minds the consequences of continuing the venture relative to what they're asked to give, and conclude that it's worth it. A leader must do what it takes to encourage competing stakeholders to willingly continue the relationship.

Three Out of Four Doesn't Cut It!

A nervous patient, worried about an upcoming operation, asks his doctor, "Will I really be okay?" "Don't worry," suggests the surgeon, "it's a simple procedure." "I know you say it's simple, but just put me at ease. When the operation is over, will my heart pump blood, my brain process information, my lungs breathe air, and my liver function?" "Of course," responds the physician, "but if I run into trouble, would you prioritize those for me?"

So far we've suggested that a leader's job is to continually find a way to balance competing stakeholder demands. We've likened the job of bringing competing wish lists into equilibrium to a balancing act. As compelling as this comparison is, it doesn't adequately capture the sometimes gut-wrenching, ulcer-inducing tension foisted upon the leader who continually runs the stakeholder gauntlet. Unlike the whimsical character found on the dust jacket (who might drop a slice of cake should he lose control), leaders face more serious consequences if they lose their balance. With living, breathing stakeholders the stakes run higher.

To expand the balancing metaphor, we're reminded of Robert Grunbers, a juggler the authors once saw in Venice Beach, California. He started his juggling act by tossing the usual balls and pins, then added a bowling ball, an egg, and an apple. If he dropped any of these items, the consequences were pretty benign. He scraped off a little sand and went on with the act. Then came the part that seems more like the balancing act required of leaders. Mr. Grunbers reached down and fired up three small chain saws and deftly tossed them in the air—blades whirling, teeth spinning. Here was a symbol of contemporary leadership. One dropped or forgotten component and *slice, chop*—incredibly bad things happen.

When it comes to stakeholders, if you lose one, the enterprise isn't simply hamstrung or perhaps wounded—it's usually dead. *Satisfying three out of four isn't good enough.* As was the case with the nervous patient who insisted that all of his vital organs be kept healthy, savvy leaders look upon stakeholder health with the same degree of concern. If *one* walks away from the venture, *all* fail. *All* must be satisfied that they're getting what they want out of the enterprise, or it's only a matter of time until the venture collapses.

It's little wonder that if one group starts to show signs of dissatisfaction, leaders have been known to be forced into a deadly slide.

When the Balance Is Lost

A reactionary is a somnambulist walking backwards.

FRANKLIN D. ROOSEVELT

Since the consequences of alienating a stakeholder are so severe, it is little wonder that leaders often act so quickly, dramatically, and decisively that they end up looking more like reactionaries than responsible stewards. To deal with symptoms of a dissatisfied stakeholder, leaders end up using expedient, but imbalanced, tactics. Fleeing customers are attracted back with more promises and lower prices. Or perhaps hemorrhaging financials are stemmed with drastic cost cuts. Maybe exiting employees are offered increased perks and benefits. Whatever the drastic strategy, the good news is that the symptoms usually abate for a time. In fact, Wall Street analysts may even applaud the heroic intervention. The bad news is that anyone who didn't ride in on a turnip truck knows what tomorrow will bring. Like a real-life version of the movie *Groundhog Day*, every time the alarm clock rings, leaders wake up to the same problems again—a dissatisfied stakeholder group knocking on their door.

Consider airline price wars. Rather than being driven by new and more effective ways of doing business, they look more like suicide pacts. One airline, in a desperate act to attract more customers, drops prices to a ridiculous level. Like lemmings, other carriers lower their prices and jump off the same cliff. In a similar vein, more than half of the knee-jerk downsizing efforts we've studied fail to cut costs in the long run. If the spendthrift culture or bloated processes aren't handled, the dismissed employees show up at work the next day as contractors—only at a higher price.

With each round of the dangerous dance, leaders dance with a new partner. As one group of stakeholders is satisfied with a short-term fix, another group becomes alienated. Now the leaders are forced into different, but equally expedient and costly, actions to satisfy a new group of people. The cycle repeats itself over and over again until one day the chain saw drops, and *plop*—a previously healthy career or even company falls to the ground.

Outside Encouragement

Since it's so patently clear that organizations need to avoid pitting one stakeholder against another, you'd think that the clarion call of contemporary scholars would be for moderation and balance. Strangely enough, the opposite seems to be true. Experts from all over the world routinely encourage strategies that purposefully build up one stakeholder at the expense of everyone else. American universities practically give degrees in the topic. Business schools continually graduate MBAs who march forth with a solemn oath to uphold their fiscal duty to owners and shareholders. While achieving profits is a noble and decent goal, it's incomplete.

In a similar display of excess, every decade or so crusaders spew a burst of rhetoric about the all-consuming importance of customers. "Trust us," they argue. "If you just take care of customers, the margins take care of themselves!" Within months, hundreds of desperate leaders rally to the customer cry by forging ahead under the banner of "the customer is always right"—often at the expense of their employees or at the cost of other stakeholder demands. But it doesn't last.

As companies bend over backward to please customers, human-resource professionals soon warn that talented employees are leaving in droves. It's not long until another group of gurus rises from the dust of sagging morale and proclaims the need to "treat employees like your best customers." Again the promise is chanted (with just a quick word-processing edit and update), "Just take care of *employees*, and everything else takes care of itself!" Meanwhile, margins go down the drain. Then what? Leaders circle back and "just" take care of margins again.

What makes this deadly cycle particularly fascinating is that there are so many outside experts offering so many different starting points. The number of narrowly focused change initiatives seems almost endless. We can reengineer, work on our sociotechnical systems, or even our architecture. We can downsize, right-size, or retrofit. If we want to be really trendy, we can create a learning organization, teach the elephants to dance, or even become revolutionaries. Then again, we might even seek a therapeutic dose of quality. Or better still, we can follow the admonition of back-to-basics aficionados who ask us to reimmerse ourselves in the "I think I can" school of organizational change. That's right. When all else is said and done, we can seek a "checkup from the neck up to get rid of some stinkin' thinkin'." Our choices seem limitless. If you want to give one or more stakeholders excessive and costly attention, you can find a long list of experts who will gladly give you a hand.

When Will We Learn?

In spite of the fact that companies and people continue to suffer from myopic, imbalanced strategies, we don't seem to be learning from history. A 1993 *Business Week* cover story hailed the new "horizontal corporation."[2] This is a company in which "customer satisfaction—not stock appreciation or profitability—[is] the primary driver and measure of performance." The assumption is that "the profits will come and the stock will rise if the customers are satisfied."

This kind of simplistic thinking eats at the heart of our political system, social fabric, and organizational health. When we hear values played off each other as if they could be chosen like flavors of ice cream, we're led to conclude that a great number of businesses suffer from a severe case of "value simplicity." Leaders and employees alike prefer "focusing on single issues" over "balancing competing demands."

The leaders of vital organizations, on the other hand, understand the need to serve multiple stakeholders. Their hearts are bigger. They embrace a commitment to the needs and aspirations of all of their key players. And they do it eagerly. They aren't dragged kicking and screaming into this commitment. They make this commitment willingly because they realize that human systems don't work unless all the humans involved feel they're cared for by the system as a whole. And if leaders are good at their job, this attitude soon permeates the entire organization.

For example, Xerox is a marvelous case study of what it takes to restore balance. Leaders saw that the company was struggling, recognized it, made a detailed and long-term plan, and turned the corner. Ford did it too. More recently, Chrysler had one foot in the grave but is now closer to vitality. All are trying to do it through balanced, long-term attempts rather than short-term programs. All are trying to find ways to teach leaders and employees alike to strike a balance with their stakeholders. All have written "value-complex" mission statements that purposefully highlight the importance of each competing constituency.

How these and other companies are finding ways to strike the balance will be covered later on. For now, we just want to make it clear that our intention is not to offer another simple solution to a narrow question. We pledge to keep our eyes wide open to the full complexity of the core job of leaders: building an enterprise that maintains the balance between competing stakeholders.

Our goal in the following pages (and there are more than a few of them—you can't handle complexity with five homilies, a clever case or two, and a fabulous book title) is to sort out the principles from the promises. In an era when so many promises come to leaders in the form of snappy books, tapes, and seminars, the timing is right for a balanced, tested, and more thorough approach. In the remainder of this chapter, we'll identify the features that differentiate the unhealthy organizations from the vital—better yet, the good organizations from the vital ones. Our goal here is to establish the groundwork that we'll use throughout the rest of this book.

THE DEATH-TO-VITALITY CONTINUUM

vitality—noun—full of life, vigor, energy

Let's start with a simple premise. Vitality isn't like pregnancy. Although you can't be half pregnant, you *can* be half vital. Every person, every team, and every organization fits somewhere on the following continuum.

Death   **Vitality**

The Death-to-Vitality Continuum represents a whole range of potential states of health. Some organizations are a lot more alive than others. They're downright vital. Others limp along for years. Completely vital organizations are easy to spot. They achieve positive results even in the face of turbulence and change. They are so filled with life and energy that even serious threats don't push them toward the abyss. Vital organizations have enough reserve that, when faced with the need to change, they can take the time required to go through long-term transformations without losing their competitive standing. Sick, dead, or really close-to-dead companies, on the other hand, are hard to distinguish.

Pygmy Insight

Natives from equatorial Africa have a view of death that suits contemporary organizations quite well. They describe illness in the following stages: hot, fevered, ill, dead, completely dead, and dead forever.[3] Given the use of Chapter 11 and other techniques to avoid collapse, organizational death might well be described in the same way—dead, completely dead, and dead forever.

How Vital Is Your Company?

Although stages of organizational health are neither discrete nor conveniently bundled into separate categories, most leaders have a clear sense of the range. They also understand that every company lies somewhere on the Death-to-Vitality Continuum—and is moving in one direction or the other. Nobody stands still. More importantly, they typically know where their company lies and in which direction it is heading.

The bad news is that precious few leaders know what it is about their company that contributes to its vitality. They have been taught for years that vitality and the traditional measures of profits, quality, safety, and morale are one and the same. These midlevel measures, it turns out, are the wrong ones. They measure neither cause nor effect.

Savvy leaders, on the other hand, have a true sense of vitality. They know it comes in two forms: Outcome Vitality and Cultural Vitality. They know that the results they want to achieve relate to Outcome Vitality. Stakeholders must be satisfied. Consequently, they don't settle for measures that only hint at or vaguely assess stakeholder willingness to continue the relationship. They are tenacious about measuring and influencing the cause. In addition, they have a deep appreciation for Cultural Vitality. They find ways to learn about what's going on in the hearts and minds of their people.

Let's look at each of these two components of corporate health. First, Outcome Vitality.

Outcome Vitality

Although traditional organizations measure vitality in terms of profitability, Statistical Process Control (SPC) charts, or other "technical" measures, we'll describe vitality in terms of human values and assumptions. With a truly vital organization, employees, customers, owners, vendors, and communities are so pleased with what they receive from the transaction that they're delighted to continue with the venture. None are waiting to leap to other suppliers or employers.

Outcome Vitality

The willingness and ability of all stakeholders to continue the relationship; a measure of *future vigor.*

As you might guess from our discussion thus far, Outcome Vitality has four parts. Each represents the net value experienced by one of four stakeholder groups: (1) investors and owners, (2) customers, (3) employees, and (4) all other stakeholders (such as communities and government agencies). Let's examine each in turn.

INV (Investor Net Value) is a measure of the net value the organization provides its owners and other investors. INV is a far more accurate measure of how likely an owner is to *continue* the relationship than traditional earnings figures. Traditional measures such as dividends and stock appreciation only serve as surrogates for owner satisfaction. In some cases they predict net value; in others, they don't. The fundamental question INV answers is "Given that investors have shared with us their precious financial resources, are they receiving enough in return to warrant continuing the relationship?" INV measures what the owners and investors are thinking and feeling about their investment.

CNV (Customer Net Value) measures the degree to which the enterprise is providing the customers with a positive net value. In this, the most salient of all the value exchanges, customers pay money and in return want similar or greater value—which can be measured in quality, cost, delivery, and relationship. The customer is likely to be thinking, "I pay good money. What I want in return is a high-quality product at a good price, delivered when I want it by people who are competent and civil." All of these characteristics are essential to getting and maintaining market share, loyalty, repeat buyers, and customers who will tell their friends. More importantly, all are essential if you expect customers to continue purchasing your products or services. CNV measures what's in the hearts and minds of an essential group of stakeholders.

PNV (People Net Value) is a measure of what employees receive (in pay, benefits, job satisfaction, and other personal rewards) for what they offer in time and effort. In this value exchange, people get paid money. But for the work they put in, they often want more. They want direction, security, opportunities to contribute and grow, etc. The measures can be *hard* (such as employee turnover or the number of grievances) or *soft* (such as perceptions of compensation, learning and growth opportunities, and control over work). PNV extends beyond traditional measures of job satisfaction and morale and goes right to the heart of the matter: "Are employees willing and able to continue the relationship?"

ONV (Other Net Value) reflects a balance that is rarely measured in formal ways. It looks at the net experiences of the remaining stakeholders. ONV explores, among other things, quality-of-life trade-offs. The community receives taxes, employee salaries that are spent in local stores, and other financial benefits. In return, it may give up open roads, clean streams, or healthy air. In some ways, members of the local community share more intimate and vital resources than anyone else involved in the value exchange. The air they breathe, the water they drink, and the accident rate they live with are all generated by local organizations. ONV tends to go unnoticed until the day community members rise up in indignation, show up at the front gate, and demand immediate action.

Outcome Vitality Looks to the Future, Not to the Past

The past is of no importance. The present is of no importance. It is with the future that we have to deal.

OSCAR WILDE

The future isn't what it used to be.

YOGI BERRA

Outcome Vitality is much more future oriented than traditional business measures. In fact, organizations that enjoy high scores on routine corporate-health scales may not be the least bit vital. For example, a high market share may not reflect current Customer Net Value. Market share reflects how customers *used to* feel about the value exchange. If you want to know how well your organization will fare in the future, you'll have to set aside historical artifacts and read the hearts and minds of consumers.

Just look at what happened to the automobile industry a couple of years back. The Japanese were seemingly unstoppable. Then, in an uncharacteristic tirade, a Japanese senator accused American employees of being illiterate and lazy. American consumers were already leery about the loss of an entire industry. Couple this with the fact that American cars were winning quality awards for the first time in a decade, and the insult hurled at the American workforce backfired. At the same time the words were leaving the senator's mouth, an unprecedented shift in buying patterns was occurring. Japanese autos began to lose market share to the Big Three.

Traditional customer-satisfaction measures did not predict such an unprecedented shift. Customary measures of satisfaction revealed that owners were quite satisfied with their Toyotas, Mazdas, Hondas, and Nissans. Interviews with potential customers, on the other hand, uncovered statements such as "We really like the quality in our Japanese vehicle. We like it enough to rank it toward the top, but we think it's about time we give an American product a chance." Customers were looking to buy a car that would help rebuild an industry.

In short, the current net value of each stakeholder group is the best predictor of whether each intends to continue the relationship. Measuring anything other than the net value is dangerous, even though other measures may be simpler and certainly more readily available, given today's measurement tools. Net-value measures, on the other hand, allow leaders to develop strategies based on predictors of intentions rather than summaries of past actions.

A leader's most important short-term report card should be an accurate measure of what he or she has done to ensure the organization's long-term strength. *Leaders should not just be measured by what they achieved yesterday but by what they will achieve tomorrow.* Too many executives, midlevel managers, and frontline supervisors build their careers by accomplishing short-term goals at the expense of long-term effectiveness. Savvy leaders not only continually measure existing results, they also carefully monitor critical stakeholder intentions. They look to the future by supplementing traditional measures with measures of Outcome Vitality.

An Example of What Not to Do

Computer science only indicates the retrospective *omnipotence of our technologies . . . and in no sense a new vision.*

JEAN BAUDRILLARD

Having said that leaders need to get into the heads and hearts of the stakeholders to assess Outcome Vitality, let's take a look at an example of a traditional, imbalanced approach to measurement.

Data, Data Everywhere. Virtually every leader in today's organization pores over the same stack of data. The numbers are different, but the source is the same. Most are convinced that the numbers currently pumped out by their computer are the ones they should be worrying about. Why else would they pore over them? For example, consider an operating committee the authors have worked with for the past five years. They do a fairly good job of measuring the organization's vitality. Let's put it this way—*they do what just about everyone else does.* They routinely meet and discuss how they're doing and what they can do about any problems they see on the horizon. To assist with their analysis, they use piles of data. Their routine printouts literally cover the top of an enormous table. They measure cost, quality, and schedule results—to two or three decimals.

Now, this particular group is made up of smart people who feel comfortable sharing their opinions in an open forum, so a lot of problems are brought to the surface. They don't run off half-cocked when a single measure goes south, nor do they place excessive emphasis on a single score. By today's standards, they're at the top of the heap. However, if they were to take a more focused, formal, and balanced approach (one with more complete stakeholder net-value data), they would have a better picture of their Outcome Vitality.

Using a four-stakeholder, net-value approach, here's how they currently stand in the marketplace.

INV (Investor Net Value). Here they have pretty good numbers, because accounting is a function that every company has. Investors demand accurate, current data. Of course, the leaders still don't know about softer measures such as perceived social contribution or satisfaction with their relationship with the leadership team. Right now, the assumption is that if profit figures are kept at a certain level, investors will be happy. Although the measures of profitability are accurate, they only provide a partial picture.

CNV (Customer Net Value). For this measure, the company relies on vague measures and a theory born out of desperation—as long as vocal complaints are low, we're okay. Their current data consists of a handful of measures of satisfaction, most aimed at product features. They sit in the same position as hotels that ask, "Was the food okay?" without asking, "Did the desk clerk treat you like dirt?" They aren't asking the right questions. Without complete and accurate measures of Customer Net Value, the company is quite vulnerable to the consumer version of a Dear John letter. Everything seems to be going along just fine until one day *bam!*—your customers decide to dance with a different partner. An American car, anyone?

PNV (People Net Value). Like most companies, here too they're not particularly sophisticated. They've done a small employee survey, they do exit interviews, they know how many leave, but much of what is needed remains invisible. In fact, they never even ask employees about their overall willingness and ability to stay in the relationship. How curious.

ONV (Other Net Value). Save for an occasional rumor, newspaper article, or surprise audit, who knows what's going on out there?

So how is the company doing? What should the leaders do to help the company become and remain vital? Given that they've only taken traditional measures, it's not clear.

What should be clear is that if the leaders looked at vital signs that measure stakeholder net value, they would have a more complete and balanced view of their health. INV, CNV, PNV, and ONV are some of an organization's vital signs.

Vital Cultures

The second measure of a leader's effectiveness is found in the behaviors, assumptions, and values of the workforce. Within a vital culture, employees don't just show up to work each day, nor are they merely excited or pleased to be part of the organization. Instead, they eagerly look for ways to continually satisfy competing stakeholder demands. Strangely enough, most organizations assess Cultural Vitality by carefully measuring employee satisfaction—while paying little or no heed to whether employees, satisfied or not, care about doing what it takes to meet stakeholder demands.

If you want to know how well you'll do in the immediate future, measure Outcome Vitality. Ask stakeholders how willing they are to continue the relationship. If you want to measure how likely you are to *sustain* Outcome Vitality, measure Cultural Vitality.

Cultural Vitality

The willingness and ability of employees to meet competing stakeholder demands; a measure of *long-term sustainability.*

Organizational Vitality: An Aggregate Score

The measure of an organization's overall vitality consists of the combined score of Outcome Vitality and Cultural Vitality. Vital organizations have stakeholders who are willing and able to continue the relationship (Outcome Vitality) and a workforce that is willing and able to continue serving each (Cultural Vitality).

A simple way of looking at overall Organizational Vitality is to explore it by using a two-by-two matrix with Outcome Vitality on one axis and Cultural Vitality on the other. The measure of an organization's overall vitality can be demonstrated in the following way:

Box 1. A truly vital organization is found in this box. Existing stakeholders are willing and able to continue the partnership. Existing employees are willing and able to supply stakeholders with what they want.

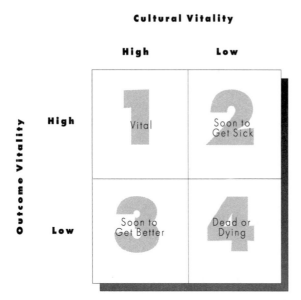

Cultural Vitality

Box 2. This is a dangerous box. Current measures of Outcome Vitality are high. For whatever reason, you've been able to keep all stakeholders satisfied. And yet when you look at your Cultural Vitality, your employees are not willing and able to keep the balance. It's probably only a matter of time until things take a turn for the worse.

Box 3. This organization sits on a precipice. Stakeholder measures are currently low, but the workforce is willing and able to do what it takes to meet their needs. Left to their own, employees would find a way to rejuvenate Outcome Vitality. After all, they're willing and able to meet stakeholder demands. It's only a matter of releasing their energy. Unfortunately, many organizations commit suicide when in this box. When Outcome Vitality scores start to dip, leaders start kicking rear ends and taking names. They sacrifice Cultural Vitality on the altar of satisfying single stakeholders. Equally bad is when they begin acting as though they're presiding over a fire sale. They downsize, centralize, and bureaucratize in ways that shore up certain outcomes while killing others. After winning what they thought were key battles on certain stakeholder fronts, they learn that they lost the war on another one.

How you act when in Box 3 determines whether you'll plunge into Box 4 (soon to be dead forever) or ascend to Box 1.

Box 4. Pass the formaldehyde. If stakeholders are unhappy and employees don't seem either motivated or able to turn this around, start sending out resumes.

Obviously there's a strong correlation between Cultural Vitality and Outcome Vitality. You'd expect organizations to fall into either Box 1 or Box 4. If Cultural Vitality is strong, you'd expect to find Outcome Vitality to match. The same is true for poor vitality measures. Notwithstanding the causal relationship, we suggest that, as Outcome Vitality starts to weaken, steps can be taken to shore up the Cultural Vitality causing it. You can count on a lag time between diagnosis and remedy. The remainder of this book looks at ways to assess both forms of vitality and steps that can be taken to bolster sagging Cultural Vitality.

Organizational Vitality

All stakeholders are willing and able to continue the relationships, and employees are willing and able to meet stakeholder demands; a **measure of *overall vigor.*** Vital organizations possess both abundant Outcome Vitality and Cultural Vitality.

Defining a vital organization is one thing; achieving it is an entirely different matter.

WHAT LEADS TO VITALITY?

Let's begin by recounting the search for vitality that's been going on for centuries.

The Search for the Key to Cultural Vitality

I don't want to achieve immortality through my work. . . . I want to achieve it through not dying.

WOODY ALLEN

Medieval legend promised lasting vitality to those who found and drank from the Holy Grail. Today's search for Organizational Vitality finds us running to and fro in a similar search for a simple key. Leaders are anxious to learn what, if anything, will guarantee a long, if not eternal, run. They ask, "What cup should we drink from to ensure that, no matter what else happens, we'll survive vicious competition? We know that in order to be vital we must keep all of our stakeholders happy. But how?

What must we think, feel, and do in order to guarantee a healthy balance?"

The answer to this question has changed over the centuries. The vitality strategies employed by Louis XIV, J. P. Morgan, and Lee Iacocca are strikingly different. The competitive challenges each faced in his day dictated what he needed to master if he expected to maintain a vital organization. One glance into history and you'll quickly learn that what used to lead to success no longer suffices.[4]

Changes in Competitive Advantage

As you drive the romantic highway that follows the winding Rhine River in Germany, you'll note that about every half mile you'll round a corner and confront a magnificent castle capping the next hillside. If you take a wrong turn, however, and head away from the river, you'll see open countryside. Not a castle for miles. Why?

Aristocrats in past centuries weren't interested in river views or rising real-estate values. They understood that the Rhine carried the commerce of the day. By owning a prime spot on the river, they could stop traffic and exact fees—sort of the I.R.S. of their time. You could make a comfortable living at such work. That was the good news. The bad news was that your position on the river was at the mercy of the ruling monarch. If you didn't know how to maintain a solid relationship with people dressed in purple, you were in trouble. Many a fallen lord or lady learned this lesson the hard way as they went from glory to guillotine in one mismanaged event. Oh yes, in those days if you failed in your business, you didn't just lose your job—you also lost your head. That tended to get the attention of other aristocrats, who began studying in earnest how to manage this "critical problem." Scholars began writing about it, and a new field of inquiry emerged—political science. Leaders at this time, if they expected to remain vital, had to own land and be politically savvy.

Real estate and relationships ceased to be the critical problems with the advent of the Industrial Revolution. If you wanted to grow up and become a robber baron, you had to learn how to acquire and manage huge sums of portable wealth. Capital became the critical problem, and a new science of finance and economics emerged to help leaders learn the skills for those days. Those who now understood *economics* as well as their predecessors had understood *political science* created vital organizations. Over the years, the sciences offering the vitality grail have shifted as each new round of leaders finds others closing the knowledge gap. What started as a need to master political science and then economics eventually transitioned to management theory and, yes, even accounting.

What's Today's Grail?

The only way to keep your health is to eat what you don't want, drink what you don't like, and do what you'd druther not.

MARK TWAIN

If you want lasting organizational health today, you have to step away from capital, real estate, and markets and do something a lot of leaders don't always enjoy—you have to get into the hearts and minds of the workforce. Contemporary leaders have to assume that their competitors have similar access to capital, markets, and technology. Any short-term advantages they have in these areas will be quickly matched by others. For instance, when Western Electric invented the transistor, it didn't bother taking out a patent. The race was on for those who could most rapidly translate the technology into products and profits. Many Japanese companies won. Why?

Today's "critical problem" is related to *discretionary effort*. Work has changed over the decades. There was a time when 80 percent of employees worked in low-discretion jobs (tasks where the amount of effort they put in was determined by the pace of the production line). Today only 15 percent of the workforce is chained to a production line. Most employees have high-discretion jobs. That is, they make choices about how they spend their time. They decide what they'll work on and with how much energy. They have jobs in which there's a huge gap between the minimum effort they can get away with giving and the maximum they could give.[5]

Even heavy industry has been dragged (kicking and screaming) to this realization. In the late 1980s, Toyota had a $1,000 cost advantage over General Motors in the production of a small car *after* factoring in differences in wages, exchange rates, and technology. Toyota had somehow learned to engage its people's discretionary efforts $1,000 more efficiently than General Motors. Its leaders were handling the day's critical problem (were drinking from today's grail), whereas General Motors was using the skills of yesteryear and moving perilously closer to death. And that's in a heavy-industry environment where worker discretion is likely to be lower than the circumstances most of today's leaders face.

The world, the nature of work, and the critical problems leaders face have changed over the centuries. Despite all of the changes, many leaders are still dressing up for yesterday's foxhunt. They'd do better if they understood that today's Cultural Vitality depends on a leader's ability to motivate and enable employees to take all of that wonderful, and yet dangerous, discretionary effort and aim it at surprising and delighting multiple stakeholders.

How Do You Capture That Discretionary Effort?

The test of leadership is not what people do in your presence but what they do in your absence.

Of course, not every leader is chasing the wrong rabbits. There are those who desperately want to focus on their employees in an effort to enhance their competitive advantage. They understand that it's through the discretionary efforts of their people that they'll eventually achieve their dreams. Unfortunately, they're operating on one of the following two fallacious assumptions:

- A happy culture is a productive culture.
- An empowered culture is a productive culture.

The first theory suggests that there's some link between employee satisfaction and productivity. The only problem with this theory is that it's wrong on two fronts. First, happiness is not vitality. For every study that shows a positive relationship between employee satisfaction and productivity, you'll find one with the opposite conclusion. How could satisfied workers be *less* productive? Depending on the values in the culture, satisfaction is achieved in different ways. For example, when asked who their heroes and heroines are, many employees tell glowing stories of people who find ways to get out of work, are able to take a good nap, and brag about sneaking a two-hour lunch every day.

Second, productivity doesn't guarantee Outcome Vitality. Even if people are working in ways that keep them fully employed and moving with great energy, many companies are chock-full of people who are giving their best efforts on products and services that don't satisfy stakeholder demands. The space between stakeholder need and employee effort is too large.

Empowerment theory is a little more complex. Most theorists list four or five characteristics that lead to Cultural Vitality, then shrug when asked why those four or five are included and not four or five others. Common candidates for inclusion in the empowerment top 10 list include items such as communication, leadership, trust, and teamwork. But then again, who *wouldn't* believe that *trust* is important? And, of course, people need to be able to *communicate*. What else is new?

These broad-brush and vacuous theories of effectiveness have the unfortunate effect of dividing families. Some leaders are willing to take the leap of faith that these noble characteristics are, indeed, the grail of effectiveness—and drink deeply. They put all of their efforts into the grail of increased trust. Others (usually the harder-headed operations managers) are more cautious. They know the legend that says if you drink from the wrong grail, the result can be death, not just disappointment. They don't want to waste time, money, and energy on dubious doctrine. We applaud their willingness to take a sometimes unpopular stand.

A Word of Caution

When somebody approaches you with a plan to improve your overall effectiveness (one that comes with a catchy buzzword and a breathy promise), but you can't figure out how the plan will serve all of your stakeholders, go with your gut. Insist that all strategies, no matter how they're packaged, have a direct and obvious link to Cultural Vitality. If not, prepare for the worst.

The True Test of Cultural Vitality

Our research has pointed to a clear and practical measure of Cultural Vitality—one that gets to the heart of the matter. Later on, we'll look at topics such as intrinsic satisfaction, communications, and trust—but as a means, not as an end.

For now, we'll link Cultural Vitality to what leaders care about deeply—Outcome Vitality. Our studies in over a dozen industries have demonstrated that the following definition (the same one we've been using all along) helps leaders focus on the variables that actually influence an organization's ability to produce significant and sustainable Outcome Vitality.

Cultural Vitality

The willingness and ability of employees to meet competing stakeholder demands; a measure of *long-term sustainability*.

Getting to the Heart of Discretionary Effort

Think for a moment about this definition. Wouldn't it be wonderful to
know the degree to which your people are motivated and able to serve
customers well? What would you give to get your hands on hard data
about the ways they are and are not able to add value to investors? How
many surveys have you taken that failed to show you the real barriers
to high employee satisfaction?

This definition of Cultural Vitality has proven immensely useful to
leaders who want an approach to leadership that is reliable, valid, and
actionable and that focuses their attention on what they know to be
important.

To make the definition more usable, we break it down into four parts:

P_p — People's motivation and ability to positively affect the net value
  received by other people within the organization
P_i — People's motivation and ability to serve investors
P_c — People's motivation and ability to positively affect customer net
  value
P_o — People's motivation and ability to positively affect the net value
  of other outside stakeholders

Putting our two formulas together, our theory goes:

Cultural Vitality leads to Outcome Vitality

or

$$P_p + P_i + P_c + P_o \implies PNV + INV + CNV + ONV$$

Cultural Vitality measures examine the values, assumptions, and
skills of employees as they relate to critical stakeholder groups, which,
in turn, directly relate to Outcome Vitality. In short, if people don't care
about or are unable to serve each of the stakeholder groups, they simply won't be served. Or, to put it another way, you're a lot more likely to
satisfy competing stakeholder demands if employees are both willing
and able to do so.

Even the most skeptical managers should find these measures more interesting, more insightful, *and* immensely more powerful than the traditional single-minded, value-simplistic measures such as employee satisfaction. You won't need a divining rod or chicken entrails to predict your future if you get right to the heart of employees' willingness and ability to meet stakeholder demands.

A Practical Application

Let's move beyond the hypothetical to the practical. We'll look at a hospital example to see how the vital signs we're advocating here illuminate critical factors and suggest solutions. Please note that we're focusing here on the *what* and *why*—we'll get to the *how* of these numbers later.

A Detailed Look at Kidney View

Kidney View Hospital has reasonable vitality measures. It's in the middle of the pack compared to others in its parent company. CNV measured at around 82 percent. This represents the summary number of a customer-satisfaction survey. INV was only measured in terms of return on investment less cost of capital. It hovers between −2 and 0 percent. In other words, in many years the company would do better to invest its money in stocks or bonds than to keep this hospital going—if all the investors cared about was their return on capital (which may be true). PNV has historically been at about 60 percent. This number also came from a survey. People like their work, but interdepartmental rivalry is tough, too many physicians are sometimes abusive to staff, and people feel insecure in their jobs. ONV hasn't been measured to date. The leaders thought about looking at things such as community support or supplier satisfaction but decided it wasn't worth the money.

Graphically, these approximations can be displayed as follows:

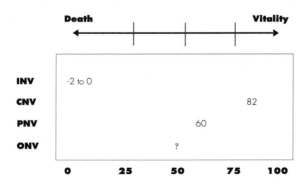

This company performs fairly well, but it desperately needs to move INV up. Four CEOs have been brought in over the past five years but have failed to turn things around. When numbers are low, headquarters reviews financial figures monthly and issues orders for staff reductions when census (in-patient) numbers are low. Other costs have not been addressed. Analysis of lost revenue opportunities is nonexistent. No rationale is ever given for staff reductions beyond "our other hospitals run at these levels."

However, when we lift up the hood to look at Cultural Vitality, we find the following more revealing scores and the supporting data that indicate employees' continuing motivation and ability to serve their stakeholders.

P_p **— Motivation: 88%** People want to overcome differences in the interest of serving patients.

P_p **— Ability: 32%** Contact between key departments is only through formal channels. Ability to work together is impeded by infrequency of contact, physical distance, and reporting relationships. Communication skills are low, particularly between physicians and staff.

P_i **—Motivation: 15%** The owners of the company are seen as insensitive capitalists living in posh houses and mooching off people's illnesses in order to support their lifestyle. This perception tends to discourage people from looking for opportunities to save on costs or to capture revenues. Charges are often not posted to patient accounts. Cost-saving suggestions come by accident, if at all. Money is administration's job—and they're in bed with headquarters.

P_i **—Ability: 18%** No one knows what anything costs. There's no system for analyzing and improving work. People do their jobs, yet they don't know how to look for ways to improve, and they have no opportunity to think about changing their processes. When a nurse in the operating room uses gloves, she takes the more comfortable ones even for short procedures. She has no idea the standard ones cost 25 cents while the nicer powderless ones that she regularly chooses cost three dollars. Opportunities for efficiency are regularly overlooked.

P_c **— Motivation: 86%** People love serving patients. Sure they get burned out on long shifts, but they're saving lives.

P_c— Ability: 52% Employees mostly want to be left alone to serve patients, but they often need help from other departments. The organizational structure makes delays, miscommunications, and missed orders frequent. Getting a patient into medical imaging for an x-ray (a 10-minute procedure) takes three hours of scheduling, waiting, etc.

P_o— Motivation: 90% As you talk with people, you get a sense that most employees have a deep commitment to serving the community. After all, these are health-care professionals. Their desire to serve extends beyond "providing health services" to "being a responsible member of the community." The hospital is located in a small rural town, and environmental sensitivity runs high. The area they tend to underplay relates to their relationship with suppliers. Nobody spends much time thinking or worrying about how to partner with them. Oh yes, and government regulators are seen as swamp scum unworthy of their attention.

P_o—Ability: 15% As much as employees worry about the surrounding community, almost no measures are taken. Without a clue about community relations (other than what they hear at the supermarket counter), employees are in a poor position to deal with any potential problems.

Where Problems Lie

This more complete view of Cultural Vitality illuminates where problems lie and where opportunities abound. Ability components of P_c and P_p could use some work. P_i is at a critical point. Bringing in a new CEO won't turn this around unless he or she deals with the huge barriers in the organization's Cultural Vitality.

As this moderately complicated health-care example demonstrates, coming to an understanding of Outcome Vitality (and its driving source, Cultural Vitality) isn't easy. We'll spend time in the next few chapters diving still further into the hearts and minds of the workforce. We'll explore how the values and assumptions of employees toward stakeholders are formed and what it takes to change them. We'll dive into this swirling vortex of ambiguity because that's where the pearls lie. Leaders who have a clear understanding of what employees are thinking and feeling know where to start a change process. They know what levers to trip and what land mines to skip. Instead of being propelled by a dull feeling that shouts "get better," they have a clear sense of *what* needs to change and *why*.

SOME PRACTICAL ADVICE FROM THIS CHAPTER

Our purpose in this introductory chapter was to introduce the concept of balance and what it takes to achieve it. We'll explore more *whys* and *hows* later. For now we want to make sure that we're all using the same vocabulary and theory of effectiveness. Let's summarize here and note some ways to incorporate these ideas:

- **Balance.** Leaders are continually caught in a never-ending balancing act that requires them to do whatever it takes to satisfy a variety of competing stakeholder demands. Some make the mistake of responding to one group at the expense of another. How often, if ever, have you done this? Why? What can you do to make sure that you keep a more balanced approach in the future?

- **Vitality.** Every organization fits somewhere on the Death-to-Vitality Continuum and is moving in one direction or the other. Get your team together. Pass a sheet around that has the Death-to-Vitality Continuum on it. Ask them, based only on their gut feeling, to place a dot where they think the organization is and an arrow to indicate which way the organization is moving. Have someone collect the papers and transfer the individual responses to a flip chart. Then lead a discussion around these questions:
  - *What are the reasons some of the arrows are moving toward vitality?*
  - *If applicable, why are some of the arrows moving toward death?*
  - *Why is our organization not as vital as it could be?*
  - *What can we do to improve our vitality?*

- **Outcome.** The first component of vitality is Outcome Vitality. All stakeholders are willing and able to continue with the relationship. Outcome Vitality is assessed by measuring the perceived net value of investors (INV), customers (CNV), employees (PNV), and other stakeholders (ONV). Do you take accurate and frequent measures of stakeholder net value? Where could you improve? What will it take for you to move *away from* traditional measures that describe where you were and move *toward* future-oriented measures that explore the intentions of critical stakeholder groups?

- **Culture.** The second component of vitality (and the measure of a leader's effectiveness) is Cultural Vitality. Employees are willing and able to meet competing stakeholder demands. To create vital cultures, leaders must find ways to capture the discretionary effort of every employee. This requires leaders to continually measure and publish both Outcome Vitality and Cultural Vitality measures. At a minimum, PNV, INV, CNV, and ONV should be tracked regularly and with discipline. Further, if you want to understand why you're getting the PNV, INV, CNV, and ONV results you've got, look at your Cultural Vitality measures, specifically, P_p, P_i, P_c, and P_o. Take stock of the measures you have and don't have. To what extent do you know the motivation and ability of your people to serve competing stakeholders? How are you doing when it comes to P_p, P_i, P_c, and P_o?

Throughout the remainder of this book, we'll look at a variety of ways to both measure and influence employee values and assumptions. We'll explore practical methods to capture the discretionary effort that is so important to future success. For now, we'll be satisfied if we're familiar with the same theory and vocabulary. To get a sense of how well you've kept up with the heavy barrage of vocabulary, take a crack at the following quiz.

A QUICK TEST

1. **What's the definition of a *stakeholder*?**
   A. One who has an interest in an enterprise.
   B. Employees, customers, investors, communities, and others who have a profound impact on an organization's ongoing success.
   C. A person possessed by a debilitating fear of Dracula.

2. **What's meant by the term *balancing act*?**
   A. Any act of leadership that requires bringing varying stakeholder demands into a harmonious or successful arrangement.
   B. The constant and challenging demand to satisfy one group of stakeholders in a way that doesn't damage the relationship with others.
   C. What it takes to drink coffee, talk on the cellular phone, put on makeup, and steer a car over a patch of ice—all at 70 miles per hour.

3. **Define *vitality*.**
   A. When measured in outcome terms, the willingness and ability of stakeholders to continue the relationship.
   B. When measured in cultural terms, the willingness and ability of employees to satisfy competing stakeholder demands.
   C. An incredibly important or essential "-ity."

4. What is meant by the term *net value?*

   A. In a resource exchange, net value is the measure of what one *receives* relative to what one *gives*.

   B. A future-oriented measure of stakeholder intentions rather than a historical measure that examines where you've been.

   C. A fast-food restaurant sanitation measure—usually expressed in terms of hairs per serving.

5. What's the *Death-to-Vitality Continuum?*

   A. A model that helps position an organization's health along a line of subtle gradations ranging from total health to final collapse.

   B. A simple tool used to assess an organization's current vitality and the direction it's heading.

   C. A controversial ride recently introduced at Walt Disney World.

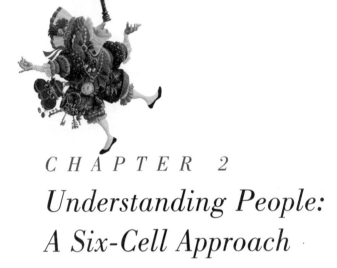

C H A P T E R   2

Understanding People:
A Six-Cell Approach

The people, and the people alone, are the motive force in the making of world history.

MAO ZEDONG

Influence and Cultural Vitality

What does it take to make a culture more vital? How do leaders impact employees in a way that changes the way employees think and feel about their stakeholders (P_p, P_i, P_c, and P_o)? To answer these and similar questions, we need to take a few minutes and look at people in general. After all, they form the building blocks of corporate vitality. Organizations don't behave—people do.

The good news is that the theory we'll develop doesn't just explain why employees do what they do; it covers all people. As we unfold our model of human behavior selection (explaining why people make the choices they make), the concepts we'll develop can be applied to employees, investors, customers, government regulators, and community members alike. We won't need different theories for different stakeholder groups. In addition, the same factors that make up Outcome Vitality (the willingness and ability of stakeholders to continue the relationship) make up Cultural Vitality (the willingness and ability of employees to satisfy competing stakeholder demands). As you might guess

32

from our definitions, we'll dive deep into the constructs of both motivation and ability as we explore human behavior selection.

Our goal in creating a model of individual behavior selection is simple. To understand the connection between employee behavior and corporate vitality, we'll eventually have to answer the question "Why is it that certain employees seem to be almost obsessed with serving stakeholders while others couldn't be driven with a lead pipe to do much more than serve their own personal agendas?" Or so it would seem. By the same token, "What does it take to enable individuals to serve stakeholders?" Let's take a close look.

IN SEARCH OF A USEFUL THEORY OF BEHAVIOR SELECTION

For every scientist (S) who studies human behavior, there will be S + 1 theories of motivation.

To understand what makes people tick, we've chosen a theory of human behavior selection developed by colleagues at Stanford University. These researchers explored how people make choices. What made this particular research notable was that it dealt with snake phobics.[1] The scientists asked the question, "How can we get people, who are terrified of even the thought of snakes, to cuddle and stroke a boa constrictor the length of a Buick?" Since most of us suffer from at least one illogical trepidation, we can relate to the topic. It's also an attempt at behavior change about as monumental as most leaders will ever face.

Finding the Really Fearful

Studying snake phobia is more difficult than you might imagine. For openers, where do you go to find people who tremble at the first sign of a slither? And even if you could locate a sizable sample of the fearful, would any of them be willing to come in for therapy? To answer these questions, researchers placed an advertisement in the *Palo Alto Times*. The ad simply explained that scholars were studying snake phobics. It concluded by asking interested parties to report to the basement of the psychology building at a specified time. (Visions of smoldering electrodes spring to mind.)

To everyone's surprise, several hundred potential candidates responded to the ad. The researchers discovered that scores of people were struggling with their fear of snakes. Many had avoided going out in the country but now faced a transfer to the suburbs. Others had put off fieldwork for years and now were taking jobs that required walking in the grass. (And we all know what lurks in the grass.) All were desperate.

Once a phalanx of phobics had been identified, it had to be winnowed. The researchers only wanted to work with the most severe cases. To premeasure the participants' level of fear, researchers asked each to assess his or her own ability to work with snakes. The researchers asked, "Would you be willing to cradle a 15-foot boa constrictor in your arms while seated alone in a chair?" (Fat chance.)

So the researchers softened the goal. "Could you touch a 15-foot boa constrictor?" One or two said they could. "Could you touch a large boa constrictor while wearing a suit of protective clothing?" Still others could. "Could you look at a boa in a covered terrarium?" Still more felt capable. "Could you stand 10 feet away, dressed in protective clothing, and look at a boa in a covered terrarium?" The researchers only worked with those who were unwilling even to look at the snake. They sent everyone else home.

Three Theories They Didn't Use

Once the researchers selected the subjects, the therapy began. To appreciate the method of influence, it helps to have a working knowledge of the theories the researchers were and weren't testing. For openers, they weren't testing behaviorism, psychotherapy, or trait theory—and for good reason.

Behaviorism

Of course, Behaviorism "works." So does torture. Give me a no-nonsense, down-to-earth behaviorist, a few drugs, and simple electrical appliances, and in six months I will have him reciting the Athanasian Creed in public.

W. H. Auden

Had the team members been behaviorists (who vehemently argue that people don't think, per se, but just react to reinforcers), they might have tried to make a subject's contact with the snake an enjoyable experience. Since people repeat behaviors that yield pleasant results, they might have employed a secondary reinforcer such as money. Of course, the researchers probably would have discovered that individuals who loathe snakes don't readily change their opinions through extrinsic reinforcers. As a therapy, giving a condemned prisoner bonbons to make his execution more attractive is a trifle weak.

Actually, many behaviorists have tried to apply their therapeutic methods to varying groups of tough subjects. Consider the work done by one research team that tried to help smokers who wanted to quit. They believed that people continue smoking because they derive some pleasure from it. (It's hard to argue with that.) They also postulated that if they could get smokers to associate pain with lighting up, people would quit. To test their hypothesis, they brought people into laboratories and shocked them whenever they reached for a cigarette. When people finished the therapy, they flinched a bit when they reached for a cigarette. Behaviorists were encouraged.

But it didn't last. Fortunately, people aren't like behaviorists' favorite subjects—rats running a maze. Humans think a lot about their choices. Unfortunately for the behaviorists, this very ability to cogitate undermined the therapy. Subjects quickly reasoned that the shocks had nothing to do with smoking. It wasn't long before they lit up again. They understood that the best way to avoid getting shocked was to quit going to the lab. What the behaviorists were most successful in creating was lab avoidance.

Psychotherapy

The mind is an iceberg. It floats with only one-seventh of its bulk above water.

SIGMUND FREUD

Had the researchers been psychotherapists, they might have followed Freud's injunction and taken the subject back to the "critical childhood event" that led to the fear. A subject might have seen a frightening movie about snakes during her formative years. Perhaps a respected adult feared snakes. Of course, to uncover the critical event, it might take years on the couch. After all, getting to the genesis of behavior can be time consuming, and it hasn't proven particularly effective either.

We don't even want to go into the way Freudian psychology or its hybrids would explain why people would put cigarettes into their mouths in the first place. This is not that kind of book. Let's just say that while the explanation makes for great conversation on Geraldo, leaders are still left asking, "So how does that help me foster new behavior?"

Applications of Freudian methods to the practical challenges of leadership have proven both suspect and ineffective, yet Freudian thinking pervades our entire culture. Few people realize that Freud is the father of such unproven ideas as

- People persist in acting in dysfunctional ways because it gives them some deep-seated payoff.
- People's problems (conflict, drug use, bulimia, kleptomania) are symptoms of some deeper underlying trauma.
- Change always takes a long time.
- If you change someone's behavior without dealing with the root trauma, the problem will show itself in new symptoms (e.g., stop philandering and you'll start stealing).

All of these are basic Freudian *assumptions*. Little, if any, empirical data exists to validate these notions, yet they hold a position in our thinking and vocabulary as if they were proven facts.

Trait Theory

Finally, the researchers might have drawn from a long line of exploration that tries to identify consistent personality characteristics or traits. Armed with these traits, the researcher could then use the information to design a tailored therapy. We include this particular theory, not because it offers a plausible solution to phobias, but because, to this day, it remains immensely popular.

Consider the spotted, and yet curiously popular, history of trait theory. For decades, scholars attempted to find stable characteristics that make up one's personality. To identify these personality anchors, researchers typically asked friends and parents to describe individuals. "Is he or she reliable, trustworthy, and hard working?" Scholars then used these descriptive labels to predict how people would behave in experiments. At least they *tried* to predict how people would behave in the laboratory. It turns out that researchers, armed with traits, could never predict more than 12 percent of the behavior in any experiment.

After trait theory slipped ever so slowly into oblivion, from the ashes of two decades of research arose not a phoenix, but trait theory's ugly cousin—labeling. Instead of relying on parental descriptions, researchers shifted to using surveys to produce personality descriptors or labels. Today's subjects are given personality titles such as "driver," "nurturer," or "blue" (for the jargon impaired), based on how they respond to a mere handful of questions. The claim of labeling theory is that once you know someone's targeted characteristics, you'll know how to treat him or her. Unfortunately, these labels, which are drawn from even more sketchy information than parental descriptions, are even less predictive than traits—although they do make wonderful parlor games.

Labels, in spite of their plausibility, like trait theory of old, just aren't predictive. In most cases you would do just as well knowing a subject's sign of the zodiac as to know how that person responded to 30 questions or the psychological box this puts him or her in. Unfortunately, labeling still remains incredibly popular. You can't go to a training conference without finding hoards of people offering and receiving labels. Some even wear them on their lapels, as if somehow they have just exposed their inner being.

It's a Matter of Modulation

Before we throw out labeling theory bag and baggage, we will concede that labels can predict some behavior. When parents and friends suggest that a person is *reliable* or *hard working*, such general descriptions *do* predict behavior—over long periods of time. Of course, years of research have taught us that these same labels don't predict a *particular* behavior. It's a matter of modulation.

If you want to predict how someone will respond throughout his or her career, a simple label may help. Leaders have been known to use labels quite effectively in performance reviews, job assignments, and promotions. Simple one-word descriptors help decision makers think about the person over the long run. However, we shouldn't try to use labels to predict what people will do tomorrow. When you crank your modulation down to the particular instance, you'll need to move from who or what people *are* to what they are *currently thinking* and *feeling*.

The practical value of a model of behavior selection is measured by how well it helps us predict, explain, and influence behavior. We haven't found great utility, although some have tried, in taking a group of 500 employees back to critical childhood events to understand why they play cards during working hours. In a similar vein, hooking people to electrodes hasn't exactly been widely accepted as a responsible leadership technique for getting people back to work. We've also found too many examples of people behaving in ways inconsistent with the simplistic labels assigned to them by trait models to believe that these labels help predict a great deal of behavior. That's why we've discarded these theories in favor of one that has proven far more useful to practical-minded leaders and to us as consultants.

MENTAL MAPS AND MOTIVATION: THE FIRST BUILDING BLOCK OF OUR MODEL

I think, therefore I am.

DESCARTES

I am what I think.

CONTEMPORARY PERSONALITY THEORY

I yam what I yam.

POPEYE

The Stanford research team rejected behaviorist, Freudian, and trait models for a more compelling, predictive, and balanced theory. They argued that behaviors are guided by thought. People carry assumptions around in their heads that tell them what will happen if they do this or that. These mental maps help them choose behavior which they believe will produce the outcomes they want. Instead of responding to innate needs or acting out traits, individuals think about what they might do and what might happen as a result. Then, based on their thinking, people select what actions they'll take. Makes sense, doesn't it? Let's sneak into the classroom and watch how one of the authors works with a class of undergraduate students to teach how this model works.

Poison, Anyone?

"Imagine a large jar full of small pink pills. Lots of them. One thousand, to be exact. Every pill is a sugar tablet. That is, every pill but one. The odd capsule looks just like the rest, but in spite of its harmless appearance it's filled with strychnine. Swallow it and you're in for a short, yet thoroughly agonizing, death. Now who would be willing to reach in the jar, pull out one pill at random, and swallow it—just for the heck of it?" Although you can't be certain of their sincerity, one or two students usually raise their hands. They must be thinking the odds are only one in a thousand (*probability* = .001) that they'll die, whereas it's almost a sure thing that they'll survive, and a lot of people will think they're daring and even cool. (Our guess is that most people would think they were daring and stupid.)

The Pot Thickens

Now, in order to encourage more takers, we sweeten the pot—only this time with something better than sugar. "Who," we ask, "would be willing to swallow a pill for, say, $10,000?" A few hands go up. "A million dollars?" Most hands go up. "Who among you wouldn't be willing to take a pill for any amount of money?" Most hands go down, and three or four hands go up.

"You wouldn't suck down a pill for, say, a billion dollars?" we ask a guy with his arm in the air. *"Nope,"* he responds, *"I'm not much of a risk taker,"* giving credence to the belief that a simple label is predictive. "Would the people who know you agree that you're not much of a risk taker?" *"Absolutely,"* he continues. *"They'd call me 'conservative'"* "So," we push on, "you're a conservative, and because of this you would not take a pill that just might kill you—for any amount of money." *"That's right,"* he states emphatically.

So the bet is on the table. He, like hundreds of theorists before him, believes that because of an inner characteristic we'll call conservatism, he'll never take a pill that might kill him—no matter how slim the odds.

"Do you have any children?" we ask the student. (We usually pick one who looks old and bedraggled enough to have kids.) *"Oh yes, two— a girl and a boy."* "And you love these children?" we continue. (By now, most of the class know exactly where we're heading.) "What if, heaven forbid, one of your children needed medicine. Expensive medicine. You've exhausted all of your financial options, and you're still $10,000 short. Without it, your child will probably die. Now, for $10,000, would you take one of these pills?" *"Of course,"* he practically shouts back. "But I thought you're conservative." *"I am,"* he continues, *"but I love my children so much that taking a pill that would certainly save my child's life without putting me at much risk is, indeed, a conservative action."*

"A minute ago you said that because you're conservative you would *not* take the pill. Now you're saying that because you're conservative you *would* take the pill." *"That's because things changed,"* he continues. Precisely, and without knowing those "things" (his map of the world, complete with assumptions and values) you simply can't predict his behavior with any degree of accuracy. Without understanding what a person assumes and values, we can't accurately predict how he or she might behave in a certain situation. Mental maps, unwieldy as they are, are our best hope for understanding, and thus predicting, short-term human behavior.

How Our Maps Work

Most behavior is multimotivated.

ABRAHAM MASLOW

At the center of everyone's thinking lie assumptions about behavior-to-outcome linkages (or mini-maps of cause and effect). These maps link behavior to outcomes. More specifically, they demonstrate what people believe will happen as a result of a particular behavior. Of course, people don't simply predict that outcomes will or won't happen. Instead, associated with each assumption about cause and effect is a probability. Rather than seeing the world in binary terms (the simple presence or absence of an outcome), people see in gray—in shades and probabilities instead of in black or white. Humans set mental odds. Such maps of the probabilities (p) of various possible outcomes could be demonstrated in the following way:

Mental Map

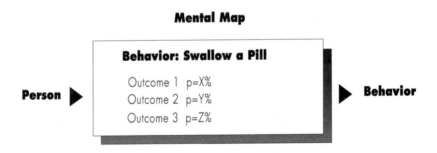

Behavior: Swallow a Pill

Outcome 1 p=X%
Outcome 2 p=Y%
Outcome 3 p=Z%

Person ▶   ▶ **Behavior**

People who volunteered to take a pill out of the jar may have held the following mental map:

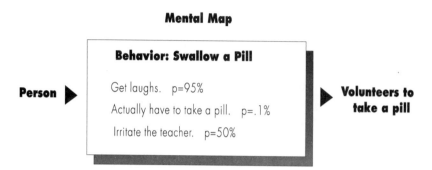

Mental Map

Behavior: Swallow a Pill

Person ▶

Get laughs.   p=95%

Actually have to take a pill.   p=.1%

Irritate the teacher.   p=50%

▶ **Volunteers to take a pill**

Volunteers assumed that the odds of getting laughs were high—perhaps they've tried to get laughs in the past and have high confidence that they know what works. On the other hand, they set the odds to be fairly low that the teacher is serious about someone selecting a pill. And finally, the risk of bugging the teacher by raising a hand when he's probably trying to make a serious point are moderate (50 percent).

Wait! We're Not Done

While this map helps us understand some of what individuals consider when deciding how to behave, it's incomplete. We still haven't asked questions about motivation. Do they care about getting laughs? Do they care about taking the pill? Do they care about irritating the teacher?

Accompanying each outcome assumption is a value (v). People either like certain outcomes or they don't. Of course, this liking and disliking come in varying degrees. If they place a high value on getting laughs and irritating the teacher (ever met or been one of these?), then you can guess how they'll behave. Let's add values to the model:

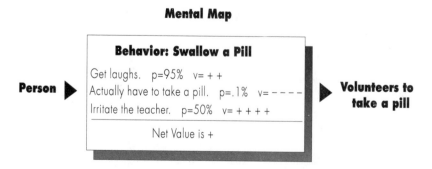

Mental Map

Behavior: Swallow a Pill

Person ▶

Get laughs.   p=95%   v= + +

Actually have to take a pill.   p=.1%   v= – – – –

Irritate the teacher.   p=50%   v= + + + +

Net Value is +

▶ **Volunteers to take a pill**

A Complicated Mix

How do people blend values and probabilities? Nobody knows for certain; however, it's fairly clear that most use some form of mental gymnastics to weigh the likelihood of the event against the value. Combined, the two yield an overall score or *net value*. If the net value is positive, people give the behavior a try; if it's negative, they don't. This, of course, is a rather structured way of looking at a very fuzzy process. How people interweave probability with value is a very personal experience and can never be completely captured with a simple formula. Nevertheless, the overall process holds true for all people.

For example, the person who considered himself "conservative" wasn't willing to take a pill under the following conditions:

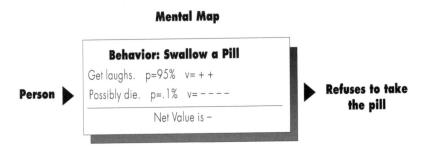

Mental Map

Behavior: Swallow a Pill

Person ▶   Get laughs.   p=95%   v= + +
           Possibly die.   p=.1%   v= – – – –
           ———————————————————
           Net Value is –

▶ **Refuses to take the pill**

For this person, the thought of dying was so negative that, when weighed against a probability (no matter how small), he still came up with a negative net value. This "low risk taker" wouldn't take the pill even if offered a billion dollars. Of course, if taking the pill for $10,000 would save his child's life, this same "conservative" person willingly agreed.

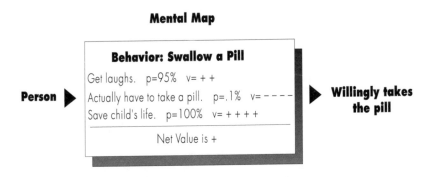

Mental Map

Behavior: Swallow a Pill

Person ▶   Get laughs.   p=95%   v= + +
           Actually have to take a pill.   p=.1%   v= – – – –
           Save child's life.   p=100%   v= + + + +
           ———————————————————
           Net Value is +

▶ **Willingly takes the pill**

Knowing whether the person was "conservative" or a "risk taker" wasn't very useful in predicting behavior in a particular situation. On the other hand, understanding outcome assumptions and the values associated with each was extremely helpful. Of utmost importance was the *net value*.

Life in the Net

Motives, then, consist of the net value associated with the expected results of a specific behavior. This is the same net value that stakeholders consider when deciding whether to continue with a relationship. Stakeholders, humans that they are, look at what they're giving up to be part of an enterprise, what they're getting in return, and come up with a net value. "I'm getting a great return on my investment, but I'm helping perpetuate apartheid—and because I worry more about the latter than I enjoy the dividends, I withdraw my investment."

Consequently, in order to understand motive, one must understand net value or a person's outcome assumptions and their relative value. Outcome assumptions alone are insufficient. For example, in one study, senior executives examined if employees believed that existing work habits would lead to the company eventually failing, and the workforce agreed.

What the executives hadn't imagined was that the employees didn't care if the company closed. Exploring expected outcomes without examining values is incomplete. Similarly, values uncoupled from their outcomes make little sense. Combined, *the interaction of outcomes with values forms net value, and net value drives behavior*.

Given what we've suggested so far, you might predict that individuals would behave differently if they held different outcome assumptions, probabilities, or values. A change in any one of these could change the net value. Consequently, any attempt to foster a new behavior should be aimed at either helping people understand that negative outcomes are less likely or that positive outcomes are more likely. For instance, that's what parents are doing when they help a child let go of a table and take the first few tentative steps. Mom and Dad are trying to help the child see that walking produces positive and not negative outcomes (e.g., happy parents, faster mobility, and better reach of attractive objects).

The practical challenge of applying all of this to day-to-day behavior change is yet to come, but for now let's return to how we can cure our snake phobics—a practical enough problem. What can we do to reshape their inaccurate maps into ones that are more in line with reality? How do we alter *net value?*

NET VALUE, SNAKE PHOBIA, AND INFLUENCING HUMAN BEHAVIOR

It turns out that reshaping mental maps is a tricky business. *Telling* people (the knee-jerk tactic) that their maps are wrong can lead to resistance: "Trust me—the snake won't bite you." "Yeah, right." Individuals are quite capable of maintaining distorted views of the world. (Seen Elvis lately?) If whole cultures can sustain myths, then certainly phobics can sustain their distorted maps. And so they do. Changing maps is going to take more than talk.

Vicarious Experiences

You can observe a lot by just watching.

YOGI BERRA

Since simply lecturing people doesn't hold much power, what if a phobic were to watch someone work safely with a snake? Could mere observation provide compelling data? Would the observer, in the face of irrefutable evidence, reshape his or her outcome assumptions? Certainly phobics could survive watching others work with snakes.

To test the power of "observational learning," researchers asked subjects to watch a research assistant "model" how to successfully handle a boa constrictor. As subjects watched the behaviors and the ensuing outcomes, hopefully their expectations would change. No longer would they expect the boa to consume them the moment they got within sniffing distance. Their mental maps would become anchored in reality. Or so goes the theory.

The "Samurai Strip"

To help soften the blow, the research assistant would first wear an impressive set of "Samurai armor" while touching the boa. The protective clothing included a catcher's mask and chest protector coupled with a hockey goalie's gloves. With time, the research assistant would discard each item, eventually cradling the boa in his or her arms with no protection beyond normal clothing. During the "Samurai strip," the snake-phobic subjects would sit in a nearby room and watch the action.

Next, the subjects would be asked to don the Samurai gear and go through the same procedure: first, standing next to the covered terrarium in full armor; next, touching the snake; next, removing the gloves—until eventually the subject cradled the 15-foot boa constrictor while seated alone in a room. Not bad for a person who originally wouldn't even look at the snake.

How long would such a procedure take? That's precisely what the Stanford group wanted to learn. Would subjects believe that they could enact the new behaviors with the same innocuous results? And if so, how long until they would be willing to try the same actions? Many outsiders suggested that it would take months, even years, of therapy. Restructuring mental maps isn't easy—especially when someone's map suggests that there's a 100 percent chance of being killed by a snake if you so much as touch it.

Success at Last

Any device whatever by which one frees himself from the fear of others is a natural good.

EPICURUS

After experimenting for a few weeks, researchers were able to reduce the therapy to two two-hour sessions. That's all. Within four hours almost every subject could be "desensitized." The therapy actually helped restructure mental maps. Eventually the Stanford group applied the process of systematic desensitization (or map shaping) to agoraphobics—individuals who feared leaving their homes to venture into the wide-open, dangerous world. Many had been housebound while undergoing traditional therapy for years. Systematic desensitization helped them as well. Within a few months they were out driving in the community. Most eventually took jobs.

Not Every *Latrodectus Mactans* Is a Friend

In partial fulfillment of an assignment for a graduate course I was teaching, one student suggested to me that she was going to "cure her husband" of arachnaphobia. When I asked her how debilitating her husband's fear was, she explained that he "refused to allow black-widow spiders to crawl on his body." We could be wrong about this, but not allowing a venomous spider to stroll across your face seems more like common sense than an unrealistic fear. To quote Ogden Nash, "If called by a panther, don't anther."

Motivation

Individual

Do I enjoy the activity itself?

EXPANDING THE MODEL: THE NEED FOR ABILITY

As elegant, practical, and effective as our model of behavior selection is, it's still incomplete; it's out of balance. When researchers worked with snake phobics, a model of anticipated consequences was all that was required. All they cared about was motivation. Their quest for a model of behavior selection could be reduced to a single cell—individual motivation.

They only needed one cell because *ability* never entered the formula. People *could* touch snakes—that was never a question. They simply chose not to. Just as models based on rodents didn't readily lead to a cognitive approach, models based on phobics wouldn't naturally explore the concept of ability. Nevertheless, without adding an ability component to the model, our view of behavior selection is incomplete. For example, had the researchers been examining why leaders don't always create vital cultures, they might have learned that not every problem is the result of inadequate motivation.

Incomplete Models Lead to Unbalanced Results

Naturally, when the model you're working with only includes motivation, you work with motivation. A more complete model of human behavior selection would take into consideration a person's ability—as does social learning theory. These learning theorists suggest that when people are considering whether or not to attempt a certain behavior, they not only look at the probability and value associated with each potential outcome, they also look at the difficulty of actually doing the required task. At the individual level, a more balanced model looks like this:

Motivation

Ability

Individual

Do I enjoy the activity itself?

Can I do what is required?

For example, should your boss ask you to sing a piece from Rossini's *The Barber of Seville* at your next corporate function, the issue of ability might spring to mind. Your boss enthusiastically suggests, "Just think how nice it would be to have a lovely aria open the session." You agree that music is always a nice touch, but you also know that you can't hum "Peter, Peter, Pumpkin Eater" from beginning to end without slipping half an octave and whipping the neighborhood dogs into a frenzy. Needless to say, you decline. Mental maps could be expanded to include ability in the following way:

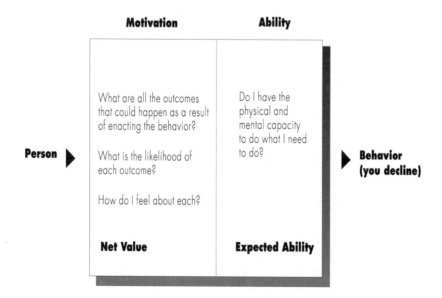

Motivation

Ability

Person ▶

What are all the outcomes that could happen as a result of enacting the behavior?

What is the likelihood of each outcome?

How do I feel about each?

Do I have the physical and mental capacity to do what I need to do?

▶ **Behavior (you decline)**

Net Value

Expected Ability

Our expanded model suggests that a person evaluates the probabilities of being able to successfully perform a behavior. This is referred to as the person's *expected ability*. As we suggested earlier, a person also assigns probabilities to each of the potential outcomes he or she thinks will happen if the behavior is enacted. These expectations, when combined with the individual's values and assumptions, produce the *net value* of the expected outcomes. The combination of (1) an individual's *net value* relative to expected outcomes (motivation) and (2) his or her *expected ability* predicts behavior.

The Fundamental Attribution Error

With malice toward none; with charity for all . . . let us strive on to finish the work we are in.

ABRAHAM LINCOLN

Using models that leave out ability hasn't been restricted to theorists. Assuming that all problems are due to motivation is perhaps the most common analytical error made by all humans—and leaders have been no exception. For 30 years, scholars have been able to demonstrate that when subjects draw conclusions about why others do what they do, they frequently violate simple rules of logic. For example, when asked why others enact certain socially unacceptable behaviors, people argue that others *want* to do it. Period. Rather than suggest that people are trapped into it (or really don't want to do it but are unable to do anything else), subjects typically explain that the person chooses to do it because he or she enjoys it.

Assuming that others almost always derive intrinsic satisfaction from what they do has been called the "fundamental attribution error." Restated: When attributing the reasons behind human action, people habitually assume that others gain immediate gratification from everything they do. Instead of being torn, having no other alternatives, or otherwise being influenced by ability or social circumstances, people do what they do in order to meet some internal, selfish desire. The term *fundamental* in the expression "fundamental attribution error" stems from the fact that the problem is pervasive. *Attribution*, of course, refers to the fact that people are assigning the reason or imputing the motive behind an action. Finally, the word *error* suggests that when people automatically assume that others are doing what they're doing because of selfish motives, they're often wrong.

> ### Fundamental Attribution Error
>
> The automatic assumption that others' actions are driven by selfish desires or motives.

I Want Names!

The most common way the fundamental attribution error is played out at work is to assume that all problems can be resolved through motivational techniques. When a boss hears that a group of employees is doing something wrong, the typical response is to "kick rear ends and take names." If the boss is more enlightened, he or she may give a motivational speech. Rather than stopping and saying, "I wonder why they did that?" or even more generously, "I wonder what in their surrounding environment led them to do that?" leaders typically respond with, "Look what they did this time!" Meaning, of course, look what they *chose* to do in order to satisfy their own selfish goals. As leaders repeatedly make the same assumption, they eventually convince themselves that their primary job is to build a fire under others. Since motivation is key to leadership effectiveness, they must become motivational geniuses. With time, leadership and motivation become synonymou*s*.

Remember the Rubber Tree Plant

You'd think that most leaders would go to great pains to ensure that they don't leave ability out of their model of human behavior selection. Unfortunately, most not only allow the fundamental attribution error to exist, they actually embrace it as a core belief. For example, you can find military boot camps all over the country proudly displaying a poster that proclaims, "Can't Means Won't!" The message behind this is clear: If you say that you can't do something, it means that you've chosen not to do something. Ability is never a factor.

While watching a TV evangelist trying to raise money, one of the authors learned that certain religious leaders aren't above the same tactic. When an elderly woman called in to the show and suggested that, despite her best wishes, she couldn't afford to send in any money, the preacher practically threw a fit. As his eyes began to bulge out of his head, he jumped to his feet and shouted, "Cain't means won't! Cain't means won't!"

Contemporary self-help gurus make a living off the fundamental attribution error as well. Some have gone so far as to have people walk on hot coals to prove their argument that people, when properly motivated, can do anything. If the point they were making was simply that people can achieve more than they initially might guess (as is the case with snake phobics), we wouldn't have a problem. It's just that most "motivational speakers" typically scream to the high heavens that people, if motivated, can do *anything*. Not only is such a simplistic approach untrue, it gives leaders (military, industrial, and religious alike) a great excuse for putting the screws on "all of those folks out there who have strayed from the formula."

Dancing with the Devil

The military services have embraced the fundamental attribution error as a credo, certain religious groups have elevated it to a sacrament, and Freud honed it to a science.

Now let's be clear. Ability isn't everything either. We aren't suggesting that "won't means can't." There are plenty of times when people *can* do things and simply choose not to because of anticipated outcomes. The traditional concept of human motivation still exists. We're simply arguing that efficacy needs to be added to the model to make it complete. We're calling for balance. When combined with outcome expectations and values, a person's sense of efficacy rounds out our model of human behavior selection. As we suggested earlier, this is true of all people—investors, customers, employees, and other stakeholders alike.

THE FINAL STEP: CREATING A USEFUL TOOL

Understanding how people make choices provides an invaluable diagnostic tool. Armed with a way of thinking about why people are currently doing what they're doing, leaders are in a better position to create the conditions that empower people to behave differently. That's the strength of the model we've developed. The weakness is that it's a bit unwieldy to think about the infinite array of mental maps a person might be carrying around. In order to organize mental maps, we've developed a model that helps leaders "bin" or combine *like* assumptions and values into six helpful categories of influence.

A Six-Cell Balancing Tool

At the top of our analytical tool are two components of behavior selection. In order to take the required action, the person must be willing *and* able. Impinging on these two components are three sources of influence: individual, social, and organizational. Each has a different effect.

Individual

This first component refers to how the individual would behave in isolation. Does the individual desire the objective (free from social pressure)? Does the person have the skills and knowledge required to complete his or her part in a given task?

	Motivation	**Ability**
Individual	1 Do I enjoy the activity itself?	2 Can I do what is required?
Social	3 How will others respond to my efforts?	4 Will others provide me with the help, authority, information, and resources I need?
Organizational	5 What formal rewards will I receive?	6 Do our structures/ systems/environment/ size block or facilitate my efforts?

Social

The term *social* can be understood at face value. What impact do others have on the person's motive and ability (social influence)? Do others encourage or discourage the required behavior? And what impact do others have on the person's ability to complete the task? Do others provide the necessary parts, services, information, and resources?

Organizational

The term *organizational* refers to the *nonhuman* elements that influence behavior selection. These elements include the organization's systems and procedures, machinery, work flow, etc. For example, at the motive level, the formal reward structure may impact individual choice. At the ability level, the work layout could influence individual ability.

A Simple Example: Using the Caliper to Get Quality

To illustrate the potential impact of each of the six sources of influence, we'll turn to an example. It comes from an actual problem we faced in an automobile-manufacturing facility. It started with an angry phone call. A customer had just been forced into a dangerous situation because the product had failed. Upon closer examination, the executive team learned that a critical quality test had never been performed. An hourly employee had simply skipped a step. An outside diameter was supposed to be measured with a specially designed caliper. The caliper hadn't been used.

Cell 1: Individual Motivation

As it became clear that the problem stemmed from not using the caliper, the management team became inflamed. The plant had just completed a quality program that had emphasized the importance of constant vigilance. "How could they have done this to us?" asked one of the managers. The rest nodded in agreement, and they rose en masse to march out to the production line—righteous indignation in hand.

Before the group made a complete exit, one of the authors asked an annoying question: "Why do you suppose the machine operator didn't take the quality measure?" "Why?" they looked on incredulously. "Because it's no fun," explained the operations manager. "Because the guy would rather be playing cards with his buddies," chimed in the quality manager. "Because he wanted to break early and take a rest," guessed the controller with a look of disgust.

This group was quick to judge the cause of the problem. Although the suggestions offered by the three managers varied slightly in tone, the diagnosis was essentially the same. As far as they were concerned, the machine operator failed to take the quality measure because he was unmotivated. He was unmotivated because he found the required task more noxious and less interesting than other things he could be doing. The executives committed the fundamental attribution error. They concluded that all problems are due to motivation, since the primary source of motivation is individual will or disposition. The cur was a lazy miscreant who reveled in making trouble for the organization, and it was about time he should be held accountable for his shenanigans.

Were they right?

Nobody knew. Of the six sources of influence, the team had immediately settled on the first one that popped into their minds—the individual's intrinsic motivation. By doing so, they had drastically reduced their capacity to discover what the real issues were. They limited their view of behavior selection to a single cell: individual motive. This doesn't mean that questioning the employee's motive was out of line. Motive *should* be explored. If not, you'd be leaving out a critical part of the diagnosis. But imputing poor motive as if it were the only source of problems is out of line, *and* it's philosophically incomplete and limiting.

It's also unfair to assume that the only intrinsic motive is selfishness. The employee might have chosen to skip the quality check in order to do something of equal importance. Perhaps he had to fix a machine glitch or avoid an unsafe work practice. Maybe the guy was motivated to do something of equal or greater importance to satisfy the customer.

Of course, beyond intrinsic motive, there was a whole host of other reasons the operator might have failed to take the quality measure. We can think of at least five other categories of factors.

Cell 2: Individual Ability

"Is it possible that the machine operator didn't use the caliper because he didn't know how to use it?" we continued to question. "It sounds crazy, given that taking quality measures is an essential part of the job, but recent tests taken in the Stamping Division showed that over 30 percent of the workforce were unable to read the calipers they use every day."

"I don't even want to think about that possibility," sighed the plant manager. "The thought that the people on our staff are unable to do their core job, after years of practice, is enough to make me sick."

"Sick or not," spoke up the human resources manager, "our recent spot check of SPC charts revealed that less than a third of the employees understood what the measures meant. Isn't that caliper one that requires interpolation? Maybe the guy is confused about how it works."

"It's possible," responded the area manager.

Cell 3: Social Motivation

"In our last quarterly interviews, I learned that a lot of the employees felt pressured by their peers to stick to their old ways," pointed out the scheduling supervisor. "When you interview employees in groups, they tend to talk about leadership problems, but when you talk to them alone, they tell a different story. Several said they were waiting on their friends before they would change."

"That's right," agreed the engineering manager. "Several people pointed out that they were reluctant to speed up their pace or increase their vigilance for fear of what their peers would say."

"Are you saying the guy didn't use calipers because of peer pressure?" asked the plant manager incredulously.

"It wouldn't be the first time," explained the operations manager. "When our supervisors sat down with their employees and taught them how to use SPC charts, several asked to keep their involvement low profile. They didn't want their friends to know that they were involved in our new quality process. Adding more measures was part of the deal."

Cell 4: Social Ability

"Speaking of group influence," muttered the engineering manager, "it could be that another operator simply borrowed the caliper and never gave it back. The things are always going twitchy, and rather than check a new one out of the tool room, they just pass 'em around. They don't want to take the time off the machine when they're on a tight deadline, so they juggle what they have rather than stop the job and go for materials."

"Are you saying that one guy's desire to get the job out the door on time could lead to someone else missing a quality check?" asked the plant manager.

"That's about the size of it," responded the engineering manager. "People are constantly being held up by their peers, and it's not always because they don't want to get the job done."

Cell 5: Organizational Motivation

"If somebody did snatch a caliper, you can hardly blame 'em," chimed in the controller. "Our reward structure encourages just such behavior."

"It does?" asked the human resources manager.

"Yeah," the controller continued. "Our bonus structure is based on group, or even individual, performance. Each area has its own goals and objectives. People are constantly pitted against each other to maximize their own goals. I once sneaked a computer from a guy across the hall to meet my own deadline, and the guy ended up getting chewed out for not doing his own job. He never did find out I was the guy who had his computer for two hours. I sneaked it back into his office the next day when he stepped out to take his licking from the division gurus."

The plant manager stroked his chin and whispered, "Maybe it's time we took a look at our bonus system."

Cell 6: Organizational Ability

"While you're looking at the bonus system," added the operations manager, "you'd better examine the basic design."

"What do you have in mind?"

"When I think about it, we put some 'go/no-go' calipers in that area. I'm not sure the guy even has the right tool. The specs we're facing require a more accurate measure than those old things can take. At the time we installed the machine, nobody had invented the right tool, but I think we now have adequate technology to get the job done. Who knows what ancient artifact the guy may be working with!"

As the managers continued their musings, it became clear to the group that the source of the problem was less obvious than they had originally assumed. It was equally clear that they would have to gather more data before making a decision. However, by asking a few questions, they had a good idea where to look.

How the Six-Cell Balancing Tool Links to Vitality

To help leaders break out of simplistic thinking, we've offered a clearer view of what really reflects and drives Cultural Vitality. We've set forth research and reasoning which argues that how people think and feel about their stakeholders (P_p, P_i, P_c, and P_o) leads to how they treat them. This, of course, leads to Outcome Vitality. Now we're adding a component that helps us get at how people think and feel. We've created a model that suggests that people make choices based on net value. That is, they look at a behavior and ask, (1) Can I do it? (2) What will happen if I do? and (3) How do I feel about it? Next we found a way to "bin" all of their assumptions and values into individual, social, and organizational categories. The resulting Six-Cell Balancing Tool helps us understand the behavior we have that either creates high or low Cultural Vitality. It breaks us out of the simplistic choice of "just" looking at organizational structure, social influence, or individual motivation as the key to changing the culture. It affords leaders a comprehensive view of the influences that shape behavior over time—within an organizational context.

This tool helps leaders understand some of the successes and failures in culture change efforts. When interventions have focused on only one or two cells, they have typically fallen flat. When all six cells have been carefully diagnosed and interventions have been made that are consistent with the diagnosis, they have often succeeded.

SOME PRACTICAL ADVICE FROM THIS SECTION

How Does This Apply to Leadership?

The cause of all human evils is not being able to apply general principles to specific cases.

EPICTETUS

As section 1 comes to a close, we should take a few minutes to reflect on the practical implications of the theories we've developed. If you choose not to read another chapter, you should be able to walk away with something at this point. Granted, most of what we've done thus far falls into the category of theory and vocabulary building. Nevertheless, the theories we've discussed have important implications to daily leadership.

Differing Views of Humanity

Contemporary behavioral and social theorists make their greatest contribution to the field of leadership not simply by providing a complex and predictive model, but by suggesting an important view of humanity. For example, to suggest that humans are nonthinking creatures who simply respond to rewards and punishment leads to highly manipulative motivational techniques. (We're reminded of a book that encourages leaders to lean forward in their chairs and smile when their direct reports give the "correct" answer, but to look the other way and frown when they're wrong.) Similarly, viewing humans as carnal animals who continually battle with antisocial behaviors doesn't exactly lead to the most compassionate leadership style.

Within a social cognitive approach, humans are characterized as thinking, anticipatory beings who can be creative, inventive, and thoughtful. They're seen as value based rather than need driven. That is, humans can learn to value goals that are both long-term and selfless. Rather than being cast as animals that respond to only the most selfish and visceral of needs, humans love, sacrifice, and in other ways work toward objectives more momentous than just satisfying their basic cravings. The old concept of a rigid need hierarchy is replaced with a model that argues that people develop unique values that go beyond a simple hierarchy. Mothers go without food in order to feed their children. Volunteers give up physical comfort and disposable income in order to work in orphanages. Political activists ignore social sanctions in order to serve their cause. Within this model there is room for both Hitler and Gandhi.

Net-Value Behavior Selection — A Healthy Blend

There can be no knowledge without emotion. . . . To the cognition of the brain must be added the experience of the soul.

ARNOLD BENNETT

The implications to leadership of a value-driven, logically sound theory of behavior selection are many. Since people respond to the net value of perceived outcomes, motivation looks more like teaching than cajoling or inspiring. A leader's job is to share mental maps until all parties share the same view—each giving and taking as the other adds valuable insights to the shared mental map. Leaders see themselves more as educators, map sharers, or even coscientists and less as cheerleaders. They give up *rah! rah!* and seek for *aha!*

Because our model includes both perceived outcomes (scientific probabilities) and values (a sense of right and wrong), we believe that leadership requires an appreciation for both science and philosophy. Effective leaders are neither heartless scientists who only concern themselves with probabilities, nor are they warm-and-fuzzy philosophers whose sole concern is feelings. Instead, skilled leaders could be best characterized as "concerned scientists." As scientists, they're constantly looking for what is correct and true. They want to be able to predict behavior. By being concerned, they place great value on respecting and dignifying other human beings.

The Concerned Scientist's Response to Problems

Concerned scientists see problems as challenges that need to be understood and not as the natural result of unmotivated or basically wrong people. They respond with curiosity rather than anger. They seek to expand their own understanding rather than self-righteously "fix" others. They replace expressions such as "Can you believe them?" with "I wonder what's going on?" They don't try to motivate or control others but strive instead to find ways to share mental maps. Rather than use "selling" or persuasion techniques to change mental maps, concerned scientists use their dialogue skills as a way to change and merge different sets of maps. They see motivation as something that needs to be captured rather than created from whole cloth. As concerned scientists move from office to home, they apply the same view to parenting. They see their job as one of helping children gain an accurate understanding of the world rather than an opportunity to finally wield power.

A Balanced Approach

Civilization itself is a certain sane balance of values.

EZRA POUND

Finally, a complete model of behavior selection helps us make a balanced diagnosis. When trying to get a handle on Cultural Vitality, rather than continually diving deep into individual motive, we can explore six complete areas, and by so doing consider a wide and balanced range of potential sources of influence. David Bradford, of Stanford University, suggests that your average person is a fairly good intuitive psychologist, a mediocre social psychologist, and a pretty lousy sociologist. We share this belief. It helps explain why leaders spend so much of their time trying to motivate others when, in many cases, a change of structure would be both easier and more effective. We hope leaders, as they try to figure out what's "going on out there," will consider a Six-Cell approach rather than always looking at the world through the lens of individual motive. Frankly, life is far more interesting when viewed from more than a single window—*and* more balanced.

It will be this complex Six-Cell view of humanity that we'll apply throughout this book. And not just because it's a noble model or because it represents the best of contemporary thinking, but because it represents the thoughts and feelings of the most effective leaders we've observed over the past 20 years. It helps harried leaders, caught between competing demands, come up with a practical balance.

SECTION 1 QUIZ

To stick to our word that we'll try to have fun along the way, use the checklist below to see if your culture is almost dead, soon to be completely dead, or not far from dead forever.

You Know You're Near Death When . . .

- The three most common adjectives used in the open-ended questions of your organization's latest survey were: *flaming*, *drooling*, and *sniveling*.

- The I.R.S. has a speed-dial number to your office.

- Your chief financial officer just renegotiated his benefits package by giving up his retirement plan in exchange for the right to be paid in cash at the end of every shift.

- Loud and annoying echoes are emanating from the area that used to be called Customer Service.

- Several TV announcements about what's happening to your company are made every week—right between the "Top Ten List" and "Stupid Pet Tricks."

- The executive committee has formed a union.

- Your dissatisfied customers don't just leave angry; they mortgage their homes and open competing businesses.

- Your Corporate Morale Team just hung banners in the hallways proclaiming, "Our customers are so dumb they actually buy the junk we make."

- Your advertising execs decided it's cheaper to print "Classic" on your products rather than introduce new features.

- After using your new product for the first time, several hundred customers wrote and asked, "Should my left leg glow in the dark?"

Taking Stock of
Your Vitality

Before jumping with both feet into change strategies, we'll ask leaders to step back from their current challenges and take stock of their present condition. Our goal will be to identify gaps between what leaders desire and what they currently have. Once these gaps are identified, leaders will be asked to design, implement, and measure change efforts that are intended to eliminate the difference between the ideal and the actual. These gaps will serve as a starting point for the change strategies we'll be discussing in sections 3 and 4.

In chapter 3 we'll start by asking you to put on the lenses of the visionary. We'll explore ways to dream a dream. For some people, this will seem alien, even contrived. This is because most leaders are so driven by daily demands to fill the holes found between their best plans and their current results that they don't dare stop and hope for more. Why dream of the "ideal organization" when your current desires to create a tolerable one are frequently stifled?

In spite of never-ending frustrations in achieving mundane results, we'll explore ways to push the envelope. We'll encourage leaders to take part in one of the most basic acts of true leadership. We'll ask leaders to craft a vision of what can be for all stakeholders. Our thesis is simple: *If you don't dream it, you won't achieve it.* To help leaders build a balanced dream, we'll look at methods for clarifying a detailed picture of both Cultural Vitality and Outcome Vitality.

Chapter 4 describes how leaders can assess their current Cultural Vitality. Cultural Vitality is the engine that drives us toward the vision. We'll examine a culture-assessment process that can be used to gain greater understanding of the values and assumptions of all stakeholder groups. We'll pay particular attention to the thoughts and hopes of employees. At the end of the assessment process, leaders will be asked to select those behaviors identified in the dream or vision that are most at risk.

The final chapter in this section, chapter 5, examines methods for taking the pulse of your culture. Here's where we put rigor into what is often a fuzzy and aimless process of culture change. We will propose ways of establishing clear and predictive measures that help leaders know:

- Baseline measures of the behaviors they're trying to foster.
- Six-Cell levers they will need to pull to increase the frequency of those behaviors.

At the end of this section, leaders will have a clear idea of how to:

- Choose a balanced, understandable, and motivating outcome vision.
- Choose the balanced culture vision that is most likely to drive the outcome vision.
- Create measures that help them design change efforts and measure progress along the path to Organizational Vitality.

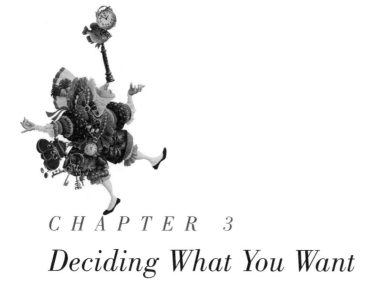

C H A P T E R   3

Deciding What You Want

In the country of the blind the one-eyed man is king.

MICHAEL APOSTOLIUS

S ome leaders shy away from the notion of dreaming or creating a vision. The very act sounds too mystical, even religious. When hearing the term *vision*, most of us conjure up images of Moses at the burning bush or a TV evangelist whose eyes gloss over (even roll back into his head) while words and images are fed to him by divine sources. Such nontraditional strategies seem ill-matched to daily business demands. Couple the mystical aura associated with the term *vision* with the fact that most business schools have flagged any act that even hints of an emotion as unprofessional, and it's little wonder that most level-headed leaders begin to shuffle their feet and look at the floor when the word *vision* is even mentioned.

Let's be clear from the start that this chapter does not concern itself with mystical visioning. Instead, we're encouraging leaders to find ways to articulate a clear picture of the "ideal organization." The visions we're proposing are similar to the one held by Martin Luther King, Jr., who told us that he had a dream. And he did. He had a detailed view of a world free from prejudice. He knew what it meant to live in a place where people were viewed not as mindless puppets pulled by genetic strings, but as distinct individuals with unique hopes and dreams. His actual experience, coupled with his ability to imagine the ideal, produced a view of a world that was at once unreal (i.e., not yet a reality) and attainable.

NOT ALL SMOKE AND MIRRORS

He's allowed me to go up to the mountain. And I've looked over, and I've seen the Promised Land.

MARTIN LUTHER KING, JR.

Dr. King's dream of the promised land wasn't made of cotton-candy concepts and warm-and-fuzzy promises. Instead, it consisted of a daily plan of action. It was filled with behaviors—both do's and don'ts. It was made up of hundreds of mental maps of how the world fits together. For example, in Dr. King's view, racial slurs would be met by a healthy disgust. Individuals would not tolerate intolerance, nor would they respond with violence. His vision consisted of a clearly articulated and detailed view of daily interaction. His dream or vision was not conjured in a pipe, but grew out of his understanding of ideal circumstances combined with what he knew was attainable. His vision invited people to push the envelope, not fall on the sword of unrealistic expectations.

Corporate dreams are made of similar stuff. They consist of thousands of mini-maps of how varying stakeholders interrelate, including a detailed array of behaviors, values, and assumptions that paint a clear picture of what healthy organizational life looks like. They extend beyond catchy phrases and popular language to detailed descriptions of daily actions. Corporate visions also come from a blend of actual experience and imagination. They are grounded in the reality of existing excellence. They grow out of moments of healthy interaction and are expanded by friends and colleagues who freely and willingly share their views of what they too have seen on the best days of organizational life. In short, they are clearly articulated maps of the behaviors, values, and assumptions of healthy employees at work. They paint a hopeful picture that encourages stakeholders to willingly continue their relationship and that stimulates employees to do whatever it takes to maintain the balancing act.

Hang with us as we dive deep into the whys and wherefores of visioning. We'll start with a detailed theory of what makes up a good vision, including common errors and fatal mistakes. And just when you're beginning to wonder if you can really do this, we'll end with a practical, how-to section that explains how the theory can be applied to your organization.

WHAT? ME WORRY?

Over the years, as we've talked with thousands of people about the need for a clearly articulated vision of the outcomes and culture they're trying to create, many wonder if it's really their job to spin a vision. After all, most don't sit atop the organization where the view is expansive and the need for vision is obvious. Instead, they lead a small team or perhaps a department or division. "Is it appropriate," they ask, "to have a dream for our group? And if so, how do we fit it into the broader organization? Are we being disloyal if what we want for our own team is different from what others want?"

To answer these heartfelt and important questions, we'll share a poignant experience. During the early 1970s, one of the authors faced the same question. This is his story.

The Border Guard

Harsh necessity . . . force[s] me to . . . guard my frontiers everywhere.

VIRGIL

In 1971 I received my first leadership assignment. After 17 weeks of torturous training at Officer Candidate School, I graduated as a newly appointed ensign. As my wife and I drove across the country to my first duty station, we talked about what I had just experienced. It hadn't been pretty. As part of our indoctrination, I and other candidates had been forced to lie on our backs with our arms and legs thrust upward, kicking and thrashing, playing the part of a dying cockroach. We were coerced to run in sweltering heat, and at least two people passed out from heat exhaustion. Terms such as *idiot*, *imbecile*, and *bonehead* were hurled at us with genuine venom. In short, we went through what the U.S. Coast Guard had deemed to be the ideal treatment for young men who were about to be commissioned officers, gentlemen, and the leaders of the future.

Love That Abuse

Rats and people learn to love the things they suffer for.

LEON FESTINGER

At first, my reaction to the treatment was predictable. I told myself it was necessary to mold me into an ensign. My wife didn't share my opinion.

She noted that I seemed less confident, somewhat cowed, and just a little twitchy. She wondered how this made me better. I couldn't even conceive of the fact that it might have made me worse.

Festinger had been right. Terrified by the thought that the abuse I had undergone was probably unwarranted, I had been trying to give it a positive spin. But try as I might, I couldn't justify it. In fact, it didn't take long until I decided that personal abuse wasn't the best way to lead people—in training or any other place. It certainly wasn't going to be the way *I* would work with people. And so, one Thursday morning while we were cruising somewhere in the deserts of Arizona in a white, 1970 Volkswagen beetle, I swore on a holy book (with my wife as witness) that I would never abuse my authority, demean people, or otherwise create a punishing environment as a way of achieving any objective— no matter how noble.

But to be true to my convictions, would I have to give up my commission?

Creating a Safe Place

The only way to predict the future is to have power to shape the future.
                                                                    ERIC HOFFER

My first job as an ensign put my conviction to a real test. I was assigned to lead a small crew of enlisted men who ran the clothing locker for the recruit training center at Government Island, across the estuary from Oakland, California. My staff's job was to outfit newly recruited enlisted men who were just beginning boot camp—recruits, as you might guess, who were shoveled heaping mounds of abuse every day. The U.S. Coast Guard, leery of being viewed as the sissy service that mostly hung around yacht clubs and hosted regattas, decided to outdo the U.S. Marine Corps when it came to abusing trainees.

The newly initiated were treated far worse than officer candidates. They were called *maggot, scum bag*, and other unsavory terms. They were forced to drag huge chains around the compound until some of the men collapsed. They were marched in full uniform into the estuary until someone nearly drowned. They routinely ran around in the heat and cold with M-1 rifles hoisted over their heads. And worst of all, they were screamed at until they were eventually frightened out of their wits. One look at a platoon of Coast Guard recruits in the early 1970s and you knew that these poor souls were on the brink of cracking.

During the first few weeks of my assignment, as I watched frightened recruits march into our stark, cold building, strip naked, and wait to be measured and given their allotted gear, I noted that the fact that they were frightened made it more difficult for us to do our job. The mortified recruits stood so stiffly that it was hard to get a fix on their true size. Worse still, I hated the fact that they were being abused before my very eyes. Their company commanders seemed to delight in humiliating and cowing their charges in front of the young ensign. This I couldn't tolerate. After all, this was the clothing locker—my turf, my dream area, my island of respect in a sea of abuse. Besides, I'd made a sacred promise. So after two short weeks on the job, I made a fateful decision. I was going to make the recruits' clothing experience relaxed, respectful, even fun. The clothing locker would be a safe haven.

But how? These guys came marching onto our turf looking like they were only moments away from needing shock therapy. And hovering nearby (with a swagger stick and a sneer that could drop a rhinoceros in midcharge) was their abusive commander. One look of disgust from him and rocks trembled.

Humor. *That* was the ticket. If I could only get these poor kids to laugh, surely they'd relax.

Oops!

Two days later, as I wandered among a group of 45 young, terrified, naked men, I tried to find something humorous—no easy task, considering the macabre circumstances. And then Providence stepped in. One of the 17-year-old neophytes put on his undershorts backward. It struck me as funny, so I pointed it out to his company commander, a boatswain's mate who made Dennis Hopper look sane. If I could parlay this incident into a clever wisecrack or two, I calculated, it was only a matter of seconds until the whole crowd would be doubled over with laughter. (What was I thinking?!)

The boatswain's mate, a man who stood 6′ 2″ and had muscles that made my teeth feel soft by comparison, walked straight over to the recruit in question. Unwittingly, in my attempt to generate laughter, I had called in the dogs of hell. The chiseled boatswain's mate stood toe to toe with the recruit in question, shoved his nose flush against the recruit's right eyeball (giving new meaning to the term *eye contact*), and told him that he had embarrassed the platoon, the Coast Guard, and simians in general. And then, when I thought there was no way that the atmosphere in the room could get any tenser, the crazed commander slugged the defenseless kid in the face, knocking him out cold.

Nobody laughed.

At that moment, in a stroke of insight born of terror, I concluded that I was dangerous—that despite my best dreams and well-thought-out plans, if I continued to try to create a haven in the midst of the terror, I could get somebody killed.

Speaking Two Languages and Filtering

No man should travel until he has learned the language of the country he visits. Otherwise he voluntarily makes himself a great baby—so helpless and so ridiculous.

RALPH WALDO EMERSON

As the wounded recruit was hauled off to the infirmary, I vowed to learn how to do things *their* way. I concluded that I couldn't create what I wanted until I first learned how to operate in the existing system, even if it meant becoming part of it. For a year I learned the ins and outs of a culture that I didn't much care for. I learned the language of control, and I learned it well. And then one day, when I felt like I had earned the right to dream my own dream, I set about the task of being a border guard.

My job, I concluded, was to sit on the border between the haven I yearned to create and the world around me. To succeed in the two cultures, I would have to speak both languages. I'd have to straddle the border between the rest of the organization and my own little world. I'd have to be able to function equally well in both cultures.

Leaders above me might give me a command in a way that was insulting, verging on pathological, but I didn't have to pass it on to my team that way. Naturally, I had to pass on the work, but I didn't have to pass on the abuse. In spite of the fact that whatever's negative or undesirable takes the path of least resistance (even in organizations), my job was to filter it out. I was to be a border guard *and* a filter.

Daring to Dream

As I grew into the clothing-locker job, I took great pains to take the organization's mission statement and blend it with my own vision. Together, my staff and I hammered out our own view of how we would treat each other and those around us. The clothing locker did become a place where recruits could relax and be accurately measured. I learned to send the company commander off to the Acey Deucey Club for a cup of coffee—my treat. I learned how to maintain control and dignity at the same time.

More important, I learned that it is okay for a group of people to dream their own dream and then do what it takes to turn it into reality. We spent hours talking about what we wanted, how to do it, and how to be loyal to the broader organization at the same time. And as we created our own vision of excellence, we became a team to reckon with. On several occasions the team rose to meet unexpected challenges, earning awards along the way. In fact, within a few short months our team became the best and most respected workgroup on the base.

In the remaining pages, when we talk about creating your own dream or vision, we're asking you to do what every person should do—no matter their position in the organization. Developing and executing a vision is a central task of every human who walks through the front doors. Of course, to create your own haven in a world gone bureaucratic, controlling, insensitive, and myopic, you'll have to be a visionary, a border guard, and a filter. It'll take courage. But that's what makes the job exciting. It's what separates leaders from managers.

Consequently, today, after having worked with hundreds of leaders who are taking the time to create their own dream, when people ask if it's okay to come up with their own vision of the organization they'd like to create, we tell them that it's more than okay. *It's their obligation*. After all, if they don't dare to dream, who will?

CREATING DISSATISFACTION WITH WHAT *IS*

Unfortunately, the balance of nature decrees that a super-abundance of dreams is paid for by a growing potential for nightmares.

PETER USTINOV

Having said that it's every person's responsibility to conjure up and live his or her own dream, it's time to look at what makes some dreams work while others fail. It turns out that a great number of leaders, in their honest desire to create a healthier organization, embrace dreams that result in nightmarish results. The reason? Many visions never translate into results, but they almost always translate into dissatisfaction. People typically prefer the demon they know to the one just around the corner.

So we caution leaders to cross the threshold of visioning thoughtfully. Creating a view of a better world isn't a process that can be whacked out in a weekend. It requires drinking deeply and often from the fountain of hope. When leaders don't take the visioning process seriously, their visions of what can be are born of wishful (and often shallow) thinking. Their dreams are conjured up in a moment of desperation and then gazed at less frequently than a high school yearbook.

These intellectual concoctions not only fail to remedy existing problems, they create new ones (feeding employees' staunch belief that their leaders are dimwits who can only pump out unrealistic and fuzzy dreams—and then only after an aneurysm). Despite their best efforts, many leaders have created visions that bear a number of common flaws.

Typically, their visions of how each stakeholder will be treated are imbalanced or dated. Their visions of what their own organization's culture will be like are selfish or fuzzy. Let's learn from each of these mistakes. As we do, begin reflecting on the outcomes and culture you'd sacrifice or suffer for to try to create.

The Imbalanced Dream

Left unattended, yesterday's Bambi becomes tomorrow's Godzilla.

Perhaps the most common dream turned nightmare is the one that grows out of the latest management fad—bowing to the whims of one stakeholder group at the expense of others. We've addressed this issue in earlier chapters, but it deserves separate consideration here.

A healthy vision contains an attractive dream for each group of stakeholders. Effective leaders refuse to be dragged into the either-or game. As tempting as it might be to snub a satisfied (and possibly fairly weak) stakeholder group in order to rectify problems with angry and dangerous stakeholders, visionary leaders find solutions that don't rob Peter in order to pay Pauline. They understand that, over the long haul, nobody can be snubbed or blown away. When asked what their dream of a healthy organization is, insightful leaders think long and hard about the end state of *each* stakeholder and the Cultural Vitality required to achieve it.

To demonstrate how "imbalanced dreams" can wreak havoc in the long run, let's consider what's happened to the most vulnerable stakeholder—the community. For years, organizations have posted mission statements that laud the importance of the community. But with what results? For nearly a century, organizations worldwide have destroyed not only rivers and streams, but even worse, families. And now, having sown the seeds of destruction, we're reaping the crop of desolation and violence.

If you doubt what we're suggesting, take a drive through just about any large city. When you cruise through Detroit and pass a KFC with bulletproof windows, you have to wonder if the automotive industry doesn't bear some responsibility for the wretched conditions. Are the pilfering, indolence, drug addiction, and illiteracy in some measure consequences of the imbalanced visions of previous generations?

Consider for a moment the visioning process executives have often used over the past years. When a manufacturing plant is established, accountants determine the peak operating parameters for expensive equipment. They point out that optimum financial returns are realized by running the equipment for three full shifts. Makes sense. So the plant hires thousands of people who work evenings, nights, and early mornings, in addition to those who work during the day. But at what cost? Interviews we recently conducted with off-hour shift employees uncovered several people who wondered how long it would be until their own children fell into crime. One single parent suggested that it was only a matter of months until his son would become a drug dealer. Another feared that her daughter was already a hooker.

Of course, the problem isn't restricted to three-shift companies. As the crunch to reduce costs while increasing output continues to hold most leaders in a vise, more and more are finding that the only way to get more done with fewer resources is to put in longer hours for the same pay. Thousands of salaried employees now work 60 to 70 hours per week. Without ever having signed up for it, they now work a job and a half—or even more.

We're left to wonder if the disintegration of families *and* the consequent decay of whole communities and neighborhoods is, in part, a result of parents who have worked for years during the only times they could have seen, influenced, and reared their children. What are teenagers doing as both parents struggle to meet the demands of a job that can only be done during off-hour shifts or in 60 or more hours? Customers and owners may benefit from increased hours and full plant utilization in the short run, but is the imbalanced vision costing more than we ever imagined?

The Cost of Myopia

The future has waited long enough; if we do not grasp it, other hands, grasping hard and bloody, will.

ADLAI STEVENSON

When you consider the financial costs alone that companies have to pay in employee-assistance benefits, increased plant security, absenteeism, and other problems that have resulted from the decay of the family (not to mention the enormous cost in increased taxes), you're left with little doubt that leaders who build profits on the back of the community will soon have to wallow in their own myopic swill. Even customers are beginning to ask if the cost of putting bars on their windows is adequately offset by the benefit of being able to buy near-perfect and quite inexpensive widgets.

Let's be clear. We aren't proposing that companies become welfare states. We're proposing balance. We're suggesting that the balancing act should include a balanced vision or detailed picture of how employment policies affect *all* stakeholders. For example, when a dear friend recently bought a manufacturing facility, he spent hours with his leadership team discussing what could be done to mitigate the impact of off-hour shifts and lengthy hours in general. Years earlier, he had taken part in heart-wrenching interviews with distraught employees and wasn't anxious to further contribute to the decay of the surrounding community.

When he first started the discussions, his leadership team was at a loss. They didn't believe that their new boss's concerns were genuine. In addition, since the topic was so new to them, they couldn't think of any remedies. Eventually they began to discuss putting in a "study hall" for the children of those working the afternoon shift. The students would be picked up at their schools, bused to the facility, and given guidance and help with their homework. They would build a club for the teenagers. Of course, they faced real trade-offs. The costs of such a plan couldn't simply be passed on to the consumer. Funds would have to come out of employee and owner profits. Would people be willing to do so?

The jury is out on what this visionary leader and his team will come up with or how it'll work. Nevertheless, our hat goes off to a leader who not only understands that balanced outcomes come from a balanced vision but who is willing to go head to head with a problem that others have suffered with but have not dared address.

The Ultimate "Undiscussable"

As we consult with leadership teams for the first time, we're often faced with a group of people who are hovering dangerously close to burnout. Unfortunately, nobody can talk about it. After putting in 10 to 12 hours at work, people actually apologize if they have to leave a meeting in order to watch one of their kids' Little League games. Many, eager to impress their boss that they're dedicated, send e-mail messages from their homes—with a 2 a.m. time conspicuously recorded next to the message. In private, many share touching stories of crumbling families. In public, they smile weakly as new assignments are piled onto a plate that's already full.

To deal with this problem, we ask team members to paint a picture of their ideal job. How do they want to work together? Describe the perfect day, week, and month at work. If we don't make the issue of excessive hours a legitimate topic, nobody talks about how much time he or she wants to put in. Nobody wants to be viewed as undedicated or unwilling to pay the price. Sadder still, nobody thinks to include *the ability to share honest concerns* in his or her view of the ideal company.

As much as people would love to be able to share their burdens with colleagues with whom they spend more time than almost anyone else, they don't *dare* dream of a place where heartfelt discussions of the home and community are acceptable. After all, people don't talk about family challenges or personal issues at work. It weakens their competitive position. And so they suck it up, pump stomach acid, and grow tumors. After all, who dares dream a dream in an organization where the very act of dreaming is discouraged and *family* is considered an f-word? Better yet, who dares to speak first?

Your Responsibility

Vision is the art of seeing things invisible.

JONATHAN SWIFT

When creating your own dream of the ideal organization, remember our friend who worried about the afternoon-shift employees. Think more carefully about all the ways you impact the communities you participate in. Even small employers have an effect on the water, environment, tax base, and employment base. All are playing an important role in family life. Do you consider these issues when making decisions? Will it ever be okay for you to talk about your life (including your family), or will what happens outside the building remain a secret? What promises are you willing to make to the community?

In this discussion of creating a balanced dream, we have focused on the community (and its subset, the family) because we know that it (among all stakeholders) is often the most susceptible to short-term abuse. We use it as an example of the need to keep all people in mind. We're calling for a balanced vision. We're arguing that a complete map of the ideal organization includes a picture of what happens to all who associate with your organization—over both the short run and the long run. We also want leaders to remember that the realities we face in today's society and in today's global community are created one social unit at a time. Corporate behavior, in a very real sense, is a building block of global behavior.

Remember also that the purpose of the vision is to knit disparate groups into a common cause. If you want your vision to engage deep commitment, it must hold great promise. If you want it to tap into deeper motives, it must link to an inspiring cause.

The Yesterday Dream

You see things; and you say "Why?" But I dream things that never were; and I say "Why not?"

GEORGE BERNARD SHAW

A healthy vision does more than look at current demands. Current demands reflect yesterday's thinking. A healthy vision anticipates changing stakeholder needs. Product designers have been long aware of the fact that if you simply give people what they're currently demanding, you can be at risk. You have to extend your present view of the world into your best-guess vision of where changing technologies and cultural mores will take us in the immediate future.

For instance, Robert Allen of AT&T has gone on record with his promise to customers:

AT&T will be the world's best at bringing people together—giving them easy access to each other and to the information and services they want—anytime, anywhere.

When Allen first made this statement, people weren't exactly clamoring to be brought together. Well, at least not in so many terms. Nevertheless, Mr. Allen looked into the future and saw the role of communications as one of covering interpersonal, informational, and entertainment needs through a variety of media. He then made a promise that he believed people will want him to keep in the future—far beyond today's simple demands for a low-priced and reliable phone service.

Having firmly planted this flag of promise on the ground AT&T wants to stand on in the future, Allen is in a better position to understand the gaps between where the company is today and where it needs to get to. A vision shouldn't consist of yesterday's hackneyed solutions projected onto tomorrow's problems.

Allen's dream opens the imagination of his company to search for ways to bypass earthbound communication technology in the interest of helping people find each other anywhere. His vision of the value they offer, independent of the means for delivering it, allows for exploration of ways to hold meetings where everyone can see everyone else without being in the same room. And by emphasizing the pure value to customers in the vision, AT&T has broken with yesterday in search of tomorrow.

The Selfish Dream

Nothing is so easy to fake as the inner vision.

ROBERTSON DAVIES

The most common error we see leaders make as they attempt to create their own vision of the ideal culture is captured by Stephanie, a character on *Newhart*. For those of you who watched the television program, you'll remember her as the self-centered housekeeper who demanded that everyone, particularly her husband, cater to her every whim. Perhaps her most memorable line came one week when her sniveling spouse, fed up with her coquettish demands, left her. When Stephanie realized that pouting, whimpering, and grousing wouldn't regain her husband's obsequious adulation, she asked (in a revealing expression of her lack of sincerity), "Okay, so what's the least I can do to get you back?" We'll refer to this as the "Stephanie Ploy"—calculating the least amount you can do to regain a disgruntled stakeholder.

What's the Least We Can Do?

No man sees far; the most see no farther than their noses.

THOMAS CARLYLE

Far too many leaders, in their quest to solve growing problems with stakeholders, spin a dream made of shallow promises and Band-Aid remedies. Rather than take the time to explore what is required to truly surprise and delight their stakeholders, they look for ways to outsmart and dazzle with trappings. Instead of looking for methods to surface needs and develop long-term solutions, they look for a quick fix supported by trivial efforts. Their dream, while never spoken aloud, is clear. They want Outcome Vitality without having to create a vital culture. They, like Stephanie, want world-class results by doing the least amount possible.

The cure for this malady can be simply stated, although difficult to execute. A vision should be a natural extension of one's honest appreciation and respect for others and not a selfish reaction to existing problems. If you want to focus on immediate problems, start with problems. If you want to avoid them in the first place, start with a clear articulation of your selfless values. Set aside your view of what is currently ailing you, sit back, close your eyes, and imagine what the ideal organization would look like. *Start with your heart*. Sure, reality will come crashing in soon enough, knocking off corners and reshaping your dream. Nevertheless, forget about the shaping forces of bureaucracy, narrow thinking, turf protecting, history, and tradition. When you start the process, begin with your most daring, selfless, and noble dream, and then let the chips fall where they may.

The Fuzzy Dream

If a little dreaming is dangerous, the cure for it is not to dream less but to dream more, to dream all the time.

MARCEL PROUST

One of the more disturbing movements in America is the current obsession with the need to express ideas in short, pithy "sound bites." Driven by the need to capture complex issues in compressed and memorable expressions that can be stated in a few seconds in a news interview, far too many people in positions of leadership have become quite adept at spouting clever truisms and "feel good" homilies at the expense of garnering in-depth understanding.

You can't throw a rock without hitting someone who is sidling up to a microphone and crooning the need for family values or who passionately promises to be tough on crime. In business settings, leaders talk with similar gusto about the need to surprise and delight customers. Others call for empowerment, teamwork, and quality. Unfortunately, many sound-bite masters know little beyond their catchy phrases. For example, while a friend was attending a workshop on *empowerment*, he asked the consultant to define the term. After stammering around for a minute, it was clear that when pushed to dive beneath the surface of warm-and-fuzzy words, the energetic (but surprisingly shallow) consultant could come up with little of substance.

In their quest for being quoted in a way that is *memorable*, consultants, leaders, and politicians alike often develop rhetoric that is long on clever and short on meaning. Although brevity of expression does not necessarily stem from brevity of analysis, if leaders are more interested in the expression of a thought than in the underlying principles and values, they can be easily dragged into a Madison Avenue leadership style that prefers sizzle over beef.

The Clever But Shallow Mission

Visions of the ideal organization are particularly vulnerable to pithy, yet relatively meaningless, sound bites. When asked to come up with mission statements or other articulations of the ideal organization, leaders typically feel compelled to reduce their vision to a handful of words that are both memorable and motivating. To be honest, they should. We have no bone to pick with those who produce clever summary statements of complex dreams.

Our concern is that, in almost every organization in which we've worked, a majority of the leaders have hammered out clever statements that represent *the lion's share* of their thinking. When pushed for a detailed explanation of a key word or concept found in their printed mission statement, leaders typically respond with an embarrassed grin, followed by a synonym. Instead of launching into a detailed view of how the concept translates into daily activity or giving a sample of what the concept does and does not mean, they respond with other catchy phrases that are intended to "warm" but rarely inform. Dreams should be undergirded by clearly considered mental maps and not by a mere handful of cute quotes. Short, pithy mission statements must be backed up by a detailed vision.

Will You Fire Their Butts?

For he who lives more lives than one
More deaths than one must die.

OSCAR WILDE

Not long ago we gave a detailed presentation to the union leaders of a rather large industrial complex. We shared with them the skills and underlying values of an upcoming leadership training program. We were seeking their input and blessing. Throughout the discussion, we repeatedly highlighted the importance of a humane and dignified approach to problem solving. After dispelling any notions that we would be teaching leaders how to manipulate, and eventually abuse, the hourly employees who made up their constituency, we talked in detail (using video examples) about mutual respect and collaboration. As the presentation came to a close, a senior official (who had been impressed with our recommendations) raised his hand and asked, "If management doesn't treat us with respect and dignity, will you fire their butts?"

Obviously this fellow had a limited understanding of what we had been discussing. He had accepted parts of our arguments but had missed vital components of the map we were trying to draw.

Fuzzy Visions Invite Criticism

Keep thy smooth words and juggling homilies
For those who know thee not.

LORD BYRON

As we start our "visioning discussions" with executive teams, we often talk of passing out T-shirts with large bull's-eyes painted on the back. We suggest that as leaders begin to jointly hammer out a vision of a new and healthier organization and then share it with others, they will soon be labeled as hypocrites. It's only a matter of time until they will be accused of not *walking the talk*. In short, they become moving targets.

The reasons behind such quick judgments are manifold. First, leaders are able to draw up and communicate a vision faster than they can turn it into a reality. Consequently, employees are often left with galloping expectations that are hitched to plodding realities.

> Every time a leader promises a better tomorrow, expectations take off with a gallop, while realities crawl along behind.

In addition, the leaders' view of the ideal organization, no matter how clearly defined and communicated, will vary from those with whom they share it.

Given that visions (even clearly constructed and carefully shared ones) are subject to multiple and changing interpretations, it's that much more important that leaders go beyond catchphrases and memorable metaphors. Vital dreams must be supported by complex and complete maps of how the world fits together. For every catchword or warm-and-fuzzy metaphor, there need to be dozens, perhaps hundreds, of supporting theories about people and how they fit into the dream.

The Backward Vision

To dream the impossible dream,
To fight the unbeatable foe,
To drive a bright, shiny Ferrari,
To hold tickets, for the very front row . . .

When you ask people what they want from an organization, the answers are fairly predictable. Most suggest that their goal is to achieve financial independence. They realize that acquiring massive wealth isn't a likely short-term goal, particularly if they're working in salaried positions. But given their druthers, they'd love the kind of freedom that comes from continuous infusions of positively disgusting amounts of disposable income. Some go so far as to explain what they'll do with the wealth. They paint vivid pictures of leisurely days on the beaches of Tahiti, late-evening strolls along the banks of the Seine, adrenaline-filled rides in a flashy sports car, and similar scenarios typically enjoyed by the likes of James Bond, Donald Trump, and Princess Di.

If you push the issue by asking what they'd love to see at *work*, visions are less forthcoming. When it comes to dreaming the work dream, people have a rather clear idea of what their work might *buy them*, but are often less certain about the work itself. Our literature hasn't exactly been jammed with examples of the American work dream. People rarely sit on their porches and spin tales of what their work environment could be like.

Wealth Is Not Health

There is a time when a man distinguishes the idea of felicity from the idea of wealth; it is the beginning of wisdom.

EMERSON

People frequently concoct mixed-up dreams because they confuse wealth with health. In spite of overwhelming evidence that the correlation between wealth (particularly at the high end) and mental health may actually be negative (as measured by suicides, drug abuse, and divorce), people still hold to the assumption that wealth begets joy. After all, doesn't poverty beget terror? Leaders often make the same mistake in logic. They assume that if they can generate high profits (meaning there's a lot of extra money to share among stakeholders), the corporate climate will improve. Wealth, they conclude, will generate health.

In some ways they're correct. Organizations that enjoy a monopoly of sorts, meaning that money practically rains from the sky, often enjoy high morale. Interview the people at Dream Works after they've shared bonuses starting at $10,000, and you'll hear stories of how great the company is. Down the road from the authors' corporate offices sits a rather large software company that has enjoyed similarly wealthy times. There were years when they turned 55 percent profit on net sales and bonuses ran into the millions. The people who worked there made Pollyanna sound depressed. But was the organization healthy?

Money Doesn't Guarantee Vitality

You'd have a hard time convincing people who have just pocketed a $100,000 bonus that their organization is actually a bit ill. Nevertheless, wealth is not health. In fact, organizations that experience inordinate profits typically enjoy some vital outcomes but often develop a less-than-vital culture. Inefficiencies in daily operations are routinely masked by bottom-line bonanzas. Golden handcuffs lock people to tasks they despise and relationships they loathe. Concern for the customer and other stakeholders is lessened as people wrongly conclude that they must be good. Why else would they be so profitable?

In a vital organization, people measure health in terms of daily interaction and not quarterly bonuses. They envision how they should treat each other, not how they'll spend their money.

THE VISION OF VITALITY: OUTCOME AND CULTURE DREAMS THAT WORK

Outcome Vision

True visionaries start their outcome vision by drawing a picture of what they want to create. They begin at the end, then work backwards. Martin Luther King, Jr., was clear about the world he wanted to bring into being. Robert Allen understands the kind of communication he wants to help make possible. Next, leaders work backward to discover what it will take to create it. The balanced vision for stakeholders is one that describes clearly the value that will be created for all those who are essential to bringing the vision into being. The vision makes a promise that is compelling, even inspiring, to each. None must be excluded. The more inclusive the dream, the more unifying its potential.

Successful leaders know as much about their stakeholders' wishes as they do about their production process or financial statements. If not, they could easily end up providing stakeholders with something they don't really want. For example, before people started paying attention to the idea of "economic value added," many leaders were happy with making a good, solid "bottom-line" profit. Cash flow or margins were thought of as ends in themselves—even by some CEOs.

A more careful analysis of stakeholder demands revealed that owners don't care squat about profits. What they care about is return on investment. They want a return on the capital they give managers that beats what they'd get in a similar risk venture elsewhere. If they don't get it, they take their money and run. Managers who didn't realize this in the 1980s found themselves sitting in the rubble of their dismembered enterprises after they were taken over by those who did.

Give Them What?

Leaders must put on their stakeholders' hats and share their dreams. Consider an experience we recently had. A group of high-level managers from various agencies who contract with the U.S. government asked us to help them brainstorm ways to determine how to deal with congressionally imposed funding cuts. As a way of ensuring they had a balanced vision of what they were trying to create, we challenged them to contemplate the frustrations, accusations, and complaints of their stakeholders. They quickly generated a list of complaints that was headed by taxpayers' concerns for cost overruns.

Since the group agreed that taxpayers were one of their key stakeholders, they began to explore what promises they should make to them. In the heat of the moment, while all were whipped into a visionary froth, one manager actually suggested that it would be great if they proposed *lower* budgets for the following year. Others looked on in horror while he, now totally detached from the reality in the room, continued with "Wouldn't it be wonderful if we were perceived by taxpayers as undeniably conscious of our stewardship for their funds—because we are always finding ways to do more with less—voluntarily!"

What had been a moment of inspiration quickly transformed into an embarrassed silence. Like moonlit skinny-dippers embarrassed by sudden headlights, all quickly put on their lopsided vestments. They spent the rest of the time determining how they'd prove to elected officials that they couldn't do with a penny less.

The visionary leader had the right idea. No vision is complete without a clear understanding of stakeholder demands, no matter how unsavory. The group really should have been trying to find ways to do more with less. They really should have led out in cost cutting rather than following their long-held tradition of spending everything they could until they were attacked by a budget-cutting team. Had the group started with the stakeholders rather than their own concerns, all would have benefited.

As you begin to put together your own vision of what outcomes you'd like to achieve, consider the following questions:

- What is our vision for each of our stakeholders?
- What complaints and attacks do we repeatedly hear from various constituencies?
- What vision, if we create it, would serve our constituencies better?
- What impact do we want to have on our communities? On society? On the world?
- What need do we fulfill today for our stakeholders?
- How are these needs likely to be different tomorrow?
- What significantly more important value could we offer that tomorrow's technology—if we can create it—will enable us to give?

Culture Vision

Leaders should understand that they aren't really leaders until they're influencing the behavior of others. Those who are skilled at the balancing act understand that their work can't stop with only a vision of what will happen to stakeholders. They also must ask, "What must we do to bring this vision into being?" They articulate their theories about what behavior will work best in a "culture vision." For some, this is a statement of value, operating principles, or management philosophy. Whatever its name, a culture vision must be *broad* enough to capture the interest of all employees, but *focused* enough to drive daily action.

To gain a better understanding of Cultural Vitality, leaders need to spend time imagining what their ideal work culture would look like. They need to spend time thinking of what they do and don't like about work relationships. They should have a clear map of what it's like to work in an environment of trust. They need a solid understanding of teams that are passionate about serving stakeholders—how they work together, what gets them excited, and how they differ from traditional workgroups.

When you begin to create your own unique culture vision, consider the following questions:

- What cultural qualities and behaviors must we foster to create the Outcome Vitality we truly want?
- What behaviors are most likely to create an organization that both employees and other stakeholders love?
- Think of your fondest work-related memory. What conditions account for that wonderful experience?
- What behaviors are required to create those conditions?
- How can you breathe life into noble terms such as *dignity, respect, trust, continuous learning,* and *collaboration?*

Taking Stock of What We Want

Changes occur in organizations only when leaders have a clear understanding of the culture they would like to create. This means that leaders must be able to think and talk about their ideal organization. They must be able to talk the talk before they walk it. They have to be able to spin a dream of the ideal workplace—complete with the behaviors, values, and assumptions required to make it function.

Dreaming dreams and creating visions doesn't come easy to most of us. So when we try to conjure up a mental map of a new and better way, we often make mistakes. We've talked about common errors and suggested some more sure-footed approaches. We've suggested that visions must be selfless, detailed, balanced, and forward looking.

Now it's time to look at how to live up to all of these fancy notions. We'll move from the ethereal realm of visioning to the more practical world of how to step outside today's description of *what is* and find tomorrow's map of *what can be.* We'll start by exploring methods for developing a vision of Cultural Vitality and end with a brief discussion of ways to create a clear understanding of your desired Outcome Vitality.

SOME PRACTICAL ADVICE FROM THIS CHAPTER

A rock pile ceases to be a rock pile the moment a single man contemplates it, bearing within him the image of a cathedral.

SAINT-EXUPÉRY

The Culture Vision

A vision of the ideal culture is usually best created after two trips: one to Paris and one to Kansas. The trip to Paris provides a chance to get off the farm and into a completely different world. Organizations that create their culture vision without first getting out of their own culture and looking at widely divergent systems end up choosing from limited options. They become culturally inbred because of limited genetic input.

The results, as you'd expect, are often both unattractive and ineffective. Since the current culture is much of what's driving our current results, if you attempt to move to a culture that is defined by those locked in the present, your choices are likely to be quite uninspiring and will probably look a lot like the past warmed over.

The Trip to Paris

Toto, I have a feeling we're not in Kansas anymore.
DOROTHY IN THE WIZARD OF OZ

The trip to Paris can take three forms. You can read about Paris, invite Paris in, or take a trip to Paris. All have merit.

You read about Paris by getting articles, books, videos, and other media that describe what leaders and others in a variety of organizations are doing to achieve their outcome visions. You can look at Baldrige winners, Deming graduates, most-admired lists, and so on to find out who's doing great things. The idea here is to generate, generate, generate—gather lots of ideas and a variety of alternatives to stimulate thinking.

You invite Paris in by getting academics, leaders, and consultants to share what they've seen and done. One note of caution: Not every good athlete is a good coach. Similarly, not everyone who has worked for a winning team can tell you what led to the victories. Pick your guests based on (1) their insights and (2) their ability to explain them. Check around before inviting anyone into your company.

Finally, you can visit Paris. Load up the truck and get the folks to see for themselves. Direct experience can have a profound impact. Seeing working models cuts through both skepticism and hype. There's nothing like a concrete experience to show nuances and details.

But before you go to Paris, you need to be primed for the tour. We've worked with many organizations who conduct visits willy-nilly and get little or nothing out of them.

Here are some tips for getting the most out of visits.

Getting Ready.   As you prepare for a "field trip," let people know what you're looking for. Your goal is to come back with one good idea that you can embrace. You want something that is different, but *could* work. *Warning:* People often visit other locations (particularly those of vital competitors) with a chip on their shoulders. One group we took to Japan went through the same emotional stages typically associated with the death of a loved one. First it was denial ("There's no way they could be this good," and they sneaked in at two in the morning to see what was *really* going on). Then depression ("There's no way we can measure up."). Finally, they settled on healthy optimism ("We can do this.").

They were able to go through all the stages because the trip lasted a week. Unfortunately, when we took a group across town for a four-hour visit, they never got past denial ("Those bozos may outproduce us, but at what cost? They're clones with no thoughts of their own. Give 'em a few weeks, and the whole thing will collapse."). When we take field trips, we share this story. It helps people keep a more positive focus.

When You're There.   We'll spend some time in the next chapter on how to conduct a culture assessment, but for now let us simply point out that when you're visiting another site, you're looking for the behaviors, values, and assumptions that make the other place tick. You won't learn this through direct questioning. People will tell you what they want you to hear. To get around this problem, request informal time. Chat with people of your own choosing, avoiding shills who have been coached. The more you can conduct off-the-cuff interviews and wander around at your leisure, the better.

After You Return.   Gather everyone together in a room, and have each person share his or her favorite observation. Allow all present to explain what they saw, why they liked it, and what they think it would take to make it work in your own organization. Your goal here is not to change policy, but to begin surfacing ideas. At this stage, follow the rules of brainstorming. Get ideas out; don't criticize them. As a leadership team, evaluate the recommendations, and then pick some "low-hanging fruit." Adopt an idea or two that is simple to implement and that will yield immediate and obvious results.

The Trip to Kansas

The trip to Kansas is a trip home. People have garnered a great deal of what they want to see in the ideal organization from their current associations. They've seen snippets of what they like, and they want more of some things, less of others. They recall a healthy situation with a previous assignment. The goal of the trip to Kansas is to get everyone's existing ideas out in the open where they can be discussed by the entire team. Of the many sad truths about organizations, perhaps the saddest of all is that most people have profoundly important dreams that they wouldn't think of sharing with their colleagues. People don't ask for what they want. This has to change.

The Dream Session. Over the years, we've developed a powerful tool for generating dreams. We sit down with a group and ask them what they want from their teammates. They each must share a one-word characteristic of what they admire, followed by a story. The reason for the story is simple. It provides clarity. People don't describe a characteristic unless it's been violated. No one asks for people to speak English. That hasn't been at risk. Instead, they ask for something they haven't always had, but dearly want. By telling a story of how their dream was previously shattered, they put meat on the bones of skeletal visions.

For example, a person suggests, "When I think of a teammate, I think of someone who is honest." At this point, people are probably assuming that the individual doesn't like to work with people who lie or steal. But he goes on to tell a story. "I once worked with people who said they liked you to your face and then bad-mouthed you to anyone who stuck their head in the door. I didn't even know that I had a problem until one day a guy delivering a package called me 'motor mouth.' That's what people had been calling me behind my back. I didn't know I had been talking too much."

After the negative story is told, the person is then asked to share what he or she would like to see happen instead. "If someone has a problem with me, I want the person to talk to me straight up, face to face. I can take it, and it sure beats hearing about your problems from a 22-year-old FedEx employee."

Such dream sessions help groups jointly share a vision of a variety of interpersonal features. Make sure that people share what they want *and* don't want from teammates. This provides a clarity that's hard to achieve in any other way. Remember, the goal is to get dreams out on the table where they can be understood, honed, and shared.

Start, Stop, and Continue. Another tool for helping people discuss Cultural Vitality uses three sheets of poster paper. At the top of each is written either "start," "stop," or "continue." Participants are given a marker and asked to write one behavior on each of the three sheets. Obviously, the title at the top of each sheet helps individuals think of three different kinds of actions: (1) those they like and want to see continue, (2) those they don't care for and want to see stop, and (3) those they've heard about, previously enjoyed, or only imagined and that they want to see start. The goal is to encourage open discussion of the daily behaviors people would like to see in their ideal organization.

Ground Rules. Typically, after openly discussing what behaviors people are looking for from their co-workers, people look for a commitment. Many teams end up creating an informal document that reflects their shared vision of how they'll work together each day. Such a document is often referred to as a team's *ground rules*. Central to the document is a list of values and actions the team embraces. Individuals tend to start with less risky items (such as how they'll share work or how they'll divide up assignments). We always insist that for every task-related item, they create one that deals with the team's relationship. Hot items include:

- How they agree to make difficult decisions
- What they'll do when they face a problem
- What happens when someone speaks ill of another
- What they'll do when someone violates one of the rules

A Behavior Fest. Most people aren't particularly good at describing behaviors. They're better at describing outcomes than actions. Consider something as simple as teamwork. People will often suggest that they want people who collaborate. But what's a collaborative behavior? After six probes, people finally come up with a behavioral example. "People need to give up on their own short-term assignment in order to pitch in and help someone facing a more important task." The test of behavioral specificity is simple. After hearing someone describe the behavior, could everyone in the room go out and replicate it when needed? As a guide to your visioning discussions, post a piece of flip-chart paper with the following question:

Will others be able to go out and do what you've just requested?

The Outcome Vision

The outcome vision is best generated through dialogue with stakeholders. Some call this an *environmental scan*. This is the process of surfacing the values, assumptions, and concerns of all stakeholders to determine what the company must deliver to keep them engaged in the relationship.

Top leaders should be intensely involved in the environmental scan. We've found this critical for two reasons. First, it improves the quality of the product. Second, the process itself has a powerful motivational effect on the leaders. It's hard to listen to data firsthand from living, breathing human beings and not care about it. When executives experience the joy and pain of various stakeholders, it's tough for them to advocate imbalance with the same fervor.

Now we don't mean that leaders should not use skilled professionals for functions such as customer analysis, constituency surveying, and so on. We're simply suggesting that leaders must have their skin in the game during key parts of the scan.

The scan attempts to answer questions such as:

- What will motivate or enable our customers to continue and broaden their relationship with our company?
- What motivates or enables our investors to provide capital and other support?
- What motivates or enables vendors, communities, and others to support our efforts?
- What will motivate or enable our employees to contribute all they can to our vision?

Depending on the sophistication of the scan, companies use a variety of techniques to gather data to answer these questions. Methods include focus groups, scientific surveys, and telephone interviews.

A FINAL NOTE

Visioning, like breathing, knows no season. Effective leaders learn that a great deal of their time should be devoted to keeping an eye open to new ways of pulling people with diverse backgrounds and interests into a functioning unit. They understand that the behavioral sciences are still in their infancy and that nothing that we suggest today is likely to last forever. They eventually learn to enjoy musing about new and better ways to get things done. At first the act of painting a dream may seem soft and gushy to some. Others can hardly sit still long enough. The thought of all the problems that are "going on out there" keeps them from being able to focus on the long-term picture.

Those who are looking for a reprieve from visioning and who want to get back to their "real jobs," might do well to consider that they don't really like leadership. Visioning lies at the very heart of leadership.

> To be brutally honest, were you to reach down into the souls of effective leaders and permanently extract their ability to dream, or were you to cut them off from the right to create a vision, you'd be left with managers.

C H A P T E R   4

Assessing What You've Got: Culture

Culture is a little like dropping an Alka-Seltzer into a glass—you don't see it, but somehow it does something.

HANS MAGNUS ENZENSBERGER

In the last chapter we explored ways to create a clear vision of your ideal organization. We'll now lower our sights from that distant horizon of what *can be* and take a look at the front porch of *what is*. To do so, we'll build on the model we developed in chapter 2, where we argued that if you expect people to try new behaviors or abandon old ones, you have to understand and then influence the values and assumptions making up their mental maps.

In the next few pages, we'll look at several methods for identifying the *shared* behaviors and mental maps that make up your organization's culture. We'll move from an individual model of behavior selection to a method of assessing the values and assumptions shared by the majority of employees. These shared values and assumptions, coupled with common skills, are often referred to as an organization's *culture*.

Savvy leaders are aware of cultural influences—how they're formed, and what it takes to measure them. They understand that traditional measures and direct techniques are of little use when it comes to uncovering and understanding mental maps—shared or otherwise. They realize that, like the mystical workings of an Alka-Seltzer tablet, culture quietly and unobtrusively works its magic—or mischief.

Because culture resides in the minds of the workforce, it can't be understood by turning a spotlight on it, it's rarely measured directly, and it's almost always inferred. More importantly, the ability to surface and understand the motivating forces behind all behaviors is a valuable tool possessed only by the most skilled of executives. We stumbled on this insight in a curious way.

Here's how it happened.

The Anthropologist President

Anthropology is the science which tells us that people are the same the whole world over—except when they are different.

NANCY BANKS-SMITH

The first time we trained the president of a large health-care corporation and his immediate staff, we were surprised to learn that the senior executive wanted to see us a week before the training was to be conducted. Since his time was allocated in 10-minute increments and we had already blocked out two full days on his schedule (something unprecedented), we couldn't imagine why he wanted to meet with us beforehand for a couple of hours. His assistant explained that he wished to go over the training material alone, free from the presence of his direct reports.

As we drove up to the president's office, we discussed what might drive him to cover the training material in advance. Since the topic was leadership and he was the top leader, maybe he was uncertain. Was he afraid of looking weak in front of his staff? Certainly someone who had risen to the position of president wouldn't worry about looking bad. But then, why? What would compel him to take two hours out of his busy schedule just to receive a personal tutorial?

When we finally met with the senior executive, we were pleased to learn that he was the picture of professionalism. He greeted us with a warm smile and carefully attended to our every word. It was obvious that he wanted to learn our material and, more importantly, embrace it. But why did he need the overview? Why couldn't he wait until the two-day session along with everyone else? Since we couldn't find a delicate way to ask him at first, we decided to keep watching his behavior.

The next week, when the scheduled training rolled around, we received our answer. He didn't dominate the session by jumping in with the right answer (a fear we're ashamed to say we held). He could have, given that he knew exactly where we were going with the content. Nor did he withdraw to the background and busily work on other projects (still another fear). He took part right alongside his direct reports.

By the first break, we finally understood his strategy. As others rushed to return phone calls, he caucused with us. What did we think about Chris? Did she seem to be onboard with the concepts? His view was that she was holding back a little. Did we agree? What could be done to draw the Southern Regional Director into the conversation? It was hard to get a read on him.

The president wanted to review the content in advance so he could devote his attention to the group process. Anyone could garner the materials by simply paying attention; and, if extra attentive, this same person might even be able to get a feel for the group dynamics as well. But this executive wanted to devote his undivided attention to the underlying group process. For him it wasn't enough to casually watch for subtext. He wanted to be able to focus on it completely.

Later we learned that the president believed that his job in any meeting was to monitor the process. The day had long passed since he was expected to be the content expert. Similarly, he no longer desired to be the one who made the decisions. Instead, his job was to work with a team of highly opinionated people who would jointly make decisions, set policy, and see to the execution. His job was to ensure that the group functioned as an effective team. This, he had learned, took a great deal of careful, real-time analysis. He explained that a course he had taken years earlier in anthropology had taught him a few things about reading underlying values and assumptions. And now, at the summit of his career, he saw himself as a cultural expert. He wanted to be one, and he worked at it full time.

Split Attention

This insightful president was right. As we've watched leaders at work for the two past decades, the characteristic that most decisively separates the leader from the content expert, manager, or individual contributor in general is the ability to process two types of information simultaneously. Skilled leaders always split their attention. They are equally involved in the content and the process of any interaction. They're very self-aware, worrying as much about *how* they say things as *what* they say. Similarly, they watch others carefully, listening for the words, and then dive beneath the content by watching for nonverbals—whatever is unstated or partially stated, the interactions between individuals, and other factors typically studied by anthropologists, communication experts, and cultural theorists.

In this chapter we'll explore the skills used by this elite group. Whether you plan to conduct a formal cultural assessment or not, the following material is designed to help leaders keep a careful eye on the assumptions and values that drive daily behavior. Our goal is twofold. By the end of this chapter, the reader should have a fairly good idea of how to conduct a cultural assessment. In addition, and probably more important, we'd like to share a handful of process skills that help leaders informally (and continually) monitor their organization's culture. We'll start with a brief review of how, after over a century, the study of culture found its way from the Trobriand Islands to just about every organization.

CULTURE: A BRIEF HISTORY

Americans first became enamored with the idea of corporate culture in the early 1980s when a handful of skilled leaders figured out how to meld the economies of scale enjoyed by large organizations with the sense of dedication and family commitment typically found in small, closely held companies. Before this monumental achievement, highly dedicated, closely knit groups known as *clans* had existed only in small, family-owned businesses. These relatively small companies achieved their goals through informal means. Their control systems consisted of shared values and assumptions. Manuals, policies, and procedures were unheard of. In short, they were lean, mean, and small.

Large companies, in contrast, were bureaucratic and unwieldy. Their size afforded them the massive resources required to play ball with the major players, but they were typically stodgy and slow to react to change. Employees often were dedicated only marginally to the cause.

It was when someone figured out how to combine the dedication and informal atmosphere historically found in small companies with the resources of multinational corporations that the word *culture* began to be bandied around. Consultants warned leaders that if they wanted to compete, they'd have to go beyond traditional mechanistic approaches and change the hearts and minds of their people. The scramble was on.

Perhaps the most astonishing aspect of the worldwide call to change culture is that it came with such speed. For over 100 years, organizations had competed with few disruptions. This isn't hard to explain. After all, every organization shared the same corporate genealogy. Competitors hired employees from the same marketplace, recruited managers from the same schools, and shared barbecue across the same fences.

Today we typically don't compete across back fences. We compete across oceans. We're forced to go head to head with organizations from countries that sport entirely different values and assumptions. Competing against people whose mental maps are markedly different hasn't been fun. These "clan members" labor long and hard, and they scare most of us to death.

To make matters worse, they aren't all from across the sea. Bill Ouchi accurately identified American-grown, clan-type cultures ("Theory Z companies")[1] situated all across America. These American-based organizations, according to Professor Ouchi, have the characteristics of clans but are homegrown. They commit to their employees over the long run. They don't typically lay people off. They rarely rely on policy manuals for control. Instead, they share a common value structure that informs choice. They carry names such as Hewlett-Packard and Procter & Gamble. Peters and Waterman described them as "excellent" companies.[2]

Whatever you call them, these clans have been so effective and vital that competing with them has been almost impossible. Whenever a clan-based organization has stepped into a competitive arena, it has grabbed huge portions of the market, often destroying the competition. To exacerbate matters, those who want to regain their competitive posture by becoming a clan quickly learn that clans are hard to replicate. In fact, at first glance it's hard to figure out just how clans differ from hierarchies. When you look at machines, designs, technologies, buildings, formal policies, products, services, and structure, clans look quite similar to typical organizations. In addition, their people often graduate from the same schools and live in the same communities as do their competitors.

To see how clans differ, you have to watch their people at work. Something happens to people as they join clans. With time, they begin to act on different assumptions and share different values. It's in the heads and hearts of their people that clans differ from traditional hierarchies. It's in their culture.

What Is Culture?

The Law of Raspberry Jam: The wider any culture is spread, the thinner it gets.

ALVIN TOFFLER

Until recently, the terms *corporation* and *culture* were rarely used in the same sentence. *Culture* to the person on the street was something related to art history and opera. To the scholar, *culture* was something studied by either anthropologists who examined the beliefs of broad social groups or by microbiologists who grew fuzzy purple organisms in petri dishes. Organizations, of course, fell somewhere between microorganisms and broad social groups.

Scholars did not apply the unique perspective offered by cultural experts until the mid-1980s. This relatively sudden interest in culture paralleled the entry of clans (often foreign) into the U.S. market. As hierarchical organizations began to lose market share to clans, culture became of interest—in much the same way you become deeply interested in your left shoe when it catches fire.

Unfortunately, in spite of the zeal to change organizations' cultures, the term *culture* has rarely been elevated to more than a sound bite. In a room full of a dozen people, it's hard to find any two who use the term the same way.

A Look into the Box

> Stripped to the bare bones, an organization's culture consists of the unique values, assumptions, and behaviors shared by its people.

Most of culture can only be inferred. Behavior, of course, can be observed, but the underlying values and assumptions that drive it can only be deduced by listening and observing carefully. For example, you observe hundreds of people in a particular facility signing up for a blood drive, and you see the same thing happen several times over the next few weeks. You have a feeling that this peculiar behavior has something to do with the culture, but you still don't know what values and assumptions are driving it. Here's where inference comes in. You have to dig around to surface the mental maps that crystallize into behavior.

So you dig a little deeper. You learn that before a new VP came along, blood drives met with little response. This makes you suspicious. You listen to people talking on the way to open up a vein and hear a few mutter, "Time to give Gardner his pint." Hmm. What does that mean? You stop a guy on the way to the drive and ask him why he's taking time out of his busy schedule to donate blood. He answers, "We've gotta take care of our own, don't we?" When you ask what this means, he explains that the new VP is a hemophiliac. When people learned that this well-liked leader was in regular need of transfusions and that over a dozen people like him worked in the area, employees began coming out in droves for the drives. The best leaders develop the skills of listening beyond the words people say to look for the meaning behind what they do. This helps them deduce the values and assumptions that eventually sprout into observable behavior.

As a brief reminder, let's restate our definitions. *Values* consist of "hot cognitions," or what people get excited about. In Trekker terms, they're the emotional side that Spock inherited from his mother. *Assumptions*, on the other hand, represent nonemotional mental maps. They provide meaning to an ambiguous world. They are the logical side that Spock inherited from his Vulcan father.

Culture or Personality?   At the individual level, values and assumptions make up personality. To the degree that individuals share values and assumptions which cause them to behave in similar ways in similar situations, they become a culture. Of course, not everybody in a culture shares every value and assumption, but they do share enough to make them a functional unit. They can communicate fairly well and share the same goals, so they choose to work together.

Since values and assumptions are used to describe an individual's personality, shared values and assumptions might be described as a corporation's *personality*. Corporations have distinct personalities (*cultures*) to the extent that a majority of their shared values and assumptions are unique to their particular workforce.

Corporate Culture or Something Else?   Most of what people carry in their heads does not make up corporate culture. Either they don't *share* the values and assumptions (they're part of individual personality rather than culture) or they're not *unique* to the organization (they're part of a broader culture rather than the corporate culture). Typically, the culture found in a specific organization reflects more of the broader national, regional, or business culture than a unique corporate perspective. The fact that American English is spoken and blue suits are worn in many organizations reflects an American corporate culture, whereas believing that if you park in a manager's parking place you'll be fired is part of a specific organization's culture.

Even within what appears to be a profoundly cohesive American business culture, you'll find striking differences. For example, when American Express transferred an operation from New York City to Salt Lake City, many of the managers who transferred commented on the differences in regions. They attributed productivity changes to differences in *local work ethic*. Companies that move from Detroit to cities in the South hope to capitalize on regional differences in work ethic.

Geography is not the only factor that influences culture. Industry cultures are frequently as strong as, or stronger than, regional ones. Companies with dramatically different work values and assumptions exist often within a stone's throw of each other. At the corner of 17 Mile and Mound Road (north of Detroit), you can find a Ford facility to the north and a division of General Dynamics to the south. Their cultures are quite different. The Ford culture is more similar to that of a GM facility in Saginaw (miles to the north) than to the defense industry across the street. As a testimony to the strength of industrial cultures, when the automobile industry recently moved several facilities to different geographic regions, the industrial culture frequently overpowered the regional work norms. For instance, employees working in automobile plants in the South frequently act more like their union brothers and sisters in Detroit than their blood brothers and sisters in the same community.

Shared values and assumptions interest leaders because they lead to common behaviors—which, of course, influence both Cultural Vitality and Outcome Vitality. Whether an organization is made up of a regional, industrial, or corporate culture is not important. What does matter is that executives learn how to understand *and* how to influence their own company's culture.

WHY DOES UNDERSTANDING YOUR CULTURE MATTER?

If you want to change your culture, you have to start with the culture you've got. "Ya gotta dance with the one what brung ya." Then, as the dance unfolds, you can change a step or two.

Over the past decade, the authors have had a unique consulting experience working with three Malcolm Baldrige Award winners. What made the experience unique was that not only did we work with these award winners, but we had the opportunity to work with their sister divisions in the same company—ones that didn't win any prizes.

As we labored in this unique environment (trying to understand why one group in an organization has spectacular success in creating vitality and another group comes short), we recognized a key variable—culture. One group tries to change the workforce, more or less attacking the culture, while the other tries to work with it, starting from their existing base and building. When leaders try to "copy" other successful change efforts, without regard to cultural specifics, they almost always fail. However, when leaders understand the current culture, they can use the existing values and assumptions to launch the charge. Consider a real-life example.

Fred! Fred! Fred!

One day while conducting interviews with a group of six blue-collar employees in a large manufacturing operation, one of the authors asked a question that yielded a rather animated response. He was trying to uncover shared values when he asked, "Who are the real heroes around this place?"

"*What do you mean?*" one of the participants asked.

"Well, who is really admired around here? Who is someone people look up to?"

A few of the more feisty interviewees traded knowing expressions, started to smile, and then chuckled until someone almost shouted, "*Fred!*" Then everyone broke out laughing. From the back of the room someone started leading a cheer: "*Fred! Fred! Fred!*" and the whole crowd joined in. He had obviously struck pay dirt.

"Why is Fred such a hero?" the interviewer shouted over the din.

"*To be frank,*" one of the employees began, looking around in a conspiratorial fashion, "*he's the only guy I know who could go back in the warehouse after an order, take a two-hour nap, and never get caught.*" The group burst out into a hoot as the chant of "*Fred! Fred! Fred!*" started up again.

It didn't take too many interviews to realize that a key value in this particular culture was the ability to beat management or circumvent the system. But there was more. As the assessment team plugged along with more interviews, another value became clear. When a group of assembly-line employees was asked the "hero" question, a fellow dressed in big overalls and shoes that looked like they were rescued off a trash heap answered in surprisingly reverent tones, "*Sarah.*" Others chimed in their approval.

"Why is Sarah such a hero?"

"*Sarah came up with an idea to improve the finish on the product and reduce a manufacturing step. She told the idea to the boss, but he said it wouldn't work or management would have already done it. He shut her right down, but that didn't stop Sarah. Oh no, not Sarah. She wrote up her idea and took her proposal to the plant manager. He looked it over and okayed a feasibility study. Now we do it Sarah's way. It saved the company money and lets us put out a better product.*"

We quickly learned that not only was "beating the system" valued, but putting out a quality product mattered a great deal to the employees as well. We also learned another widely shared assumption. People suggested that a high-quality product meant satisfied customers, which, in turn, meant continued business and (here's the payoff) eventual job security. They saw the relationship as clear as day. They linked quality products to the ability to maintain their lifestyles.

Now here's where it gets interesting. They also believed that "the system" more often than not prevented people from producing quality products and that managers were the keepers of the system. So the picture that formed over the course of the culture assessment was:

Key Assumptions
- The best way to keep jobs is to put out quality products.
- The "system" and the managers who support it prevent people from putting out a quality product.

Key Values
- Keep jobs and maintain lifestyles.
- Put out a quality product.
- Beat management and circumvent the "system."

Of course, these are but a small part of the overall culture, but if they're combined, they lead to some interesting interactions.

Now the managers of this particular facility were convinced that their Outcome Vitality was at risk. They figured it was only a matter of time until their customers jumped ship to a competitor who was producing a lower-cost product. Their desire was to improve their quality and reduce their expenses. Without understanding their current culture, they would probably have designed a Total Quality Program, "rolled it out" top to bottom, and tried to motivate the workforce to implement it. It doesn't take a Ph.D. in anthropology to predict that this plan would have been doomed. (Pictures of the *Titanic* come to mind.)

However, since the managers had taken part in the culture assessment, they realized that, to be effective, the quality improvement initiative could not be seen as a management program. Rather, all employees would have to be deeply involved in diagnosing, designing, implementing, and measuring the improvement effort. In this case, it seemed appropriate to let employees feel like they were "beating" the system by improving both the products *and* the system at the same time. Done well, management wouldn't have to "motivate the workforce." In fact, the leaders would be needed to coordinate the efforts and remove the barriers—a very different job indeed.

As the improvement initiative gained momentum and support, eventually leading to substantial improvements, the leaders decided to work on changing some of the existing assumptions and values (i.e., the ones that suggest that leaders are mindless pinheads who stand in the way of progress). However, to be initially successful, the change effort had to begin where the culture was. And then, after gaining some respect, they were in a better position to change a step or two.

Of course, in order to build from the existing culture, the leaders had to understand it—and living in it didn't guarantee that they knew it. Values and assumptions are so much a part of people's thinking that it takes a special effort to bring them into view. That's why effective leaders go to extraordinary means to assess their own cultures. Throughout the remainder of this chapter we'll explain how this can be done. The good news is that the skills used to surface, understand, and then work with values and assumptions serve leaders at every turn. The better news is that leaders can learn to do it relatively quickly. We'll cover only the highlights in the following pages.

WHAT IS *YOUR* CULTURE?

Cultural anthropology is not valuable because it uncovers the archaic. . . . It is valuable because it is constantly rediscovering the normal.

EDWARD SAPIR

For over two decades it was believed that an organization's culture could only be assessed by outsiders. Three reasons were most often cited for this reluctance to involve leaders. First, employees aren't likely to be honest in front of a leader. It takes an outsider to create a safe climate. Second, even if employees were willing to speak their minds, nonprofessionals wouldn't be able to see the culture. They'd be focused so much on the content of each discussion that the underlying values and assumptions would go unnoticed. Third, culture is so difficult to discern that it takes experts with years of study and experience to truly understand it.

Although these three barriers are, indeed, a risk in every assessment process, they can be overcome. In fact, we've worked with literally hundreds of leaders who now successfully conduct their own assessments. In fact, we've learned how to train insightful leaders to become effective culture assessors. What is remarkable about this feat is that through the use of video-based instruction and some follow-up and coaching, an entire leadership team can learn to assess a culture in a day of training. On the following pages are some critical components of this method.

Unobtrusive Measures

The Village Tour

The easiest way for a leader to eliminate "reactance" (subjects' unnatural responses to people in positions of authority) is to leave people out of the process. For example, in one hospital we asked staff members to walk through their facility and look at the layout, read the signs, and otherwise look around—only with the point of view that they knew nothing about medicine. One sign prominently placed at an entrance stated *Ambulant Patients Only.* More than one patient avoided the portal because he hadn't arrived by ambulance.

It didn't take long for the health-care professionals to realize that they had designed the signs for the staff and not for the patients. In spite of the fact that they constantly suggested that customers were the center of everything they did, it was apparent that they didn't always put on their customer hat. In fact, when they conducted a small test, they learned that 65 percent of the words used on the signs were not understood by college seniors. Astounding.

On a village tour you can learn a great deal about a culture by looking at things such as:

- What is allocated a lot of space or very little space
- What or who is given prominent or poor placement
- What kinds of things are displayed or not displayed (personal items, posters, announcements)
- Who sits next to whom and who is far from whom

For example, a village tour of Salt Lake City would show that the tallest building is a church's administration building. A similar tour of New York City would discover that the tallest buildings are related to trade and commerce. From this, one might begin to infer the values of the local cultures. Similarly, if in an organization you notice that people in positions of authority occupy floor space on the top floor and are separate from everyone else, you might infer that the culture (1) assumes leaders' interaction with one another is more critical than with others in the organization and (2) values authority in and of itself.

Thematic Analysis (What Do People Write?)

Another inconspicuous method for bringing values and assumptions to the surface consists of gathering a sample of common documents and examining them for themes. It's easy to do and can actually be pretty entertaining. Simply pull together a sample of memos, letters, newsletters, announcements, bulletins, reports, anything you can find pinned to a bulletin board, and any other written material you can think of. You can also pull up memos, notes, and any other public documents off the computer network. Probe for themes. What topics are constantly repeated? What's the tone of the writing? What elements are given emphasis?

When assessing your own culture, look for inconsistencies between the key elements of your vision and what your documents reflect. For example, if you're interested in treating people with respect and dignity, do memos routinely carry accusations and threats? If you espouse careful analysis, do people respond to problems by immediately assuming that all problems are due to motivation? If you're desperately trying to increase employee involvement, do published documents reveal that leaders are more comfortable making most of the decisions?

Consider the following note taken off the computer screen of a human resources specialist we were working with one day:

```
To:   All hands
From: The accounting office
Re:   Expense reports

This is the third time we've had to say this, but
so far it's clear that nobody has paid any atten-
tion. Stop using the old expense forms (F231) and
start using the new ones (F337)! If you continue
to pay no heed to our advice, we won't reimburse
you for your expenses. Don't count on a penny.

In addition, who was the idiot who submitted the
request to be paid for the cost of repainting the
hood of his car that was parked in the parking
lot because, "after a bird deposited its break-
fast on it, it left a stain that couldn't be
removed"? Very funny. We've got enough work
without a bunch of clowns sending in stuff like
this.

Oh yes, and one final note, Mr. Crenshaw had
another wonderful idea we'd like to pass along.
He suggests that if you're interested in starting
```

```
up a Christmas fund, it makes sense to start now,
early in the year. As he's been known to tell us,
the early bird gets the worm!

P.S.
We'll be shut down during lunch hour from now on.
Please stop by our office from 8:00-11:30 or from
1:00 to 3:30.
```

Although no single message reflects an organization's culture, what can you tell about the person who crafted this memo? What were his or her assumptions and values at the time? If you find dozens of pieces that contained similar work, what might you start to wonder?

Obtrusive Measures — The Culture Interview

A more obtrusive, yet effective, way to assess culture is to train a team how to surface values and assumptions during a 90-minute group interview. Although the best method for learning the process is to go through fairly intensive training, the next few pages highlight a few of the more salient issues and skills. Later in this chapter we'll follow a manager around as he tries to understand his company's culture.

A Marriage of Science and Art

A culture interview requires a careful blend of science and art. The science aspect involves carefully selecting a representative, random sample of the organization. Targeting an overall sample of 10 percent provides a good picture of the organization's overall culture. It may be wise to increase the size of the sampling in areas where resistance to change is more likely. Where it is known that critical cultural issues need attention, 100 percent sampling may be desirable. After an initial assessment, further efforts can focus on some of the subcultures and key demographic groups.

The art of a culture assessment lies in the ability to infer values and assumptions from interviews and observations. Developing these skills is not as difficult as it might first appear. By learning about culture and understanding the skills of the culture-assessment process, leaders can readily discern some of the more obvious values and assumptions. Then, by pooling insights during a data debriefing, the team can validate specific inferences and interpretations. A combination of education, skill development, and continued practice helps hone the art. Combined, the science and art of culture assessment provide leaders with a profound understanding of their people's widely shared and deeply held values and assumptions.

Conclusions from the assessment interviews are shaped by the assessment team into a culture report that points out the prominent themes. This report becomes the basis for all of the Cultural Vitality work that follows, as well as a baseline for future comparison.

Mixed Composition

Your assessment team should be made up of a mix of internal and external personnel. Each group brings distinct skills and perspectives to the team. Insiders are typically better at filling in the details. Outsiders, usually consultants who specialize in conducting culture assessments, ask tougher questions, probe for more details, and compare the organization with more outside points of reference.

Those being interviewed should also be put into mixed groups. The ideal group size is around eight. By selecting a random sample of people across the organization, the topics discussed usually remain fairly broad. Don't mix levels of the organization very often. If you want to see the impact of leaders on the group, conduct a multilevel assessment. However, most interviews should be of people of similar rank but from different departments.

After you've conducted several interviews of mixed composition and have started to develop a handful of theories, pull together some homogeneous groups, and check for subcultural differences.

Indirect Questions

Rather than ask for values and assumptions, trained specialists ask questions that stimulate examples rather than conclusions. As individuals share stories of the nature of work, the observers draw conclusions about values rather than about the individuals being questioned directly. For example, you might ask: "If you were made the head of this company, what is the first thing you would change?" or "If one of your own children or a family member came to work here, what advice would you give?" A summary document of the entire process is available from The Praxis Group. Please check the order form at the end of this book for details.

Management Involvement

The ultimate goal of a culture assessment is to *increase* Cultural Vitality, not just to understand the culture. The culture assessment ought to be done in a way that increases the motivation of managers and other leaders to take action to bring about change. Researchers typically leave managers out of culture analysis. Unfortunately, if you leave managers off the team, those conducting the assessment have to find a way to communicate their findings to those who have the power to do something about them. Generally, this means an assessment team spends hundreds of hours collecting valuable data and then shares the conclusions in a couple of hours. The data deserve more.

Most organizations don't change simply because outsiders hand executives a report. Researchers must include managers if they want them to be involved in the change effort. Involvement increases commitment. For example, U.S. citizens sent far more money to Ethiopia in private donations than to Sudan, yet both countries were in many ways in equal need. Why the difference? You and I *saw* firsthand pictures and documentaries about Ethiopia. Hearing isn't enough. Experiencing the data gives leaders more motivation *and* ability to take action.

Managers, when paired with human resources specialists and outside consultants, can bring to the surface the same issues that nonmanagers alone might. With a few hours of instruction and a practice session under their belts, managers can learn to encourage honest opinions and can then hear the same controversial discussions that outsiders typically hear.

Example Based

The key to bringing values and assumptions to the surface is to find ways to encourage examples or stories. As long as individuals are telling you what they think you want to hear, you're at the mercy of their translation. Encourage them to tell stories of a typical day at work, and you can draw your own conclusions. Ask who the heroes are and why. Push for stories. Probe for the underlying meaning.

TRICKS TO UNDERSTANDING CULTURE

Practice Anthropology

To get a good look at your own culture, you must do more than conduct an interview. You have to be able to examine people and their values and assumptions up close. This isn't easy. In fact, most of us would make lousy anthropologists. If we were dropped in the middle of a Paraná wedding ceremony, we'd probably write "really weird" in our notebooks. Rather than assess the tribe's behavior or norms, we'd pass judgment or miss the significance of the experience. Not that anthropologists are the only ones worthy of studying group behavior, but we could learn from the more objective approach of trained professionals.

Without going into great detail, let's simply suggest that skilled students of culture are effective at dipping below the surface of an interaction. They don't take every observation at face value. They're as interested in the *why* of any discussion as they are in the *what*. They withhold judgment—as well as one can. Rather than respond with "how disgusting," they record what they see and wait for *long patterns of observation* before drawing any conclusions.

"Fresh eyes" see things that people who are part of the culture never see. Practice watching a group with "fresh eyes." If you're interested in practicing this skill, check out the movie *Witness*. Watch the scene in which the Amish community helps a young couple build a barn. As you watch, look for behaviors that you might see with your "fresh eyes." Ask yourself these questions: What are the assumptions and values these people carry around? How do they influence their behavior? How do they differ from the traditional workgroup?

Watch for "Value Footprints"

Emotions are the footprints of values. Any time a person expresses strong emotion, it's a sign that an underlying value is being satisfied, threatened, or accessed. Skilled students of culture watch for signs of emotion and discern strong energy in the tone of voice, body posture, and frequency of reference to a particular subject.

One of the easiest ways to recognize shared values in a culture is to identify signs when one is threatened. Some signs of a threatened value include sarcastic jokes, derogatory references, complaints, conflicts, and subject avoidance.

If people exhibit these signs, the culture observer should dig deeper to discern the value that's being violated. For instance, a department that complains bitterly about the lack of support it receives from higher-ups clearly values support, a service attitude, and demonstration of commitment. As you ask more questions about the lack of support, you'll discover more precisely the reason there is emotion around this issue.

Satisfied values, on the other hand, show up in positive emotions such as pride, enthusiasm, and commitment. For instance, people may have a value for delivering what the customer wants when they brag about a heroic instance of satisfying a deadline.

Examine Conflicting Subgroups

If you want to extract the meat from a nut, look for a crack in the surface. The same could be said for understanding culture. To bring values and assumptions to the surface, watch subgroups in the middle of a conflict. Conflicts occur when individuals have either different values or different assumptions. Such differences lead to arguments. During arguments, people cling to and articulate their values and assumptions. In short, you can see culture as it cracks under pressure. Bring together groups made up of people who are typically in conflict. As you conduct the interview, watch for differences of opinion. Ask yourself what the arguments tell you about the culture.

Look for the Heroes and Heroines

Although people typically find it difficult to talk about their core values, they do find it easy to discuss the heroes and heroines who embody their values. Ask people *who* they most admire in the organization and *why*. In one company the responses were almost always the same. The heroes were people who figured out how to beat the system. People told stories of how some of their most admired colleagues had placed clothing lockers in an elaborate configuration that made up a maze—leading to a hidden area where people played cards. Stories of heroes and goats do a far better job of bringing values to the surface than do direct approaches.

Listen for Your Vision

The purpose of the culture interview is to create circumstances in which leaders can observe firsthand how well the values and assumptions expressed in their vision have been embraced by the workforce. We've waited until now to point this out because we don't want leaders to jump right in with questions such as "So, do you really believe in and support our mission statement? Are you willing to do what it takes to satisfy competing stakeholder demands? What do you honestly think about our customers?" As tempting and direct as such questions are, they simply won't surface honest, accurate answers.

To get at your most important values, approach them indirectly. For example, if you're interested in your employees' customer orientation, listen for how often they discover barriers to serving customers. If they're frustrated about bureaucracy, red tape, or lack of empowerment because it keeps them from doing what it takes to meet or exceed customer expectations (stated or otherwise), you know that they care about customers. If, on the other hand, the word *customer* is never mentioned or if people seem more than satisfied with existing circumstances, you might wonder if they really worry about surprising and delighting their customers.

Remember, the opposite of love is not hate; it's apathy. The stronger the emotions are, the more likely your employees have strong values. The frightening interview is not the one punctuated by emotional statements; it's the one that looks more like a group nap than a discussion.

Watch for What's Missing

Sherlock Holmes is famous for once solving a crime by noticing that a dog *wasn't barking*. Sir Arthur Conan Doyle included this clever twist in one of his stories because he appreciated just how difficult it is to notice the absence of behavior. We share his opinion. After culture interviews are completed, it's rare for leaders to talk about what they *didn't* hear. They should. After conducting, say, three or four 90-minute interviews, if not a soul has mentioned anything even remotely related to your espoused key values or stakeholders, you ought to take note.

Pull Yourself Out of the Content

When you're in the muck you can only see muck. If you somehow manage to float above it, you still see the muck but you see it from a different perspective. And you see other things too.

DAVID CRONENBERG

As part of culture-assessment training, we ask participants to observe a group of people in the throes of a heated discussion. By design, the topic is always controversial. The purpose of having participants observe a group argue over an interesting topic is to see to what extent trainees can pull themselves out of the muck of the argument and shift to observing the process. It's actually quite difficult. Imagine how much more challenging it is to observe a group of your own employees discuss a problem without getting equally sucked into content.

In some ways, examining culture is akin to looking at a computer-generated three-dimensional design. You know the kind. You're supposed to focus on an imaginary point beneath the printed design until a 3-D image appears. When conducting a culture interview, pulling yourself out of engaging or entertaining surface issues is a similar act of will. If you don't purposefully remind yourself of your intent and continue to look past the surface for the underlying pattern, you'll be listening to the arguments.

Practice the observing process by watching daytime talk-show debates. Videotape a few and then pore over them with members of your family. It can be a lot of fun. Train yourself to see beneath the arguments. Focus on process. Ask yourself what values and assumptions are at play.

Learn from Our Experience

As we've conducted interviews, we've often noted similar cultural dimensions. We'll share a few with you, not because we're certain you'll face similar issues, but because they're rarely noted by nonprofessionals and because they deserve your attention.

Value Simplicity

Are people continually suggesting that they want to be given simple answers? Do they yearn to return to the "good old days" when all they had to do was manage a few tasks? Do they fall into either-or traps? ("Do you want volume or do you want quality?") Do they continue to seek imbalanced approaches to solving their problems? Do they willingly abandon one stakeholder in order to satisfy another?

Mistrust

Do participants continually speak of people in ways that suggest they don't trust others' motives, ability, or both? Does it take a long time before anyone opens up? Do eyes flit around the room to see how others are responding to problem descriptions?

Unflattering Labels

Do participants willingly label others in the organization? Do they routinely make the fundamental attribution error—simply assuming that problems stem from "unmotivated," rather than "unable," colleagues? How strong are the negative adjectives?

Inability to Engage in Dialogue

How do participants treat each other during the interview? When opinions differ, do people jump in and tear each other apart? How skilled are participants at talking about differences of opinion?

Deference to Authority

Does the presence of leaders stifle the conversation? Does it take a long time before anyone takes a risk? Do certain leaders uncover different information than others? That is, are some leaders able to get the group to open up while others are not?

Helplessness

How do people talk about problems? Are they spoken of in ways that suggest that things can never be changed? Do people speak of *they* and *them* all the time—as if there's a mysterious, unapproachable group that runs the organization? Do they use "victim" language?

Frustration

Are people noticeably upset with their inability to achieve what they'd like? Remember, frustration is typically a sign that employees value getting their jobs done. Don't see anger, disappointment, or other strong emotions as signs of an unhealthy culture. Fear apathy, not anger.

Missing Stakeholders

Is the silent "barking dog" of your interviews the complete and utter absence of any reference to certain stakeholder groups? Granted, you'd expect employees to be most concerned with those with whom they closely relate. Nevertheless, are the terms *productivity*, *yield*, *profits*, and *continuous improvement* dirty words? Are family issues never brought up? If people are working the afternoon shift or extended hours, do they appear comfortable talking about this aspect of their lives? Do they talk about life outside of work at all?

PATRICK McDUFFY, ANTHROPOLOGIST AT LARGE

We've provided an overview of the types of actions to take and elements to look for as an overview of the culture-assessment process. We've given particular attention to common mistakes leaders make so you can avoid all of them (okay, most of them). Now, let's look in on Patrick McDuffy, a real-life anthropologist leader, and see how some of these ideas can be put into action and serve a leader on a daily basis.

Seeing the Invisible

Hypocrisy, the only evil that walks Invisible . . .

JOHN MILTON

Patrick McDuffy, full-time senior manager and part-time cynic, was concerned. His latest worry had started when he and other members of the management team had decided to push quality to the number one priority for the coming year. The idea of improving quality wasn't so hard to swallow—it was what went with it that made him nervous. Over the past few months, Patrick had been reading all about quality. He had covered everything from *Quality Is Real Cheap* to *Dress for Quality*, and all the authors had suggested that quality never improves until employees are heavily involved in the process. Participation is the key.

His team had tried to involve employees once before and had failed miserably. The last time they looked in the suggestion box months (make that years) ago, there were only two suggestions, and both made some sort of snide reference to "where the sun don't shine."

McDuffy's nagging question was simple. Would his company's culture support the change that leaders were committed to create? He decided to walk around the place and see what cultural evidence he could find. His first stop was at the lobby rest room. Sure enough, the messages scratched into the metal stalls echoed the same themes that had shown up in the suggestion box, only with visual aids. At least he wasn't named personally.

The Culture Quest

Instead of pondering, or even reacting to, the content of the message, he began asking himself questions he thought might help him determine the culture.

- If that's what they say and do, what are they assuming? What do they value?

- How representative are these assumptions and values? Are they widely shared?
- How important are these values? Are they deeply held?

As he walked into the hallway, Patrick decided to be more proactive. He'd give the culture a poke and see what happened. If people were supposed to create a participatory culture, how willingly would they share their opinions? Would they come clean after a disagreement with, say, a boss? Henry, an analyst who worked for one of Patrick's direct reports, was walking by. Why not give him a try?

"Say, Henry, do you have a second?"

"Certainly, Mr. McDuffy," replied an obviously startled Henry.

"I just wanted to bounce an idea off you." Then Patrick came up with an outlandish notion just for the fun of it. "I've been thinking that Germax"—their largest and most faithful customer—"is getting too pushy. They're costing us too much in money and emotional strain to service them. Maybe we ought to drop them and focus on the customers with greater margins. What do you think?" (This anthropology thing was turning out to be fun. You get to mess with people's heads in the name of scientific inquiry.)

Henry looked surprised, then thoughtful. Finally he responded, *"I see your point Mr. McDuffy. And I think you may be right. Would you like me to run the numbers on it?"*

Patrick feigned a pensive pose and then shook his head, "No, let me get back to you on that." Henry looked relieved as he hurried down the hallway.

As the frightened analyst scurried away, Patrick repressed the desire to label him as a spineless wimp and asked himself, "What were his assumptions and values?"

Next, Patrick grabbed a tray and walked through the lunchroom line. People looked surprised. "Hello, Mr. McDuffy," they responded when they got too close to comfortably avoid him. "What brings you down here today?" they asked—obviously referring to his presence in the lunchroom instead of the executive dining room reserved for the management team.

"Oh, just having lunch," he casually replied.

As he walked out into the eating area, he selected a strategic location near a partition where he could hear the conversation at the next table without being accused of snooping. There was an animated conversation being held by a group of midlevel managers.

"But what can we do? If they don't get us the information, we can't meet deadlines. It's totally out of our control!" one of them complained.

"Yeah, and then we miss the schedule, and everyone says it's our fault."

"It's not fair!" another piped in.

"If someone doesn't do something about it, we'll miss it again next month. And you know who'll catch the blame."

As the managers gathered up their trays and exited, Patrick shifted his sense of disappointment for their obvious feelings of helplessness and once again asked his assumptions-and-values question. "What in their mental maps causes them to act this way?" And then he added another question, "And what are we doing to help keep these maps intact?"

The next day in the top-management team meeting, Patrick watched his boss in action. She was a woman who described herself as "aggressively participatory," and Patrick agreed with half of her self-assessment—she certainly was aggressive.

"Folks, this is a critical decision, and I would like everyone's ideas," his boss kicked off the meeting. "Let's decide as a team. I personally believe the second option is the better of the two because we've done it before, but I could be wrong. What do you all think?"

There was a long stretch of awkward silence. Then, one by one, various team members voiced their support for option two. The boss then announced, "Since we're all in agreement, let's go with the second option." From that point on, she made 15 decisions over the next hour. Sometimes she "involved" others by asking for their input after she announced her conclusion. On other occasions she just made the choice by smiling and pointing out what was going to happen. Most of the decisions were around trivial elements such as how many flip charts would be used at the all-hands meeting. All was done in a pleasant, even friendly, tone.

The pattern looked strikingly familiar. Patrick wondered what people were thinking as they sat quietly and deferred to her. What were their assumptions and values? Only in this case, *he* was one of the people who was sitting quietly and sucking it up. He knew, however, what he was thinking: He liked his job. Stories abounded of people being shut down for not being a "team player"—meaning not doing what the boss wanted. He believed the adage his former boss often quoted: "Those who acquiesce ascend." And he really wanted that next promotion.

Later that afternoon, as Patrick sat alone in his office, he pondered his experience over the past two days and marveled at his transformation. Normally he would have been pulled into the content of what he had seen, and he would have gone to immediate action, telling people what to do and how to fix the surface problems. Now, after having asked questions about values and assumptions, he had a different perspective. He was in a better position to work on the roots—values and assumptions—and less likely to hack away at the branches of behavior.

He started creating mini-theories. It appeared that people, himself included, were deferring to those in authority. There was an obvious reluctance to disagree with people who had control over vital resources. Were others assuming, as he was, that open disagreement was likely to yield disastrous results? Did they believe that only the terminally naive would be stupid enough to push back on a boss's idea?

Then there was the matter over lunch. Midlevel managers appeared as if they were assuming they had no control over their work. They continually used "victim" language. Why? Were they assuming that the organization was a massive monolith? That nothing they could do would change anything? That if they went to the trouble to try to change things they'd just be wasting their time and maybe even get into trouble? They seemed to value meeting their deadlines, or at least not being blamed for missing deadlines. Could these "helpless" assumptions be related to the deference shown to authority?

Finally, he began to think about what he *hadn't* seen. This, quite naturally, wasn't something that immediately came to mind. The whole idea of looking for what *wasn't* there was a bit alien to Patrick, a natural born, shoot-from-the-hip action taker. To make the invisible more visible, he thought of what he hadn't seen—in light of the plan to increase employee involvement. People weren't exactly bursting with new ideas and suggestions. Pushing back, challenging, discussing alternatives, taking responsibility, searching for solutions, the use of personal pronouns (I, me, we), and other actions of initiative and involvement were conspicuous by their absence.

Patrick didn't know the answers to the questions he had been raising, but by looking beyond single events and the immediate content of interactions, he was starting to see patterns and possibilities worth testing. He did come to two conclusions. One, if his musings and mini-theories were correct, the quality initiative was in jeopardy. Two, he had better test his theories by adding to his sample. So he decided to form a team and conduct a series of interviews throughout the organization. He had to learn if the assumptions and values he had been seeing were accurate, widely shared, and deeply held. Without that knowledge, he didn't know what they were facing or what corrective actions to take.

Patrick wondered briefly if he should involve others in the decisions to conduct culture interviews. After all, the precipitating event of this whole experience had been his fear that he and the other managers wouldn't be able to create a culture of involvement. As he thought about involving his team, he imagined the following conversation with his own team of direct reports.

The Sycophantic Cycle

"I've been thinking about getting a better feel for what's really going on in this company by conducting in-depth interviews with small groups of employees. It's always good to know what people are thinking. But I don't want to do this without first getting your input. What do you think? Would it be a good idea?"

"Absolutely!" responds his personal assistant. "The idea of getting input from others is positively inspired," chimes in someone else. "Brilliant," two others exclaim.

"Wait a minute. I'm not really sure it's the right thing. I just want your honest appraisal. This could be a mistake, taking up everyone's time on such a risky venture."

"Absolutely!" responds his personal assistant. "What were we thinking? It could be time consuming and risky," suggests another. "It would be a real mistake," two more chime in.

"Now wait a minute. I get the feeling you're just agreeing with me because I'm the boss."

"Of course!" they exclaim in a single voice—as if unabashed toadying were a precious corporate asset.

"You don't seem to be tracking this argument. You see, I don't want you to treat my ideas any different from your own. I want you to stop deferring to me. Would that be okay?"

"Is this a trick question?" ventures his assistant.

"No," responds Patrick. "I really do want you to stop treating me as if everything I say is correct."

"Got it, boss!" exclaims his chief accountant.

"We'll stop doing it right now!" insists the marketing director.

"How are we doing?" inquires the quality manager.

Ugh, thinks Patrick to himself. As much as you'd like to zoom ahead to a new set of values and assumptions (at least *some* new ones), and no matter how much you'd like to reach out and perform a frontal "culturotomy," one fact remains inviolate: When it comes to culture change, you have to start with your existing culture—ya gotta dance with the one what brung ya. It seemed like he'd read that somewhere before.

IN SUMMARY

Our goal in this chapter was twofold. First, we wanted to share several techniques for conducting a culture assessment. We provided several hints on how to complete a successful group interview. These interviews make up an important step along the road to Cultural Vitality.

Our second goal was to familiarize the reader with observational skills in general. Our intent was to share methods for continually measuring day-to-day realities against one's vision. The ability to watch for and pick up on underlying, often masked, values and assumptions is invaluable. The health-care president we referred to at the beginning of this chapter is our model of the ambulant anthropologist. More importantly, he strikes an entirely new balance. Every day he walks that fine line between getting caught up in the content of any discussion and observing the process. He continually toggles between what people are saying and what it means about their values and assumptions. In so doing, he keeps familiar with the issues at hand, gains a feeling for people's values and assumptions, and is constantly monitoring his organization against the stated vision.

Today's visionaries realize that organizations need leaders with not only a clear vision but with the ability to monitor their progress. A vision that is not carefully and accurately monitored is nothing more than a wish list that will one day be posted on the front gate by angry employees who feel cheated by hollow promises. On the other hand, a constantly monitored vision is a leader's most reliable road map to what needs to be changed to strengthen Cultural Vitality.

A PRACTICE ASSIGNMENT — LAYING THE GROUNDWORK FOR A CULTURE ASSESSMENT

Before you jump full barrel into a culture assessment, try a walk around. Listen to what people talk about, read your posted memos, watch for what excites people. If you lead a small workgroup, draw people together and ask a couple of questions: "If you could change one thing . . . ?" "If a family member came to work here, what advice . . . ?" Listen for values and assumptions.

Those with larger responsibilities would do well to formalize their approach. Invite a cross-section of leaders to read this chapter. Complete a village tour, and analyze written documents. When your team feels comfortable, pair up and conduct group interviews. After you've all completed three or more, meet and discuss what you've learned.

Practice at home by spending an evening listening for values and assumptions. As people talk, see if you can determine the underlying values or assumptions driving the conversation, being careful not to commit the fundamental attribution error while you're listening and observing. To receive more information on the culture-interview process, see the order form at the end of this book.

CHAPTER 5

Assessing What You've Got: Pulse

If you keep measuring what you've been measuring, you'll keeping getting what you've got.

One of the working titles of this book was the *Renaissance Challenge.* Our reasoning was simple. We ask leaders to embrace skills from a wide range of disciplines. For example, in chapter 3 we asked leaders to step outside traditional business-school topics, put on their philosopher hats, and create a vision. In chapter 4 we suggested that leaders need to be walking anthropologists. Now we're going to propose that leaders should know enough about surveys and research techniques to be able to continually monitor the vitality of their company.

Uh-oh.

Surely we've gone too far. Now, not only are we encouraging leaders to take on the skills of still another discipline, we're asking them to enter a field that most people (how should we put it?) *loathe.* The very thought of the word *survey* makes many executives nervous. When the expression "employee feedback" finds its way into a conversation, they break out in a sweat. The whole idea of taking "soft" survey data makes them queasy.

Here's why.

What Do You Mean I'm Hard to Approach?

It's a Monday morning, and you've just heard through the grapevine that it's time to administer your organization's biannual Corporate Health Survey. The thought of one more three-decimal assault makes you nauseous. You find it ironic that the mere thought of a corporate health survey makes you and most other leaders sick.

The first time you had a leadership survey filled out on you and your team was back in the 1970s when you were the morale officer on the USS *Enterprise*. It had taken weeks for the crew to fill out all of the survey forms. The completed surveys literally filled the back of a flatbed truck.

At first you fretted over what your results would be. Then, as weeks turned into months, you forgot about the whole thing until another rumor came down the line. Within a couple of days, a fat manila envelope appeared in your in-basket. You stared at the thing for a couple of minutes until you finally mustered the nerve to open it. Your results hadn't been so bad. Your team scores, as judged by other workgroups, had been mixed. Some people liked the relationship you had developed and others didn't. The results seemed capricious.

Your personal leadership scores, as judged by your direct reports, had actually been good. Compared to your buddy Jim, a fellow front-line officer who had honed his sarcasm skills to an art form and used them to continually take cheap shots at the people who worked for him, you did great. Jim's direct reports had written in zeros and negative numbers on his survey. Ones weren't low enough for him. On the open-ended part of the questionnaire, one of his employees wrote, "I won't rest until I know the route your children take to school." Jim hadn't been amused.

Jim's low scores had kept up your spirits for a while, but, true to your normal uptight style, your two low leadership scores (5.2 and 5.4 on a 7-point scale) started to grate on you. Just what did your direct reports mean by insinuating that you were "hard to approach"? And what gave them the notion that you were a bit forceful? You asked the fellow officer who shared an office with you if he thought you were standoffish and forceful, and he just averted his eyes and darted out of the office. Go figure.

Finally, you tracked down a couple of your direct reports and asked them what they had in mind when they gave you the low score. They stammered nervously and swore that they didn't do it. The next morning, you took a real tongue-lashing from your boss for "going on a search-and-destroy mission." You pointed out that you were just seeking clarity, not trying to track down the guilty.

After a couple of months of inaction, you were able to put the whole thing behind you until a memo came down from headquarters asking everyone to hold a formal meeting with their direct reports, discuss the survey results, come up with a plan, and send in form RT649E reporting the result. You put that meeting off for as long as you could until, fearing a reprimand from the forms control officer, you finally called your 14 employees into your office.

Your team's scores were quickly handled. Nobody could figure out what they meant. Some liked their relationship with you; some didn't. (What else is new?) When it came time to review your leadership scores, people stared at their fingernails and snickered nervously. A couple of brave souls ventured a comment or two while you wrote furiously on the flip chart. Their peers became *real* interested in their fingernails when somebody said that you had a tendency to force your ideas on others. You would have thought that cuticle reading had been elevated to a sacrament. Finally, in spite of the nervous silence that followed, you came up with some vague plans and sent the report in. Fortunately, nobody followed up on the meeting, and your boss never mentioned a word about it again.

Now you're about to start the whole process again on your new job. You'd rather inhale ammonia.

Where Did We Make a Wrong Turn?

There is nothing like a good, painstaking survey full of decimal points and guarded generalizations to put a glaze like a Sung vase on your eyeball.

S. J. PERELMAN

It's little wonder that people aren't real fired up to administer leadership (or any other kind of employee health) surveys. Most are time consuming and relatively useless. For example, traditional measures either (1) barbecue leaders, (2) simply look at satisfaction (do you like your pay, benefits, and other perks?), or (3) provide interdepartment smiley or frowny faces. The leadership data, as you know from personal experience, hasn't always been all that helpful, and the employee and interdepartment satisfaction measures don't come close to assessing Cultural Vitality. Actually, both types of surveys often cause more harm than good. When they turn ugly, they don't just provide vacuous, guilt-inducing data—they also take time, raise expectations, lower esteem, and lead to witch hunts.

But let's not throw out the baby with the bathwater. The idea of using surveys is solid. Once leaders have dreamed their dreams and laid out a course of action, they need to assess how well they're doing. They must measure the gaps between their dreams and reality. To do so, leaders have to find a way to get their finger on their company's pulse. They need to measure what people are thinking and feeling—their assumptions and values. If they can't measure gaps in behaviors, values, and assumptions, they can't track and fix the important parts of Cultural Vitality.

There's more. Taking survey measures isn't enough. Leaders have to do it frequently and quickly—that's why we've chosen the pulse metaphor. Taking your organization's pulse means getting regular, quick, and accurate measures of cultural health. Many leaders take financial and other operational measures daily. However, since they only assess what people are thinking and feeling every couple of years, it's little wonder that these "soft" measures are not part of a leader's daily, weekly, or even monthly regimen. When you think about it, it seems a bit odd to be looking at quality and cost measures with the setting of the sun and Cultural Vitality measures every time Mars completes an orbit (687 days). But then again, when you remember that your typical culture measure is painful, expensive, and laborious, it's little wonder that leaders refuse to take "soft" measures more often than they change their carpets. Who wouldn't?

Stop the Insanity!

In order to track Cultural Vitality efficiently (beyond leadership scores and interdepartmental relationships), leaders have to institute a system that quickly, accurately, and effectively tracks what people are thinking, feeling, and doing. More specifically, they must dive into employee attitudes about each of the stakeholders.

Once again, we're not suggesting that leaders become survey or research experts. However, they must know enough about the process to direct and judge it. They must understand (and this isn't going to make us a whole lot of friends in certain quarters) that there's a fair chance that many of their professional staffers don't know any more than they do about how to generate *useful* culture data. If they did, why in the heck would they be passing around that noxious cultural probe (i.e., the leadership survey) every two years?

This has to stop, and you just might have to be the one to stop it. To find out what leaders should be doing, let's take another look at what many organizations have been, and shouldn't be, doing.

WHAT WE TRADITIONALLY DO

A precedent embalms a principle.

BENJAMIN DISRAELI

Traditional, ineffective measures of Cultural Vitality typically have gone unchallenged by leaders because most aren't trained consumers of social science research. Although they may have a hunch that the material they've been asked to use is of dubious value and has no clear evaluation criteria, they're left registering complaints that sound more like whining than thoughtful criticism. Worse yet, they look defensive. (Did your department get a low score? No wonder you don't like the survey!) Unarmed with a careful way of thinking about survey research, most leaders sniff the instrument suspiciously, smile warily, and then take their stripes.

Useless Contraptions

Because many leaders know so little about survey methods, they often end up using instruments that look alarmingly like an appliance collection one of the authors stumbled upon one day when he came across the humble home of Tu and Ari, twin brothers who lived and fished on a remote island in the South Pacific. Their home, once a simple make-shift hut, had mutated into an agglomeration of add-ons, wings, and extensions—all constructed to house the newfangled gadgets that passing salespeople had convinced Tu and Ari they simply couldn't live without. The two fishermen had acquired this bizarre collection of appliances after placing a fish trap in just the right place, generating a veritable fortune. Fishing they knew. Appliances they were less sure of. Actually, they weren't the least bit confident that the ever-growing mound of high-tech wares would be useful, but both agreed that they sure looked good. As money rolled in, they grabbed up Wurlitzer organs, big-screen TVs, massage recliners, and top-of-the-line juicers. They hoped one day to have electricity.

Far too many surveys end up looking like Tu and Ari's appliance collection because leaders, unaware of the underlying theory of survey design, add on a bell here, a whistle there, and a nifty new scale toward the end. They, like the two Polynesian fishermen, eagerly snatch up the latest wares offered by passing human resources professionals, consultants, and business leaders. And what do they get for their efforts? They end up with a fancy survey that is virtually powerless for guiding change.

- Without a careful and thorough culture assessment, leaders find themselves asking survey questions that have been precipitated not by solid research, but by a single poignant event, a frightening rumor, or possibly a senior executive's latest whim.
- Without a stakeholder-based theory, leaders end up measuring items that only tenuously link to Outcome Vitality. Inspired by ardent gurus instead of clear theory, they burn millions of dollars on the altar of "blind faith," believing that if they just (insert your latest trend), they'll soon sip from the grail of Cultural Vitality.
- Without a vision-based focus, leaders dilute their energy and efforts by aiming at dozens of issues surfaced through hundreds of questions.
- Without behavior-based questions, leaders generate gaggles of guilt without stirring up a whisper of hope for change.

MASTERING MEASURES OF CULTURAL VITALITY

Given that it's quite easy to construct fancy-looking survey instruments that are virtually powerless to either guide or inspire change, we recommend the following strategies.

Build on the Culture Assessment

When contemplating a survey, start with the data from your culture assessment. Instead of grabbing popular off-the-shelf survey measures that may have nothing to do with your organization, use the culture-assessment process to show you where to focus your surveys. As you're finding out what's really going on "out there," also be looking for key issues and gaps. Based on what surfaced during the interviews and on your observations during the culture assessment, select your change targets from the top two or three gaps you observed. These targets can then be used to (1) design survey questions and scales that are tailored, powerful, and relevant and (2) guide the overall change process.

To help you reduce a host of issues to a handful that will guide both the change strategy and the design of survey questions, we recommend the following process.

- **Nominate.** Ask each person who took part in the culture-assessment interviews to nominate a behavior he or she would endure 1,000 paper cuts to see more of—obviously, these should be behaviors that would significantly enable the organization to provide greater PNV, INV, CNV, and ONV.

- **Post.** Write each behavior on a sticky note, and post it on a wall.
- **Clump.** Look for themes. Move the sticky notes to form groups of behaviors that seem to be similar in nature.
- **Label.** As the leadership group begins to feel comfortable with the groupings, establish labels or names for the groups. Choose labels that are interesting and compelling.
- **Select.** Choose two or three areas to work on. These will be the topics you'll turn into useful measures and work toward improving.
- **Anchor.** Finally, anchor your two global areas to concrete behaviors. Make a lengthy list of actual behaviors that turn the compelling label into daily action. Without a list of behaviors, you won't know what to measure, teach, and encourage.

For example, Mike Miller, a senior manager at AT&T, worked with his leadership team through just such a process. After conducting a thorough culture assessment, the team grouped the behaviors and assumptions they had surfaced into four or five categories. The two they decided they'd be willing to make significant sacrifices to foster were Personal Engagement and Openness. Under these two interesting and compelling headings they listed a number of very specific behaviors.

Jack Welch, the CEO of General Electric, chose Openness and Boundarylessness as his Cultural Vitality focus. Of course, to bring meaning to these labels, he and other leaders identified specific behaviors that do and do not represent these cultural characteristics. Welch, Miller, and other top-notch leaders select only a couple of targets and translate them into daily behaviors that can be taught, encouraged, and measured.

The point we're making is that you can't be "focused" if you have a list of 10 or more cultural goals. Likewise, you're aiming in the dark if you can't name the specific behaviors that will tell you if the culture is changing or not. Don't proceed past the original culture assessment until you've narrowed your list of challenges to two or three categories, each supported by a long list of clearly defined behaviors. Remember, behaviors form the anchor of everything you'll be doing to encourage change—from measurement to training.

Don't Gather Conclusions

Now, having said that the anchor of the change process in general (and of survey items in specific) is a carefully crafted list of desired behaviors, leaders had better know how to distinguish a useful behavior from everything else posing as one. It turns out that this task is not as easy as it first appears. Actually, this behavior quest must start with dozens of mini-theories that relate behaviors to desired outcomes. If you don't know what behaviors lead to what results, then you don't know where to start. Without a theory linking action to outcome, you end up selecting behaviors on the basis of hunch, history, and happenstance. As obvious as this sounds, most of what has been done with surveys over the past few years hasn't been based on anything close to careful theory. If anything, it's been based on vague homilies that tenuously (*very* tenuously) link behavior to outcomes.

Actually, professional survey work took a real turn toward vacuous, guilt-inducing fluff several years back when questions started measuring conclusions rather than behaviors. Researchers began asking questions such as, *"Does your boss include you in the appropriate number and level of decisions?"* To the average survey designer this sounded like a reasonable question. Similarly, had you asked most leaders whether they agreed this question was important, they would have caved in quickly and encouraged you to include it. After all, employee involvement is important, right?

The problem with this particular question is not with the idea of involvement per se but with how it is operationalized and with the reactions it engenders. The real trouble starts after the survey is administered and the data are returned. The poor leader who is staring at a low score in "employee involvement" is not unlike a parent on Christmas Eve trying to assemble a remote-control racer and one of the instructions states: "Now, build the drive shaft." No pictures. No details. No hints. Just do it. The leader, either by direct command or insinuation, is told to improve his or her "involvement score." No pictures. No details. No hints. Just do it.

But do what? The leader looks at the question that led to the low score and asks, "What do you mean I don't include them in the *appropriate* number of decisions? What decisions? Didn't I just hand the whole marketing plan over to them? Where did this come from?"

Unfortunately, since the survey typically comes back in nifty binders and is reported to three decimal places, leaders, while left wondering what to do, don't demand more clarity. After all, the results look so impressive and so. . . uh . . . numeric. Hogwash!

> Measuring fuzzy conclusions to three decimal places is akin to putting a caliper on a dust bunny.

Don't be influenced by dazzling decimals, impressive significance scores, and artistically displayed standard deviations. The fact is, fuzzy questions lead to fuzzy results, no matter their packaging. *If you want the numbers you're gathering to actually mean something, don't measure conclusions. Measure behaviors.*

Here's how.

Creating Behavioral Measures

behavior—noun—recognizable and reproducible bundles of motor responses

You'd think that describing a behavior would be a piece of cake. It's not. Every time you describe a behavior to someone, you're taking a huge number of minute activities and placing them into a bundle. If the bundle isn't recognizable and reproducible, it's useless. Let's look at each of these concepts, in turn.

Bundles. No behavior consists of a discrete or single action. For example, consider the seemingly simple action of raising your hand in class. Without going into the detailed physiology of lifting one's arm, suffice it to say that hundreds, maybe even thousands, of tiny actions must occur before an arm climbs into the air. Heaven only knows how much information must be relayed over the human information highway (the nerves and spinal cord) just to start the process. And that's just for something as simple as hefting a limb.

Now, how about something more complicated and subtle—say, flirting. How many minuscule actions go into this common activity? A young woman shouts to her beau, "Stop flirting!" He responds, "I wasn't flirting." What if he doesn't know what she meant? Should he not "talk" with other women? No, that's not it. Was it wrong that he smiled? Not actually. Well, then, what was it? It was in the *way* he smiled. "Ah," he says, "it was in the *way* I smiled."

Our point? When you choose to describe a behavior, be it part of your vision statement, a term you use when coaching another, or a word that you place in a questionnaire, be warned—the larger the bundle of subtle behaviors, the less likely that others will understand what you mean by it. (Which leads us to our next point.)

Recognizable. For survey purposes, bundles must be recognizable groupings of motor responses. That is, after hearing the behavioral description, an individual would be able to differentiate the presence or absence of the behavior in question when observing others. This turns out to be no simple task. We learned this over 20 years ago when we first tried to capture leadership behavior on video. The actions scholars had been describing for decades in popular leadership texts turned out to be subject to a vast array of interpretations when ultimately demonstrated on video. Actions such as "open the discussion with a warm greeting" turned out to be difficult to create. After producing an example on videotape, you could scarcely find two people who would agree that a particular action was warm. One found it warm, the other cloying.

Reproducible. When you get right down to it, the real test of a behavior description is whether the person can reproduce it upon hearing the description. Even when researchers are able to capture behavior bundles that everyone agrees hold a certain property, the behavior bundles are often hard to reproduce. It's a great deal easier to train critics who can recognize the presence or absence of a particular behavior than it is to find actors who can replicate them.

The implications of this bundling discussion to the leader (as survey expert) should be clear. More often than not, the bundles contained in your typical survey offer little instruction to the person reviewing the data. The catch expressions are neither recognizable nor reproducible. Consider the problem a couple of the authors once faced when working with a senior executive who had been repeatedly described by his direct reports and colleagues as "arrogant." Watching him at work, you might conclude that he was indeed arrogant, but to him the term was a painful label with little useful information. He had a sense for what people were concluding, but didn't know what he was doing that led to the conclusion. As we watched him at work, we repeatedly saw him take certain actions that others might label as arrogance. For example, when talking to him about a TV show, he responded, "I don't have time for such mindless activities as watching TV." When a colleague was giving a presentation, the manager in question started filling out paperwork on another project. When speaking of another division, he referred to his colleagues as "simpletons."

Combined, the actions led others to conclude that perhaps he thought that he was smarter than others or that his time was more important. Rather than deluge him with a litany of minute behavioral descriptions, people bundled their conclusions into a single, neat, yet impossible to comprehend, term. He was "arrogant," and everyone agreed. The leader, of course, was left clueless.

To coach the executive in question, telling him to be "less arrogant" was not the least bit helpful. Telling him that many of his problems stemmed from actions such as calling others "simpletons" or working on his own projects during an important presentation *was* helpful. He understood these behaviors. For the first time he could see how others could formulate an opinion of him as they had. His behavior began to change immediately.

When it comes to behavior descriptions, insightful leaders create a vision made up of discrete, recognizable, and reproducible bundles of behavior. Their measures of success include items that are equally clear. For example, knowledgeable leaders wouldn't dream of including an item in a survey that leaves the person or group in question with a sense of guilt but no real understanding of what needs to change.

When reading potential Cultural Vitality survey items, expert leaders ask, "If the team, department, or individual in question received a low score on this item, would it be immediately obvious to any of them what they need to do in order to improve the score? If they're able to recognize what they're currently doing that's wrong and exactly what they need to do instead, would they be able to enact the requisite behaviors?" These are the ultimate tests of the power of a survey item.

Anchor Everything to Your Vision of Vitality

If you don't care where you're going, "then it doesn't matter which way you go."

LEWIS CARROLL

The Cheshire Cat was right. If you don't care about what you're trying to achieve, it doesn't matter what path you take—and it certainly doesn't matter what you measure. But leaders do care. That's why it's so important to have a clearly articulated and detailed vision. If leaders follow the advice in chapter 3, if they develop a detailed vision of what they're trying to achieve with each stakeholder group, they'll have a wonderful starting place for assessing the relevancy and effectiveness of their measures. With this clear vision in mind, leaders can carefully design measures of PNV, INV, CNV, and ONV. Other books in this leadership series will be devoted to these stakeholder measures. For now, we'll simply suggest that if your organization has a biannual employee-health questionnaire, three dozen measures of profitability, a six-item customer-satisfaction survey, and nothing that measures the community, you're out of balance.

Link Behaviors to Vitality

Next, when looking at what to include in an employee survey, turn to your vision of Cultural Vitality. This too should be filled with dozens of behavior descriptions. Here's where theory can be enormously helpful. Sooner or later, every question included in a survey must link your measures of Cultural Vitality to Outcome Vitality. Rarely has this been the case. In fact, one of the reasons that a great deal of the effort to measure human values and assumptions has been so singularly unsuccessful is that most surveys have been void of this much-needed theory. For example, when human resources professionals were first asked to assess people, most ran out and gathered measures of employee satisfaction. Do they like their jobs? Do they like their pay? Do they like the benefits? Do they like each other? The word *like* was bandied about quite a bit. Underlying this unrelenting drive to measure satisfaction lay a simple theory: If people are satisfied, they'll do whatever it takes to get the results back to where they ought to be.

It turns out that this popular theory was based on quite a leap of faith. Scholars later showed that the relationship between job satisfaction and profitability was mixed. Sound thinkers took one look at the whole mess and concluded that in the gaping maw found between employee satisfaction and profitability, there was a lot of wiggle room. It didn't take a degree in rocket science to conclude that a more finely tuned theory was called for.

As leaders face the daunting task of building vitality, they need to be armed with dozens of theories that relate employee behavior to Cultural Vitality. For instance, when conducting the culture assessment we referred to earlier, Mike Miller discovered a common and dangerous pattern of behavior. It was called "playing chicken." If individuals assigned to a critical part of a larger project were falling behind schedule, they were loath to admit it publicly. Instead, they waited for someone else to admit that their part of the same project was late. Consequently, everyone would sit around as the due date barreled closer like a speeding train, not wanting to be the first to jump off the track by admitting they were late. Once someone else begged for more time (thus pushing the train's arrival time further away), all those who didn't fess up could heave a sigh of relief and benefit from the reprieve.

Mike and his leadership team believed (this is the mini-theory) that the cost of this behavior was enormous. If no one spoke up about delays, they would end up shipping hastily packaged goods that would practically fall apart on the customer's doorstep. The cost of rework and end-of-project crises was much greater, they believed, than evenhanded development over time—which could be achieved if people were candid about schedule and resource needs.

Miller and his colleagues started a campaign to encourage "openness." That is, they required absolute candor about schedule, quality, and resource issues with top leaders, peers, and direct reports. These were the behaviors the leaders were after. To be sure they didn't forget the business rationale, they explained why these behaviors would help improve customer and economic outcomes. They are currently testing this mini-theory. Month in and month out they carry out interventions designed to foster greater openness. They measure the behavior and check to see if increased behavior coincides with improved customer and economic outcomes.

Examine Blocks to Vitality by Completing a Six-Cell Analysis

Perhaps the least popular part of surveys is the fact that most are based on the fundamental attribution error. Behind every question is the assumption that if people learn that they have earned a low score, they'll be motivated to change. Consequently, surveys are often used as clubs. "Hey, Ms. Hide-Your-Feelings, it's time you started opening up and sharing what you think!" or "Okay team. Our customers don't think we treat them with dignity. Get to it."

How different it would be if individuals, after being asked how often or effectively they do something, were asked what prevents them from doing what has been asked. Consider Mr. Miller's groups who were routinely "playing chicken." Miller and his fellow leaders could have simply announced, "Stop 'playing chicken.' Start letting people know the minute you're falling behind schedule." But they didn't. They decided to take a balanced look at what was causing the behavior. More specifically, they were interested in determining what was encouraging people to remain silent when they started to lag behind schedule. They conducted a Six-Cell analysis. Potential barriers they decided to measure included:

- They're afraid of what the boss will say when they announce they're behind schedule. (Cell 3)
- They don't know how to talk about falling behind without looking like they're giving up an important goal. (Cell 2)
- They're rewarded for always staying on schedule. Thus, let someone else take the heat while keeping your performance review clean. (Cell 5)

- Their scheduling skills are lacking. They make promises they can't deliver on. Not out of fear, they just don't predict well. (Cell 2)
- The current development process they're using doesn't help them make accurate scheduling estimates. (Cell 6)
- Colleagues aren't getting them the information they need to help them with the planning cycle. (Cell 4)
- They fall behind because other teams are so worried about their own goals that they don't provide them with the support they need. (Cells 4 and 5)
- New projects are added on after schedules are set, pushing everything else back. (Cell 4)

You get the idea. To understand the causes behind today's behavior, brainstorm possible Six-Cell influences. (This will be easier after you've read the later chapters on each cell.) After considering each cell, develop a survey that not only measures behavior, but the causes behind it.

When the Six-Cell data returns, you're in a strong position to design initiatives that attack barriers cell by cell. As you carry out these initiatives, continue to take behavioral measures (e.g., how often are people talking candidly with bosses about schedule or staffing concerns?) to see if the barriers you're removing are actually enabling the behaviors you want to encourage.

These behavior measures then allow you to check out your mini-theories. In other words, as the number of open discussions about scheduling challenges increases, are PNV, INV, and CNV increasing? Are customers more satisfied with the product they're receiving? Are people happier with their work? Are revenues increasing or expenses declining? If the answer is yes, you begin to suspect that the actions resulting from your Six-Cell diagnosis are paying off.

Having completed a Six-Cell analysis, you're on your way toward avoiding the black holes most culture-change efforts get sucked into. You started by identifying a handful of target behaviors. These came from comparing your vision of Organizational Vitality to what you observed in the culture interviews. Next, you clearly stated your beliefs or mini-theories about how each of these targeted behaviors would help drive better outcomes. Finally, you gathered data about what was routinely blocking these behaviors. All that's left is determining the "pulse" or behavior scores you want to measure on a regular basis to track your ongoing progress.

Don't Confuse Numbers with Vitality

"But his cholesterol count was so low!" wailed the widow as she stood over her husband's lifeless body.

After you've clarified your vision, created behaviorally anchored measures, and conducted a Six-Cell analysis, someone is bound to look at the averages of the scores and ask, "What do the numbers mean? How are we supposed to interpret the fact that we received a 1.5 under the category of Openness?" To answer these queries, you have to return to the original survey questions. Researchers often collapse data into huge bundles, give them labels such as "Openness" and "Integrity" which sound important, and then fret over the findings as if they really meant something. Don't fall into this trap. Return to the original questions and ask, "What does an increase or decrease in the score for this question mean about our ability to satisfy competing stakeholder demands?" ("How much more frequently are people speaking up about potential scheduling risks?")

Never separate the results from the actual questions.

Having identified the question that leads to the numbers, compare each score to your vision or mission statement. The natural tendency is to compare your numbers to those scored by other divisions, departments, or companies. Don't compare your numbers to external benchmarks unless you're certain that they're comparable and relevant. When it comes to comparing survey results between organizations (or even work areas), you're often comparing apples and oranges. People interpret the questions differently. Worse yet, you may be comparing yourself to a group that is close to being dead forever. Having a temperature that is 15 degrees higher than your average cadaver is hardly worth celebrating.

Given that external benchmarks do little to shed light on the numbers, where should you turn? Benchmark yourself against your dream. That's why you created your vision or mission statement in the first place. It, and only it, can explain why certain scores matter a great deal and others don't amount to a hill of beans. For example, based on your dream, some scores *should* be low. You haven't focused on them, and, in fact, you've done nothing to improve them (and would only chalk it up to chance if they improved). In contrast, other numbers that are relatively high should disappoint you because they're core to your mission.

For instance, the authors once worked with a team that celebrated the fact that their overall customer-satisfaction score was two-tenths of a point higher than every other division in the company. The celebration came to a halt when one of the team members pointed out that they had poured all of their change efforts into that score, and despite their comparative advantage, they were still scoring only a 5 on a 7-point scale. That simply wasn't good enough.

Rely on your mission statement, not your raw numbers, to provide meaning.

Let Your Vision, Not the Computer, Determine Significance

There are three kinds of lies: lies, damned lies, and statistics.

BENJAMIN DISRAELI

If ever there was a word that was yanked from typical usage and misapplied to a specialized jargon, the term *significance* has to lead the list. When the mean scores of two populations are compared and found to be different, the first question people ask is, "Are the differences *significant?*" That is, are we significantly better than the other group? Are we significantly better than we were before? Has our "Openness" score improved significantly?

Unfortunately, the question of significance could easily mislead someone into believing that what is being asked is, "Are the differences *important?*" After all, isn't that what *significance* usually means? Actually, when you say that a finding is statistically significant to the .05 level, you're really talking about *odds* and not *importance*. You're saying that if you were to produce survey results using a roulette wheel, only five times out of a hundred would you expect to achieve the scores you received.

We mention this because the concept of significance has eluded enough people for long enough that it's common for leaders to assign importance to a finding that deserves little attention. The computer suggests that the differences are *significant*, so people begin to think they're important. The truth is, it's fairly common to report a difference that is statistically significant to .05 but that is theoretically insipid or, worse still, has little to do with an organization's vitality. For instance, with a sample of 500 people, mean scores of 4.3 and 4.5 respectively on a 7-point "Openness" scale could be significant to the .05 level. However, leaders who are worrying about people "playing chicken" may not be thrilled by an improvement of only two-tenths of a point.

The solution to this misinterpretation is simple. Start by looking at questions that are core to your mission. Next, look at mean differences. Find ones you believe are important enough to deserve your attention. On a 7-point scale, differences of a full point are usually worth examining. Then bring your statistics into play. Check the odds on the differences you've deemed interesting. Then, and only then, can a significance score be used in the way it was originally intended. Let the computer calculate the odds, allowing true "significance" to flow from your mission statement.

Take Frequent Measures

If you don't measure, you can't learn.

As leaders continue to take actions to improve their vitality, they have no way of knowing how well they're doing unless they take frequent measures. Three types of measures help leaders know whether they're gaining or losing ground. All three need to be taken with enough frequency that they not only guide routine performance, they symbolically communicate that leaders really care about the results.

Outcome Vitality

We hit on this pretty hard earlier. Complete and accurate PNV, INV, CNV, and ONV numbers are important because moving stakeholder satisfaction measures into the stratosphere guarantees future vitality. Stakeholder measures should not only be taken, they should be posted publicly and often. For example, an amusement park we're aware of takes a simple customer survey daily. Perky park personnel poll people as they leave the park, asking them three questions that support their strategy. "On a scale of one to ten," they ask, "how enjoyable were the rides? How friendly were the employees? How clean was the park?" The previous day's measures are posted immediately for all to see— how elegant in its simplicity!

Cultural Vitality

These are surveys that gather data regarding how frequently people enact the handful of behaviors you've selected as your focus. If these surveys are longer than 20 to 30 questions, then you don't have a focus—you have potpourri. The brevity of the survey allows you to frequently check (at least quarterly) to see if desired behaviors are increasing. Some behaviors (such as frequency of making improvement proposals or cold calls) can be tracked without surveys and, consequently, can be tallied and reported even more frequently. If you've just spent a few grand on sales training (hoping it would result in more cold calls), either these measures should improve or you should be scratching your head asking, "What do we need to learn from this dismal failure?"

Initiative Effectiveness

Finally, leaders should be taking initiative-based measures. They ought to put the same kind of discipline in their behavior-change initiatives that they put into everything else. For example, a couple of the authors recently sat with an executive team that was planning to hold a regular top-management conference. In all, they would spend $100,000 on travel, accommodations, and speakers. When we asked what would be different after the conference, someone mumbled, "We'll have another one of these things over with."

At the end of a rather animated discussion, the organizers realized that the proposed conference was, in fact, an intervention. People were being brought together to influence behavior, values, and assumptions. The team then turned to what they wanted to change and how they would measure it. They then produced a five-item questionnaire that was administered before and after the conference. The discipline of identifying measurable goals forced a few items off the agenda and returned a few items previously discarded.

If accounting is the language of business, then surveying is the language of culture change. Leaders who want to know whether they won or lost in various culture-change efforts do well to demand clear, concise, and quick measures of culture-change results.

Take Control

Don't put your success in the hands of strangers—especially ones who seem to be living life in slow motion.

One of the reasons surveys are not administered very frequently is leaders don't have the resources to gather the information they need. Consequently, they rely on outside experts to conduct the lion's share of the work. The good news is that the leaders are saved a great deal of effort. The bad news is that the work is usually completed outside their control and at a snail's pace.

To help solve this problem, the authors have designed a software tool, Corporate*Pulse*, that helps manage survey work from the initial questionnaire design to the final diagnosis. In the back of this book we've included an order form for a sample disk of the software. This software makes it possible for leaders to develop stakeholder outcome measures, create behavioral and Six-Cell questions, print out surveys, analyze data, and produce visual displays of the results—all with the click of a finger (or a mouse, actually).

Leaders will never keep their fingers on the pulse of their Organizational Vitality and Cultural Vitality as long as the process takes weeks to deliver and can only be conducted by outside "experts." Turn this around. Take control over your own vitality measures by insisting that you and your trained professionals create a system that makes it easy to "pulse," or quickly and conveniently measure values and assumptions. If you don't, count on being driven by the mounds of operational measures that you're currently gathering daily. Remember, when it comes to changing organizations, if you keep measuring what you've been measuring, you'll keep getting what you've got.

IN SUMMARY

If leaders expect to keep their fingers on the pulse of their vitality, they must take concise and focused survey measures. After visioning, completing culture interviews, and developing careful mini-theories of which behaviors will best drive results, leaders must work with their human resources specialists to create instruments (and a system for administering them) that continually monitor behaviors at risk. To ensure that these measures are sound, leaders must insist that:

- The Cultural Vitality survey is focused on no more than two or three key areas (selected from the culture assessment).
- The survey measures behaviors, not conclusions.
- Long-term change-process measures assess behaviors *and* include Six-Cell questions that assess barriers.
- All important initiatives are "pulsed" or measured to see if behavior, values, and assumptions change.

If leaders don't establish these standards, they're likely to end up with a survey process that comes out of the Tu and Ari school of design—if it looks good, throw it in.

Of course, none of this is easy. Frankly, in most organizations, getting leaders to design and develop reliable culture measures is like getting them to drink curdled milk. This need not be. With a clear understanding of what's required to assess behaviors, values, and assumptions, survey design and administration transforms from a loathed, mysterious task to a valued activity. With time and practice, Cultural Vitality measures become such a vital part of routine data gathering that most leaders can't believe there was a time when they only assessed people every other year.

A PRACTICAL ASSIGNMENT — GETTING GOOD AT DESCRIBING BEHAVIORS

Let's work on an important skill—one that is needed for visioning, coaching, and measuring: the ability to tell the difference between a behavior and a conclusion.

A good way to develop the skill is to think of a few people you know. Start by listing some of their qualities. List some ways you'd describe them. These descriptions typically are going to be conclusions such as "reliable" or "short-tempered."

Now, take one quality and answer the question, "What does this person do or not do that causes me to conclude this about him or her?" For instance, "What does Cynthia do that makes me conclude she's a 'team player'?" Check your answers to see if they're conclusions or behaviors. Remember, a behavior is a bundle of actions that can be observed, recognized, and replicated. A conclusion, on the other hand, is a judgment. A behavior is what you can *see* ("She offers to lend a hand when she hears I'm on a tight deadline."). A conclusion tells you what you think about that behavior ("She's helpful.").

After listing possible behaviors, review each to see if it's an action you can observe or a judgment you've made. For those that don't pass the "behavior" test, push your thinking further by asking, "What does this person do or not do that causes me to conclude this about him or her?"

Prepare for a conversation with someone who could improve his or her performance or your relationship. List the conclusions you hold about this person and his or her work. Then list the behaviors that cause you to draw these conclusions. If you actually hold the conversation, notice how helpful it is to be able to give behavioral examples. We'll dive deeper into the topic of coaching in chapter 8. For now, you should be able to recognize a behavior in order to assess the quality of your Cultural Vitality questionnaires or surveys. If you really want to go for the throat, take a look at each question on the corporate health survey you've traditionally used and hold it up to the test of behavior or judgment.

SECTION 2 QUIZ

In section 2 we've asked you to take stock. What is your vision, and how well are you measuring up to it? Let's see how much of the material has stuck.

1. What's the best way for a leader to create a corporate vision?

A. Meet with outside experts, and ask them to share the best of what they've experienced.

B. Pull key people together, and ask what they'd like to see happen in their own workgroup.

C. Take nine Seldane tablets, eat two peyote buttons, lick the back of a Colorado River toad, and let the games begin.

2. What is meant by an organization's *culture?*

A. The unique values, assumptions, and skills of a workforce

B. The deeply held and widely shared mental maps of the workforce

C. A measure of how many employees, when asked to pass the gravy tureen at the annual company banquet, first plop a handful of mashed potatoes on their plate.

3. How does one properly use the term *survey?*

A. It refers to an instrument that, when properly constructed, measures the behaviors (not your conclusions) of those being assessed.

B. It's a specialized tool used for discovering the forces behind existing employee actions, both positive and negative.

C. It's the title you should use when addressing Tony Vey—after he's been knighted.

4. In what way can leaders be "border guards"?

A. By carefully filtering out values and assumptions that don't fit the organization's vision

B. By insisting that outsiders don't treat their team members in a manner inconsistent with the team's espoused values

C. By tackling anyone who walks into their work area without a visa

5. What is meant by the term *significance?*

A. A statistical term referring to the probability of a false rejection of the null hypothesis in a statistical test

B. An expression describing how many times out of 100 the results you've achieved would occur at random

C. Who knows? By the second day of their statistics classes, most students are in a coma.

Influencing the One

The owner of a small restaurant in an inner-city barrio was approached by a group of local thugs and "encouraged" to pay for protection. He flatly refused their attempts at extortion. Twice again they approached him, and twice again he refused. Finally, after a fourth visit, the restaurateur agreed to pay the monthly fee—but only after the hoodlums suggested that if he didn't pay, they would break his arms and legs. When asked by a friend who had been paying the fee for quite some time why it took him so long to capitulate, he answered, "Nobody ever explained the benefits package."

It's time to shift gears. We'll assume that the reader has begun both the visioning and assessment processes, has a fairly good idea of his or her organization's peculiar gaps, and is eager to move from thinking and measuring to reaching out and trying to reduce the gaps. It is to this task we'll now turn our attention. Our goal will be to present the best of current theory and practice as it relates to influencing behavior—remembering, of course, that people choose to do what they do based on the net value or overall results associated with an action.

Unlike the thugs in our anecdote who achieved their goals through threats of arm-and-leg breaking, we'll look at other less-intrusive means of influence. We'll start in chapter 6 by examining a model of how values and assumptions are formed and influenced. From there we'll look at specific methods for impacting an individual's motivation and ability. Chapter 7 examines what leaders can do to enhance intrinsic motive, while chapter 8 explores steps leaders can take to surface and resolve ability problems. Our goal in this section will be to provide both a way of thinking about influence in general and a handful of specific tools for encouraging individuals to change.

C H A P T E R   6

Encouraging People to Change

The human mind treats a new idea the way the body treats a strange protein; it rejects it.

P. B. MEDAWAR

Maggie's Turn at the Helm

Maggie McFerson sat staring at her clock radio. It registered 2:00 a.m. A graveyard-shift supervisor had just called to let her know production was down to 200 units. Average shifts ran 900 parts. *What!* she wondered, *Is it possible we're being hit by a slowdown?* She felt her entire world crumbling around her.

Two months earlier, when Maggie had received the news she would finally be running her own plant, she hadn't imagined that, in addition to a sumptuous office and a luxury car, the job would carry with it 2:00 a.m. wake-up calls. When she'd been promoted from area manager in Cleveland to plant manager in Houston, all she could think of was the host of improvements she would be able to bring about. For years she had been taking notes on what could be done to reduce waste, increase yield, move up productivity, build teamwork, escalate quality, and so on. This was to be her chance at the helm. Lately, though, it seemed more like her time on the rack.

When Maggie first walked around the plant in early June, it was clear that most employees were not working an eight-hour shift. They were

141

taking money for eight hours, but they put in only about six. At any time of the day or night you could find people standing around in small groups talking about sports, taking bets, and skylarking in general. People didn't actually walk from place to place. They ambled.

To get work practices back on track, Maggie dusted off an operations-research book from her MBA coursework and figured out just how many people it should take to meet their daily production schedule. After adding a 10 percent buffer, Maggie announced that the plant could be running 1,400 parts per day with 53 fewer people. Nobody actually applauded, but, hey, who could argue with carefully calculated numbers?

To achieve her ambitious goals, Maggie communicated production targets to each area and shift and instituted tighter accountability to be sure everyone knew what was expected. She set up incentives for those who cut waste or found ways to reduce costs. It had been a busy 60 days for Maggie. All that was left was to sit back and enjoy the improvements.

Maggie had not gone into the job blindly. She had envisioned the improvements clearly. In fact, she saw her visioning skills as among her best leadership qualities. In her view, people would return from lunch on schedule. Shifts would start and end on time. Repair crews would move swiftly to downed equipment and have it up and running—pronto. Card games in the middle of shifts would cease completely, and people would stay at their machines during working hours. Better still, people would eagerly move to other tasks if their help was needed. It was a beautiful picture.

Then came the phone call. Not only had past practices not changed, they were getting worse. Production was dropping to 500–600 parts per shift. Downtime on equipment was lengthening. And now, a full-fledged slowdown. The workforce was sending her a clear message: "We're not dancing to the new tune."

Maggie thought about how she had frequently criticized so many of her past plant managers. The explosive, controlling, authoritarian actions she had once abhorred, she now considered giving a tumble. Well, she wouldn't take names and kick rear ends—yet.

Knowing "What" Doesn't Guarantee "How"

This world is run by people who know how to do things. They know how things work. They are equipped. Up there, there's a layer of people who run everything. But we—we're just peasants. We don't understand what's going on, and we can't do anything.

Doris Lessing

Maggie's problem is clear. Although she has a distinct picture of what she would like, she is not the least bit certain how to get there. When she started the new job, she thought she was clear about what needed to be done, but now, after eating a double helping of humble pie, she's fairly certain that announcing, even carefully planning, changes doesn't guarantee them.

Maggie is in good company. Most of us have a lot clearer idea about what we want from others than we have about how to get it. We're not particularly good "intuitive change agents." Just walk into any Kmart and take a look at amateur change agents at work. One person tries to get a clerk to take back a defective toy—he whines in a tone that would raise the hair on the back of your neck. A child attempts to get her mother to buy her some kind of gum that squirts out of a tube—she sticks her lower lip out so far you could put a bowling ball on it. A man clutching the arm of his sweetheart tries to get her to end her shopping trip faster. Someone at the entrance solicits donations for an orphanage, swinging a nerve-jangling bell in your face.

Everywhere you turn, people are trying to influence someone else. In fact, we work most of our waking hours trying to influence the behavior of others in one way or another. Leaders may not describe it in those terms, but every memo, speech, policy, decision, meeting, or conversation they hold is intended to impact the behavior of one or more people. Now, let's be clear. We're not talking about manipulation—an unhealthy subset of influence. We're talking about honest, well-intended, and aboveboard attempts to encourage others to modify their mental maps and, therefore, their behavior.

We have no bone to pick with the fact that people try to influence each other. Humans would be irresponsible not to attempt to make the world a better place. We're just not very fond of how most of us go about it. Maggie was so inexperienced at trying to bring about change that she actually created new problems. One of life's great ironies is that although people spend a tremendous amount of time trying to get what they want from others, they aren't very good at it. Maggie, Kmart customers, and just about everybody who ever licked an ice cream cone (meaning the Western world as we know it) are, at best, marginally effective wielders of influence.

This paucity of practical influence skills is curious when you consider that humans have had thousands of years to develop their interpersonal repertoire. However, it's less curious when you consider that although people are bent on getting what they want from each other, they've also learned to be equally adept at resisting most forms of influence.

So, How Come We Aren't Getting Better?

Given that people treat each other's influence strategies as invading viruses, you'd think that getting better at "having our way" would be one of our most important school subjects. In ancient Greece, it was sometimes the *only* subject. Of course, there were no lawyers at the time, people had to defend themselves in front of the senate, and a loss could mean having to spend some quality time being tortured. Ancient Greek influence classes had a waiting list.

Today, the average citizen doesn't take so much as one course in interpersonal influence. Although the consequences of failure are less salient than being tortured, the results of our interpersonal naiveté are similarly costly. The U.S. divorce rate is over 50 percent; child, spousal, and most forms of interpersonal abuse are on the rise; and close to two-thirds of the inmates in prison for a capital offense are first-time offenders—not career criminals, but people who simply didn't know how to get their way short of killing someone.[1] Astounding. The final statistic alone is enough to give you the heebie-jeebies.

> Many prisoners who have been convicted of murder are in prison because their influence repertoire is limited.

Since our influence skills border on functional illiteracy, one would hope that we'd at least walk away from our social science courses with a grasp of applied social skills. Fat chance. Most of us remember almost nothing from psychology, save a dim memory of how catatonics actually sleep with their head four inches above a pillow. Leadership courses haven't done much better at teaching practical skills. They mostly rely on cute homilies or vile trickery. The cute ones fail to develop helpful skills and models. The vile ones include such terms as *sharks*, *Attila the Hun*, and *intimidation*—in their titles, no less.

In short, there's scarcely a book, leadership workshop, social science course, or Kmart customer out there that wouldn't benefit immensely from a close look at what skilled people do to influence others—which is exactly what we'll discuss next. We'll start by returning to our target of influence—mental maps. Understanding how mental maps are formed goes a long way in helping us develop influence techniques.

HOW MENTAL MAPS ARE CREATED

In my writing I am acting as a map maker, an explorer of psychic areas . . . a cosmonaut of inner space.

WILLIAM BURROUGHS

We're Born with a Somewhat Clean Slate

Humans, unlike most organisms, are not born with very many values and assumptions. Unlike guppies that are born "aquarium wise" or caribou that are on their feet and running for cover within hours, humans are born with little of the knowledge they'll eventually need to survive. Instead, the process of developing a distinct personality (a complex array of values and assumptions) accelerates outside the womb. Although it's true that humans are prewired in some ways (i.e., we do have *some* "instincts"), a great deal of the human personality is learned concept by concept, one day at a time.

The organizational implications of the fact that humans are born with a nearly blank slate should be clear. Leaders have a greater potential to impact values and assumptions than many imagine. Employees don't mysteriously walk through the gate with preprogrammed work ethics. Unhealthy attitudes can't be blamed on genetics. By the same token, individuals who care deeply about providing customers with quality service don't develop this value during their first six weeks of life. Values and assumptions—good or bad, healthy or sick, productive or counterproductive—are learned over an entire lifetime. Even if work habits and other organizational assumptions and values have been largely developed before people fill out a job application, what is learned can be unlearned or expanded—particularly if you understand how this world (our campus) teaches values and assumptions.

Filling in the Slate

The world is more than a stage (no offense, Shakespeare); it's a classroom. Every time we wake up in the morning, we crawl out of bed and step into the front row of the school of hard knocks—the one that teaches values and assumptions. Fortunately, humans are wonderful students— particularly children.

Consider a child whose mother punishes her for trying to stick her finger into an electrical outlet. Her fingers are too large to fit in the tiny holes, so she receives no shock, but her mother yells at her anyway.

Moments later, the little imp pokes a different finger at the same outlet. Rebellion, you say. No, simple curiosity. She's trying to find out for what specific crime she was punished. Was it wrong to put a particular finger into that thing, or does the rule apply to all fingers? After getting punished again, she tries a pencil. Same result. Then a different outlet. More yelling. Finally, after a rather lengthy and elegant experiment, she concludes, "Sticking anything into any of those things gets you into trouble around here." She adds a page to her ever-growing mental map.

Hours later, this same curious two-year-old scientist opens the front door and toddles onto a newly waxed entryway. Her older sister, who has just finished the wax job, yells at her and tells her to use the back door. She concludes that the front door is now off limits (knowing nothing of the evils of wet wax). For several days she enters only through the back door (operating from a misguided map), until one day when she runs another experiment at the front door and nobody yells at her. She concludes that yelling is random.

A few weeks later, she steps onto another newly waxed floor. Only this time it's her mother who has just completed the job. Her mother says, "Honey, I just waxed the floor. When you walk on wet wax, it leaves footprints." Our little explorer looks at the footprints and thinks to herself, "Aren't those neat?" She steps onto the floor and continues her artwork. Her mother continues, "Don't walk on the wet wax. Footprints are ugly." Later that week, the child tells her friend who tries to walk on a newly mopped floor, "Footprints are ugly. Bad footprints." As her mental maps continue to grow, so do her values.

Attention Please!

As our young friend continues to expand her mental maps, a variety of sources of influence continue to add information to her ever-increasing database of values. Of course, not everything around her has an equal impact. Of the millions of data points surrounding our intuitive scientist, only a select few make it through her attentional screen. Contrary to popular myth, she is not taking mental photographs and storing images of everything she sees. Instead, she is allowing only small portions of the never-ending barrage of stimuli around her to filter through her mental screen.

Fractured Fairy Tales. As much as we would like to believe that each of us is an ambulant repository of the audio and video images of our entire lives (just waiting to be played back), it turns out that it takes a lot more work to make it through our thick skulls than just pointing our eyes at something. Yes, much of what we take into memory is stored away and is later accessible from our mental vaults. We've all heard stories of a 90-year-old who laid his tongue across a car battery and his entire fourth birthday party flashed before his eyes, but this shouldn't be taken as evidence that *everything* we've ever seen or experienced is similarly hidden behind the veil of recall. It turns out that if we don't attend to something, if we don't *pay rather close attention*, it is unlikely to make it into memory in the first place. Try studying for a test if you believe otherwise. Better yet, try getting through to a recalcitrant teenager.

The notion that data more or less sneaks into our brains and works on us in mysterious ways has been repeated so often that most of us believe it when we hear stories about how people are readily manipulated through subliminal techniques. Just about everyone over the age of nine has heard the tale of how a group of researchers exposed movie audiences to hidden messages that urged them to eat popcorn. Since the messages were flashed on the screen at a speed that made it impossible to read, the unconscious mind had to be put to use. After only a few minutes, the crowd practically ran to the snack bar, begging for popcorn.

If you thought about the wild claims of subliminal learning, you'd begin to wonder why we don't use similar techniques to achieve more important goals than encouraging moviegoers to consume fat-covered grain. Actually, people have tried to reduce tension, teach languages, lose weight, and achieve a variety of other objectives through subliminal techniques. They just haven't worked. Truth be known, crowds of people never actually ran to the snack bar. Nor do people learn languages or lose weight while they snooze. Oh, you can buy tapes to play while you sleep. You can even find people who swear by them. What you can't find is a single piece of reputable research that verifies the same. U.S. army researchers, who thought it would be pretty handy if they could teach soldiers in their sleep, couldn't find any evidence, and they looked for three years. (Insert your own military cheap shot here.)

Information Flows through Three Important Conduits

Information networks straddle the world. Nothing remains concealed. But the sheer volume of information dissolves the information. We are unable to take it all in.

GÜNTHER GRASS

As we continue our quest to influence someone's mental map, let's assume we've left subliminal techniques to others and have gone to great pains to gain our subject's undivided attention. We've fired a cannon, grabbed the subject's head, stared into his eyes, and are about to release a barrage of data. Now, which methods of sharing information are effective, and which ones aren't?

Researchers have learned that data flows from external sources into our internal maps through three distinctly different information conduits: (1) personal experience, (2) vicarious experience (observation), and (3) verbal persuasion. None of these conduits is new to us. In fact, not only have we provided examples of each, we'll demonstrate that they are not equally influential.

Conduit 1 — Personal Experience

Of these three data conduits, personal experience is the most influential. As individuals touch, taste, smell, hear, see, and otherwise directly gather data, information flows directly (and with few sources of distortion). It's hard to deny what happens to you personally. For instance, you stick your finger in an outlet, and you receive a rather noxious shock. It'll take some pretty slick talking to convince you to do that again. You touch a boa constrictor and learn that it doesn't always bite you. You might just try that again.

Conduit 2 — Vicarious Experience

Vicarious experience can also be an influential means of transferring information. It was the principal means of influence used in the snake-phobic labs. Subjects watched someone else handle the boa and thought to themselves, "I could do that." Vicarious experience is an efficient and powerful way of generating new data for others to put on their mental maps. For example, children have been cured of their fear of interacting in social settings by watching films of other shy kids who slowly move into play groups and eventually have a lot of fun. As subjects observed people "like them" taking actions they themselves had feared—and getting good results, they began to modify their outcome assumptions and try new behaviors.[2] Of course, observations are less trustworthy than personal experience. When you see someone else having an experience, you have nagging doubts. Three important assumptions can lessen or heighten the power of vicarious experience.

Relative Ability. First, you may ask yourself, "Could I do that?" This may sound silly with simple actions such as touching a snake. Nevertheless, with many activities, it's not easy to enact the behaviors—particularly when the size of the behavioral bundles grows. For example, a co-worker makes a significant improvement in a core business process that results in double-digit quality gains. You may value the contribution and even envy the recognition. Overall, you'd love to behave the same way. But you don't believe you're as skilled at statistics and process mapping. Just because *someone* does it doesn't mean *you'll* be able to do the same. Consequently, observing others succeed is less influential than personal success.

Relative Outcomes. In addition, you may question the outcome. Perhaps you can do everything your quality-obsessed colleague did, but would you get the same result? Maybe your friend is a special case. Perhaps he has a better relationship with other departments. Maybe the boss gave more support because he favors him—pulled some strings and whatnot. Another person's outcomes may not predict your own.

Relative Value. Finally, you may question whether you value the outcome to the same degree as the other person. For instance, if you drive by a bungee-jumping platform and see people similar in age and physique leaping from a platform without getting hurt, you still may decide not to jump. When you observe others, you're still left with the question, "Will I like what they like?" Maybe getting a "rush" experience is not a valued outcome for you. You may change your mental map about the *risks* of bungee jumping through vicarious experience *and* still place a low value on the outcome (and, therefore, not try it).

Although vicarious experience doesn't exactly have feet of clay, it is subject to erosion. As you watch others and learn, you're still left questioning relative ability, outcome, and value. Could I do that? Would I get the same result? And if I did, would I like it?

Conduit 3 — Verbal Persuasion

Verbal persuasion, the final means of map building, does have feet of clay—at least when compared to personal or vicarious experience. Of the three forms of influence, it's the only conduit that comes with a gatekeeper. By passing the data through another person, the conduit has more potential sources of contamination. When someone tries to convince you through verbal means, written or spoken, a whole new set of doubts comes into play. Not only do you wonder if the experience is relevant, you question the ability and motivation of the person sending the message. Does she really know? After all, I didn't see her have the experience. Maybe she misinterpreted what happened. In addition, she may have some motive for fooling me. Maybe she's misrepresenting the world to achieve her own self-serving goals.

Not All Information Is Sticky

As influential as conduits are in transferring information to mental maps, the method of transmittal is not the only factor that impacts the power of data. The information itself, irrespective of the conduit, has certain properties that affect credibility. As values and assumptions are taken into a person's mental map, they stick with varying degrees of tenacity. Some come sheathed in Velcro®. They quickly become attached to an entire array of values and assumptions. Others are coated in Teflon®. They're distinct or new enough that they don't readily stick to anything. Once again, an example might help.[3]

Every afternoon for a couple of weeks, your boss asks you if he can pick up something for you at the cafeteria. You tell him, "No thanks. I brought my lunch." It's a fairly meaningless question, but it's consistent. You assume that it'll happen tomorrow. One day you decline, and your boss comes back with, "All right, that's it. I ask you every day, and you never need anything. That's the last time I'm asking you." He smiles and exits. The next day you figure he's not going to ask you, and he doesn't. You never give it another moment's thought.

Contrast this with a boss who is routinely abusive. He returns from a leadership seminar "born again" and announces that he's going to quit his punishing ways. This time you don't believe he'll change. First, abuse covers a lot of territory. It's a rather large behavioral bundle. In addition, you're suspicious that your boss actually gets rewarded for being abusive. He might even enjoy it. Throughout your entire life you've assumed that bosses are abusive. Your parents taught you at their knee. Your assumption that bosses are abusive is linked to dozens of other assumptions and values that cut across all six cells. When assumptions link to an important nexus in your mental map, they aren't going to change easily. In fact, should a centrally linked assumption come under attack, individuals typically find ways to restructure new data to fit their point of view rather than the other way around. Consider the following example.[4]

I'll Be Darned!

Myrna, an eager psychotherapist fresh out of school, arrives at her first assignment (a state mental institution) with an air of confidence, even enthusiasm. Her colleagues, battered by years of harsh reality, find her enthusiasm nauseous. In an effort to stifle her sickening energy, they assign her to an incurable case—a man who thinks he's dead.

For months Myrna employs every therapeutic technique imaginable. The patient remains unchanged. Nothing Myrna says or does convinces him that he's not dead. Nothing. In fact, the harder the therapist pushes, the more convinced the patient becomes. Although the more the staff finds the eager therapist's failure reassuring, the more Myrna finds it humiliating. Finally, as it becomes increasingly clear that she's not going to be successful and is likely to be the butt of a lot of jokes, Myrna tries one final strategy. She asks the patient, "Do dead people bleed?"

The patient responds, *"No, they certainly don't. After all, everyone knows that dead people don't have blood."*

"Are you certain?" she asks.

"Absolutely," he replies.

Armed with this logic, the eager psychotherapist reaches into her smock, pulls out a scalpel, and makes a small cut on the patient's hand. Of course, he bleeds. The patient, seeing the blood flowing from his hand, bugs his eyes with a look of astonishment and proclaims, *"Well, I'll be darned! Dead people do bleed!"*

When it comes to highly interconnected assumptions, it's easier for humans to restructure data to fit their personal views than it is to destroy a cornerstone of their being. Of course, it only follows that since values are often nothing more than bundles of highly interconnected assumptions, they're just that much more resistant to disconfirming data. The following statement captures the stable nature of values in a humorous way.

> *"I'm sure glad I don't like broccoli, because if I did, I'd eat it, and I hate broccoli."*

Most individuals can't even conceive of holding different values. As a cognitive element becomes interwoven with other assumptions and closely held values, they become quite difficult to displace. Interwoven assumptions, inextricably glued together by logical linkages, can't be altered in isolation. They can change only by altering several components in concert.

> Centrally linked elements on a mental map can be changed only by displacing an entire mental neighborhood. Think of it as a paradigm shift.

INFLUENCING MENTAL MAPS

I am a firm believer in the people. If given the truth, they can be depended upon. . . . The great point is to bring them the real facts.

ABRAHAM LINCOLN

We've talked about preparing to take action long enough. It's time to *take* action. Well, not quite yet. It's time to develop an action *plan*. Knowing why people are doing what they're doing (understanding the sources and resilience of their values and assumptions) helps us think about what*is*. It still doesn't tell us what actions to take in order to create what*can be*. It's time we looked at several potential strategies that are effective at empowering others to change their course. It's time to turn our energies from understanding existing maps to helping create new ones. At the conclusion of this chapter, we'll see what we can do to help Maggie, the new plant manager. We'll apply what we learn here to her attempt to get managers to hold people accountable without triggering a slowdown.

As we sit perched on the threshold of doing something, we have to at least glance at the question of ethics. After all, who died and left us in charge of shaping maps? Actually, if you're a leader, it's your job. If you're a human, it's your responsibility. Social creatures owe each other the benefit of their best thinking. In either case, as long as you're considering the impact on all stakeholders and are aboveboard with your attempts to alter net value, you're on safe ground.

We'll begin looking into varying influence strategies by examining what people typically do. This we'll follow with a half-dozen chapters that explore effective influence strategies. For now, let's examine the most typical map-changing strategy. It makes for an interesting story.

"The Law of the Hog"

There is no human problem which could not be solved if people would simply do as I advise.

GORE VIDAL

While conducting research at a plywood plant in the Northwest, David Maxfield, a colleague of one of the authors, experienced the cost of using ineffective influence strategies in a way that has become legendary within leadership folklore.

As David pulled up to the plant, he couldn't help but notice an ambulance parked out front. The plant manager explained that the person being loaded into the vehicle was an hourly employee who had been punched out by his boss, a frontline supervisor.

Later that day, when David asked hourly employees what happened when they didn't have a particularly good relationship with their boss, they answered, "The hog!"

Not far from where David was conducting the interviews was a small shack that housed a terribly powerful and frightening machine that ground up scrap wood. That ominous machine was "the hog" to which the employees referred. Its sole purpose was to take wood and turn it into pulp. The sound and fury of the blades struck fear into the hearts of the bravest of employees.

Noticing the look of horror on David's face, the hourly employee quickly pointed out that when they didn't get along with their boss, they didn't throw their boss into "the hog." Instead, they waited for him to leave and then threw perfectly good veneer into "the hog." In so doing, they ruined the productivity and yield figures by which the supervisors were measured. Of course, the bosses knew this was going on, so they took to climbing the rafters to catch people in the act. Employees, aware of their bosses' subversive activities, took to posting spies to watch the rafters. (Fun place to work.)

From this incident emerged the expression, "The Law of the Hog." To the extent that ineffective or insulting influence strategies are used as a means of getting things done, you'll incur unpredictable, and often costly, non-value-added consequences.

When leaders threaten, punish, or bribe, they're attempting to change behavior by hefting weights onto the scale. For example, when legislators punish drug smugglers with life in prison without parole, they're trying to add a massive negative outcome to criminals' mental maps. Since legislators typically believe that criminals' current behavior is driven by intrinsically evil motives, they don't waste time trying to change current values. After all, it would be futile to try to get criminals to stop valuing huge profits or start valuing the welfare of others. Instead, lawmakers simply tack on big negatives.

Of course, for this strategy to work, not only do criminals need to know that life in prison is a bad thing, they have to believe that they might actually get caught *and* have it applied to them. The risk is that if they *do* attach a negative value to the outcome of "heading to the Big House" *and* believe that the *probability* of that ever occurring is minuscule, then the "net" is still in favor of a crime.

Remember Maggie, the plant manager dealing with the slowdown? She's running the same risk of feeding "the hog." If she guesses that people are doing what they're doing because of selfish motives, her behavior will be driven by these assumptions. Like the legislators, she may throw her hands in the air and give up hope of restructuring people's current values—after all, they're "selfish and lazy" people. She may move quickly to tacking on huge penalties. This, of course, could lead to a wide range of responses.

The one consistent and useful finding emanating from behaviorism is that negative reinforcement leads to unpredictable results. (Meaning, if you punish people, it's hard to tell how they might react.) They might do what you ask, or they might feed "the hog." Besides, who wants to be the kind of person who reaches for the whip every time someone could benefit from map sharing? Most of us have spent years vowing not to become that person who can hardly wait to put on spiked boots and hike off into the land of aggressive influence.

TRY THIS INSTEAD

I know no safe depository of the ultimate powers of the society but the people themselves; and if we think them not enlightened enough to exercise their control with a wholesome discretion, the remedy is not to take it from them, but to inform their discretion.

THOMAS JEFFERSON

Avoid a One-Cell Model

When you consider that the fundamental attribution error received its name from the fact that people routinely assume all problems are due to motivation, it should be of little surprise that solving the problems stemming from this error would be an important contribution to any leader. Our research has repeatedly proven this to be true. You'll have a golden moment when you stop and say to yourself, "Now wait a minute. I know this person looks guilty of just not doing what I asked, but maybe I should stop and ask what really happened and the underlying cause." Which takes us to our first practical point—avoid a one-cell model. Is the person not doing what is required because he or she is unmotivated or because he or she is unable? If so, what's the source of motivation and what's supporting or thwarting the person's ability? Knowing the difference is important.

Now, having said that problems stem from both motive and ability, we'll take on the more difficult of the two in the next few pages—motive. We'll leave discussions of ability to later chapters. For now we'll assume that the person you're working with simply doesn't want to do what's required. What can you do?

Work on Net Value

People make a common mistake when trying to figure out how to change another person's behavior. They think the other person must change his or her values. Wrong. All you have to do is change the outcome assumptions people tie to a particular behavior. By doing so, you change the *net value*. This is an important distinction deserving a more complete explanation.

Spinach, Yuck!

Let's work with a common example: a child dislikes the taste of spinach. Dad says, "Spinach tastes good. Eat it." The child takes a bite and gags. Maybe *Dad* likes it, but *she* doesn't. What can Dad do to get her to change her *values*, what she feels good about, or what she likes? How can he get her to actually enjoy spinach? Dad cuts a deal. Rather than lecture her on why she should like it, or even worse, try to convince her that she really does like it, Dad offers an incentive. He tells her that if she eats five bites, he'll read her a bedtime story—one of her favorite activities. Although she may not immediately change her opinion or value for the taste of spinach, she willingly chokes down the greens because the new net value is worth it to her.

With time, Dad hopes that she'll develop a taste for spinach. He works on the long-term value of spinach by adding to the short-term value of eating it. He attacks the only thing he can work on: net value. He does it by either adding new outcomes with positive values or pointing out existing ones that she might not be aware of. In this case, he sweetens the pot by linking her "unvalued" behavior of choking down a nasty-tasting vegetable to a bedtime story. By adding the incentive, he reframes the activity. Now, instead of merely forcing down something that she doesn't like, she's earning a reward. She's pleasing Dad and getting a bedtime story to boot.

Dad doesn't know how to get her to like spinach. (Does anyone know how to directly affect such intrinsic values?) But he understands the effect of piling on incentives. He figures that if he can just get her to do what he wants by using external rewards, she'll learn to develop a taste for the flavor of spinach on her own. This same strategy applies to just about everything Dad tries to get her to value. "If you read every day for an hour, I'll take you to the movies on the weekend."

Most of us spend a great deal of our lives doing things that we may not enjoy per se, but we hang in there for the long-term result. We go to work, diet, exercise, clean toilets, take vitamins, and a whole host of other activities, not because we enjoy completing the immediate task itself, but because we like the net value of the associated outcomes.

Within organizations people learn to tolerate, even enjoy, their jobs by linking them to meaning and purpose beyond the immediate task. The bricklayer who lays every brick as an important part of creating a temple has a different experience than the bricklayer who sees every brick as five pounds of terra cotta needing to be hefted and cemented.

Human beings live life in the "net"—net value, that is. It's the "net" that supports our every action. It's the "net" we have to influence if we expect to change behavior.

Link to Valued Outcomes

Parenting: Thirty years of teaching moles to fly.

As we try to figure out how to change someone's existing net value, we often assume that the only way to do so is to pile on consequences. We pay our kids to eat spinach or threaten to take the car keys if they continue to talk back. Perhaps a more careful approach, given the potential for feeding "the hog," would be to explore the other person's mental map and try to find a way to link to his or her existing values. This is not to suggest that a person never adds to another person's mental map by manipulating outcomes. Our goal is simply to start with what we currently have rather than leap in with extrinsic rewards or our power base. We assume for a moment that the other person is capable of actually caring about what we care about. Their net value will change as we help them make new linkages. Consider the following example of linking to existing values.

Kelp Huggers Meet the Heartless Profiteers

One of the more interesting cases of trying to balance community needs with corporate desires for profits occurred when a large oil company proposed offshore drilling near a sleepy coastal tourist town. When the petroleum executives held their first meeting at the town hall, the results were predictable. Seated on one side of the room were what reporters called "kelp huggers." These were the oceanographers, biologists, ecologists, and others who saw themselves as keepers of the environment. Seated across from them were the oil-company representatives, shop owners, entrepreneurs, gas-station attendants, and anyone else who figured to make a buck off the huge influx of revenue the company promised the community. As the two groups slipped into a heated argument, fur flew.

Finally, in an almost pathetic wail, one of the oceanographers shouted, "You don't get it. One tiny spill and you might just kill our bay's entire starfish population." With this pronouncement, the environmentalists all gasped in horror. Their profit-oriented opponents broke into poorly concealed chuckles—shoulders heaving—as they tried to conceal their indifference. You could almost hear their silent musings—"Let's see, we make more money than Aristotle Onassis, and it might cost us some starfish. Gee, should we take the risk?"

At this moment, when it looked as if the two groups would never find common ground, one of the few people in the audience without an ax to grind asked an important question. "I don't know much about starfish. I'm not even sure if their dying is such a big deal, but I can tell that it matters a lot to you. Why's that?" (In other words, please share a larger portion of your mental map.)

At first, the oceanographer seemed taken aback. The fact that starfish would be harmed—that fact alone was enough to throw him into deep depression. But rather than accuse the questioner of being an insensitive klutz, he decided to explain the big picture.

"Actually, starfish are the canaries of the bay. When the ecosystem goes awry, they go first. After they're gone, there's a slow, but highly likely, domino effect. One by one, other species will perish, until one day this lovely bay that we, our families, and thousands of tourists enjoy each year will be turned into a filthy, stench-filled quagmire. The smell of rotting sea life will carry for miles."

With this explanation, the tide turned. After a flurry of questions and answers, several business owners took up the cry, "Save the starfish." The next week, T-shirts with the slogan began to appear on the boardwalk. The platform was not erected.

Now, how is it that people who had originally appeared uncaring and only profit driven would eventually take up the cry to save the starfish? Because they saw how the demise of these harmless sea animals linked to outcomes they cared about. Who knows? With time they may have even taken a liking to the creatures themselves, but irrespective of their feelings toward marine echinoderms, they linked their life cycles to their own. No starfish—no tourists—no income.

The challenge of any parent, king, supervisor, or fast-food clerk facing a person who doesn't want to do what should be done is to find a way to link the target behavior to *existing* desired outcomes. Actually, that's what parenting is mostly about, trying to encourage here-and-now children to see beyond the immediate gratification of an act to the long-term consequences it might yield. We have to continually remind our offspring of basketball coach Denny Crum's immortal words: "Most of our future lies ahead." Of course, it isn't easy to always be making links to other outcomes. Many people tire of asking questions or suggesting potential linkages and simply resort to name-calling and threats. The choice is yours. Make links, or feed "the hog."

Leverage Your Actions

Of all the diagnoses a leader completes in a day, knowing how to examine to what extent a particular behavior is resistant to change ranks at the top of the list of usefulness. Informed leaders, when exploring resistance, ask, "To what extent is the current behavior motivated and enabled?" and "To what extent is the replacement behavior the same?" Consider the following Leverage Grid.

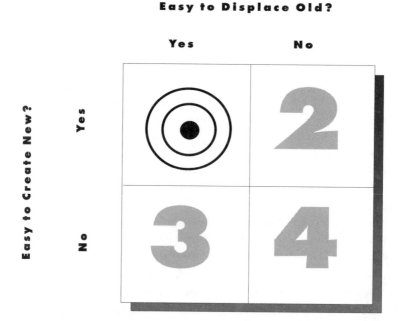

Easy to Displace Old?

In this particular matrix, we're simply applying the Six-Cell Balancing Tool to the old and the new behaviors. On the one axis we ask, "To what extent is the old or existing behavior empowered? Are the assumptions we're dealing with deeply held and widely shared? Are their ideas linked into a worldview that has been constantly reinforced through actual experience? Or are we taking on a notion that is uncoupled from any big picture and is based on verbal persuasion?" On the other axis we ask, "To what extent will the new or replacement behavior be easy to empower? Can the assumptions be taught through vicarious or even actual experience, or will we be forced to rely on verbal persuasion? Are the behaviors themselves hard to learn and enact?"

If you're looking for targets of change, start with those where the new behavior is readily empowered and the old one isn't particularly strong. It's astounding to watch leaders who start a change project by doing just the opposite (i.e., they go for the jugular by attacking old mental maps that are based on years of personal experience and by asking for replacement behaviors that are quite difficult to either motivate or enable). Let's see how this grid applies to a typical problem.

McDuffy's Challenge

Let's say you're our old friend Patrick McDuffy. You've just had that frightening conversation with Henry, the analyst who you stopped in the hallway. You floated a ridiculous idea by him (drop your biggest client), and he agreed out of fear. At first you pointed out the problem, encouraging him to express what's on his mind. After all, how else can you make the best decisions? He smiled knowingly and said, "Whatever you say boss"—hardly the reaction you were hoping for.

As it becomes apparent that Henry isn't going to change his behavior at the drop of a hat, you're left wondering, "Just what is the source of resistance, and how deep and wide does it run? First, how motivated is the person? Does he find the undesired behavior itself rewarding or the replacement behavior punishing?" (Cell 1) "Probably not, it's not as if deferring to the boss is a pleasant task in and of itself. How about social factors? There's probably a lot to be considered here. Does he fear reprisal from peers? Is it the boss himself he's worried about?" (Cell 3) "And what about the formal reward system? Are people really rewarded for being open with their ideas, or is honesty praised in public but punished when it comes to performance reviews?"

As you look at all of these potential sources of influence, you must also ask, "How were these assumptions formed? Were they based on actual experience confirmed over time, or are they fairly new ideas that have been shared mostly through verbal persuasion? Is Henry a phobic who fears something that will never happen, or has he been repeatedly beaten up for sharing his opinions until he's now the frightened person I find twitching before me?"

Next, ask, "To what extent is the current behavior enabled? Is the person quite good at relating his opinions in ways that don't arouse defensiveness in others? Has he honed his 'masking skills' to an art?" (Cell 2) "Do others feed him with information about what is politically correct?" (Cell 4) "Are there systems and policies in place that subtly encourage compliance? Do people, because of their work locations, interact so infrequently that they're unlikely to risk difficult conversations?" (Cell 6)

Actually, when it comes to ability, it may be more effective to explore to what extent the replacement behavior is enabled. "Does the person know how to express a differing opinion without looking disloyal or excessively aggressive?" (Cell 2) "Does our organization provide training classes or a formal mentoring process that would help individuals learn the new skill?" (Cell 6)

Leaders frequently underestimate how difficult it can be to enact replacement behaviors. For instance, when the authors are invited into a consulting project, leaders almost always assume that whatever they're asking others to do is fairly easy to enact. After all, if you reduce behaviors to small enough chunks, anyone can do them. We're typically brought in to help with a change project because leaders are puzzled by employees who aren't doing what is required. They've been put in teams, but they aren't "collaborating." They've been asked to make consensus decisions, but they keep getting into arguments. They've been requested to create a learning environment, but nobody seems to come up with very many new and creative ideas. What's wrong with these people anyway?

Once again, the fundamental attribution error rears its ugly head. After a rather quick diagnosis, we routinely learn that the people aren't doing what they're asked because they don't really know how to do it. Since it's politically unsafe to utter the deadly words "I don't really know how to do that," leaders continue in their belief that their employees are unmotivated and need a good kick in the pants. Maybe a motivational speaker would help.

Our conclusion?

> Never assume that any human interaction skill is easily understood or readily replicated—no matter how "simple" in appearance or widely demonstrated by others.

Choose Your Targets with Care

In any attempt to influence behavior, skilled leaders choose their targets carefully. They understand that it makes a lot more sense to attack behaviors that are only loosely empowered than ones that are core to one's belief structure. Rather than go for large bundles that might possibly lead to huge results (and are also likely to be resisted tooth and nail), they go for small wins. For example, in one company where leaders were trying to eliminate racism, they gave up demanding that people "think only good things about each other." Instead, they prohibited the telling of racist jokes. Here was a simple behavior rather than a global value. Not only was the action easier to eliminate, it was easier to measure. In fact, they eradicated it in two weeks.

Similarly, insightful leaders realize that it's safer to encourage actions that can be readily empowered than ones that are difficult to support. Why ask for behaviors that are difficult to replicate or that only can be encouraged through verbal persuasion when other actions are easy to perform and can be encouraged through both vicarious or actual experience? (Which takes us to our next point.)

Replace Verbal Attacks with Actual Experience

Lecture is a form of attack.

Voltaire

Most of us have a hard time recovering from our education. School systems are based on a strategy of creating a credible source known as a teacher and then having this source give lectures. After years of exposure to the education system, most of us have come to believe that if you want people to change their opinion, simply give them the correct facts. Consequently, when faced with the need to bring about a change, most leaders launch into lectures without giving the matter a second thought. Of course, parents draw on this strategy as well. During the early years, the strategy works. Children hang onto every word as if it were God's own truth.

But the adult world doesn't usually respond like small children who are thirsty sponges just waiting to be filled with facts. People cling to their old beliefs like rag dolls. Teenagers learn to question adults. Voltaire was right. Most adults do treat lecture as a form of attack. That's why enlightened leaders have learned to rely less on verbal persuasion and more on vicarious and actual experience. They are "conduit sensitive." Naturally, when information is not the least bit controversial, leaders continue to rely on the shorthand of verbal persuasion. But when employees are asked to do something that might not be all that popular at first glance, savvy leaders think twice before launching into a lecture. Some get quite creative.

The Power of Personal Experience

We learn through experience and experiencing, and no one teaches anyone anything. This is as true for the infant moving from kicking to crawling to walking as it is for the scientist with his equations.

VIOLA SPOLIN

Consider the actions of a close friend of one of the authors. He was trying to convince his son to take more care when riding his bike in the streets. The boy had just learned to master the two-wheeler and was taking far too many risks—at least, that's what the dad thought. After telling his son of the dangers of cars and watching the information roll off his back, he took another tack. He asked his older son to mount the bike and ride it in the street. Then he climbed into the driver's seat of their car, placed his young son on his lap, and asked him to steer the car near the bike. As the boy drove precariously close to his brother, he could see how easily the car might swerve out of control. Up until that point his mental map was filled with assumptions about how cars more or less ran on safety tracks. Now, aware of the true dangers of riding his bike too close to cars, he was committed to keeping a safe distance— the point of his father's original lecture.

Leaders have learned the same principle. For instance, we worked with a group of automobile employees who had been asked to shift to a team environment. For months the leaders had talked of the Japanese competitors and how they were more collaborative and, consequently, more productive. On just about every bulletin board you could find a printout of the two sacred numbers—output per employee and machine utilization. Both sets of figures showed how the Japanese were anywhere from 5 to 40 percent more effective than their American competitors.

When we asked the employees to what extent they thought it was necessary to increase their output per employee, they suggested that there was no pressing need. When asked about the published figures, they explained that the numbers had been contrived. They were "sick to death" of hearing about the Japanese and refused to believe anything about them.

Finally, the leadership team decided to send a large number of the employees to visit a Japanese plant. When the group first arrived in

Osaka, they didn't want to believe anything they saw. As they were taken on tours, they quickly discounted the presentations on efficiencies and effectiveness as hype. At the end of the first day, one of the consultants suggested that they pierce through the veil of hype by sneaking into the plant that night and watching the "real employees" at work. That evening, when they saw the same level of activity and energy they had seen during the programmed tour (only this time without the tour guide), they were convinced that their Japanese counterparts were, indeed, far more collaborative and seemed to be getting a lot more done—somewhere between 5 and 40 percent more. What the leaders' verbal tactics hadn't been able to do in months, actual experience was able to achieve in one day.

Create Vicarious Experiences through Stories

All human beings have an innate need to hear and tell stories and to have a story to live by . . .

SEYMOUR COX

Most leaders not only rely on verbal persuasion as their primary means of influence, they also draw only from a subset of the verbal repertoire. They rely heavily on facts, figures, and statistics, while completely forgetting about their most powerful verbal tools—the simple story. But who dares share anecdotes in an environment where storytelling has become verboten? The message from the business schools is clear. Stories are for the uneducated, the weak minded, the illogical, and the naive.

Hardly. When Joanne Martin and other researchers at Stanford University gave three different groups of MBA students the same information but through three different modes of presentation, they learned that stories were more influential than any of the other means of persuasion. All three groups were given a policy statement about a winery, and they were then given one of the following: (1) a story, (2) a table of statistics, or (3) a combination of story plus statistics. When asked to evaluate the credibility of what they'd read, the students exposed to the story placed more confidence in it. That was the most revealing part of the research. In spite of the "perceived" bias of these students toward facts and figures, they actually believed the story more than the numbers. However, she also found in her research that stories can backfire or be dismissed as propaganda if they're seen as inconsistent with the hearers' prior knowledge or experience. To be powerfully persuasive, stories "must be congruent with prior knowledge."[5]

After learning about this interesting research, one of the authors visited his brother-in-law who managed the concessions at Yellowstone Park. Listen to his story.

Where the Buffalo Roam . . . at Great Speeds

When my family and I first entered the granddaddy of all national parks, the ranger on duty handed us an orange-colored page that warned visitors of the dangers of hot pots and animals. I wasn't sure what the statement "hot pots and animals can be dangerous" actually meant, so I asked my brother-in-law to clue me in. "It's awful," he went on to explain. "Less than a month ago, a nine-year-old boy was running along the raised, wooden walkways near one of the hot pots when he tripped. His momentum propelled him over the low fence and into the boiling water. Since the water is forced out of the earth under extreme pressure and across hot rocks, it averages over 200 degrees. The boy not only died instantly, but his flesh separated from his bones. His parents stayed around for over a week, trying to convince the Park Service to erect more substantial barriers so that other families wouldn't experience a similar tragedy."

"What about the animal warning?" I asked. "They can be equally dangerous," his wife chimed in. "About a month ago, a tourist decided it would be great fun to pull on a buffalo's tail while his wife videotaped him. She now has a videotape of her husband being trampled to death by a buffalo. The thing that most people don't realize," she went on to explain, "is that buffalo, cute and awkward looking as they may be, are actually quite violent and can run about twice as fast as any human."

As I heard the frightening and heart-wrenching stories, I pointed out that the clipped facts stated on the warning sheet weren't nearly as powerful as the vignettes. Perhaps the Park Service should tell the stories and not just publish the number of people killed and the cause. This, of course, might frighten people away, but it seemed the least the government could do to prevent similar tragedies. After telling the story of the research just completed at Stanford, my brother-in-law agreed to help put the story of the park deaths in print. Two years later, the number of deaths in Yellowstone Park dropped to an all-time low. The poignant stories may well have been a part of the important change.

Back at the Plant

When the group of American automobile employees we mentioned earlier returned from their trip to Osaka, they were assigned to share their findings with their co-workers. The original plan was to expose around 25 percent of the employees to an actual experience with the Japanese threat, and then have them convince their friends that the threat was real. One group, somewhat frightened by their overseas experience, immediately ran out and warned their buddies that "the Japanese really did produce more at work." The reaction was predictable. The recently returned employees found themselves in the middle of a heated argument. Their friends didn't want to believe the findings and did what they could to resist their conclusions.

The plant human resources specialist, seeing what was happening, encouraged the remaining employees who had visited the Japanese facility to give presentations that consisted of a story. "Don't jump to the punch line, but do what you can to create the same emotional reaction you experienced in Japan," he coached them. "Tell how you went on tour and doubted what you were being told. Share the feelings you had as you were being ushered through the building by the rigid, peppy guides. Explain what happened that night as you sneaked in. In short, help the others have the same experience. Don't immediately share your conclusion. Let members of the audience draw their own."

The goal was to move away from verbal persuasion and toward vicarious experience. Stories, well told, put people into the middle of an event. They help others make deeper connections and hook their emotions. The strategy worked. The reaction to the new story-based presentations was quite different. Employees quickly moved from being out-hustled in Japan to trying to find ways to increase their own competitive advantage. With rare exception, the fact that the Japanese were producing more was never questioned. The story or vicarious experience was accepted as fact without being treated as less-compelling forms of verbal persuasion usually are (ones that are chock-full of cold fact and are often treated as invading organisms).

Share the Complete Story and Not Just the Punch Line

When one is frightened of the truth ... then it is never the whole truth that one has an inkling of.

LUDWIG WITTGENSTEIN

Although telling a poignant story can bring a depth to a mental map that you might not be able to create through other verbal means, the importance of stories is magnified only when leaders find themselves caught between competing stakeholder demands. When you can't satisfy one group without offending another, it's time to tell the entire story. For example, consider a company that recently reached a production level that made it financially expedient to start a second shift. To remain price competitive, the company needed to take full advantage of the machinery. Customers would buy from competitors who were running their machines at least 16 hours a day, and there were plenty to be found. The employees, on the other hand, didn't look forward to being away from their family and friends from 3:30 p.m. until midnight. In fact, they abhorred the thought.

The leadership team agonized over the tough choice. For hours they debated the pros and cons of the two choices—buy new machines and keep everyone on days, or use the machines across two shifts. Since this particular group of leaders had come out of jobs where they had worked second shift, they were painfully aware of the social costs of being separated from loved ones during this time. Many had seen their own family lives disintegrate when they themselves had worked second shift, and they were loath to force the same circumstances on their own employees. But the financial considerations were incontrovertible. Either they added a shift, or they faced financial ruin. Choose your poison.

After hours of gut-wrenching discussions, the leadership team called a plantwide meeting. Without so much as a preamble, the plant manager announced that the leadership team had decided to put on another shift. In order to reduce the burden to any one person, everyone would be asked to rotate onto second shift every other week. Not once did he or any of his staff talk about the torturous process they went through to reach the decision. Not once did they describe the tough personal trade-offs that they had worried about. Instead, they focused only on the financial need—sharing only half of the picture. They obviously feared that if they shared both sides of the agonizing decision, they would undermine their eventual choice. Virtually every leader hammered away at the financial advantage, even necessity, without mentioning a word about the disastrous effect on the employees' personal lives.

What a mistake. Employees were already suspicious that leaders in general only care about the bottom line. The decision (and the subsequent discussion) confirmed their worst suspicions. The cost to morale and leadership credibility was astronomical. Arguments, slowdowns, fistfights, a tightening of the antimanagement stance, and a whole host of other costs were incurred. Why? Because leaders who had agonized over a decision were unwilling to share the whole picture.

What would have happened if the leadership team had taken the workforce through the entire logical process? Imagine what would have taken place if the leaders shared how they had lain awake nights worrying about the tough choice. Unfortunately, they worried so much about looking strong that they ended up looking selfish. Had they worried less about their appearance and more about an honest and full explanation, they would have looked both strong and humane.

After making tough choices (even after you've involved as many people as you can), explain the entire thought process and not just the conclusion. Tell the story. As part of the story, tell what you were thinking and feeling. Never agonize over a decision that is bound to have negative effects and then share your conclusion as if you were a computer spitting out numbers. Share both sides *and* why you ended up where you did. Share your struggle to find balance. Explain how the decision links to your vision. Continually remind people of the delicate balance you walk between competing stakeholder demands. Avoid reinforcing value-simplistic conclusions by continually focusing on single values. Stories provide a wonderful medium for bundling complex values into thoughtful, real-life accounts of people caught in conflict.

Sure, those who are on the receiving end of the bad news aren't going to jump with joy over the decision, but they aren't going to think you are a heartless machine either. It's a lot easier to live with bad news when you understand the big picture.

HOW ABOUT MAGGIE?

Let's return to Maggie, the plant manager who needed to increase production levels. If you recall, she'd seen plenty of evidence that people were vacationing on the job. To solve this problem, she had tried to introduce more accountability by holding area managers to higher targets. The result was a slowdown. Union employees weren't buying this "speed up" strategy. That's where we left her at the beginning of the chapter.

We now pick her up at a point where she's decided that perhaps she needs to take a more careful approach to change. First, she's concluded that not all problems are due to intrinsic motivation. Second, she decided to enlist help from the rest of the leadership team. She began by calling together a group of the more senior and experienced leaders.

She asked them what they thought was going on. At first, they seemed reluctant to share their opinions, but when she continued to remain cool and collected, even when they suggested that she had made some poor choices, ideas began to flow. After an hour of brainstorming, the conference room walls were covered with flip-chart paper filled with suggestions about potential problems.

As people began to jump in with solutions, she slowed the process down by asking the question of leverage. Which of the problems could be readily resolved? The team immediately turned to ability problems. The machines needed more routine maintenance; the distance to the tool bin was too far; some of the newer supervisors weren't sure how to balance the schedule. The group decided to go for the low-hanging fruit by working on problems that could be resolved with a policy change, the investment of a few dollars, or by putting together short training sessions.

Next, the group turned to the other half of the Six-Cell Balancing Tool. Surely there were some motivation problems that could be dealt with. Here's where the concept of leverage was given a good workout. Maggie suggested that they only consider working on assumptions that weren't deeply held and widely shared. For example, many of the leaders suggested that the workforce was afraid to speed up their efforts because they thought the top bosses were heartless idiots who took joy in watching them suffer. Maggie wasn't sure how these ideas were formed, if they were accurate, or what to do about them. As she dove deeper, she learned that many employees feared that if they moved too fast, some of them would be laid off.

Had this happened before? No. Did it have to happen? Absolutely not. What if they were to meet with the union leaders and offer a guarantee? Nobody would be laid off if productivity improved. They could handle any extra personnel through attrition. The workforce was aging, and many were close to retirement.

Next, Maggie held an all-hands meeting. She announced the changes they would be making to help remove many of the barriers she had become aware of, and she encouraged employees to keep sharing their concerns and issues so they could continue to make life easier for themselves, as well as become more efficient. She then explained that as improvement continued, nobody would be laid off. She didn't just talk about the deal. She talked about how she valued people. She told a story of how her own father had been taken advantage of by a company that had wrangled ideas and improvements out of him until he and half his friends were fired. She told how she and her siblings had been devastated as a result of the sudden loss of income and how she vowed that she would never be party to such an action. The head of the union then stood up and explained the deal they had arranged.

With this symbolic event, Maggie and her leadership team started a long process of healing. They continued to work on high-leverage items, avoiding long-held values and doing everything they could to ask for behaviors that could be easily enacted or taught without great effort. Gone were the harangues, the recriminations, and the accusations. She did pick one deeply held and hard-to-change assumption. When she learned that employees had been offering ideas for years, only to have them rejected, she put together improvement teams—and then bent over backwards to implement every feasible suggestion. She then went public, talking about each suggestion and how it was put in place.

Behavior did begin to change. As people saw how serious she was about removing barriers, their desire to get along and go along increased. As she did everything in her power to listen to recommendations and to always deliver on her word, no matter how painful, people began to trust her and the rest of the leadership team.

As time went on, Maggie became quite "conduit sensitive." She refused to rely routinely on verbal persuasion by sending memos or giving announcements. Instead, she looked for ways to create vicarious or even personal experience. For instance, when one of the cross-functional teams suggested that the plant change to a new inventory system and the idea met some resistance, she hand-picked opinion leaders and had them visit a sister facility that was using the new system. Then, these opinion leaders were asked to share their experience with the rest of the workforce. They were encouraged to tell the whole story.

Over the period of a year, her plant began operating at close to the level her earlier estimates told her it should. And she enjoyed working with her union colleagues to boot.

IN SUMMARY

Our goal in this chapter has been to introduce a set of strategies aimed at influencing net value. Our focus has been on leverage. The idea is to attack behaviors that are only weakly supported or empowered and to supplant them with ones that are readily supported or empowered. Obviously, you don't always have the option to work only on the easy targets, but at least it gives you a place to start.

In addition to worrying about leverage, we've recommended a handful of strategies for dealing with the motivation side of net value. We have reserved our discussion on influencing efficacy expectation (how effective something will be) to later chapters and have focused on what it takes to influence both outcome assumptions and values. We suggested that values are best approached through the least intrusive means possible. Piling on negative outcomes was equated to feeding "the hog." Instead, we turned to ways of influencing values by considering net value. Our preferred method was to link behaviors to existing valued outcomes.

Our approach to changing assumptions drew from a simple theory. Assumptions change most readily through actual experience. We pointed out how most change strategies start with the least powerful lever: verbal persuasion. After suggesting ways to provide actual experience, we then examined how to create vicarious experiences through storytelling. Finally, we explained that when verbal explanations are given, it's helpful to tell the whole logical history rather than simply jump to conclusions.

Of course, dealing with mental maps is never easy. If you don't go to great pains to explain what you're thinking and why, if you're not both lucid and credible, and if you don't rely on powerful conduits, you may end up with the following experience (as told by one of the authors).

Liver — One Scoop or Two?

One day when my daughter was about five years old, I overheard her trying to convince a friend from the Far East to taste ice cream for the very first time. Her friend staunchly resisted. I couldn't imagine why. After all, this was ice cream, the universal satisfier. Then I remembered an incident from my own childhood. My mom had given me the same line my daughter was using, "Trust me, you'll love it." Only the food was liver. My daughter's friend had probably had a similar experience and had learned to be skeptical. Such is the risk you take every time you try to share your maps of the world. You talk "ice cream," but the other person hears "liver."

Of course, in this case the problem was quickly rectified. The little girl eventually took a lick of the ice cream, and personal experience took over where verbal persuasion left off. Chocolate worked its magic.

C H A P T E R   7

Improving Intrinsic Satisfaction

Happiness is an imaginary condition, formerly often attributed by the living to the dead, now usually attributed by adults to children, and by children to adults.

THOMAS SZASZ

I t's time to turn to the six cells and look at a variety of means for influencing each. We'll start with Cell 1. This is the cell that explores to what extent a person gets satisfaction out of a behavior itself. It deals with the part of motivation that is built into the job—independent of social sanctions or formal rewards. It answers the question, "If this person were left alone in a room, would he or she enjoy doing what is required?"

That's right, people can *want* to do their work. Despite clever comments to the contrary, people do find happiness—even in their jobs. This doesn't mean that

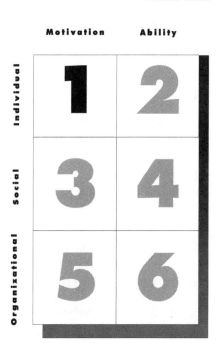

171

employees will be insulted if you pay them for a job they want to perform. On the other hand, pay doesn't have to be the only source of motivation. When leaders assume that all performance problems stem from a lack of motivation (as if there were no such thing as ability), they draw their influence tools from only three cells, instead of six. As costly as this error is, it's made worse when leaders overlook *intrinsic* motivation. Dropping intrinsic motivation from the formula further reduces the sources of influences from three to two. The irony of dropping Cell 1 is that it is the most likely source of motivation for keeping people energetically about the task of meeting stakeholder demands. It's the only cell that requires no leadership support and serves as a source of motivation 24 hours a day.

When people want to do their actual jobs (or at least most of the elements), they tend to work with more energy, passion, and attention to detail. In addition, they typically bring an upbeat tone to the culture and demand far less attention than those who despise their work. Imagine what it's like when every member of a work team enjoys his or her job. Better yet, how about the entire division, department, or company? When intrinsic motivation rules, the task of leadership is no longer to encourage the workforce, but to remove obstacles and provide resources.

It should come as a surprise to no one that organizations staffed by employees who receive great satisfaction from their jobs are remarkably efficient. Imagine two companies competing side by side in the marketplace— one filled with employees who are excited about their work and one where employees would rather take a beating than show up each morning. Which do you suppose has the highest productivity? Duh. Which has the higher payroll costs? Duh again.

Hewlett-Packard serves as a living example of the power of intrinsic motivation. Over the years, leaders at HP have developed a marvelous working atmosphere—allowing individuals to *want* to do the work itself by creating a veritable utopia for engineers and scientists. People take such satisfaction from their jobs that the company has been able to keep top performers in spite of higher offers. While HP salaries are competitive with those of other industry leaders, excessive compensation isn't what keeps employees' loyalties. And HP continues to be a remarkably creative, highly productive, and powerful player in the marketplace.

Doing the Right Thing for the Right Reason

Money is better than poverty, if only for financial reasons.

WOODY ALLEN

There's a certain irony in the fact that we've chosen to talk about the importance of creating intrinsic satisfaction as a means of generating increased profits. Woody Allen, in his own twisted way, was right: Money should be restricted to the realm of finance. Vital leaders worry about creating an environment where people enjoy their work simply because they want people to enjoy their work. They don't need increased productivity, cost savings, or quality measures to inspire them to create a workplace where people enjoy their daily routines. They want people to be satisfied with their job—as an end in itself. After all, people often spend more time at work than anyplace else.

Most leaders can remember a time when they shoveled chicken manure for a summer or slaved away at something equally disgusting. They recall, with not-so-fond memories, what it was like to drag themselves out of bed every morning to face a noxious task. Consequently, good leaders worry about the quality of the jobs they ask employees to perform. They allow themselves a feeling seldom experienced by the harried manager. They allow themselves the luxury of feeling compassion.

Actually, of all the acts of leadership we'll discuss in this book, perhaps the purest and most noble acts are those aimed at creating healthy and productive jobs. Compassionate leaders don't simply throw money at problems. Instead, they take the time to fashion jobs that provide intrinsic satisfaction. They worry about jobs because they honestly care about people. Whether they're a young frontline supervisor trying to meet daily production schedules or the president of a mammoth organization attempting to battle offshore competition, truly visionary leaders share a common quality—they dream of creating a place wherein excited employees work with passion toward a shared goal and go home at the end of the day with a feeling of accomplishment and pride in a job well done.

Visionary leaders refuse to be hypnotized by the haunting belief that "most work is intrinsically numbing." Visionary leaders hold out for more.

Perfuming the Pig?

If you want people motivated to do a good job, give them a good job to do.
FREDERICK HERZBERG

But what does it take to create an organization with jobs people actually enjoy doing? Was Herzberg right? Is giving them a good job to do the only way to motivate people to do a good job? And if this is the case, what makes a job good in the first place? Does it require lots of excitement, glamour, and stimulation? Perhaps Thomas Szasz was right. People can only imagine *someone else* being happy at work. Hourly employees envy managers, who, in turn, envy hourly employees.

But then again, it doesn't take years of studying philosophy to conclude that the goodness of a job doesn't lie in the job itself. It lies in the mind of the person performing it. In fact, experience alone suggests that different people working in the same job have very different reactions to it. One produces widgets with a smile, while the other dreams of greener pastures. One designs circuit boards as if doing so were infinitely entertaining, while another counts the moments until he's home in his garden.

Of course, you have to admit that some jobs are viewed by just about everyone as despicable. For example, Florida is currently resurrecting chain gangs (prisoners forced to work on public projects). The chain gangs perform certain jobs that public-works officials can't get others to perform short of pointing a gun at them—draining snake-infested swamps, for one. With similarly filthy, disgusting, back-breaking, dangerous, or mind-numbing tasks, it's hard to imagine a way of making them intrinsically satisfying.

Maybe.

Before we quickly come up with our top ten 10 list of truly deplorable jobs, let's take a look at a task that most of us would not consider a whole lot of fun. One of the authors studied it while conducting a culture assessment at a large mine in Wyoming. Here's his story.

The Best Damn Miners

Happiness doesn't depend on outward conditions. It depends on inner conditions. It isn't what you have or who you are or where you are or what you are doing that makes you happy or unhappy. It is what you think about it.

DALE CARNEGIE

As we pulled up to the entrance of a large Wyoming coal mine, I noticed a handwritten wooden sign on the gate. It read, "Beyond this gate are the best damn miners in the world!" Later that day I interviewed a driver who was a living, breathing embodiment of the message captured on the sign. He drove an earthmover with eight-foot-high wheels that was capable of moving the equivalent of a New Jersey mountain with each load. I interviewed him on his break as he casually leaned against his "mover."

"What exactly is your job?" I asked.

"I drive."

"How long have you been driving here at the mine?"

"Twenty-two years."

"Where do you drive?"

"Here," he said, pointing toward the mine. "Same route every day; load up at the bottom; drive to the top and dump; drive back to the bottom. Twenty times every seven hours and 45 minutes."

"How do you feel about your job?" I questioned.

"It's a good job."

Here was a miner describing as a "good job" an extremely repetitious task he had been doing for more years than the average person spends from birth to high school graduation. The next question almost asked itself.

"Doesn't it ever get boring?"

"No, it's fun," he said with an almost whimsical smile.

"What makes it fun?"

The miner paused as if he'd never considered the question before. Then his face brightened. "I get to drive *this*," he said with a burst of enthusiasm as he patted the huge machine. "And we set a new record last week—80,000 tons hauled in one shift. I carried over 4,200 tons of that myself. Here, let me show you." The miner climbed up the metal ladder to his cockpit. I followed. He grabbed a clipboard, thick with dirty pages, from under the seat. Each sheet was covered with neatly printed columns and figures. This was a record of his tonnage by haul, by shift, by month—over the last year. The record-setting day was underlined in red.

"Are you required to keep these records?"

"Nah, but I like to track things. You know, see how I'm doing. Look what else I have here." He pointed to a cassette player on the seat and pulled out a plastic case that he opened to reveal a horde of cassette tapes. "I listen to these a lot. Great books on tape, self-improvement stuff, country western. And I got this," he said, pointing to a CB radio attached to the dash. "Me and my buds turn into real chatterboxes depending on how Cowboy football [University of Wyoming] is doing."

As I climbed down the ladder, I had a fairly good understanding why this particular crew was the best-performing one in the company. If you were to assess their culture, you'd learn that Cell 1, intrinsic satisfaction with the job itself, was quite high. They had found ways to turn repetitive, dirty, often exhausting jobs into something they enjoyed and, in so doing, saw themselves as "the best damn miners in the world."

"Want To" Versus "Have To"

Give a man health and a course to steer, and he'll never stop to trouble about whether he's happy or not.

GEORGE BERNARD SHAW

A useful way to categorize motivations is in terms of those things people *want* to do and those things people believe they *have* to do. "Have to" tasks are those that are completed either to avoid a punishment or to gain an extrinsic reward. Either way, the person does not wish to engage in the activity per se, but feels he or she must do so to avoid a greater cost or gain rewards. Although the person may intellectually believe that he has a choice in the matter, emotionally he or she feels as if the task is mandatory. "Have to" tasks are often referred to as work, burdens, obligations, sacrifices, duties, and responsibilities.

"Want to" tasks, on the other hand, are activities the person chooses to do because he or she desires to do them. These types of tasks are often referred to as play, fun, pleasure, hobbies, interests, challenges, desires, careers, excitement, and freedom. Because the person is "doing what he or she wants to do," there is a heightened sense of choice.

At this point we must avoid the tendency to inappropriately categorize "have to" as "work" and "difficult" while assuming that "want to" is "play" and "easy." On the contrary, whether rock climbing, running a marathon, or laboring 24 hours straight on a project at work, "want to" tasks are often extremely challenging and leave people exhausted, yet feeling fulfilled. With "have to" tasks people often expend the same amount of effort and concentration (feeling similarly exhausted) and yet describe themselves as burned out, trapped, and unfulfilled.

It's shocking to discover how many people can hardly imagine that work and play can be one. For three years one of the authors ended his organizational behavior course by giving a short, animated speech on why students, while they were young and still fairly mobile, should seek work they intrinsically enjoy. He told of how his own father had trudged home at the end of every day and unknowingly taught his children that paying jobs were something to be despised. In spite of the tragic, silent lessons, the son stumbled on a career he loved. Each day he would wake up with a renewed excitement for the field. "Be advised," he would tell the students, "your vocation and avocation *can* be the same. If you don't like what you're currently studying, what makes you think you're going to enjoy doing it eight to 10 hours a day?" After giving this mini-lecture for three years, the head of the accounting department stopped him in the hallway and told him that about a dozen students would drop out of accounting each year at the end of the "intrinsic motive" lecture. They hated the field, loathed their homework, didn't enjoy anything about the topic, but had settled in on the major for the money. Obviously they hadn't read Woody Allen.

One of a leader's primary jobs is to create a climate where fewer tasks are seen as "have to" while most are viewed as "want to." Leaders need to find a way to allow earthmovers, secretaries, programmers, department managers, and dockworkers alike to derive intrinsic satisfaction from their jobs.

SO, WHAT'S A LEADER TO DO ABOUT CELL 1?

As a leader, how do you create intrinsic motivation in your workforce? The answer is, you don't. You can't. In fact, people are already motivated to act. People already have intrinsic motivation and do not need a leader to give it to them. So, when it comes to Cell 1, what's a leader's job? *The leader's challenge is to create those conditions that help people find intrinsic satisfaction in their jobs.* The areas where a leader can have an impact on Cell 1 include choice, enrichment, leveling, linking, and reveling. Let's see how a leader can influence each in an effort to create a climate where intrinsic satisfaction is the rule and not the exception.

Choice and Involvement

Whatever does not spring from a man's free choice, or is only the result of instruction and guidance, does not enter into his very being, but still remains alien to his true nature; he does not perform it with truly human energies, but merely with mechanical exactness.

KARL WILHELM VON HUMBOLDT

For years philosophers have argued over what really constitutes freedom or personal choice. Most suggest that by the time we're aware of a thing called agency, we have little left. Our language has been determined, our thought-processes fully formed, our values mostly complete—so choice is a mere illusion. Tell that to a dockworker who's just been told that she *has to* work Labor Day weekend.

We'll suggest that most people prefer to be involved in decisions that affect them. They don't want to feel like objects that simply respond to changing stimuli, but prefer to be the "captains of their fate"—imagined or otherwise. Let's be clear about our motive here. Individuals prefer to be involved in decisions because they rightfully think they have important information that can improve the quality of the choice. Yes, people feel more committed to choices they've been involved in, and this plays a factor as well, but it shouldn't be the sole reason for involving people in choices. The primary reason for involvement deals with ability and not motive. Data improves the quality of a decision, and more *people* generally provide more *data*.

It's Not All Smoke and Mirrors

We pause to make this point because a great deal of the decision-making literature is strikingly manipulative and patronizing. For example, in one often-quoted study, a group of employees complained about their "hot and poorly ventilated" work area and wanted something done about it. Their foreman discussed the problem with the engineers and with his superintendent, and they all felt this was a "trumped-up complaint" and that installing air conditioning would be too costly. The employees, however, came up with a proposal of their own—to buy large fans to circulate the air around their feet. And even though the foreman "felt that the fans wouldn't help much anyway," he hesitantly agreed to their proposal "since it seemed that the fans could be used elsewhere after their expected failure to provide relief." After trying out various arrangements of the fans for several days, the work-group finally settled on a configuration that worked best for them, and they were "completely satisfied with the results."[1]

This particular study is certainly open to alternative explanations. Perhaps the engineers, foreman, and superintendent didn't have enough relevant data. Perhaps the employees knew their own feelings better than they knew broad theories of air flow and thermal dynamics. Perhaps they, in fact, as users of the product, were privy to information that was too subtle for traditional metrics. Perhaps they weren't kidding themselves into thinking that their own choices were better when they weren't, but instead they were able to consider data that others would never see. Not every human being is a childlike creature who throws a tantrum, makes a poor choice, convinces himself or herself that the choice was better, and then lives with the consequences for years.

We suggest that people like to be involved in decisions because they believe their insights will be useful. We agree. Now, this doesn't mean, however, that people want to be involved in *every* decision, but they do want to be involved in *some*. A leader's job is to determine *which* decisions and then allow as much involvement as possible.

Four Types of Decisions

As we take a look at ways to increase the quality of people's work life through involvement in decision making, it's helpful to understand the four types of decision making and when each is best used. The four types include command, consensus, consultation, and individual choice.

1. Command. Command decisions are the ones most people worry about, but they're actually easy to deal with. They consist of decisions that have already been made and simply need to be implemented. Commands are handed to every leader, work team, and individual by other stakeholders. Customers say they're only willing to pay a certain amount of money. It's not open to debate. Government agencies simply won't allow certain work practices. They're too unsafe. Communities won't allow companies to dump their waste just anywhere. Leaders decide on certain business strategies. They aren't about to open the product line to debate. A great deal of what reaches the workforce has already been decided. It comes in the form of commands.

Leaders make two mistakes when it comes to commands. First, they pass on the constraints as if these were their own idea—giving the impression that they're making demands when they're not. Nobody likes it when choices are limited by what seems to be the whim of the boss. Employees have enough demands placed on them without the head cheese making up a few of his or her own, just for the heck of it. Astute leaders describe constraints as just that. Don't say, "Give me 300 of these by noon," implying that it's the boss's idea based on who knows what. Instead, suggest, "Our customer needs 300 of these on her dock by four o'clock. This means we'll have to get them out of our department by noon." Place commands within their natural context by giving credit to the stakeholders in question rather than owning every decision as if it were of your own making.

Second, leaders mistakenly give the impression that, in order to embrace the "employee-involvement movement," people are going to be involved in every decision. No longer will anyone be given commands. Leaders can no more do away with command decisions than they can do away with the need for oxygen. They can do away with *capricious* command decisions, that is, ones that *could* involve more people, but they can't do away with stakeholder demands. During the early stages of any "employee involvement" program, leaders must take care to explain the four kinds of decisions and why they exist. If not, given the current language of involvement floating around, employees might mistakenly conclude that they're now going to take part in every decision. Nip this dangerous thinking in the bud.

How, not what. Once a command or constraint has been given to an employee or workgroup, it doesn't mean that all decisions have been made. At this point it's up to those who complete the task to decide how to do it. They won't be deciding what to do—that's come as a stakeholder demand—but they will be deciding what processes and methods they'll be using. To be frank, the employee-involvement movement should focus in this domain. Employees should be involved in the *hows* after the stakeholders determine the *whats*.

Size matters. Given that opportunities now exist for choice, there are three ways they can be made: consensus, consultation, or individual choice—depending on the size of the group affected.

How does one decide the size of the group?

- **Principle.** Those affected by the decision should be involved in it.
- **Principle.** The larger the group affected, the more complex and difficult the decision-making process.
- **Conclusion.** Involve everyone who is affected by a decision, but not one person more.

For example, 14 programmers were brought together to help lay out the initial design of a new piece of software. The idea was to get as much input up front as possible, so the project manager invited every programmer he could lay his hands on. The only problem was that several of them would be contributing nothing to the finished product. Nevertheless, they had plenty of opinions. Enough so that it took hours to make even simple decisions. It took almost 90 minutes just to choose a meeting time, and this decision was continually revisited. Finally, one day when the group was about to burst with frustration, somebody asked, "Does everyone in this room really have to be involved in this project?" Within 10 minutes the group was cut in half, and the remaining seven programmers made more progress in the next meeting than they had in the previous five.

2. Consensus. As organizations face increasingly complex tasks, it's common for leaders to create groups of people or teams who are highly interdependent. That is, what one person does affects the others. Instead of isolating people, surrounding them by buffers, and then allowing them to act as islands, employees are thrown together into small groups of people who depend on each other to complete their work. They often rotate tasks and almost always need input from teammates to finish their work. This, by the way, should be done when tasks are complicated, new, and constantly changing—requiring multiple heads and hands.

When co-workers are interdependent, most decisions will be made by consensus because everyone is affected. With consensus decisions, everyone shares his or her opinion and eventually everyone agrees to a single choice. This, of course, requires an understanding of the decision-making process and no small amount of skill in managing groups. As we've observed teams form over the past decade, most have fallen into a common trap. Certain team members express their opposing opinions, eventually agree to a choice, and then don't support it. They go out and try to talk other teammates into their point of view—after the fact. Worse yet, should the decision not pan out, they can't wait to say, "I told you so."

These problems can be fixed in one of two ways. First, team members need to understand and agree to the principle that every person will stay with an idea until he or she has been convinced of another point of view. Once team members have agreed to a new choice, they will support it as if it were their own. They won't "just live with it," they won't "just give it a try," they'll *support* it. Second, team members must be trained in the skills of open dialogue. People frequently try to submarine an idea in private because they aren't very skilled at expressing their opinions in public. After continually "losing an argument" in a group discussion (but still holding to the same opinion), they give up and wait until a time when they can discuss the issue one on one. If your discussions are routinely followed by a variety of postmeeting lobbying efforts, you can count on the fact that your group has insufficient dialogue skills.

As a leader, you must take two important steps. First, ensure that everyone involved in a consensus decision buys into and supports the idea of consensus. Second, provide training and skill building in the art of dialogue. To throw people into teams, demand consensus decisions, and not train them in dialogue skills is to court disaster.

3. Consultation. Sometimes decisions affect so many people that it's too hard to bring everyone together, hammer out the issues, and come to consensus. We don't make laws by consensus. We select people who represent us and allow them to make the choices. Cross-functional teams represent the business form of the consultation process. Representatives from affected groups are brought together into a short-term decision-making body and asked to wrestle with an issue. They then make a consensus decision for the larger group.

Mistakes in this process are fairly easy to predict. Groups are brought together and make decisions for the broader population, but the decisions are simply passed on by the leaders—leaving the impression that only the top bosses were involved. To avoid this problem, select a representative body, inform those who will be affected so they can put in a word with one or more of the people on the team, and have the decision-making body make and announce the decision.

Perhaps the most common mistake made in the consultation process occurs when those who are part of the decision-making team ask others for advice, but don't make it clear that they're only asking for advice, while reserving the decision for themselves. Leadership teams fall into this trap quite often. When everyone in the organization will be affected by a choice, the operating committee is asked to make the decision—after all, it represents every person and function. Leaders go astray when each polls his or her direct reports without letting them know of the broader process. For instance, an engineering group meets and brainstorms how the new parking lot slots should be assigned. They unanimously suggest that the plant should hold a raffle and make assignments by lot. Since the physical facilities fall more or less into the engineering realm, team members believe the choice has been made. In the meantime, the comptroller's team is recommending "first come, first serve," and the human resources team has just settled on a formula that links distance from the main entrance to how often a person comes and goes each day. Each leader involves his or her team, and none thinks to tell them that they will only be making a recommendation. The next day, the operating committee meets and cleverly comes up with a hybrid of the various suggestions. When the final decision is announced, virtually everyone is surprised. Many have already made plans on the basis of their recommendations. All feel violated. The fix is simple. When asking for advice but reserving the right to make a decision based on a broader pool of data, let people know what you're doing up front. Try to walk away with more than one idea. Remind people of what you're doing as you leave the group, recommendations in hand.

Sometimes leaders use a consultation approach when they see the decision as their own but don't have the specialized information they need. In these cases, the leaders, instead of assembling a representative body, gather a team of experts who have specialized knowledge and can make recommendations. Here again it's essential that expectations are clearly set up front. Will the experts decide, or will they make a recommendation to the leaders who will decide? If this is not understood up front, count on violated expectations.

Finally, don't give misleading limits of freedom. It's common for leaders to turn a decision over to a group, but to *hope* for a particular outcome. They have a strong opinion, are worried about appearing too controlling, and turn the choice over to a team—hoping all along that their choice is selected. This is an accident waiting to happen. When giving a group of people several choices from which to select, make sure that you'll support *any* of the choices. If you have restrictions, explain *what* they are and *why* they exist. Never allow direct reports to make a decision that you can't willingly support.

4. Individual Choice. Actually, a great deal of what a person does during the day is subject to his or her own choice. Since no one else is affected, individuals choose what to do on their own. For example, as you type, you set the keyboard where you want it. You tilt the computer screen to your eye level. You adjust the chair to your height. You make dozens of similar choices every hour concerning personal issues. The rule here should be a simple one: When others are not affected and options are available, individuals should be allowed to make their own choices.

Over the past few years this particular principle has been pushed into a corner. Japanese efficiency experts routinely study the way a particular job is "best done" and then demand that everyone does it the same way. If a certain bolt is best locked down with the right hand, all employees, including the left-handed ones, will do it with their right hand. American firms, cowed by their impressive foreign competitors, have attempted similar strategies to standardize the work process, only to learn that their workforces prefer more choices. American employees don't buy into the fact that somebody else has studied the process and decided for them how every step along the way needs to be handled. The debate for and against process routinization will rage for decades (with good reasons on both sides), but here's a rule of thumb. Ask "Can a task be completed in a variety of ways and still yield the same long- and short-term results?" If the answer is no, explain the reasons for the fixed process, and demand consistency. If the answer is yes, allow for individual choices.

Several groups we've worked with have assumed that, since people *enjoy* being involved in decisions, they should be involved in most decisions—certainly every decision affecting them. It's part of the North American "more is better" philosophy. The fact is, people don't always want to be involved in every decision. They are either genuinely indifferent to the choices or trust others to represent their opinion. More often than not, people are so busy in other parts of their work that they willingly let others make some decisions for them. Whatever the reason for wanting to turn the decision making over to colleagues, it makes sense to start the decision-making process by determining who wants to be involved. This doesn't mean that teammates and leaders won't try to convince individuals to provide their best thinking, or in some cases even demand it. Our point is it makes sense to allow people to have a choice in the choices they make.

Finally, when it comes to decision making, the issue is not *which* is more effective: command, consent, consult, or individual choice? Each form has its purpose. The real issue is, which is *best suited* for a given decision? The key to effective decision making lies in deciding how to decide *up front*. Before deciding, agree on how to decide, and make sure that everyone understands. One of the authors observed a good example of this process at the Saturn division of General Motors. The team leader started the meeting with, "We've got a critical decision to make today. Our partners need our answer by 11:00 a.m. I would prefer that the decision be made by consensus. If, however, we have not reached consensus by 10:30, then let's make this a consultation process, meaning, I'll decide based on the dialogue we've had. Does that sound okay to everyone?" Everyone nodded in agreement.

By taking the time up front to decide how to decide, everyone is clear on the decision-making process. People now know how to contribute and what to expect. Misunderstandings are less likely, and effective teamwork is more probable.

Job Enrichment

Idleness, indifference, and irresponsibility are healthy responses to absurd work.

FREDERICK HERZBERG

With some jobs, having a choice offers little respite. The job itself is so noxious that the only real choice the person cares about is choosing to do something else. Sure, deciding whether you use your left or right hand to shovel chicken manure is helpful, but it's still a boring, dirty, back-breaking, and nose-vexing job. You're shoveling, and chicken manure to boot! Of course, the human spirit has an infinite ability to turn the most repetitive and mind-numbing tasks into engaging competitions, personal challenges, and similarly noble conquests. (Our dirt-moving friend and thousands like him have shown us this.) But this doesn't mean that leaders should purposefully keep people in grungy, disgusting, and routinely despised tasks just so they can uncover the irrepressible human spirit. There is no honor in insisting that people find a way to see a nine-tenths-empty job as half full.

During the late 1960s, Frederick Herzberg and others began to explore ways to make jobs that were generally not very enjoyable into ones that were.[2] Their solution was a straightforward one—change the job. More specifically, enrich the job by adding activities that are more enjoyable. One of the reasons leaders have achieved dramatic improvements in productivity through sociotechnical approaches, quality initiatives, and team structures is that each of these strategies has enriched the tasks employees perform. When jobs are made inherently more interesting and challenging, using more of people's talents and abilities, intrinsic motivation increases dramatically.

Herzberg and others argued that there's no reason to think of jobs in traditional ways that limit people to boring and repetitive tasks. For years companies combined activities into abstract constructs that eventually became concrete jobs with clear borders and lives of their own. With time and familiarity, leaders began to see these arbitrary constructs as something sacred, complete with borders that needed to be defended against outsiders who naively wanted to pervert them by shaping them into new forms. Leaders today need to bypass these traditional borders.

Forget the notion of a job. Instead, look at what needs to be done in order to satisfy competing stakeholder demands, and then explore dozens of different ways to combine the varying tasks into healthy combinations. The current movement to redesign work does just that. Employees themselves create their own job descriptions. As long as your starting point is stakeholder demands, leaders should be open to how tasks are combined.

In a similar vein, rethink the whole idea of a career. College courses, on-the-job training programs, trade techs, and other job-preparation programs need to be seen as starting places, not as career boxes. Throughout this book we've been asking leaders to stretch beyond their traditional jobs and develop skills in visioning, cultural anthropology, rhetoric, drama, and a variety of other areas that can't and won't be addressed in any business school or MBA program. We're asking leaders to rethink their careers. We're asking them to reshape their boxes.

In today's "learning organization," executives aren't allowed to sit in their offices with dictating machines. Instead, they're being asked to log on and make use of their computers. They've been asked to reshape their boxes. Typing and first-round editing once done by a full-time secretary are now picked up by the executive who does it while he or she creates the first draft. A step is cut out of the process, and the secretary is free to do other tasks. This works only when (1) executives buy into the notion that the expanded skill increases their competitive advantage and (2) secretaries buy into the fact that they now are free to do more complex and varied jobs.

To survive in today's diversified environment, careers must be organic. People are being asked to learn several fields, not just one. They have years to gain the knowledge, so why restrict them to the box their initial education put them in? Healthy organizations allow individuals to continually enrich their jobs by taking on the challenge of learning new skill-sets on the job, at home, or anywhere else they can develop new ideas and abilities. Today's leaders must believe in the trite graduation speech that suggests a commencement is, indeed, a commencement and not an ending.

To help people discover the "want to" reasons for adding value to organizations, leaders should work with employees to design jobs that step out of traditional, restricting boxes and shape them into ones that:

- Provide opportunities for growth, new experiences, and learning
- Offer variety and variation (rotation, swapping, cross-training)
- Enable people to acquire and demonstrate competence
- Allow for increasing degrees of responsibility
- Encourage measurement, tracking, goal achievement, and success
- Encourage fairness and equitable treatment
- Match individual abilities and interests with job requirements

Leveling

Philosophical rules to live by: Seek pleasure; avoid pain.

We've suggested that jobs can be made more enjoyable by allowing individuals to embrace more intrinsically challenging or stimulating activities. We'll now explore a method we refer to as "leveling"—combining desirable with undesirable tasks to create an overall job that isn't so hard to survive. For example, kids are a lot more willing to muck out a stall if part of their job consists of riding the horse.

Now, let's be clear, with *leveling* we're dealing with the net value, not with the intrinsic value of any one part of the job. By spreading negative aspects across jobs that are largely positive, you end up with a job that "has its negative aspects, but all in all is a good one to have"— as is the case with yours, ours, and just about everyone's job.

We mention leveling because it hasn't been the preferred tool of leaders and scholars, yet it deserves more consideration. For example, those who preached the religion of *job enrichment* also spoke eloquently and vehemently against the concept of *job enlargement*. They rejected the temptation to just pile on more of the same—maybe even add a noxious task or two—instead of adding something particularly interesting or stimulating. The reasons against such a strategy are self-evident. If you don't like liver for breakfast, you won't be more satisfied eating it three times a day.

Over the past few years, we've watched as several companies created a team environment wherein jobs were rotated among all team members. In so doing they bucked years of tradition that assigned jobs by seniority. The back-breaking or boring jobs (particularly those linked to a production line) were always done by the newest employees (in several plants these were people with 15 or more years of tenure), whereas tasks that allowed for "free choice," required more skill, and were completed at a slower pace were always snagged by senior employees.

In order to enhance a workgroup's flexibility, it was argued that every employee should know how to do every task. That way, should someone transfer, retire, go on vacation, come down with the flu, or otherwise be unavailable to do a job, anyone else on the team could step in without a drop in productivity. The principle was simple: Customers are better served when costs are kept low, and costs are kept at their lowest when there is no start-up time. Since it was hard to argue against the value of serving customers, teams (certainly the older members) reluctantly agreed to rotate jobs to keep everyone up to speed on every task.

It turns out that overall job satisfaction increased. Sure, there are always a handful of employees who would prefer to work only one job. However, a surprising number of people who thought they preferred a single task, holding on to it like an old baseball glove, found that they preferred rotating. Of course, virtually all of the newer employees were delighted with the change.

By the way, as part of the agreement, employees who were asked to structure jobs to include both popular and unpopular tasks were all paid the highest job rate—since they could all complete any task. This, of course, only works when the team does reduce costs by eliminating start-up times. If not, raising the average salary without increasing productivity only increases the cost of doing business in an environment that calls for cost savings. People "knowing their stuff" isn't enough reason to justify greater pay. Would you be willing to pay $200 for a haircut just because it was done by an out-of-work brain surgeon?

The most common argument against leveling—combining a large group of jobs into a single job category—is that it keeps people away from the task they're best at. Not everyone is as efficient at every operation. This argument, when made against a background of "we can't make enough parts as it is," often wins out over the call for flexibility. Often, given the need to put out work at the highest level, individuals settle in on jobs that maximize efficiency and minimize flexibility.

With time, the teams we worked with came to realize that they had to manage the tension between the need for flexibility and the need for efficiency. They refused to be dragged into an either-or argument. Instead, workgroups quickly assigned people to their most efficient jobs during times of high production demands and then shifted around when demands dropped to normal.

Linkage

Yes, I do lay brick day in and day out, but it's not a boring or inconsequential job. You see, I'm not laying brick; I'm building a cathedral.

Picture a job requiring people to crawl in the mud, endure freezing temperatures, eat lousy food, and face the risk of death. How could people in this situation discover intrinsic satisfaction in the job? What if they weren't just crawling in the mud but were defending their country and preserving its freedoms? For most people, a meaningful, even noble, purpose changes the meaning behind difficult, even unpleasant, tasks. Most humans are willing to sacrifice their very lives for a cause, if it's one they see as vital to their values. Jobs, careers, tasks, and noxious activities change in value as they're linked to a higher meaning and purpose.

Herein lies an important key to leadership—a key that has fallen into disuse and has often been labeled as outdated or even corny. Nevertheless, when you think of great leaders, you think of those who inspire people with a compelling vision. They can "rally the troops" around a common cause, even in the face of adversity. Whether it's marching in the face of persecution in Selma, Alabama; marshaling the best scientific minds to reach the moon in an impossibly short time; or teaming to build Saturn automobiles in Spring Hill, Tennessee, effective leaders help people link their personal tasks and results to a higher meaning and purpose.

They'll Be There Monday

Consider an example from corporate America. Two of the authors were part of a research team conducting a culture assessment at a large insurance company in the northwestern United States. One of the researchers observed a group of claims-processing clerks whose job was to receive claim forms, evaluate them, and place them in one of two piles for further processing. The researcher noticed that on Friday afternoon, with 20 minutes still remaining on the shift, many clerks stopped working. One sitting nearby cleaned her desk, made a "to do" list for the weekend, then punched out at five o'clock.

Two weeks later, the researcher had the opportunity to interview her. He started off with, "I noticed two weeks ago that you quit working at 20 minutes to five, but didn't punch out until five. Why was that?"

She replied, "Well, we have a policy that we can't leave until five."

"No," stumbled the researcher. "I mean, why did you stop working with 20 minutes left in the shift?"

The clerk shrugged and answered, "It was the weekend."

"Are you aware that you still had six more claims in your in-basket?"

She nodded. "They'll be there Monday."

The researcher paused, then asked, "Do you know the company's mission statement?"

"Sure." Then she looked at a framed poster on the wall and read in part, "Maximize the return on investment for shareowners."

"Does that inspire you to do a good job?" asked the researcher.

The clerk looked at him incredulously. "Is that a serious question?"

Later that month, in our report to the division executives, we identified that employees felt they were paid fairly and that they had a good benefits package (Cell 5). They agreed that they worked with nice people and were treated well by the bosses (Cell 3). However, there was little or no sense of meaning or purpose (Cell 1). This, of course, often led to unproductive behaviors. We recommended that the leaders create a shared sense of vision throughout the company. The leaders responded that they already had a mission statement. We acknowledged that there was something posted on the walls, but that the people had not discovered in the statement any real sense of meaning or purpose that mattered to them. They saw little evidence that it mattered to the leaders or anyone else.

From that moment on, the leadership team began to ask some difficult questions about the company. What do we think is important? What do we want to do and why? Do we contribute anything to society that matters? Who benefits from our efforts? Is that important to us?

One of the vice presidents began reading through speeches given by past presidents to see if she could find any clues to the early leaders' vision. She eventually found a speech given by the founder in 1904. He had stated: "The purpose for our enterprise is to reduce financial hardship and human suffering. And to the degree we do it well, we shall prosper."

As the vice president considered the words of the founding leader, her assumption that the purpose of the company was "to invest premiums" began to expand. She realized that the company not only had responsibilities to serve owners, policyholders, and employees, it also had a responsibility to serve the larger society.

After musing over the company's mission for several days, she took the founder's statement to the executive committee and began a conversation about responsibility, purpose, service, and leadership. To shorten a yearlong story, the company's leaders created a draft mission statement that said, in part, "The purpose of our enterprise is to reduce financial hardship and human suffering." The draft was then sent to every member of the company along with a cover letter that said, "Here's a rough draft of the division's mission statement, written by the executive committee. We're not happy with it yet. What's missing that should be added? What should be removed? Please give us your best thinking on the matter." The committee read every employee response.

In addition, every team was asked to review the mission-statement draft and send in a team report, identifying modifications. All of the recommendations were gathered, considered, and eventually used to create a new document. The usually invisible leaders then "hit the road"—meeting several times a week for six months with groups of employees, sharing their feelings and insights, and advocating the division's purpose.

Finally, each team leader met with his or her team and jointly identified how what they did served the mission or failed to serve it. Then, each team submitted a summary of its discoveries.

Leaders throughout the company were asked to visibly and frequently reference the mission, use it when making tough decisions, and evaluate team performance in light of the vision. As gaps were identified, several change projects were initiated.

Eighteen months after the first culture assessment was held, another one was conducted to determine if key assumptions and values had changed. The same researcher was assigned to observe the same processing clerks. This time he noticed the clerk he had interviewed 18 months earlier work on a Friday afternoon until five, punch out, return to her desk, work an additional 25 minutes, then go home.

Two weeks later he interviewed her.

"I noticed a while back that you punched out at five, then worked an additional 25 minutes before leaving. Why?"

"Well, we're having some overtime pressures, so they've asked us to punch out at five."

"What I mean is, why did you work an additional 25 minutes after punching out?"

"There were still seven claims in my in-basket," she responded.

"They'll be there Monday," the researcher suggested.

The clerk became very serious as she explained, "Oh, you don't understand. Oklahoma suffered a series of tornadoes, and those people really need their checks."

The researcher asked, "Do you know the company's mission?"

"Yes," she replied, and without looking at the wall recited, "To reduce financial hardship and human suffering. That's what my job is all about."

Now that she could relate to the mission, its purpose was filled with emotion. Instead of simply linking to profits, it linked to something she could identify with, brag about, and take pride in. Of course, the cynic on reading this story might suggest, "This meaning and purpose stuff is just a clever way of wringing more out of your people." However, a serious student of leadership will realize that by linking to a higher meaning and purpose, people find satisfaction in their jobs and in their lives.

Who benefits from such a change in perspective? Certainly the company, which realizes greater productivity, and the customer, who receives improved products and services. But the employee benefits as well. When the job of laying brick turns into the work of love associated with constructing a temple, the routine task of hoisting terra cotta turns into a mission of importance.

It's inspiring to watch an employee on an automobile production line vigilantly look for the smallest deviation—to ensure that "a defenseless person isn't stranded someday if one of our parts should fail." In contrast, it's depressing to watch individuals who loathe the "mindless task of watching for minute deviations." Satisfaction is indeed in the eye of the beholder, and when the beholder can see how his or her job links to higher meaning and purpose, satisfaction soars.

To help people discover the "want to" reasons for adding value to the organization, leaders need to courageously link jobs to inspiring, even noble, goals such as serving society, taking pride, and being the best.

Revel in Excellence

One of the reasons that Cell 1 is often overlooked, even battered, is that leaders are so concerned with rewarding positive performance that they inadvertently undermine the intrinsic value of an action. The good news is that if you take time to recognize a certain performance, it sends the message that the performance is highly valued. It clarifies to others what you care about.

But there's more. You might also send a dangerous message. When you choose to reward something, you might unconsciously imply that the behavior needs to be rewarded, otherwise it might not continue. You might be saying that the activity is boring or even noxious. Why else would someone make such a big deal?

Now, if you want to send this message, you're okay. But what if you don't? In fact, what if the opposite is true? What if the activity you're rewarding is just about the most important thing you can ask people to do? And what if it *should* be intrinsically rewarding? Then you're in real trouble. If you keep telling people, "Congratulations, you just did the most important [read 'noxious'] job of the day," and that job is supposed to be naturally rewarding, you're praising and sending the wrong message at the same time. This can be a huge problem. It too has been studied in the laboratory.

Testing the Overjustification Hypothesis

The only reward of virtue is virtue.

RALPH WALDO EMERSON

In the early 1970s, Mark Lepper, a researcher at Stanford University, sought to measure the unintended effects of positive reinforcement.[3] He worried about unforeseen messages. More specifically, he wondered if rewarding people for doing something they already enjoyed doing would send the message that the task was not really so desirable, thus diminishing the intrinsic value of the activity itself. Lepper postulated that, after receiving a reward, a person might look at himself or herself much like an outsider and conclude *"I must be doing this not because it's enjoyable, but because I'm getting rewarded."* Dr. Lepper set out to measure this theory.

For several days, a research team carefully watched children who were attending the Bing Nursery School, conveniently housed just down the street from the psychology department. The researchers vigilantly watched the children to see which toys they each played with the most, as well as which snack they each preferred. The unsuspecting children were then rewarded with their preferred snack every time they played with their favorite toy. Then, after an intermediate period of no rewards, the researchers noted the toys the children played with during their free time.

The results supported his hypothesis. The children actually played *less* with their preferred toy after the reward period than children who hadn't received rewards. Perhaps, Lepper concluded, rewarding people for doing what they want can detract from the activity's intrinsic value.

Now, let's be clear. The effect Lepper found was quite subtle. It took repeated trials and unique circumstances to replicate the findings.

Why? Because the effect is subtle. Although people may (under certain circumstances) lessen their interest in an activity that has been rewarded, the opposite can also be found. A person may think, *"Wow, and I get paid too!"*

We cite Lepper's study because we find the question interesting, not because we believe it accounts for most behavior. However, to show the effect in action, consider two different strategies for teaching kids to read books.

We shouldn't teach great books; we should teach a love of reading.

B. F. SKINNER

Try It, You'll Like It. One of the authors once lived next to a couple who wanted their children to read more. To sweeten the pot, they paid their offspring five dollars for every book they finished. Their offspring have grown and left home by now, so the experiment is concluded. One boy left with a sound system that he bought with his reading money. He purchased no books, but his CD player is top of the line. His brothers are equally uninterested in reading for the fun of it. Obviously, the plan didn't yield the results the parents had hoped for. At no point did the intrinsic value of reading take over for the extrinsic reward. The subjects never learned to like books. If anything, they merely increased their appreciation for the utility of money. Neither parent read much, but they figured if they made reading attractive enough, their boys would eventually pick up the habit.

Contrast this strategy with a couple who did nothing more than love to read. Both parents would cuddle up with books in front of a crackling fire and lose themselves in the written word. Both shared stories from the books. Both were devoted to reading. They never thought to pay their offspring for reading. In fact, the thought of paying someone to read would have been offensive to them. Reading was its own reward. Their children, to nobody's surprise, are also avid readers.

The Catch-22 of Extrinsic Rewards

We continually face the problem Dr. Lepper studied.[4] It's never easy to know *when* and *what* to reward. You face a catch-22. If you really want someone to do something, reward it, right? But if you reward it, you unintentionally may be stating that the target activity is intrinsically undesirable. This is exactly what you *don't* want to communicate.

A Lesson from Japan. Paying people to do what should be naturally rewarding plays itself out in interesting ways at work. Consider what happened to a group of hourly American employees who were preparing to work a production line in a green-field (start-up) Japanese automobile assembly plant. One of the trainees asked the Japanese liaison if the new plant would start an employee-suggestion program.

In halting English, the foreign executive cheerfully explained that the company prided itself in recognizing exceptional performance. He promised that there would, indeed, be a suggestion program. The employee, encouraged by the news, asked for more details. "What can we expect?" he probed. The questioner, of course, was pushing to see if the program would be equal to the one offered by the American car companies. The Big Three paid up to $10,000 and a car for worthy and verifiable cost-saving suggestions.

The Japanese executive reached into his pocket and pulled out a pen. He held it up with obvious pride and explained that in special cases executives would give employees a fine writing instrument. It looked like it might cost about five dollars. After a brief pause, the employee explained that the local car companies gave out cars and thousands of dollars for qualified ideas. Perhaps, suggested the employee, the company would implement the same strategy in this new facility.

The Japanese executive was stunned. There's no better way of putting it. And it wasn't because of the amount of money involved. It was because of the message behind the amount of money. He couldn't understand why anyone would make such a big deal over suggestions. After all, suggestions were their own reward. They made up the very fabric of the Japanese company's *kaizen* (continuous improvement) program. Certainly, you wouldn't pay a bird to sing or a flower to turn its face to the sun. Why, then, would you pay someone for coming up with ideas for improving a product? It was only natural to do so.

The Japanese executive still doesn't understand why American car companies pay employees extra for doing what they're expected to do. Most of the American laborers still think that the company's suggestion program is cheap. Both are suffering from culture shock.

Embrace Old-Fashioned Values

Only the mediocre are always at their best.

JEAN GIRAUDOUX

Perhaps one of the biggest challenges current leaders face is the one offered by today's unending push to provide continuous external rewards for tasks that should be intrinsically rewarding. You can't throw a rock without hitting a salesperson who is hawking a glossy incentive program or an author who is singing the praises of prizes. Insightful leaders aren't taken in by the glamour of extrinsic rewards. They understand that it's okay to talk about intrinsically satisfying, yet old-fashioned, values. They share stories of previous successes and willingly get excited about "outdated" concepts such as pride, competition, and the feeling of being the best you can be.

For example, one of the authors once worked as a clerk in a grocery store. As part of his assignment, he toiled alongside 16-year-old boys whose job it was to take bottles that had been returned for the two-cent deposit and place them in their respective wooden boxes. After watching several young men complete the job as if it were torture, the clerk started turning the job into a competition. Who could get done the fastest? He didn't do this as a ploy, but because it was what he did personally to make the job more enjoyable.

The clerk had learned from his parents that there is joy in a job well done. He liked to find quicker and better ways to do a mundane task. This way, the task, no matter how boring, always allowed him an intellectual challenge—how could he do it better and more efficiently? He learned that no task, no matter how mundane or repetitive, can ever be separated from what is a true characteristic of any job: It can always be done better, faster, or smarter. Although the deposit boys had historically quit about every six weeks, within months, several of these young men had been promoted to clerk, arriving each morning with a spring in their step.

Years later we learned that these same old-fashioned values helped employees go through tough changes. We found that the best way to inspire employees to switch to lean, mean, customer-driven teams was not to talk about past failures or future threats, but instead to talk about excellence, pride, serving customers, and being part of the best team. When employees were told to change their behaviors or lose their jobs, they didn't believe the threat and were generally insulted. On the other hand, when they were asked to be the best, to find ways to surprise and delight customers, and to continuously find ways to work smarter, they rose to the challenge.

> One of the great tragedies of today's organizations is that many are being led by leaders who are ashamed to talk about the intrinsic satisfaction one experiences in pride of workmanship, striving to be the best, and turning every job into a never-ending quest to provide greater value.

Mitigate Extrinsic Rewards

Occasionally, in spite of your own commitment to enhancing intrinsic satisfaction, you may find yourself in a situation where extrinsic rewards are a big part of the culture. For instance, you may be asked to work with a formal reward system that bestows prizes or expensive awards for behaviors that should inherently satisfy. When this happens, attend to the action as well as the reward. The reward wouldn't have been given if the action wasn't important in the first place, right? Unfortunately, if the reward is obtrusive enough, it can overshadow the action or possibly suggest that it's noxious.

Consider how an admired colleague handles a situation the school system hands him regularly.

But Did You Learn Anything? One day, as one of the authors worked on a research project at the home of Dr. Gene Dalton, Gene's oldest daughter bubbled into her father's study. She eagerly announced that she had received her junior-high report card. Her grades were impressive, certainly worth celebrating. However, instead of applauding the grades, her father asked about each class. He wanted to know if it was exciting and if she was enjoying the topic. He shared with her his enthusiasm for the classes, telling an anecdote or two about his memories of similar coursework. His joy of learning was evident, his message clear: School is for learning, and learning is its own reward.

For Gene, grades were a scorecard, but not the important one.

As Gene's enthusiastic daughter exited, he explained that he didn't want his children to get caught up in the quest for grades. It wasn't the quest that bothered him (although it *was* annoying), it was the fact that grades might overshadow the joy of learning, and *that* had him disturbed. He, along with Mark Lepper and the Japanese executive, worried about rewarding what should be intrinsically satisfying. To avoid the trap, he focused on the action he cared about (learning). He didn't dwell on the extrinsic reward (grades) that someone else had imposed on him and his family.

Skilled individuals realize that formal, "big-deal" rewards can overshadow intrinsically satisfying activities. Therefore, they turn a spotlight on the activities and downplay the rewards. They understand that Cell 1 can be destroyed as Cells 3 and 5 are allowed to dominate. They still appreciate and use both social and organizational means of support, but they couple these two extrinsic forces with compelling intrinsic elements in order to create a whole *and balanced* motivational package.

Oh yes, extrinsic rewards can be used, and used well. We'll dive deep into the effective use of praise and other subtle forms of reward in chapter 12. For now, we'll try to keep in mind that extrinsic rewards, poorly used, can undermine the intrinsic satisfaction inherent in most jobs.

SOME PRACTICAL ADVICE FROM THIS CHAPTER

Over the past few pages, we've looked at steps leaders can take to ensure that the intrinsic satisfaction (Cell 1) associated with various jobs and task assignments is enhanced rather than destroyed. To do so, we've recommended five strategies.

- *Allow for choices.* When individuals are allowed choices, they're more likely to mold an activity to their own liking. When expanding the number of choices offered to employees, set expectations up front. If you don't, employees can mistakenly assume they will no longer be told to do anything and can pick and choose what they do. Teach the difference between commands, consensus, consultation, and individual choice. By clarifying the four types of decisions and how they relate to stakeholder demands, employees can be increasingly involved in more choices—without being disappointed when they're not permitted to choose *what* to do but only *how* to do it. If necessary, hold a class with your leadership team to cover the ins and outs of decision making and choices. Have them cascade the training throughout the organization.
- *Strive for job enrichment.* Throw out the traditional notion of fixed boxes. Replace it with the idea of combining a variety of interesting and challenging activities into a set of tasks that help serve stakeholder demands. Involve employees in jointly hammering out how jobs are fashioned.
- *Encourage leveling.* Although intrinsic satisfaction with a specific task may not be easily changed, the net value associated with a job can be improved by combining undesirable tasks with desirable ones. Current efforts to maximize job flexibility have gone a long way to ensure that both desirable and noxious tasks are shared by all team members. In so doing, they have turned lousy assignments into reasonable jobs. Level your jobs.
- *Link to higher meaning and purpose.* Of all the methods focusing on intrinsic satisfaction, perhaps the most overlooked

are the steps a leader can take to link routine jobs to outcomes that have higher meaning and purpose. As leaders began to be replaced by managers throughout the 1960s and 1970s, the concept of leadership slowly atrophied, while the belief in sharing noble purposes was shot through the head. Today, organizations cry out for leaders (from corporate presidents to frontline supervisors) who are willing to share inspiring visions and talk about noble goals and lofty purposes. In so doing, intrinsic satisfaction is allowed to be an important part of any job. Tasks turn into jobs, jobs transform into careers, and careers blossom into immensely rewarding lives. Gut check: Do you talk about greater purposes, or has that part of your job gone the way of polyester jumpsuits?

- ***Allow people to revel in their intrinsic satisfaction.*** Finally, many intrinsically satisfying tasks are dealt a serious blow as they wither beneath the shadow of extrinsic rewards. Formal reward systems, although well intended, often have devastatingly destructive side effects. Tasks that are satisfying in and of themselves are inadvertently labeled as dissatisfying and as requiring extra incentives. Allow employees to revel in the afterglow of success for its own sake. Nurture intrinsic satisfaction.

CHAPTER 8

Building Individual Ability

Knowing what you can not *do is more important than knowing what you can do.*

LUCILLE BALL

In the last chapter we looked at the question of intrinsic motivation. We'll now turn to Cell 2, the domain of individual ability. Surprisingly, a great deal of what leaders want to see happen isn't taking place because employees simply don't know how to do what's required of them. For example, hospital employees may not answer ringing phones as they pass through other departments because they don't want to look like yammering fools when asked simple questions they can't answer. In an insurance company, underwriters may not cross-sell into other products because they

	Motivation	Ability
Individual	1	**2**
Social	3	4
Organizational	5	6

don't know much about them. In a software development group, people may not raise concerns about others' competence because they don't know how to do it without causing more problems than they would solve.

In this chapter we'll talk a bit about why Cell 2 problems are often invisible. We'll also talk about what leaders must do to resolve Cell 2 barriers. We won't spend much time pointing out the obvious solutions to technical competence deficits. Our focus instead will be on subtle interpersonal behaviors and how to turn Cell 2 from an invisible barrier into a potent tool for moving toward vitality.

Can I Ride a Horse?!

Cell 2 problems surface when you ask the question, "If other people supply you with the necessary resources, can you do your part of the job?" That is, Cell 2 problems surface if people give you a straight answer. Unfortunately, they often don't. Allow us another story.

A group of actors sat around sharing horror stories of downright dangerous stunts they'd been asked to perform in the past. Eddie Carroll (the voice of Disney's Jiminy Cricket) told of a horrendous job he'd once had when shooting what he thought was going to be a simple beer commercial. The part he tried out for required him to sit in a bar and talk about beer. He could do that! At the end of the audition, the producer asked him if he could ride a horse. "Can I ride a horse?!" he exclaimed.

When Eddie received notice that he had won the part, his initial excitement was dampened by the haunting question of his equestrian skills. You see, he wasn't exactly a horseman—unless you count carousels, but who counts pink plastic palominos? Notwithstanding his lingering suspicions, he eagerly showed up at the studio at the appointed time to shoot his part. Sure enough, as the script indicated, he merely sat around and talked about beer. Getting paid for the job seemed almost criminal. Just when he thought he was home free, Eddie was told to show up the next day at a large barn to shoot the "final scene." Uh-oh.

Early the next morning, Eddie drove up to a bucolic ranch located just outside Los Angeles. One glance around the place made him realize that he was facing one of those good news/bad news situations. The good news was that he didn't have to ride a horse after all. There were no horses at this ranch, just Brahman bulls. You can guess the bad news. In the final scene of the TV commercial, Eddie was supposed to sit, legs splayed, on top of a Brahman bull named "Killer" and ride off into the sunset. The scenario was the writer's idea of a snappy ending. Eddie had a different opinion.

At first, Eddie couldn't even stay on top of what he described as a "gyrating, muscled platform." To solve the problem of Eddie's inconveniently plummeting to the ground and ruining the scene, an innovative wrangler cinched a rope around the animal's ample girth and then painted it black so it wouldn't be picked up by the camera. By clutching the rope, spreading his legs at a near-right angle, and holding on for dear life, Eddie helped the production team finally get the shot in the can. "Speaking of *cans*," Eddie finished the story, "I wasn't able to walk comfortably for days." In retrospect, he was sorry he'd uttered those fateful words, "Can I ride a horse?!"

I Don't Know

Fifty-one percent of being smart is knowing what you are dumb about.
ANN LANDERS

When faced with questions of competency, almost everyone gives the same answer. They're competent, what else? For instance, if you want a job, you say you can do what's required: "Can I ride a horse?!" And after you have a job, after you've been taking money home for a couple of pay periods, you can scarcely admit that you don't know how to do what's required. That would be like confessing to stealing. In some organizations, particularly heavy manufacturing, employees are so unwilling to admit to a skill deficiency that many have successfully hidden the fact that they're illiterate—for decades. Given that a great number of safety features and important warnings are offered only in print, you're left wondering how people survive.

As a leader, it's important to know just how pervasive and sticky this problem is. You can scarcely expect to be an effective change agent, completing accurate diagnoses, if you mistakenly assume that you're going to be able to surface personal ability (Cell 2) problems with a well-placed question or two. To extract honest answers about employees' skill levels and knowledge base, you have to undo years of presocialization that usually starts just after weaning and receives a powerful boost when a child enters the loving care of the school system.

Unlike some cultures that teach children the dignity and sheer practicality of being able to say "I don't know" (opening the door to honest inquiry), U.S. schools prefer a different approach. By the second day of class, every American child understands the rule. Knowing is good. Not knowing is bad. Eventually, after years of garnering kudos by knowing the right answers, fighting for attention by giving the correct response, and struggling for grades by repeating back the acceptable solution, anyone with an IQ greater than an art-gum eraser knows that saying "I don't know" is a bad thing. A very bad thing.

This problem rarely gets better with time. For example, it usually takes consultants about two to three months of rather close work with an executive team before a team member pulls the outsider into an isolated alcove and whispers, "You know that training you're designing on managing meetings for the workforce? It wouldn't be a bad idea to pass the leadership team through it as well—and not just to show our support. I'm not sure we're very good at running meetings either." The nervous executive then darts his eyes around to see if anyone has caught him admitting to imperfection.

The Cost of Perfection

Striving for perfection is rejuvenating. It gives us purpose and warms our thoughts as we doze off each night. Not being able to say that we have reached perfection, on the other hand, really busts our chops.

The cost of having to know everything extends beyond the inconvenience of preventing leaders from diagnosing Cell 2 problems. The real dollar expenses—or the "insecurity costs"—run into the billions. For example, in one exceptionally insecure company one of the authors worked with, as leaders prepared for monthly cost meetings, they asked their staffs to spend hundreds of hours preparing tomes jammed full of facts and figures—just in case a top-level boss asked an obscure question. Why? Because the unspoken rule is: You have to know everything.

During one of these tense monthly meetings, when a midlevel manager was being grilled about a ridiculous detail that no one would ever know, he uttered words that every executive should hear. As every eye took in his countenance, he slowly rose to a standing position and delivered the following soliloquy.

"You may find this shocking, but not only do I not know the answer to that question, I'm surprised that you would think I *should* know. In fact, I'd be nervous if a person in my position actually worried about such drivel. You know, this fear of not knowing everything has gotten out of hand. To give you an idea of how severe the problem is, last month I was stopped in the hallway and lectured by a salaried employee who told me that by his calculations we had spent $75,000 creating a book of meaningless data in case one of you asked a question we might not be able to answer. We never opened the book. That $75,000 expenditure, as we all know, had to be passed on to a customer base that is growing increasingly price sensitive. This same person pointed out that not two weeks before he and a rather large staff completed the numeric masterpiece, we had denied him reimbursement on a $25 book he had purchased to update his skills. We refused him the money on the grounds that we needed to keep our costs in line. All of which leads to a burning question. How much longer will we be forced to act like a bunch of visionless cretins who are penny wise and pound foolish? I'll tell you. I know exactly how long. As long as it remains career limiting in this company to say, 'I don't know.' Well, let me break with tradition. Not only do I *not* know the answer to your question, I don't think I *should* know."

Okay, so he didn't give this persuasive speech. He thought about it for months. He mused about it in the shower. He practiced the words as he dropped off to sleep at night. And then one day, when he was grilled one more time for a piece of minutia that would put a library scientist into a coma, he ran down to the human resources manager's office and recited his speech. He spoke the words as if they were a mantra, even a sacred prayer.

We share his passion. The cost of not being willing to say "I don't know" is sapping organizations of their precious Cultural Vitality and resulting in an Outcome Vitality that's moving many organizations precariously close to death. This one weakness costs billions of dollars in "insecurity costs" every year, and, returning to our original point, makes a Cell 2 diagnosis just that much more difficult to complete.

I Didn't Know I Don't Know

Ignorance is bliss. That's why ignorant people are so happy. They're too ignorant to realize they're ignorant.

STANLEY MYRON HANDELMAN

People don't often admit to skill deficiencies for another reason. Sometimes employees are unaware that they're deficient, particularly when leaders are calling for change by asking for a new and often ambiguous set of behaviors. For example, a group of executives we worked with was genuinely interested in empowering the workforce. At least, they were excited about the possibilities of achieving greater success through allowing those closest to customers to make more choices. Intellectually and emotionally they bought into the concept.

However, from a pragmatic point of view, most didn't have a clue what the change required of them. If you were to ask them if they had the skills they needed to involve others, they would have been insulted. In their minds, the skill of employee involvement consisted of asking, "What do you think?" and forming a few focus groups. Who couldn't do this? Few of the leaders had thought through the behavioral implications of what they were proposing. Without going into the skills required in "empowering others," suffice it to say that there are virtually dozens of necessary actions, and not many of them are easily performed. In fact, a great deal of what is done to make employee-involvement programs work is a product of "style." And when it comes to interpersonal style, the have-nots don't acquire it very easily.

Actually, when you come right down to it, many of the problems leaders experience as they attempt to strengthen their Cultural Vitality relate to their inability to articulate the behavioral parts of their dream. Leaders know exactly what they want—happy stakeholders. They have a fairly good idea of what it takes to keep them satisfied and possess a vague idea of what employees are supposed to do, but they're almost blind to the requisite daily behaviors. Ironically, few leaders understand or believe this.

If you want to test this thesis, ask a leader who is supporting a team approach to describe half a dozen "team behaviors." Remember, our definition of a behavior is a bundle of actions that can be understood and *replicated*. Most leaders can give a fairly lengthy list of selfish behaviors (those they've seen) but do a miserable job of describing the flip side. They'll talk about desired outcomes until the next popular leadership movement comes on the scene, but typically they can't come up with a single positive behavior—nothing that, upon hearing, a person could go out and do. It is little wonder that people are generally unaware of their own skill deficiencies. If they don't know what's expected, how can they be held accountable for knowing if they have what it takes to get there? Given the ambiguity, they respond, "Of course I can do what's needed." To suggest otherwise is practically unpatriotic.

How Can a Leader Surface Cell 2 Problems?

To help create a climate where Cell 2 problems can be brought into the open and resolved, leaders must (1) clarify exactly what people need to do, (2) make it safe for others to say "I don't know," and (3) willingly admit that they themselves aren't omniscient.

Clarify What's Required

People don't know that they can't do what you're asking of them if they don't know *exactly* what you have in mind. As you identify your dream, explain precisely what skills are needed. Describe both your desired outcomes and the actions necessary to achieve them. For example, a group of bank tellers was asked if they would be comfortable being "empowered." This meant they would be allowed to take over some of the tasks the supervisor traditionally performed. The desired outcome was obvious—by sharing some of the responsibilities, the tellers could enrich their own jobs as well as help reduce costs. Everyone eagerly agreed. However, when it was pointed out that this meant they would have to talk to each other about interpersonal problems they were experiencing—that is, talk face to face with people they weren't getting along with—they quickly suggested that maybe they didn't want to be empowered after all. They couldn't envision themselves confronting a peer without causing a brouhaha—not, at least, without some kind of assistance.

After hearing about a targeted action, people should know exactly what's required of them. If people are given only a vague description of what's demanded, most assume that they'll be able to do whatever is required. When leaders make glowing promises of results and offer only weak descriptions of what will be demanded, employees don't know that they need assistance until they're engulfed in problems, and then it's often too late, or at least far more expensive to rectify.

Make It Safe

When you're unable to admit that you have a Cell 2 problem, half of the solution is in knowing the problem. As you conduct culture assessments and administer questionnaires, don't ask people straight out if they have the skills they need. Instead, watch for evidence of frustration, working hard but not getting done what's needed, and simple failure. When formulating questions, make it safe to say "I don't know." For example, if you ask, "Do you have the skills necessary to do your job?" people usually will come back with a resounding "Yes!"

If, on the other hand, you use a little finesse by taking responsibility for your part of the problem, you get a more honest answer. Ask, "To what extent is the organization providing you with the training you need to keep up with changing job demands?" This allows people to say they need help in a way that's politically safe. You've pointed out that the world is changing, meaning it's only natural that everyone needs more training. In addition, you've suggested that if employees aren't getting it, it's not their fault, it's the organization's. You've made it okay for people to say "I need help."

Model the Behavior

I don't get it.

TOM HANKS (AS THE CHARACTER JOSH IN THE MOVIE *BIG*) AS HE WATCHES
A DEMONSTRATION WHERE A TOY ROBOT TURNS INTO A BUILDING

It's been refreshing over the past few years to watch leaders free themselves of the burden of perfection. As they begin to realize that it's all right to say "I don't get it," and as they become increasingly comfortable taking part in classes or even personal coaching, not only do they remove a tremendous burden from their shoulders, they make it safe for others to do the same.

Lyle's Learning Environment. One of the authors was particularly impressed with Lyle, a senior executive who was striving to create a "learning environment." When given the opportunity to receive coaching in how to conduct a plantwide meeting, Lyle jumped at the chance. As the human resources specialist prepared to bring in a renowned speech coach, thinking that she would start with a generic presentation, Lyle volunteered to receive one-on-one coaching—in front of his entire team of direct reports. From that day on, other leaders asked for similar help.

Several weeks later, Lyle and his team met with his boss and a group of other senior executives in a rather tense quality meeting. When one of the senior managers eventually asked a question that bordered on minutia, Lyle responded with, "I don't know. I know who can get the information, but I certainly don't keep track of it." He didn't act indignant or take shots at the person asking the question; however, he did let his bosses and his own team members know that he felt okay about not having his finger on every little detail.

Within a few weeks at the recommendation of the marketing director, Lyle's operating committee began each meeting with, "What do we have to get better at?" The team members automatically assumed that the turbulent environment they were facing was constantly serving up new demands that required new actions and, possibly, new skills. They looked upon the need to change as a growth opportunity and not as a threat to their self-worth. No longer did they believe that a lack of omniscience was grounds for dismissal. With time, Lyle transformed what had started as an "uptight, cover your tracks, never stick your neck out" culture into a healthy learning environment where Cell 2 problems were readily surfaced and fixed.

ONCE YOU KNOW

To be happy is to be able to become aware of oneself without fright.
WALTER BENJAMIN

Let's assume that you've taken pains to create an atmosphere that allows Cell 2 problems to come out in the open. People are aware of and talk about their training needs. Now it's time to take action. People need to be trained, taught, and coached. What's a leader's role?

Greater than many imagine.

It's Not My Job

Many leaders assume that training needs should be handled by the training department. In large part that's true. Leaders certainly wouldn't be expected to tackle any legal or medical problems that might arise. They'd count on the expertise of their lawyers and medical staff. Nobody's arguing that when an employee has a stroke at work, bosses should roll up their sleeves, grab a letter opener, and perform brain surgery. The same is true with training demands. Human resources professionals need to be allowed to work their profession. However, there is an important difference. When it comes to training how to be a leader, or to discussing key elements of the organization's vision, leaders must take an active role in both the leadership and delivery of the training.

Frankly, trainers, no matter how good their presentation skills, don't have the impact of a leader—at least when it comes to leadership topics. It's an issue of credibility and support. Leaders are seen as the people who (1) know what it really takes to work out there on the floor and (2) are going to hold the trainees accountable for doing what's being taught. After the last word is pronounced by the trainer and everyone hustles back to work, it's the leaders who will either reward or punish those who actually try to implement what has been taught.

To study the impact of who conducts leadership training classes, researchers examined training delivered by (1) a leader, (2) a highly skilled professional trainer, and (3) a leader who had once rotated through a training job. When the researchers looked at traditional measures of satisfaction, the professional trainer did the best of the three. His abilities to explain, keep the energy level high, and entertain were rated tops. In fact, the course itself received the highest rating when he taught it. It also was judged most useful and practical.

However, when the researchers measured how much those in the class changed as a result of the training (as judged by their direct reports), the leader who had once worked as a trainer was the most successful. He was followed by the leader who wasn't exactly a strong trainer. The trainer, the fellow with the high training marks, had the least effect on actual behavior on the floor. Once the training was over, he stayed behind while everyone else returned to work. The two leader-trainers walked out with their trainees and direct reports, modeled the desired actions, and reminded people of the need and opportunity to use the new skills. With leaders at the helm, the training stuck. We may love the content of the training for the trainer's sake, but we do what's asked of us out there on the floor for the boss's sake.

Great. Another assignment.

REASONABLE EXPECTATIONS

Disappointment is a sort of bankruptcy—the bankruptcy of a soul that expends too much in hope and expectation.

ERIC HOFFER

At this point many leaders get nervous about all the jobs they're being given. "You want us to be visionaries, philosophers, and now *this?* You expect too much. We hire trainers and human resources specialists to conduct our training. Leave us alone to fight the battles between competing stakeholders. It's enough to keep two people busy for a lifetime."

No matter how unpopular the notion, leaders can't strip themselves of their responsibility to teach, coach, and train. When it comes to their vision in general and to leadership in specific, no one is better suited to the task. The only question is, "How can leaders take on the job without crushing themselves with one more assignment?" To respond to the never-ending time crunch, we'll suggest that leaders (1) teach in real time, (2) train in short bursts, and (3) coach to solve problems.

Teach in Real Time

Teaching is not a lost art, but the regard for it is a lost tradition.
JACQUES BARZUN

Any parent knows that teaching children isn't best done from a podium. It happens during critical "teaching moments." Kids aren't nearly as interested in hearing about the life cycle of a butterfly at the dinner table as they are when they stumble across a cocoon during a picnic. Savvy parents leap on teaching moments. When a child's curiosity is afire over how a squiggly caterpillar can turn into a delicate moth, it's time to talk about metamorphosis rather than discuss why tennis shoes need to be kept clean. Savvy teachers build on each student's interests rather than blindly follow a textbook.

Savvy leaders make good use of the same principle. Rather than give long lectures or look for special forums, the leader-as-teacher leaps on teaching moments, builds on employee interests, and sneaks lessons into the moment-to-moment situations found in the fabric of daily life.

Did You See What I Did There?

Those of you who saw the movie *Mr. Saturday Night* with Billy Crystal will remember his favorite line. Throughout this story of an aging comedian and his brother, every time Billy sets his sibling up to think one thing and then pulls out the rug in a comedic tug, he stops and talks about what happened. "Did you see what I did there?"

Effective leaders follow Billy Crystal's example. After important teaching moments they ask, "What just happened there?" or even "Did you see what I just did?"—particularly if whatever they're talking about didn't go well. Effective leaders pounce on the chance to say something every time an employee is caught between competing stakeholder demands. They leap at the opportunity to talk about what just happened when someone unwittingly thumbs his nose at the organization's mission. They go to great pains to teach a mini-lesson every time a brave employee steps away from the pack and tries an action that supports the new dream.

For example, an exceptionally adept leader did a remarkable job of doing "real-time" teaching after conducting a meeting where he and his direct reports made long-needed progress on a staff-reduction plan. The plan was nine months late and was putting budgets at risk. After the plan was clear, the talented leader stopped and asked, "Now, let's talk about how we got here. What kept us from completing the plan effectively, and what did we eventually do to succeed? Most importantly, was there anything I did that either helped or hindered the process?" A rich conversation followed. The nonpunishing way he raised the question made it a learning dialogue rather than a witch hunt. He could have waited to talk about the issues at another time, but they probably would never have surfaced.

To be able to teach in "real time," effective teachers continually pull themselves out of the heat of the moment and switch from talking about the subject at hand to analyzing what happened and why. It's a gift. Few people have the capacity to yank themselves out of daily concerns and step back to look at what's going on. Teachers have to do this to survive. Effective leaders leap on teaching moments by stopping the overwhelming momentum of daily problems and talking about what just happened. They talk process, strike when interest is high, give the lessons in "real time," and then move on.

Train in Short Bursts

Training is everything. The peach was once a bitter almond; cauliflower is nothing but cabbage with a college education.

MARK TWAIN

There are times when leaders need to do more than informally teach. They must also help out with routine training. Not everything can be taught in "real time," nor can leaders reach a wide audience by teaching only on the job. Consequently, training specialists design instructional modules that dive deep into tough topics that can be delivered to a wide audience. When these training topics touch on the organization's mission or delve into the ins and outs of leadership, leaders must take part.

Perhaps the most palatable way to participate in this type of training is to do so in short bursts. Rather than cotrain an entire session, take part in the kickoff. Start the session by explaining that you've already gone through the training, you support the principles, and you're trying your best to implement them. Just as a reality check, suggest that you aren't perfect yet, but you're not using this as an excuse for not trying to get better. You too are a student and hope they'll take the topic as seriously as you do. Then exit gracefully.

In effective training sessions, usually near the end, the agenda shifts from theory to practice. What are participants going to do to transfer the concepts from the training room to the work setting? Here's a time when it's helpful for leaders to step back into the room. They can lead a discussion of "next steps." When leaders help participants brainstorm action plans, they're letting everyone know that they expect something to happen. They're also in a position to help link the action plans to the normal work cycle. The new actions don't have to be taken out of everyone's hide if the leader is there to help develop realistic goals and link them to the routine job cycle.

By restricting their involvement to the kickoff and final action planning, leaders are able to maintain an important presence without having to spend huge chunks of time. They get to train without having to be "trainers."

Coach to Solve Problems

Where no counsel is, the people fall; but in the multitude of counsellors there is safety.

PROVERBS 11:14

The easiest way for leaders to personally help out with Cell 2 challenges is to turn problems into coaching opportunities. Since problems are always with us, if leaders can solve them by coaching others, not only are challenges met, but skill deficiencies are eliminated at the same time.

Coaching differs from teaching in that it's aimed at a specific individual or behavior. It's a subset of teaching. Teaching can be defined as the sharing of mental maps—explaining behavior-outcome beliefs and sharing values. Coaching is more closely linked to cybernetics. It's the set of activities that provides individuals feedback about their current behavior coupled with advice on what it'll take to achieve different outcomes. It's one of the most important services a leader can provide to a direct report. Unfortunately, most leaders don't take the time to provide much coaching, and when they do, they do a poor job. Here's why.

The Ostracized Coach

Leaders frequently find themselves in an awkward situation. They have access only to their direct reports' results. Computers dutifully spit out summaries of what outcomes are being achieved. Frightened by the numbers, leaders call in their direct reports and remind them of little more than the blatantly obvious. Rather than provide help, leaders simply point out from their positions of power what their direct reports already know: The results are unsatisfactory.

Leaders typically end up in this role of "portrayer of the painfully obvious" because they're cut off from critical data. Their position is similar to that of a basketball coach who can see only the scoreboard. In the halftime discussion, she is limited to making banal comments such as, "You're going to have to find a way to score more points." Without seeing exactly what the players are doing, the coach can't give behaviorally specific advice. Without observations, the coach transforms from coach to cheerleader, stuck in a role of giving trite motivational speeches. She also might transform from coach to critic, pithily and acerbically pointing out the need for better results.

Of course, coaches aren't usually in a position where all they can see is the scoreboard, but leaders are. They're given a constant stream of output data (the "scoreboard"), but their jobs rarely place them in a position to watch the person at work. Consequently, they have to guess what people are actually doing. This can be tough.

Surrogate Observation — The Verbal Reconstruction

When most leaders learn about poor results, they don't immediately lapse into lectures or threatening attacks. They prefer the more humane and scientific approach of filling in the missing observations by asking a series of questions—ones that help diagnose where the person has gone wrong. In essence, they ask their direct reports to paint a picture or verbally reconstruct what happened so they can then jointly discover where the problems are arising. By reconstructing the situation, the direct report provides the leader with valuable information about the situation that can then be used to give feedback. Done well, the two can jointly come up with a new plan, and the leader can offer suggestions or advice. Of course, to pull this off, the questions and following discussions must be done in the spirit of dialogue. Both parties must have equal right to share their point of view and offer their best thinking. Done poorly, the questioning becomes an inquisition.

Producing a verbal reconstruction helps others see how they might have *thought* about the problem differently, but it usually does little to provide behavioral feedback. Most postmortem discussions focus on the details of the decision-making process. This is particularly true of leaders of hourly employees who rely on after-the-fact analyses to help their direct reports learn better ways to think about solving problems. Did you do A? Did you look at B? Did you notice if C was E-ing? Lead-

ers of employees who work on metal parts and other tangible products
become quite skilled at teasing out detailed after-the-fact pictures and
then playing them back in a way that allows for a slow-motion, play-
by-play analysis that helps their direct reports think about what they'll
do the next time they face a similar problem.

The Coach's Coach

Unfortunately, as leaders are promoted to be leaders of leaders, reviewing
how their direct reports thought about a particular problem often provides
insufficient feedback. It's fascinating to watch leaders who are tremen-
dously good at teasing out how to think about problems with processes and
parts trying to apply the same techniques with their direct reports who are
working with people rather than metal objects. Their entire discussion
focuses on the content of the problem. Did you do A? Did you look for B?
Etc.

A coach's coach has to do more than help others think about the mental
steps involved in the problem-solving process. A coach's coach has to know
exactly how the other person is treating his or her direct reports in order to
provide helpful feedback. The emphasis of these problem-solving discussions must shift from the *what* of the conversation to the *how*. For example,
consider the following problem where a leader has a view only of the
scoreboard.

May the Force Be with You

A CEO lamented that she was receiving a barrage of anonymous notes
about her CFO. Most of the notes likened the CFO to Darth Vader, concluding that he "did not share the CEO's values." Some recommended a
public flogging; most wanted him canned as a testament to the CEO's sincerity in supporting the new culture.

Here was a culture-defining moment. Making a sacrificial lamb of
the CFO would gain some symbolic benefit, but the CEO didn't believe
the feedback—at least not the conclusions. She had seen too many examples of the CFO's defending investments in people, community, and
other stakeholders to believe that this was a person with an evil heart.
Clearly he was intense, even driven. When critical issues were at risk,
he would talk more than he listened. The CEO decided to try coaching.

The first conversation was more frustrating than fruitful. The CFO
expressed a willingness to receive feedback. But when the CEO coached
him to be "more respectful" and "a better team player," the CFO drew

a blank. He needed examples. He needed behaviors. None of the poison-pen letters shed any more light on the matter. The CEO agreed to begin observing the CFO in meetings and give more direct and regular feedback. She also agreed that if people approached her in the future with criticisms about the CFO, she would encourage them to, at least, specify behaviors that were a concern and, at most, sit down with the CFO and coach him directly. There were few takers.

After a few weeks of observing the CFO in action, she'd gathered a fascinating list of behaviors and was able to tell the CFO the following:

When people disagree, you avert your eyes and begin tapping your pencil. When someone is taking a long time to make a point, you begin rocking back and forth in your chair. You make jokes that others can't make back—jokes about their job security and future opportunities in the company. You make joking comments about others' jobs that they take as demeaning and derogatory (bean-counters, gearheads, grease monkeys, etc.). When you make strong points, you aim your finger at people and lean forward. When others are talking, you shake your head at times and cut them off before they finish.

We are all blind to behaviors that cause others to conclude we're "evil incarnate." All of us do things that lead others to resent us, avoid our company, and plot our demise—things that we don't intend in the way others are taking them and that don't serve our purposes well.

Real-time coaching (like that given by the insightful CEO) is best done by leaders who have a view of the game and the behavior, not just the scoreboard.

The Up-Front Contract

Wise leaders take pains to ensure they have opportunities to watch direct reports in action. Consider what it was like when one of the authors took his first job as an associate professor at a university. His boss approached him the first day at work and talked about how it was the department head's job to help the newly appointed faculty member succeed. He would do everything in his power to bring together whatever resources and support were necessary to create an environment that would yield earthshaking results—meaning publishing an article or two and receiving teaching reviews of 5.5 or more on a 7-point scale.

Of course, to provide the necessary support, the department chair needed to provide helpful feedback along the way. If the new faculty member didn't mind, he'd be sitting in on his class occasionally. After all, how else could he provide useful feedback? Oh yes, and he'd interview graduate students who were working for him to see how that relationship was developing. Naturally, he'd also need to take part on at least one of the research teams the novice professor would be leading in order to watch that part of the work as well.

In short, the leader contracted up front to do more than stare at the scoreboard. He didn't want to simply look at teaching evaluations filled out by students. ("On a scale of 1 to 7 you received a 3.7 on 'knowledge of the subject.' Fix it.") He was similarly unwilling to hear graduate-student rumblings in the hallways and pass on the rumors. He understood that if he was going to be of any help at all, he would need to make personal observations and then provide behaviorally specific feedback.

If style were an important ingredient of the young faculty member's success in the classroom and on research teams, it was doubly so for the department chair. To provide delicate feedback, the department chair had to be skilled. He was. He knew what it took to create a helpful learning environment rather than one of mistrust. He succeeded because he had great respect for the recently hired faculty member, and this respect permeated the conversation. The young professor left feeling incredibly supported *and* eager to do his best.

Since most leaders of leaders or of skilled professionals don't know how to hold such discussions with direct reports, they don't. They don't contract to make observations, they don't make observations, and they end up as scoreboard watchers who do little more than provide an occasional reminder of the painfully obvious. They end up providing no feedback at all or stooping to such hollow expressions as "straighten out your relationships." As a last resort, many hire consultants or ask their human resources staffers to take certain people aside and "fix their interpersonal skills."

Effective leaders break this blind, insulting cycle by contracting to coach. They suggest that it's a leader's job to do whatever it takes to make the person successful and contract up front for opportunities to watch the person at work. They watch their direct reports in meetings and when they're working one on one with staff members, solving problems, and working through differences between competing stakeholders—and then provide helpful feedback.

Know How to Give Feedback

Once effective leaders make the effort to watch their direct reports on the job, they give them timely, helpful feedback. To do so, they establish a positive tone, leave room for self-discovery, and separate observations from conclusions.

Establish a Positive Tone

You give me powders, pills, baths, injections, and enemas—when all I need is love.

WILLIAM HOLDEN IN THE BRIDGE ON THE RIVER KWAI

All feedback must be given within an atmosphere of mutual respect. This isn't as hard as it might sound, providing that you possess one characteristic. You must admire the person with whom you're talking. When you allow yourself to focus on the person's many strengths, a feedback discussion can actually be enjoyable. Once you've opened yourself up to a person's *strengths*, you'll see that most, if not all, of his or her *problems* are natural extensions of his or her abilities and skills.

For example, consider Robert, a highly energetic, almost frenetic plant manager a colleague worked with a few years back. His direct reports were quite fond of him, but were upset because he tended to "dominate every meeting he was in." As our colleague got to know Robert, it was clear he took so much airtime in meetings, not because he was the big boss, but because his mind ran at a million miles an hour, and he could hardly spout his ideas fast enough. Criticizing Robert for dominating the meeting wouldn't have been nearly as helpful as opening the discussion with a description of one of his positive attributes— his ability to come up with and share lots of ideas—which is exactly what our colleague did. From there he was able to make the transition to how those special skills were leading to problems.

Our goal is not to perfume the pig. When you build from a strength, you're not trying to cover up a raging weakness. Instead, you're attempting to help the other person see how a legitimate strength can turn into a problem when not carefully monitored. For example, creative people can drive their colleagues nuts with their spontaneity and lack of structure. On the other hand, extremely well-organized people can drive their friends to distraction should they come across as robots who can't ever shoot from the hip. Here's where feedback can be helpful.

But feedback isn't feedback isn't feedback. Over the past couple of decades, the authors have been asked to take a person aside and deliver bad news. People allow problems to build up for years, and then an outside consultant is asked to help fix whatever is wrong. This doesn't work. You can't go into a feedback discussion with the idea that you're there to help "fix" the other person. You can't see people as wrong and bad and yourself as the person who has been sent to set them straight. First of all, they aren't wrong and bad. They aren't even wrong. They're just pushing an asset a bit too far, and your job is to help them see when they should pull back. Second, if you continually focus on problems, the people you work with will begin to twitch every time they see you walk in the room. "Oh boy, here comes my favorite boss with another patiently delivered, carefully thought-through emotional enema."

Skillful coaches spend enough time with the people they're working with to be able to see their many strengths. By doing so, they're in a position to give helpful feedback rather than simply dump bad news. As long as coaches can see how the problems they're about to discuss are linked to an individual's strengths, they need not pace the halls worrying about the repressive discussion they're going to have to lead. By seeing what's good in others, the conversation takes on the tone of a friendly and helpful coach who is focusing on microbehaviors ("step just a little closer to the plate") rather than a psychoanalyst who is continually forcing a patient back into his or her dark childhood.

If you become good at coaching others, no longer do your clients smile grimly when you walk in the room. Instead, when you meet with them one on one, they often eagerly switch the topic to self-improvement. They know you see them as talented people, and any feedback you're offering is nothing more than the advice of an admiring friend. You're simply tweaking the edges. When the conditions are right, and when the feedback helps the people you work with resolve ongoing, nagging problems, you can bet they'll be asking for your help. But, once again, you can't do any of this if you don't legitimately admire a great deal about the person to whom you're providing feedback. Without respect, feedback turns into criticism, and from there it's all downhill.

> As you prepare to coach someone, ask yourself: Do I admire this person? Can I see how his or her strengths are leading to problems?

Leave Room for Self-Discovery

I have come to feel that the only learning which significantly influences behavior is self-discovered.

CARL R. ROGERS

As you make the transition from strengths to challenges, it works a lot better if the other person helps paint the picture. For example, with Robert the conversation went as follows.

"I get the impression from your body posture and energy in meetings that your mind is running about a million miles an hour."

"You've got that right."

"You're wanting to rush on, but the group seems to be going almost in slow motion. You've thought through the ideas and worked out what you think is the best way to go, and then others seem to drag along—almost as if you're trying to swim in molasses. Is that right?"

"I couldn't have put it better myself."

"What danger do you suppose you run at that moment?"

"I move on too fast or seem like I'm forcing my ways on others?"

There's an art to setting up conversations where others can come to their own conclusions, but it's worth taking time to develop the skill. Think of how much better the conversation went by allowing Robert to come to his own conclusion rather than using the following traditional approach.

"As I watched the meeting yesterday, I noticed that you were moving faster than everyone else. It gave the impression that you were trying to force your way on others."

Guess the reaction.

Or better yet, imagine how an even more common treatment would have fared.

"People are tired of you taking over the meeting and ramrodding your way through." (Which, by the way, is how Robert was described when the consultant first came onboard.)

Truly masterful teachers and coaches continually find ways to allow people *the sweet experience of self-discovery.* Carl Rogers was right: "The only learning which significantly influences behavior is self-discovered." It's the ultimate and final form of personal experience.

Share a Combination of Observations and Conclusions

If all economists were laid end to end, they would not reach a conclusion.

GEORGE BERNARD SHAW

Most of us, unlike economists, draw millions of conclusions—so much so that we fill our coaching sessions with them. These sessions would improve greatly if we provided a balance of observations and conclusions. If, when giving feedback, you share only conclusions ("taking over" and "ramrodding"), you're likely to end up in an argument. Skilled coaches separate conclusions from behaviors and then share them in a helpful package. They understand that, by simply providing conclusions, the other person is left with a poor understanding of what he or she is doing. This gives little help or hope for improvement. In addition, many conclusions expressed in isolation aren't exactly heartwarming. They lead to hurt feelings and bad blood.

Savvy coaches start with descriptions of observable behavior: "In the meeting yesterday, I noticed that you cut three people off in the middle of a sentence." If people are beginning to draw conclusions about the behavior, the conclusions are stated tentatively and are always linked to the behavior: "I'm not sure what's going on, but I'm beginning to wonder if you really want to hear what others are saying. I'm not sure what you intend. Can you help me understand?"

Finally, as this example demonstrates, the person ends by inviting the other person to explain his or her point of view. Skilled individuals invite disconfirmation of their hypotheses.

This Isn't Easy

Before we move on, it's important to realize that the behavioral description part of the discussion is the hard part. First, most of us aren't very good at teasing out what part of an overall interaction is the part that isn't working. We know we don't like what just happened, and we can even describe the feeling it gave us, but we don't know how to put our finger on what the person *did*. Second, even when we get a handle on the behavior we do or don't like, we aren't very good at describing it.

To be honest, the authors had no idea this was the case until we started producing video snippets of "good" and "bad" interactions a few years back. Say, for example, you're showing what a skilled technical-service representative shouldn't do when first showing up at a client's door. We actually prepared this exact training from a group of technical geniuses whose job was to repair multimillion-dollar machines that produced computer chips. To design the training materials, we watched both effective and ineffective reps at work and then taped do's and don'ts on video. Our first clip captured the worst offender in a single, one-minute scene entitled "The Nerd."

You can probably imagine what the vignette entails. The fellow shows up at the door, opens it a couple of inches, looks through the crack as if peering into a grade school principal's office, and then bursts into a waiting room in a tumble of briefcase, spare parts, luncheon fruit, and flying papers. Half of his shirttail is hanging out the front of his pants, his white shirt-pocket contains 17 pens of various colors (held neatly in a plastic protector), his glasses are made of thick black plastic, and everything he's wearing is made of petrochemical derivatives whose multisyllabic names end with the suffix "-on." After gathering up his material, he walks haltingly over to the nearest waiting-room chair, looking all the while at a point two feet in front of his left foot. All of this happens, quite naturally, in front of a receptionist. At this point the conversation starts. The technician speaks haltingly, continually apologizing for his presence. The number of problems that follow are legion and predictable. You know this guy.

Following the vignette, we pose a challenge to the training audience. You're this fellow's immediate supervisor. He's a wonderfully talented technician, but as you can see from the video clip, he isn't very strong when it comes to interpersonal skills. He knows that he's more comfortable with circuit boards than he is with people, and he's asked you to watch him at work so you can provide him with some much-needed coaching. Now, having seen him for only a minute, what would you tell him?

Having completed this and virtually dozens of similar exercises countless times, we can tell you what happens next. Two dozen hands fly in the air, and the first five people eagerly share a conclusion. "The guy's obviously nervous." "What can I say—he's a real geek." "He's never going to get any respect until he stops looking so awkward."

At this point we jump in with another ground rule. Select a single action of this guy, something that he could easily fix. Now give him some feedback. Our goal, of course, is to compel people to give a behavioral description. In almost every case, someone eagerly says something such as, "You need to show more confidence when you enter the room."

After we give three more probes, someone finally understands that we're after a useful blend of conclusions and behaviors (not just a conclusion), and comes back with, "As I watched you enter, I got the feeling that you were nervous, even uncomfortable. Rather than look the receptionist in the eye, you looked at the floor. In fact, I'm not sure you ever took your eyes off your shoes."

Voilà. Something the technician can use to improve his performance.

Teaching people how to move from conclusions to behaviors is one of the largest challenges we face with any training audience. It's also a skill that helps the coaching process improve enormously. Fortunately, if you're willing to spend some time, it can be learned. Try practicing on your own. Make a video copy of any of a dozen talk shows running on TV every weekday. Watch the largely dysfunctional guests interact. Most of them fall into the ever-popular category of "Really annoying people to whom we can feel superior."

Complete This Entertaining Assignment

Now, having made a copy of a talk show, play the game we play. Your job is to coach one of the guests on what it would take to be more interpersonally effective. Choose a behavior the person might change, and give him or her some feedback. Provide a delicate blend of behaviors and conclusions. Do it in a tentative way. Get good at this.

> The ability to give useful feedback by blending behaviors and conclusions in a tactful way separates effective coaches from well-intended, yet largely useless, bosses.

To prepare for the game, take a look at a sample round we made up just for this purpose.

"Name That Dysfunction"

It's the *Ricki Rivera Show*. Today's program is entitled "Young Drug Addicts and an Audience That Really Hates Them." A teenage boy who is sporting a purple mohawk haircut, wearing clothes that have more holes than material, and who is continually tinkering with two nose rings is at this moment screeching at a member of the audience who has just encouraged him to get off drugs. The teenager shouts, "It ain't my fault I'm on drugs. I can't get no decent job. I was fired from the only good one I ever had 'cuz the zit-faced dork in charge said I was takin' money from the till. All I snaked was a couple pocketfuls of small change, and he fires me! Go figure. Besides, I like smoking crack. It gives me courage and makes me more attractive to the chicks."

At this point most audience members have to be restrained to prevent them from storming the stage and ripping the kid to shreds.

As the audience settles to a seething mob, Ricki Rivera holds the microphone in front of you. It's your turn to say something to the troubled young man. Okay, so you can't fix this guy in a few seconds, but you do want to say something. Your goal? To try to engage the young man in an actual conversation or, if all else fails, to avoid making a complete fool of yourself on national television. To help you with your remarks, consider what audience members typically say.

Warning: These are bad examples. Audience members rarely provide a delicate blend of behaviors and conclusions delivered in a tactful way. Here's what they typically offer.

- **Most likely response from an audience member:** "Listen, you filthy little worm, with that kind of an attitude you're lucky we let you live!"
- **Second most likely response:** "Maybe if I was to come onstage and rip your head off you'd be able to kick the habit."
- **A likely response from someone who somehow remains calm:** "I can see you're having troubles in your life. Did you ever stop to think that it's because you dress like a junkyard exploded in your face?" (Smiles politely and sits down.)
- **Remarks from the therapist onstage:** "You're obviously full of a lot of anger. If you'll just read my best-selling book *12 Steps to Self-Mastery and Financial Independence by Buying Several Copies of This Book and Giving It to Your Messed-Up Friends*, I'm sure you'll be off drugs in no time flat."
- **Ricki Rivera's reaction:** "I wish I could just reach out and give you a hug. But first a word from one of our sponsors."

More Helpful Responses

By dint of railing at idiots we run the risk of becoming idiots ourselves.

GUSTAVE FLAUBERT

We could easily sit back and make fun of what appears to be a highly dysfunctional group of people, but we'll take a different route. Your job is to say something that might lead to an actual conversation. It's clear that a conclusion dump isn't going to do any good. You honestly care about the young man's well-being. Sample topics and responses include:

- **The clothing:** "When you wear your hair in a mohawk, many potential employers might feel that you're a high risk. They might be wrong, but have you ever considered that the way you look might be keeping you from getting a job?"
- **The denial:** "You say that your drug use is not your fault because you can't get a job. I wonder if that's all that's going on here. After all, there are a lot of people who are out of work, and yet they don't all do drugs. What's your opinion on this?"
- **The grammar:** "I couldn't help but notice that you used expressions such as 'ain't' and 'I can't get no decent job.' Are you aware that from your use of nonstandard language many people might conclude that you're poorly educated and would therefore avoid hiring you?"

- **The attitude toward women:** "You ended your complaint about not being able to get a job by saying that cocaine 'makes you more attractive to chicks.' I, for one, am offended when you use terms that tend to degrade others. Did you know that a good number of people are probably disturbed by the language you use?"
- **The attitude toward stealing:** "I find it interesting that you say 'all you did was steal change.' I personally wouldn't want to hire anyone who took so much as a penny. If you had a small business, would you want people taking money from you?"

Each of the above examples appears excessively focused. The fellow needs help in so many areas. Nevertheless, your job is to start somewhere by describing both behavior and conclusions and do it in a way that is tactful. We've picked a rather bizarre setting for demonstrating the skill, but don't let the circumstances undermine the importance of being able to provide others with a tactfully delivered blend of behaviors and conclusions. The skill is enormously important to the leader-as-coach.

Come Up with Replacement Actions

Let's add one more element to the coaching process. After you've identified what's going wrong by providing a helpful mix of behaviors and conclusions, you have to either recommend or jointly come up with an alternate behavior.

In some ways coming up with replacement behaviors is the easiest part of coaching. In others, it's the most difficult. It depends on the behavior. Moving one's eyes from the floor to the receptionist's eyes is an obvious fix. But occasionally the replacement behavior isn't obvious. And one thing's sure—ineffective actions don't have simple polar opposites. For instance, consider the annoying behavior of saying, "Yeah, but." A colleague says she agrees with you and then habitually ends by negating the agreement with "but."

If you read the dialogue literature, you'll learn not to use "yeah, but." What you don't learn is the fix. For example, if you believe in what a person has said, yet fear that important elements have been left out (elements that make the issue a bit more complex), you don't end with "but," you transition with "*and yet.*" It's a simple replacement behavior that turns a potentially caustic expression into what feels more like collaboration. Now, how many people know this? Most of us know we don't like "yeah but," and yet we're not sure what to say instead.

We provide this example because it demonstrates the behavioral complexities of effective coaching. Basketball coaches don't just say, "Quit passing the ball with your thumbs down." They tell you where to put your thumbs instead. Leaders-as-coaches need to be equally helpful. As you prepare to coach someone, think of the behaviors that are leading to your conclusions. Identify what would work better. If you can't immediately come up with something, watch people at work until you find a replacement action. Now you're prepared to move from boss to coach.

IN SUMMARY

We've taken a slightly different approach in this chapter. First, we've started by suggesting that it isn't easy to surface Cell 2 problems. Second, we've spent a great deal of time diving into the details of becoming an effective teacher, trainer, and coach. We've spent more time in the microaspects of leadership than we have up until now because we've learned that these are the areas that need attention if people want to make the transition from boss to leader.

We know that the average reader won't be able to spend a great deal of time on each of the chapters in the book. However, this chapter ends by asking you to do what the authors do with their families. Watch talk shows. Tune in to any show that pits groups of people or individuals against each other. Sunday morning offers up a great selection. Jointly observe what's working and what isn't. Become an expert at teasing out behaviors from conclusions. Turn it into a game.

For example, when one of the authors was asked to help a group of Boy Scouts earn their Communications merit badge, he popped in a video of a group of people who were screaming and yelling at each other and asked, "What should these people do to be more effective?" The 12- and 13-year-olds had a great time. Many of them realized how difficult it is to separate behaviors from conclusions. We'd be lying if we said they immediately grabbed onto the skill and mastered it. It's hard to learn. The point is, it can be fun to practice. More importantly, Cell 2 problems will be greatly reduced as leaders—in fact as all employees—become competent teachers, trainers, and coaches.

SOME PRACTICAL ADVICE FROM THIS CHAPTER

- ***Make it safe to admit to Cell 2 problems.*** Help create a learning environment where saying "I don't know" is acceptable. Find five opportunities in the next week to admit ignorance. Sacrifice your ego in behalf of the value of learning.

- **Teach in real time.** Think of two or three situations where your direct reports behave in ways that don't match the culture vision. Think of what you can do in those moments to provide respectful real-time teaching. Make a note to cue yourself so you'll remember your teaching goal ahead of time.
- **Train in short bursts.** Join in leadership and vision training classes by helping out with a segment or two. Try kicking off the sessions. Step in at the end to answer questions and to help develop action plans.
- **Coach to solve problems.** Choose a person who might benefit from your coaching. How will you contract to provide the coaching? How and when will you make observations so you can tactfully deliver a balance of behaviors and conclusions? Practice by writing out a script. Use tentative language, and try to involve the other person by ending with a question that invites him or her to give input.

SECTION 3 QUIZ

Let's see how much of the last three chapters has taken.

1. What is the meaning of the expression "The Law of the Hog"?
   A. A clever metaphor suggesting that if you use ineffective influence strategies, you can count on a variety of non-value-added responses
   B. A story that serves to remind leaders that if they draw down on their power base, they may end up paying later
   C. A complex algorithm used in predicting pork-belly futures

2. What are three conduits of influence?
   A. Verbal persuasion, vicarious experience, and actual experience
   B. Three different means through which people draw data into their mental maps
   C. Thumbscrews, employee-of-the-month awards, and keys to the washroom

3. Is there such a thing as subliminal learning?
   A. Get a life.
   B. No, so the next time you come back from a theatre snack bar with a 50-gallon drum of buttered popcorn, you can't blame your sudden craving on those "nasty hidden messages."
   C. Yes, and it works through a network of space aliens.

4. What are three targets of influence?
   A. Efficacy expectations, outcome expectations, and values
   B. Three different elements of one's mental map which, when combined, make up the human personality.
   C. A group of soft spots just below the solar plexus

5. Define the expression "the overjustification hypothesis."
   A. A psychological term meaning that if you provide extrinsic rewards for an activity that is intrinsically rewarding, the activity can lose some of its natural appeal
   B. A concept first observed when preschoolers were given their favorite snack every time they played with their favorite toy
   C. Paying lifeguards to work at a nude beach

6. What are the high-leverage tools leaders can use to increase intrinsic satisfaction at work?
   A. Choice and involvement
   B. Enrichment and reveling
   C. Bartles & James

Influencing

the Many

It would be difficult to exaggerate the degree to which we are influenced by those we influence.

ERIC HOFFER

In the past two chapters we examined a person "locked in a room alone." It's time to release our subjects from the confines of intrinsic motive and ability into the swirling confusion of society. This will take us five chapters. In chapter 9 we'll examine the subtle but powerful ways social influence almost invisibly shapes behavior. We'll try to make these invisible forces more visible so leaders can recognize when Cell 3 forces are at play.

We'll take our model of behavior selection, wherein individuals are said to make decisions based on anticipated outcomes, and look closely at social outcomes. What will people do to me if I take a certain action? How will they treat me? By adding social dimensions to our model of behavior selection, we're still left with an individual weighing outcomes and coming up with a net value. Our basic model won't change just because we add more people to the formula. Social psychology doesn't exist separate from its cognitive cousin—psychology. Nevertheless, social outcomes tend to carry a tremendous amount of weight for the average decision maker. We'll try to show why this is true and what can be done in light of it.

Once we've teased apart several of the elements involved in social influence, we'll look at the role of social influence in the change process. In chapter 10 we'll explore a line of research that examines how new ideas spread successfully through groups. We'll explore how to make the best use of strategic players in the social process. Since individuals typically pay more heed to certain colleagues than they do to leaders, what will it take to identify and make use of key human change levers? Given that verbal persuasion is the weakest lever, particularly when spoken by leaders whose motives are often considered suspect, what can be done to capture the power of individuals who are already credible? Who are the opinion leaders and how can they best be engaged?

In chapter 11 we'll follow our analysis of opinion leaders (peers and colleagues) as change levers to the direct actions of leaders. We've repeatedly pointed out that verbal persuasion (particularly from the lips of leaders) is far less convincing than vicarious or actual experience.

Consequently, what can leaders do to influence mental maps without constantly falling back on lectures, memos, and speeches? More specifically, what can be done when the values or actions in question are suspect? What if you've spoken of the importance of quality for years, but really haven't done much about it? Now you really want to do something but find you've "cried wolf" for so long that people no longer believe you. Chapter 11 examines how to use symbolic action to breathe life into dead values.

In chapter 12 we'll dive deep into a specific act of leadership influence. We'll examine praise—the heart of Cell 3. In our look at praise, we'll explore a beautiful, delicate, and widely abused form of human interaction. We'll analyze simple expressions of thanks and appreciation and discover why such actions are so deeply needed and yet rarely used. In a later chapter we'll look into formal rewards (Cell 5)—pay, benefits, job assignments, and perks.

Finally, in chapter 13 we'll explore what it takes to encourage people to share resources, skills, and information. We'll look at what it takes to turn groups of people who are interdependent and often annoyed at each other into collaborative teams.

CHAPTER 9

Understanding Social Forces

The strongest man in the world is the man who stands alone.

HENRIK IBSEN

During our teenage years most of us were painfully aware of the piercing, powerful siren call of peer pressure. It affected our every waking hour. We rarely talked about peer pressure per se; however, we constantly worried about being "cool." Being cool was a full-time job. Of course, to be cool we had to act in ways that others liked. Cool *never* came from within. Instead, it reflected the shared norms of the highly visible and popular few. It prescribed language, dress, and interpersonal action. In our efforts to

	Motivation	Ability
Individual	1	2
Social	3	4
Organizational	5	6

be cool, some of us wore our trousers slung precariously low, risking the threat of being "pantsed," because it was the thing to do. We applied Butch Wax to get our hair to stand straight up, a battle seldom won but always fought. We sewed felt images of poodles on skirts supported by yards of crinoline, because it was in. We believed that torn, ratty sweatshirts were attractive. How could they not be? After all, they were cool.

And then one day, usually around the time we graduated from high school, like canaries escaping from their constraining cage, we laughed at our ridiculous need to be accepted by a handful of "in" folks and forever released ourselves from their tractor beam of unrelenting social demands. Soon we hung out with a new crowd—maybe at work, or perhaps with college roommates. With this new group, one of our favorite pastimes consisted of looking back on those corny high school years and poking fun at how we were once social clones. And then, as if in a single movement, we hung up our letter sweaters, set aside our cheerleader pom-poms, and quietly slipped into chinos, penny loafers, and cashmere sweaters. Free at last.

With the passing of years, we became suspicious of peer pressure and counseled our own children to fight against it. Naturally, if one of our kids didn't quite "fit in," we did what we could to help him or her find a niche. It was the *bad* peer pressure we worried about. Good peer pressure, in contrast, would shape them into the model citizens *we* had become. One day we captured our greatest fear of bad peer pressure in a single slogan—"Just say no to drugs." Had we the space on those T-shirts and TV commercials, we might have added: "Just say yes to good grades, athleticism, and strong family values."

The fact that we formulated the expression "Just say no" is proof that most of us had forgotten just how enticing peer pressure can be. As we swapped our ragged tennis shoes for penny loafers, we convinced ourselves that we had somehow freed ourselves from the compelling forces of social pressure and, worse still, that it wasn't really that compelling in the first place. How else could we have come up with and supported the expression "*Just* say no"?

We were wrong on both counts. Saying no to peers—those precious few who can grant us acceptance, give us love, and verify our worth—may be one of the most difficult challenges most of us will ever face. And contrary to our public expressions, adults still worry a great deal about acceptance. They just don't talk about it as much. In spite of the paucity of adult conversations about the challenges of fighting off peer pressure, the need for acceptance doesn't vanish along with the need to use Clearasil.

For example, consider what you might do on your typical morning. You wake up and tiptoe quietly out of the room. You go through your bathroom rituals and head downstairs to read the morning paper. You eat a bowl of cereal and then take off for a walk. Later you carpool to work and grab a cup of coffee at the office. Let's stop here and see what you've done.

How much of your behavior was shaped by your desire to fit in, be well thought of, be liked, be loved, be seen as cool, or be part of a group? You tiptoed quietly, left the toilet seat up or down, wiped the streaks off the bathroom mirror, exercised, read and noticed certain things in the newspaper, used lower fat milk, ate a particular brand of cereal, rode with a group to work, then had coffee. Let's readily acknowledge that many of these decisions have intrinsic benefits. You read the paper to be informed. But could part of it be a desire to *look* "informed"? Come on, now—it's fun to be the first to notice who's recently had liposuction and which world-famous singer just declared bankruptcy, isn't it? Okay, so we do exercise and watch our fat intake because it "feels" better and reduces the likelihood of disease. But isn't a good chunk of our motivation the satisfaction we get from being able to say, "I walk every morning" or knowing that others notice when we order skim milk? Don't we want to have a nicer-looking body because of how others will see us? Even picking up coffee in the morning—isn't having a cup in your hand and drinking "together" with others a social custom?

Practically every time you cock an eyebrow there's some social reason for doing so. Social influence is like air—it's always around us, and we draw it in regularly. Even those who seem to be swimming upstream—the antiestablishment, "independent" types—are only fooling themselves by claiming not to care what others think. If that were true, they wouldn't spend so much time and effort demonstrating to others how little they care about what the establishment might think. They are just as hungry for social response as others. They just get it in a different way.

But what's going on here? Why this driving need for acceptance? Is that all peer pressure is about, or is something else going on? In addition, why do social psychologists describe social reactions in such nonflattering ways? One group studies *compliance*, another looks at bystander *apathy*, still others look at *deference* to authority. Your average bloke doesn't exactly want to be characterized as compliant, apathetic, or deferential. Surely there's a richer and more evenhanded way to examine social processes. Are we all codependent social lemmings who will go anywhere to get nurturing?

To gain a better understanding of what's happening each time a person faces a social reaction, let's take a look at a handful of studies. However, rather than simply conclude yes, we are indeed subject to influence, let's try to get into people's mental maps and see what's really happening as responsible, rational folks just like you and me respond to social signals. As we examine some of the studies, we'll learn that people aren't simply compliant, apathetic, and deferential. The same people could just as easily be described as respectful, sensitive, and socially savvy.

THE POWER OF SOCIAL INFLUENCE

I am a rock, I am an island.

SIMON AND GARFUNKEL

Let's begin with something as mundane as washing your hands in a public rest room. What effect does the presence of others in the rest room have on the likelihood of you washing your hands? While still an undergraduate student, one of the authors was faced with the challenge of designing an experiment in social influence for an upper-division psychology class. Without going into disgusting details, his experiment demonstrated that when people believe they're alone in the rest room, about four in ten times they will wash their hands. If another individual is present, the odds jump to eight out of ten. It doesn't take much upstairs to figure out what's going on here.

This "bathroom behavior" study was designed to build on a long line of research started by Solomon Asch in the late 1950s.[1] Perhaps you recall his original work. Imagine that you're asked to participate in one of his experiments on "judgment and perception." The design is simple. You sit in a group where you and seven others are asked to judge which of three lines is equal in length to a given line. The correct answer is obvious, even to the most nearsighted observer. But the other seven people choose an answer that is clearly incorrect. Now it's your turn. The experimenter waits for your reply. What percentage of people do you believe will match the group's incorrect answer? Even more importantly, what would you do?

Dr. Asch found that about a third of the participants made clearly wrong choices more than half of the time. Seventy-five percent of subjects made incorrect choices at one time or another. Three out of four readers of this book (and the authors as well) are likely to have made similar errors. By the way, when one of the authors sat in on a lecture that Dr. Asch gave at Stanford University after he retired, the scholar, 72 years old but still feisty, argued that he had been studying *independence*, not conformity. The fact that his work had long been labeled "conformity studies" bothered him. He had been fascinated by the 25 percent who always stood up for their belief in spite of enormous social pressure to do the opposite. However, when you couple his work with that done by Stanley Milgram, you begin to see why conformity, not independence, became the catch-expression of the day.

A Shocking Discovery

To do exactly as your neighbors *do is the only sensible rule.*

EMILY POST

Many readers will remember the opening scene of the movie *Ghostbusters*. The character Bill Murray plays is conducting an experiment on the effects of negative reinforcement on extrasensory perception. In reality, he ends up torturing a young male subject with electric shocks, while "putting the moves on" a female participant.

This silly setup likely was inspired by serious work done by Stanley Milgram beginning in the late 1960s.[2] Imagine that you're asked to be a paid participant in an experiment on the effects of negative reinforcement on learning. You and another participant are led by a Yale professor in a white lab coat to a room where you see a chair equipped with straps and wires. You're told a particular theory argues that punishment for mistakes in learning helps improve memory and recall. This experiment will test the theory. You begin to feel a little nervous as the experimenter points out that one of you will be strapped into the chair. Electrodes will be attached to your hands, and when you make mistakes when recalling word pairs, you'll be given a shock. You become a little sweaty, but relax when you're told the decision about who sits in the chair will be made by drawing lots. You're feeling lucky, though you do worry about your cohort. He sat next to you in the waiting room and told you that he hoped the work wasn't too tough, because he has a weak heart.

Next you're led to a separate room where you see a panel of switches labeled *15 Volts—Slight Shock* at the low end to *450 Volts—XXX Danger* on the high end. You're told that with each error, one of the two of you will increase the voltage applied in order to see if negative reinforcement enhances learning. Now you're *really* sweating bullets. The lots are drawn and, not really so luckily, you're assigned the role of "shocker" rather than "shockee." In actuality, the lots are rigged, and the other participant is a confederate (colleague of the experimenters) who will not really receive shocks. You are the subject, and the question is, "How far will you go?"

As the person on the chair makes mistakes, you continue to apply shocks. At 75 volts the "victim" begins to moan. At 150 volts he asks to be let out of the experiment. Your thoughts turn to his talk of a mild heart condition. At 180 volts he cries out that he can't stand the pain. At 300 volts you hear no more responses. The silence is frightening, but you're instructed to continue applying shocks.

So there's the experiment. The question Milgram asked before beginning his work was, "What percentage of people will go all the way?" How many will continue through 450 volts under these conditions? A group of 40 psychiatrists at a leading medical school predicted that only 4 percent of subjects would continue to the end.

In actual tests, Stanley Milgram found that a startling 62 percent of subjects would continue through 450 volts. These were businesspeople, college students, homemakers, and other handpicked normal people. They were found to be completely normal on standardized personality tests. They weren't sociopaths who loved inflicting pain. In fact, most were in various states of nervous disturbance at the end of the experiment. Several underwent therapy after the experiment concluded. (When they were told that they really hadn't harmed anyone, they were still left with the haunting realization that they thought they had been inflicting pain or worse, and they still went on. Today researchers aren't allowed to engage in this kind of intrusive research without first gaining permission from "Human Subjects Committees," and you can bet the farm that nobody would allow similar studies to be conducted again.)

Many subjects needed a great deal of prodding from the experimenter to get them to continue. But eventually they complied when the lab-jacketed researcher mentioned those now-famous words—"the experiment demands that you must go on." But most didn't do so without pause. As subjects continued to escalate shocks, they would frequently turn to the experimenter and ask, "Are you going to take responsibility if that guy's hurt?" Then they would reluctantly proceed.

What has made this line of research so compelling, in addition to the fact that it raises questions about our ability to be readily influenced, is that it was replicated in a variety of highly creative (and now forbidden) ways. For about 15 years researchers who studied obedience to authority had their day in the sun. For instance, one group of subjects was asked to thrust their hands into a vat of acid. Others were asked to throw acid into the face of a research assistant. These particular research trials, by the way, were originally completed in order to demonstrate that people who were crazy enough to risk an acid bath or to scar a stranger complied only because they were hypnotized. Nobody ever believed that the control group—nonhypnotized subjects—would ever comply. Most did![3]

Perhaps the most creative research into compliance was conducted at a time when a group of divinity students had been asked to record a speech as part of their graduation requirement. As they walked to the other building, they encountered a "victim" slumped in a doorway, coughing. If the students had been told to hurry because they were about to be late for the taping, 90 percent failed to stop and assist the victim. With only a little prodding ("your tight schedule demands that you must go on"), almost all of the students abandoned the helpless person in order to record the speech on the assigned topic—"The Good Samaritan."[4] We told you the study was creative.

Before we stand back and chuckle at these seemingly spineless folks, let's look at a line of research that raises even more questions about the susceptibility of people to social influence. This particular body of work has been dubbed "bystander apathy" research. It helps us understand even more of the features that go into "compliance."

Bystander "Agony"

The torments of martyrdom are probably most keenly felt by the bystanders.
RALPH WALDO EMERSON

Many of you will remember the brouhaha that occurred over the Kitty Genovese incident.[5] You'll recall that one fateful evening in New York City, Ms. Genovese was stabbed three times over a 30-minute period while 38 people watching from their apartments didn't so much as lift a finger to help. Nobody opened a window and yelled at the perpetrator. Nobody dialed the police. Nobody ran out and threatened the mugger. Instead, everyone sat "apathetically" in their rooms and let the poor woman die.

The event not only led to newspaper editorials and TV commentaries, it opened a whole new line of research into what was called "bystander apathy." In one of the studies inspired by the Genovese incident,[6] male subjects were asked to sit in a room quietly and take a test. As the test proctor exited the room, she always insisted that they stay seated in their places until she returned. After a short while, the subjects could hear an audiotape recording of what sounded like the proctor entering the adjacent room, climbing onto a chair, falling, injuring herself, and calling for help. When left alone in the room, nearly every subject (70 percent) bolted from his seat to give a hand. However, when seated next to a friend or a confederate who was paid to sit quietly and continue his exam, few broke ranks. Once again, this line of study was replicated in dozens of different ways. The results were always the same. When faced with colleagues who appeared unruffled by a potential emergency, subjects rarely deviated from their peers.

In spite of the obedient responses of subjects, it's amazing that they could be referred to as apathetic. If anything, most of them sat in agony, torn between taking action and breaking from the ranks. But why? Why wouldn't they simply follow their intuition and lend a hand? Are total strangers so mesmerizing in their influence that your average person can't break from their power? Were they so worried about "what others would think" that they sold out their value for compassion? To answer this question, consider an experience of one of the authors. Here's his story.

Burning Evidence

One day while working in my grandfather's tiny mom-and-pop grocery store, I noticed that a barn not a block away was engulfed in smoke. My first thought was to call the fire department. In fact, I even reached for the phone and began to dial the number. But then it struck me that somebody else surely must have called. If I called, the harried operator would curtly let me know he or she was already aware of the problem. So I hung up the phone and watched.

Soon the smoke broke into flames. But there was still no sign of a fire engine. The nearest branch was only four blocks away, so I thought surely I'd soon hear the siren. The flames now reached into the sky, and I could see other people standing in doorways watching the disaster. Obviously they had called by now or they wouldn't be standing so casually on their porches. Of course, I was standing on the porch of my grandfather's store, and I hadn't called.

For the next 10 minutes, as the barn went from smoke to flames to ruins, I remained torn between the sight of the barn and the black dial phone mounted on the wall. I never called. By the time the fire truck finally arrived, the barn and all of its hay had been consumed. The short article in the paper the next day reported that the fire department had arrived within a couple of minutes after receiving the first phone call, but had been tragically late. This news didn't exactly soothe my guilt-ridden conscience.

What was it that prevented me from making the call? By the same token, what prevented "bystander apathy" subjects from helping out a wounded person who obviously needed their help?

Actually, several forces were at work, and none could rightly be labeled "apathy." In my case, the whole idea of being chastised by a stranger was daunting. I was a teenage boy, still insecure in my standing, and the thought of being told "We already know, stupid" wasn't something I looked forward to. Couple this with the uncertainty of the call to action, and you end up with a person torn between making a phone call and sitting quietly—if not calmly.

Individuals in the bystander research faced similar circumstances. They were never totally certain that the situation warranted their leaving the room and lending a hand. There was always the chance they had misheard the situation or somebody was already jumping in to give aid. This fact alone wouldn't have kept people from helping out. In order for people to stay glued to their seats, it required at least two more elements. First, adults had to have learned that showing alarm when the facts are uncertain isn't a mature way to act. Only kids readily show fear, anxiety, and apprehension. Adults learn to mask their initial suspicions. After years of effort, they learn to "keep their cool."

Next, individuals need to show faith or trust in others' judgment. Faced with an ambiguous situation, they look to their colleagues to see how they react. If one other person so much as shows the slightest anxiety, the subject will bolt from the room. But all sit quietly keeping their cool. Either they're confederates who have been told to show no sign of concern, or they're normal folks who have mastered the art of cool. In both cases, the subject faces an uncertain situation, looks to others who are giving no signs of anxiety, and takes counsel from their cues. They mask their own emotion and then feed off each other's mask.

How about the Asch studies?[7] What happened there? In postinterviews with subjects who routinely said that a line was similar that was clearly of a different length, the researchers found two different reactions.

Reaction One

The subject sits quietly listening to the simple instructions until the first series of three lines is revealed. The first (line A) is five inches long, the second (line B) is four inches, and the third (line C) is 6½ inches long. The "standard" line is five inches long. The researcher then asks the first person at the table which line the "standard" line is similar to. The first person suggests line C, the one that's 6½ inches long. What's wrong with this guy? Anyone can see that it's the same as line A. Next, much to the subject's surprise, the next person says line C as well. What is this, twin idiots? When the third person chimes in with the same response, the subject isn't sure what's going on. Either a whole bunch of incredibly stupid people are gathered in the same room by some quirk of fate, or they're all falling in line to avoid looking different. By the time it's our subject's turn, the subject, against his actual opinion, shouts out "line C" in order to avoid causing a ruckus. Being wrong isn't that big of a deal, but acting different may cause some kind of a problem.

Reaction Two

After listening to the instructions and concluding that line A is the right answer, this subject is surprised to hear the first person say it's line C. *Hmm. It sure looks more like line A.* When the second subject, a rather distinguished-looking fellow, chimes in with C, it starts looking a little closer in length. Actually, although A looked to be the correct answer at first glance, it could be C. Now the third person agrees that it's C, then the fourth, and the fifth. By the time it's our subject's turn, he has convinced himself that line C is the correct answer and shouts it out with some confidence.

When the subjects' peers presented clearly differing opinions, some subjects (the ones Asch was interested in) held to their opinion and broke from the ranks, some chose to agree to avoid causing an incident, and some actually changed their opinion. For some, this phenomenon known as "social influence" was clearly a matter of worrying about acceptance, while for others it seemed to change their perceptions.

Before we examine these important differences, let's turn to the Milgram studies.[8] What was going on there? These poor subjects faced far worse circumstances. First, the situation was ambiguous. They were never totally certain that the other person was in any danger. They were suspicious, but uncertain. Second, the stakes were high. A life was at risk. Third, the authority figures showed no alarm whatsoever. They were obviously trained experts who had been involved in many similar circumstances and were not the least bit worried. Fourth, they didn't want to cause problems or make waves. They certainly didn't want to look like naive alarmists, nor did they want to be chastised by their individual "bosses." (Each was being *paid* to participate in the study, so it was a job—not a particularly fun job, but a job nonetheless.)

Like subjects in the bystander apathy research, the subjects in the Milgram studies were also very concerned. They were torn between confronting the authority figure by stopping the shocks and risking the health of a fellow subject by continuing the treatment. On the one hand, this was a person who had a mild heart condition; on the other hand, it was a scientific study and couldn't be altered without disastrous results. So the subjects, torn between competing demands, almost always sought data. "Don't you think we should stop and see how the other person is doing?" This question was always answered with, "The experiment demands that you must go on" (meaning, "Don't fret, we know what we're doing"). "I think the guy is hurting. Don't you think we should check? Were you aware that he has a heart condition? Are you going to take responsibility for what happens here?" But the answer was also the same: "The experiment demands that you must go on." In other words, "Trust us. Don't worry."

Deadly Sheep?

There can be a true grandeur in any degree of submissiveness, because it springs from loyalty to the laws and to an oath, and not from baseness of soul.

SIMONE WEIL

At this point in the analysis, most researchers conclude that normal human beings will do ridiculous things if asked by a person in a position of authority or a respected peer. The original work was reported under the title "Obedience to Authority." The subjects were compared to Germans in Nazi Germany who forced their neighbors into ovens. But there's more going on here than obedience, blind or otherwise.

The fact that the person is wearing a lab jacket and is described as a researcher carries a great deal of meaning beyond "I'm the boss." Here is a person with substantial information. He has extensive knowledge about actual outcomes and probabilities. As a leader of the research project, he understands that if a subject were to be harmed, he and his colleagues would be in big trouble. He probably knows a fair amount about the impact of high-voltage shocks on human beings. And *he* doesn't look worried.

After all, wasn't it one of his compatriots, a lab-jacketed science teacher, who put his hands on a Van de Graaff generator and showed that, although his hair stood on end, he experienced no damage? He pointed out that the current was of high voltage but low wattage. Watts, not volts, cause damage. Volts can sting but by themselves don't cause any real harm. These are volts here, right? Just harmless old volts. This researcher should know. He's a scientist, for crying out loud. Besides, who knows what other vital information he possesses? Maybe there's someone on the other side of the wall monitoring this whole thing. The impact of the voltage is unclear, and the probability that the experiment will be rendered useless if you quit is a near certainty. And to top it all off, the researcher, a veritable repository of relevant data, certainly seems to want you to continue.

When faced with this sort of ambiguity, 62 percent of the people relied on the implied expertise of the experimenter. Were they wrong in trusting the knowledge and values of the researchers? No. They didn't have the facts right, but that's the whole point. Uncertain about their facts, they relied on the researchers' insights. The researchers knew that the person wasn't getting shocked and acted accordingly. The subjects, uncertain as to the overall picture, believed that the researchers were neither maniacs nor idiots. They *trusted* that the men in lab jackets knew what was going on, were certain that it wasn't actually hurting anyone, and would not lead them astray. Obviously, as responsible adults the researchers weren't about to allow someone to be harmed. And they didn't.

The fact that the researchers then categorized the subjects as compliant or frighteningly obedient (a little too entrapping for most of our tastes) is evidence that the researchers were unaware of what was going on in the hearts and minds of the subjects. The fact that most subjects continued the shock treatment is *not* evidence that all people are sheep who will do anything to stay in the flock and will even go so far as to kill someone should the shepherd demand it. While the experiment *does* suggest that social influence can provide data that leads people to change their minds (as their cognitive maps change), it *doesn't* demonstrate that we do so solely because we want to be liked.

If you don't characterize humans as efficient processors of social data, you might end up assuming that they can too easily become mindless, obedient killers. On the other hand, if you see them as cognitive creatures who are continually gathering data—overt, subtle, and otherwise—the Milgram studies confirm our belief that humans not only hunger for data, they place a great deal of trust in information provided by credible sources. The fact that virtually all of the subjects worried about the other person demonstrated their compassion and value for human comfort and well-being. Many had sweat rings down to their belly buttons at the end of the experiment—they were completely unsure of how to reconcile the conflicting data they were getting. The fact that they trusted in the authorities suggests they had

not completely lost faith in others. This rather pedestrian interpretation of the findings, while not likely to make the cover of *The National
Enquirer*, provides a far more accurate view of social influence.

I Need Data

*The decisive psychological fact about society is the capacity of
individuals to comprehend and to respond to each other's experiences
and actions.*

SOLOMON E. ASCH

What's important to realize from these experiments is that there is more
to social influence than the desire to belong or to avoid social sanc-
tion. Certainly, most of us don't like to be chastised by people in
authority, nor do we like to be laughed at by bosses, peers, friends, or
strangers. But there's more to social influence than acceptance. That's
why we prefer a broader definition. We think of *social influence* as *the
process through which critical information is shared.*

Common to each of the experiments we've cited in this chapter was
a fair amount of ambiguity. Did the person in the next room need help?
Was the shock hurting the person on the other side of the wall? Was the
technician who would record the speech anxiously waiting? Would a
couple of minutes one way or another ruin the chance to record the
speech? As ambiguity increases, the need for data rises as well.
Human beings often provide the handiest, deepest, and most interac-
tive source of information. They're a veritable repository of complex
mental maps—each providing information about outcomes, probabilities, and values. They serve as living oracles who willingly share vital
facts. Consequently, humans, the supreme learning organisms that they
are, rely on others for highly needed information. This reliance on others starts with parents and never ends. As we examine social influence,
it will be this information-sharing aspect that we'll study most carefully.

I Need to Belong

*For a crowd is not company; and faces are but a gallery of pictures;
and talk but a tinkling cymbal, where there is no love.*

FRANCIS BACON

Now, having said that social influence is about data, let's return to the
very special form of data known as *acceptance* or *rejection.* Obviously,
one of the sources of information proffered by others is whether or not

they approve of your behavior or decision. You turn to colleagues to see if they'll support you after you make a tough call. You worry about whether you'll incur the disdain of your co-workers and friends. And yes, people *do* worry a great deal about being loved and accepted. It's this quality that makes humans able to survive in a world of scarce resources. It has a high value, a very high value indeed. For many of us, the need for acceptance sits at the top of the list of things we care about.

In addition, the information people share with you about how they'll treat you is generally quite accurate. The facts they believe about any situation may be tenuous, even questionable, but when it comes to their own reactions, they're experts. For example, say your boss has done something you don't like and you've decided to write her a memo telling her off. Now, your colleagues may not know if sending a harsh memo to the boss will result in what you're looking for, but they do know how they feel about the action. Of this they're certain. Consequently, both the probabilities and values associated with acceptance are generally quite high. We deeply desire people's approval, and *they* clearly know if they're going to give it. Perhaps this is why the social influence literature tends to focus almost exclusively on the *belonging* aspects of influence while paying little heed to the broader *information-sharing* component.

To gain a clearer understanding of how both the acceptance and information components of social influence combine to form a compelling force, let's take a look at what happens when social pressure rears its head in the workplace.

From the Laboratory to the Work Floor

They came to me and said, "See here, Fred, you are not going to be a piecework hog." I said, "You fellows mean that you think I am not going to try to get any more work off these machines? I certainly am. . . . " They said, "All right then, we will give you fair notice you will be outside the fence inside of six weeks."

FREDERICK W. TAYLOR

In 1928, as Elton Mayo and his colleagues were conducting their groundbreaking studies in the Western Electric Hawthorne plant, they discovered a paradox.[9] They found that employees who were paid by piecework actually chose to work slowly, at the expense of a higher income. Employees who exceeded this measured pace were quickly punished by the others in informal ways. They were labeled "rate busters."

The shocking discovery that people would actually make choices that appeared to conflict with their best financial interests illustrates the power of social influence in the work setting.

Researcher after researcher has confronted this same dilemma. Fritz Roethlisberger, who participated in the Hawthorne studies, described how "operating within this group were [some] basic sentiments . . . (1) You should not turn out too much work; if you do, you are a 'rate buster.' (2) You should not turn out too little work; if you do, you are a 'chiseler.' (3) You should not say anything to a supervisor that might cause harm to one of your associates; if you do, you are a 'squealer.' " These social norms influenced behavior more than the incentive systems did!

Two other social psychologists, Coch and French, found the same dynamic in a similar setting.[10] A new "presser" in a factory took 13 days to master her craft. At that point she began exceeding the rate of her team, which was about 50 units per hour. Soon the woman was the scapegoat of the group. She was ostracized. It wasn't long before her production dropped back to about 50 units per hour. What a coincidence! After 20 days, the group was broken up for other reasons. The scapegoat operator was left to produce on her own. Immediately her production shot up from 45 units per hour to 96 units per hour. With the Cell 3 barrier gone, Cell 1 and Cell 5 took over again.

When co-workers threaten to reject a peer, many will seriously reconsider their current behavior—and they'll trade a lot of pay to do so. Most people don't want to work in a world free of conversation. In fact, when job-redesign experts threaten to space people further apart, most fight to be placed next to co-workers where they can carry on conversations. Of course, it isn't just the fear of being lonely or not belonging that has such a compelling force. Along with "not being accepted or liked" come a variety of potentially devastating consequences that people want to avoid.

In one organization we studied, rate busters were labeled, yelled at, spoken of in despicable terms, and threatened. They were told that their cars would be the first to suffer. After having their vehicles scratched, several found sugar in their cars' gas tanks. In another company, individuals who decided to step ahead of the production norm were physically battered. And today, with an increasing number of job-related attacks and murders, the cost of not getting along keeps going up.

The consequence of being cut off from co-workers doesn't just mean you won't be asked to dance at the annual company party. You won't simply be excluded from the occasional group hug. With today's climate of violence and abuse, when your co-workers turn on you, there's some chance that your physical safety could be at risk. In addition, unless you don't care an iota about belonging or being liked and accepted, your emotional safety will continue to be vulnerable.

To the extent that others have control over valued resources, social influence increases in strength. That's why people tend to defer to persons in positions of authority. With the stroke of a pen they can put one's house payment in jeopardy. Every opinion from a boss, no matter how minute in its scope, carries with it the implied statement, "I am the person who signs your checks, writes your performance reviews, recommends you for job assignments and promotions, and decides how the bonus will be distributed." In fact, most leaders have to struggle with employees who are *so* eager to please that they defer to their boss's opinion as if it were *always* true. But then again, this isn't always the case. In fact, it's rarely the case when people are asked to do something new and complex, such as take part in a systemwide culture change. That's why we've taken the time to write this book. You can't simply put on a lab jacket, announce that the job contract demands that you must go on, and expect employees to obey. It doesn't work that way. It takes more.

It Ain't All Bad

Every society honors its live conformists and its dead troublemakers.
                                                    MIGNON McLAUGHLIN

It's easy to fall into the trap of discussing social influence as if it were some kind of evil power. The term *peer pressure* is rarely used in a positive way. And yet, the desire to be accepted, loved, and validated is one of the major forces that makes marriages last and keeps societies from collapsing. At work, people who want to belong and who care about co-workers' opinions form strong teams. In spite of the fact that movies, books, and TV shows continually laud the rugged individualists who stand up in the face of public ridicule, it's important to remember that *everyone* who strikes out against the norm isn't a hero. Criminals come to mind.

Of course, when we praise individualists, it's always people who had a unique insight, fought for it, and, *in retrospect*, proved to be correct. Movies are particularly well-received when the heroes were, at first, publicly ridiculed or even punished, and then, years later, while confined to wheelchairs, shown to have been right all along. It's not *individualism* that we admire; it's the ability to be the first to come up with a correct conclusion and be vindicated after the fact. We enjoy individualists best when we see them on the big screen (where they pose no real threat to our beliefs) or when they lived during our grandparents' youth (when they could do us no harm). In short, it takes the protective distance of time and space to transform nonconformists from trouble-makers into heroes.

Now, we're not suggesting that we'd all be better off if we acted like preprogrammed birds that instantaneously turn in midflight the moment a colleague veers. We simply believe that wanting to fit in or belong isn't all bad.

Will the Real Kramer Please Step Forward?

A couple of the authors became acutely aware of the importance of social influence one day when we were interviewing employees at a plant renowned for its poor production record. To be honest, most people just didn't work very hard. Employees had been abused for years, and when they finally gained some respect through organizing, they worked hard to protect themselves from abuse—except that the protection took a turn south when shop stewards and others began to protect employees from work. The point is, few of the employees went home every night with a warm feeling about how much they had contributed to the organization's success.

Then one afternoon, a fellow who was literally wearing one red and one blue sock entered the room where we were conducting interviews. Immediately he launched into an attack on the work ethic. He told story after story of how he was continually encouraging and eventually fight-ing with his peers to get them back to work. On the one hand, it was a relief to finally stumble onto someone who was willing and gutsy enough to take on the unproductive norm. On the other hand, the guy was scary. He looked a great deal like Kramer on *Seinfeld*. Not only did his hair appear as if he had just survived the electric chair, but his eyes had that same wild look. You'd swear that one eye actually spun as he fran-tically told his harrowing tales of taking on the rest of the workforce. He would yell at his co-workers, and they would threaten him. One day he caught someone fudging his numbers and turned him in. The accused followed him to his home in a high-speed chase and threat-ened to break his legs. To him, battling the poor work ethic was his chance to step onstage and play the role of hero. His was the "just cause," so *they* were the bad guys.

People who take on their peers are rarely heroes. Even when they have heroic causes, they're still rarely heroes. Instead, they're usually deviants. They care so little about what most of us hold precious and dear that they have little hope of ever fitting in. Of course, they rarely care about that anyway. The point is, when we start speaking of social influence as peer pressure and conclude that those who give in to its compelling force are somehow weak, we do injustice to the pure, simple, and possibly noble, desire to belong. Without it, without the glue that unites people from widely different backgrounds, organizations will fall apart in a heartbeat.

Cognitive Cockroaches

Long after the bomb falls and you and your good deeds are gone,
cockroaches will still be here, prowling the streets like armored cars.

TAMA JANOWITZ

As we suggested a few pages back, our desire for social acceptance is only half the power of Cell 3. The other half is what makes human beings the cognitive version of the cockroach. Our *mental* capacities make us true survivors—and we do it through social learning. We use each other as efficient tools to narrow down to a manageable few the thousands of options available to us moment by moment. Most people don't read the *TV Guide* from cover to cover to decide what to watch. They channel-surf some, and they also talk to friends. They use friends' recommendations—especially the ideas of those they see as like themselves—to narrow the field. It's the same with the clothes we wear, the cars we drive, the vacation places we go. Most of us reduce the many to the few by asking those we believe care about similar things and then decide from there. We are social learners.

When it comes to the job, we take cues from each other in social situations about what behavior is appropriate, desirable, or effective. Savvy people spend the first few weeks on a new job watching others in various settings and taking cues from them. A new hire learns quickly how candid you can be, what dress is acceptable, what pushes the boss's buttons, and where to go to really get something done. Many of these learnings don't come firsthand; they come from watching the behavior of others. They come from social learning.

Cell 3 gives us a way of looking at how those around us shape our mental maps. By listening to and watching others, we modify our outcome assumptions, our ability assumptions, and even the degree to which we value some outcomes over others. A respected peer tells me to avoid contact with a certain leader—"He's got quite a temper." I now have a new outcome assumption—"Challenge that person and you'll be hurt." This belief influences behavior toward that person from here on. A teacher in grade school becomes frustrated with my slowness in memorizing a poem—and tells me. Her feedback forms itself into an ability assumption about myself—"I don't remember well." That new assumption guides many of my future career, project, and assignment choices. A trusted friend comforts me when I'm passed over for a promotion. He reassures me that, "No one on their deathbed ever regretted not spending more time at the office. It's family that matters most. This is no big deal." This comment subtly influences my priorities. I slightly change my mental map. Although it may be continually attacked at work, living a balanced life can lead to long-term satisfaction.

Bosses, peers, family, direct reports, customers, friends, and others exert tremendous influence on our outcome and ability assumptions. Because we trust their judgment and motives, we give them free access to our mental maps. As we choose from an array of potential behaviors, we turn to others for valuable information. What are their beliefs? Can they provide reliable information about the real odds of success? In addition, how will they respond? Will they approve of the action and thus continue to provide us with physical and emotional support? Will they withdraw approval, attack, talk to the boss, or what? By talking with others, whether they be lab-jacketed researchers who implicitly reply, "Trust us, things will be just fine," or a sister-in-law who suggests, "If you paint your house pink, you're likely to get a lot of flack from your neighbors," humans provide the priceless information that forms the fuel of social influence.

IN SUMMARY

We decided as an authorship team that our goal in this chapter would not be to teach specific skills or to provide a list of useful hints. These will come next. Instead, we chose to start our exploration of Cell 3 with a blend of theory and philosophy. The theory we developed was simple—social influence is largely an information-sharing process. When all is said and done, people continually provide each other with vital information about how things work. The philosophy we embraced was similarly simple, and perhaps somewhat old-fashioned. We suggested that humans don't respond to others' actions simply because they have to look like everyone else or because they mindlessly obey people in authority. Humans aren't like wild animals waiting for a nod from a person in a lab jacket in order to be released on their peers. Instead, they share a deep social bond and rely on each other's insights to survive a hostile world. At least when at their best, that's how humans respond. We've chosen this philosophy because, first, we believe it, even want it to be true, and second, if people don't desire to both bond with one another and share information, organizations don't stand a chance.

We hope we've made it clear that not only does social influence glue people into functioning social units, but that all of us (at least those of us who don't have one eye spinning and wear one red and one blue sock) are subject to its compelling force. We *don't* outgrow the need to associate with and learn from others when we graduate from high school. In social cognitive terms, the value we place on acceptance doesn't go away with age. In social learning terms, the need we have to draw upon each other's mental maps is essential to survival.

When individual decision makers exit their cloisters and walk into the pulsating world of human interaction, they enter a forum richer with data than all of the libraries of the world combined. Leaders who see employees as mobile scientists who draw heavily from living repositories of values and assumptions are in a far better position to influence the flow and eventual interpretation of data than those who view humans as compliant, sheeplike creatures who just need to be stroked. (Wow! I'm employee of the month? And all it took was 20 hours of unpaid overtime. Thanks for the nifty certificate!) And by affecting this perpetual flow of data, they effectively and efficiently influence mental maps, and this leads to change.

In the next four chapters we'll replace our philosopher-theorist robes with the sneakers and workgloves of the practicing change agent. We'll look at how insightful leaders draw on the power of their social environment, master the flow of data through credible conduits, and transform from *cynics* who treat social influence like an embarrassing disorder to *effective change agents* who use social mechanisms to fuel the fires of change.

CHAPTER 10

Making Effective Use of Opinion Leaders

Leadership in today's world requires far more than a large stock of gunboats and a hard fist at the conference table.

HUBERT H. HUMPHREY

Leaders today face an interesting challenge. As they look onto an organization chock-full of individuals with distinct mental maps, they're left wondering, "What can a handful of people at the top of the organization do to influence widely shared and deeply held opinions?" As they spend hours hammering out a balanced vision—complete with values, assumptions, and behaviors—many leaders make the mistake of assuming that once they've come up with a clear idea of what they're about, they need only pass the word

	Motivation	**Ability**
Individual	1	2
Social	3	4
Organizational	5	6

through clever memos and spiffy talks. Their job is to come up with the dream, while the workforce must make it a reality. As it turns out, however, what takes hours, even days, for executives to come to grips with can't be handed off in a few well-chosen words.

In virtually every change effort we've ever been part of or studied, the time people spent thinking about and discussing the organization's vision was directly proportional to their organizational position. The higher the organizational position, the greater the time spent (especially in formal settings) on the vision. Executives spent months, midlevel managers spent weeks, frontline leaders spent days, and the troops—those who have to make it happen—only spent a few hours talking through *what* needs to happen and *why*.

Consider a decision as mundane as how long people should spend working on a newly established midnight shift before rotating. Should individuals who are being asked to rotate between days, afternoons, and now midnights spend one, two, three, or four weeks on a shift before switching? If people spend a week, they don't feel trapped on a terrible shift. On the other hand, if they rotate weekly, their sleep patterns are so disrupted that many never adjust. It's not only unhealthy, it's dangerous. This being the case, should employees even be involved in the decision? At what point for reasons of health and safety do leaders step in and make a command decision? And if leaders make a command decision, what will it take for employees, who've been promised empowerment (read "involvement"), to understand that they haven't been railroaded? And what do you do about the fact that older employees prefer rapid rotation and the newer employees want to establish longer sleep patterns? Do you allow tenure to rule the day again?

The last time we were involved in this particular decision, it occupied the combined union and management leadership team for several days, off and on, over a two-month period. Once the combined leadership decided to rotate monthly, the decision was announced in an all-hands meeting. Although the leaders tried to share some of their reasoning, most of the employees experienced the announcement as a shot across the bow. For the next few months, the time that employees *didn't* spend in the decision process earlier on was spent in small groups—bad-mouthing both the decision and the method for arriving at it. Instead of talking about the pros, cons, philosophy, and rationale (the topics the leaders had discussed), employees talked about how simpleminded and controlling the leaders were and why they were really a bunch of raging hypocrites.

The leaders had hoped people would implement and support the decision in an orderly and efficient manner. What they got was increased absenteeism, loitering during shifts, slower responses to downed machines, and more filing of grievances over petty issues. The "intervention" of simply announcing the decision resulted in the leaders' worst nightmare. In frustration one manager lamented, "It's like no matter what you do, they'll assign the worst motive they can imagine. And they have great imaginations."

In retrospect, the leaders weren't sure what they should have done differently. They had spent days in open and often animated discussion. Surely the average employee couldn't devote the same amount of time to the decision. Besides, leaders are paid for making the tough choices. When a decision ends up making some people winners and others losers, shouldn't the leaders make the controversial call rather than pit employees against one another? These and other arguments convinced the leaders that although the reaction to their choice wasn't very positive, it was the best they could expect. But was it?

If the leaders had been able to tap into normal social forces, a fair number of the problems they experienced would have disappeared. But how? Leaders certainly can't stop the train, pull onto a sidetrack, and involve every employee in activities that normally are handled by the executive team. Customers don't care about who gets to be involved and who doesn't. They want products and services, and they want them *now*. Investors and owners don't get warm feelings when they learn that leaders have to hold endless meetings to soothe employees and nursemaid them into agreement. They want lower labor costs and higher profits.

Here's where the information-sharing component of Cell 3 comes into play. As we suggested in our last chapter, people rely a great deal on the word of their friends and colleagues. We also know that these same friends and co-workers often serve as sounding boards and discussion leaders. Unlike one-way memos and speeches, informed employees can answer questions, share ideas, and jointly hammer out opinions. And the good news is that they already talk in the hallway, over lunch, during breaks, and across desks and machinery, making use of the mental "open space" found in every workday. We all know that the grapevine approach is the fastest and most pervasive method of sharing information. What if leaders, instead of making announcements and then praying for good treatment from the vine, had a way of ensuring that the information was shared openly, honestly, and fairly? What if leaders were able to move from being passive victims of the social network to being active managers of the informal system?

It can happen. We already know a great deal about individual decision makers. People look at all the things that might happen as a result of an action, note the probabilities of each potential outcome, weigh them against the value, and come up with an overall score. Either they'll give it a try or they won't. When poring over and formulating their mental maps, they place a great deal of credibility in data derived from personal experience, a fair amount in something experienced vicariously, and quite a bit less in information that comes through verbal persuasion.

This we know. What we haven't discussed is what happens as an idea passes through the social network. In our last chapter, we pointed out that friends, colleagues, and others often serve as vicarious sources of data, telling firsthand stories and serving as surrogates. They also serve as credible sources of verbal persuasion, some more so than others. Let's take the time to bring together social cognitive theory and a branch of communication theory known as "diffusion of innovations." Combined, they'll help us understand how to make the best use of social networks.

Not the Guy in Bermudas

I do desire we may be better strangers.

WILLIAM SHAKESPEARE

To examine how ideas flow through an organization, we'll turn to one of our favorite scholars, Everett Rogers.[1] Early in his career, he developed a very clever way of studying and thinking about innovations as they flow through organizations. His area of emphasis grew out of necessity. Here's how.

One day Dr. Rogers found himself working as a county agent whose job, among other things, was to help farmers embrace new crops and technologies. At first glance it would appear to be a dream job. Thousands of biologists, botanists, agro-economists, and others had labored away at producing nifty strains of cash crops and clever processes and devices. His job was to help spread the word about the new discoveries. It turned out, however, that farmers received the word of county agents in much the same way your average citizen receives a door-to-door salesperson. It wasn't an easy sell.

At first Rogers was shocked to learn that people didn't eagerly accept his advice. For example, he knew that a particular strain of corn was not only more prolific, but also more drought resistant than the one currently being used. Everyone who knew anything about the new strain had eagerly accepted it. Everyone, that is, but the farmers in his district. They were more comfortable with the devil they knew. Sure, the pamphlets carried a lot of fancy charts and figures, but the farmers preferred familiar products to risky ones suggested by a passel of strangers.

Verbal persuasion didn't carry a lot of weight, particularly when offered by some college kid "outsider" who had never brought in a crop.

After telling his story around the county for weeks, Rogers finally stumbled onto a farmer who would listen. The bad news was that this was not your run-of-the-mill farmer. He had inherited the farm from his father, had been to college, actually belonged to the country club, drove a Cadillac, and, in the place of bib overalls, wore Bermuda shorts. He listened to Rogers, experimented with the new corn, and brought in a bumper crop. Now here was some proof.

But the hands-on experiment didn't do Rogers much good. The other farmers didn't trust the fellow in the Bermuda shorts any more than they trusted the young county agent. Rather than help win over more converts, the first person to sign up actually hurt the cause. People seemed to become more resistant. They didn't want anything to do with the guy who drove the Cadillac and played golf. They drove their pickups, hung out at the local Grange, and held on tightly to their old crops.

Through this and similar experiences, Rogers began a systematic exploration into what came to be known as the "diffusion of innovations." He looked at every kind of new behavior you could try to foster. He examined what encourages doctors to begin using new drugs, what inspires farmers to begin using better farming techniques, what motivates you and me to buy a VCR for the first time, how new management techniques are adopted, how fads such as hijacking become popular, and so on. He examined 3,085 behavior-change studies. And what did he learn? He discovered that 84 percent of the population is unlikely to change its behavior based solely on arguments of merit, scientific proof, great training, or jazzy media campaigns. The majority of those who try new behaviors do so *because of the influence of a respected peer*.[2]

LESSONS FROM ALL KNOWN STUDIES OF CHANGE

Most of us are about as eager to be changed as we were to be born, and go through our changes in a similar state of shock.

JAMES BALDWIN

In reviewing all available information about affecting change, Rogers discovered that:
- Change is always slow, then fast, then slow.
- Different people adopt the change in different ways; early adopters are the key to everyone else.

- Your influence and that of local peer leaders works as a one-two punch to create adoption.

Change Is Always Slow, Then Fast, Then Slow

Lesson number one from Rogers's "metastudy" is that change always follows an S-shaped curve.[3] Change begins slowly, and progress comes grudgingly at first. As many CEOs pursuing the elusive "new culture" know, the process takes years. It seems to move at a snail's pace when you're the lone voice in the wilderness. Gradually you win over a few converts. If they're the *right* converts, when enough of them accrue, the process accelerates. That's where the S-curve steepens. Later, as you've reached most of those who are easy to moderately difficult to engage, the curve levels back out, finishing off the S. Progress past this point slows again, requiring great effort.

Consider a common challenge, such as attempting to introduce the use of "quality tools," like fishbone diagrams, process mapping, and Pareto analysis. Leaders find that the S-curve describes precisely what they experience. Some people buy in fairly quickly, creating a false sense of momentum. The true picture emerges when the initial euphoria wears off and leaders realize that, behind the few faithful who are giddy about these new tools, no one else is standing in line. A few influential managers later begin using the ideas in meetings and advocating process-mapping in some of their less effective departments. These few gain pockets of support. The adoption curve climbs slowly for about 18 months. This is the stretch of road where the faint of heart poop out. Most leaders just quit pushing at this point, declaring the effort an unofficial failure.

If the top leaders persist, they'll enjoy the rewards of the steeper part of the curve. This is where many begin to move past simple "awareness" to actual adoption, which increases social support for others who are on the fence. At about two to three years into the change process, the new practices become part of the culture, but leadership attention and reinforcement are still necessary. Countless experiences like these point out the need for (1) persistent leadership attention and (2) support of respected others throughout the organization.

Whether the S-curve levels out or nose-dives later eventually depends on the intrinsic benefits of the new behavior. If the quality tools actually add value to people's work, then people will continue to use them. If, like pet rocks, they're simply a fad, the curve eventually drops. Seen any *Baby on Board* signs lately? Many quality tools have been similarly overapplied. When the hoopla dies down, those still using the tools (or some hybrid of them) are the folks who found benefit in doing so.

It's interesting that intrinsic benefits have much less to do with *attempting* a new behavior than with *sustaining* the behavior once started. Even with a no-brainer behavior like prescribing a new miracle drug, most physicians won't do it until influenced to do so by respected peers. In the 1950s a new antibiotic called Gammanym was made available to doctors in a small New England area. All 228 doctors tracked were *aware* of the drug. They had read in credible journals and heard from pharmacy "detailmen" about its benefits, yet many took over a year and a half to begin using it. It wasn't until the more innovative doctors began prescribing Gammanym—eight months into the study—that the S-curve began taking off. The social influence of distant leaders (researchers and pharmaceutical firms) was important, but it was the influence of local leaders (peer doctors) that fostered real adoption.[4]

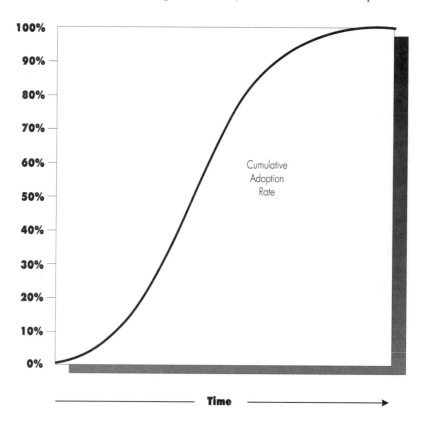

Source: Reprinted with permission of The Free Press, an imprint of Simon & Schuster, from *Diffusion of Innovations*, Third Edition, by Everett M. Rogers. Copyright 1962, 1971, 1983 by The Free Press.

As you labor to bring about change in your organization, expect it to follow this kind of curve. Expect the process to be slow, agonizing, and lonely. Unless, of course, you can gain the support of key people early on. If you take the right actions, you can speed up the curve rather than let it take its normal, painfully slow course. But how? To speed up the process, it's helpful to understand Rogers's second finding.

Different People Adopt Change in Different Ways; Early Adopters Are the Key to Everyone Else

One of the greatest pains to human nature is the pain of a new idea.
WALTER BAGEHOT

So predictable is the pattern of change that Rogers gave names to those who adopt at each stage. Your target population—be it a team, division, or nation—divides out as follows:

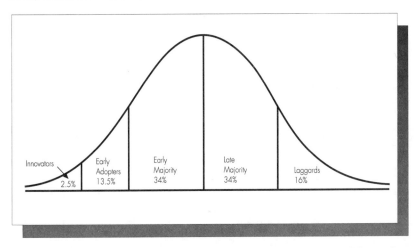

Source: Reprinted with permission of The Free Press, an imprint of Simon & Schuster, from *Diffusion of Innovations*, Third Edition, by Everett M. Rogers. Copyright 1962, 1971, 1983 by The Free Press.

To successfully take advantage of this adoption curve, it's helpful to know something about the various categories.[5] *Innovators* are the venturesome folks. This small percentage of the population is often not well connected with the rest of the pack. They are odd ducks, strange birds. They would be the ones on your block who in the 1970s built geodesic domes or installed huge wind-powered generators built from recycled milk cartons. These people are pretty much open to anything.

Leaders should not feel too encouraged when they persuade this 2.5 percent of the population to support their ideas. In fact, in some ways they need to ensure that their ideas aren't too closely associated with these mavericks. These should *not* be your change agents. In the example we gave earlier, those who were first to embrace the quality tools fell into this category. They almost squelched the adoption process. When you start a change project, don't look for the guy in Bermudas. He'll slow up the adoption rate every time.

For example, the CEO of one organization tried to influence people to look for cost-savings strategies. He asked volunteers to be part of a communication committee. Those who volunteered were an enthusiastic group. To a person, they were smart, motivated, and passionate. They were also seen as brownnosers by many of their peers. Never forget this point. Not all social influence is created equal. Just because people are motivated to help doesn't mean they'll be effective.

As you involve others, don't reach out and grab *any*one who wants to take part. Your job is to find people who are seen as rational, relevant to, and respected by the masses. In the last chapter we suggested that social influence has both a belonging and an educational component. When innovators embrace an idea, other people look on and ask, "Will I be seen as one of them if I try the same thing? Will I be labeled a geek and rejected?" When innovators eagerly grab onto a new process or are willing to try out a new behavior (and they usually do), they send their co-workers a mixed message. On the one hand, they let others know that what has been encouraged can be done. On the other hand, they inadvertently communicate that only weirdos are doing it. This alone can suck the life out of a new idea.

Early adopters are the people leaders need to co-opt. These are your *opinion leaders* who, if they sign up, will be the key to the S-curve accelerating. If you miss with these, you miss completely. According to Rogers, this 13.5 percent of the population consists of the gatekeepers to the now remaining 84 percent. They provide the powerful social influence that pushes others over the hill from awareness to adoption. They talk with their peers, and their peers tend to believe them. Your job is to get to them. They may be formal leaders or they may not. They may be union officials or they may not. They are respected by many and are easily identified. Most everyone answers with their names when asked, "Who is the most respected person around here?"

Early adopters can be identified by certain personal characteristics as well. They tend to be a little more literate and slightly more educated. They're a bit more rational, cope with uncertainty better, have more favorable attitudes toward science-based findings, and hold higher personal aspirations. Interestingly, they do not differ from later adopters in age.

Team with Early Adopters

The early majority, late majority, and laggards (i.e., everybody else) are more deliberate, skeptical, and traditional. Access to these people comes through other people. You will not convince them directly to adopt the new idea. Only interpersonal contact with those already close to them will interest them in trying the new thing. Whether you're an aborigine chieftain trying to encourage someone to move from a stone ax to a steel one,[6] a government agricultural expert trying to share new farming techniques, or a high-level executive trying to involve people in quality improvement, you will succeed only to the degree you get early adopters practicing and talking about your innovation.

Your Influence and the Influence of Local Peer Leaders Work as a One-Two Punch to Create Adoption

Another Rogers discovery clarifies the relationship between a leader's and an opinion leader's role in directing change. Rogers discovered that people go through consistent phases when deciding to adopt a new behavior. As it turns out, a leader's primary role happens in the earlier phases. Opinion leaders take over during the later of the five phases.[7]

Awareness comes first. In the medical example cited earlier, we learned that most physicians were aware of the benefits of the drug Gammanym long before deciding to actually use it. Awareness was important, but insufficient to create mass adoption. Most doctors heard of the drug through advertisements and mass media. Disseminating information and creating awareness are a leader's key role in encouraging the new behavior. To do so, leaders must "talk the talk" until they're blue in the face.

Although media reports and scientific arguments helped some in the persuasion process, most doctors decided to act only after one or more of their peers shared his or her experience with the drug. The S-shaped curve of this study in small towns took eight months to take off. Awareness took almost no time. Persuasion, decision making, and implementation occurred slowly through dialogue with peers and through encouragement from individuals' social networks.

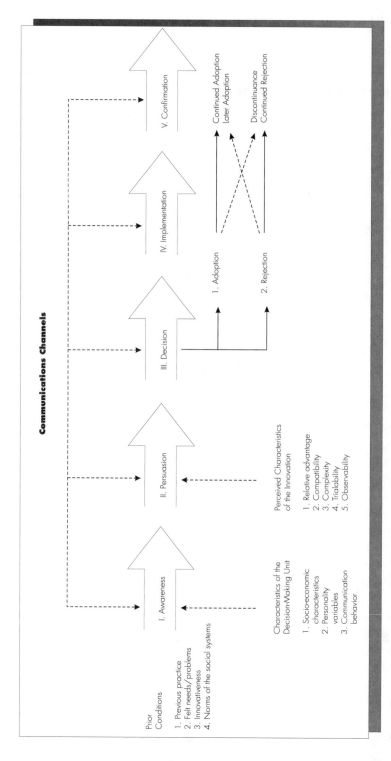

Communications Channels

Prior Conditions

1. Previous practice
2. Felt needs/problems
3. Innovativeness
4. Norms of the social systems

I. Awareness

II. Persuasion

III. Decision

IV. Implementation

V. Confirmation

Characteristics of the Decision-Making Unit

1. Socioeconomic characteristics
2. Personality variables
3. Communication behavior

Perceived Characteristics of the Innovation

1. Relative advantage
2. Compatibility
3. Complexity
4. Trialability
5. Observability

1. Adoption

2. Rejection

Continued Adoption
Later Adoption

Discontinuance
Continued Rejection

Source: Reprinted with permission of The Free Press, an imprint of Simon & Schuster, from *Diffusion of Innovations*, Third Edition, by Everett M. Rogers. Copyright 1962, 1971, 1983 by The Free Press.

The last step, confirmation, takes place when individuals experience the tangible benefits of the new approach. Here the individual is on his or her own. Neither the top leaders nor the more local peer leaders are involved at this stage. Gains are made or lost based on the positive consequences people receive from their practice of the new behavior. Once again, personal experience is the most important source of influence.

For example, a great deal of SPC (Statistical Process Control) training has *not* led to sustained change in behavior. Many people have discovered that these highly technical processes are an example of the cure being worse than the disease. The incredible amount of effort it takes to create measures, collect data, and plot outcomes on posted diagrams seems excessive—particularly when you're a convenience-store clerk. A less sophisticated quality check might be in order.

Wise leaders experiment with new behaviors in smaller units of their business in order to test tangible benefits and staying power. This way they can be sure that when people first try the behavior they'll receive confirming evidence that it's worthwhile. If not, organizations are destined to go through a painful process only to learn that the new behaviors have yielded no fruits and have been cast aside.

An Enormous Example — Mao's "Barefoot Doctors"

Being naked approaches being revolutionary; going barefoot is mere populism.

JOHN UPDIKE

To get a feeling for how the various elements of social influence come into play in an actual change attempt, let's take a look at what Mao Zedong did some 30 years ago.[8]

On June 26, 1965, Mao Zedong lit a fire under the Chinese Ministry of Health, citing their poor record in improving health practices in the far-flung rural regions of China. Rather than wait on the stodgy ministry and medical institutions to solve the problem, Chairman Mao engaged 1.8 million change agents in the cause (sounds like a lot until you realize he had the best part of a billion people to influence). Mao zeroed in on the precise characteristics of the ideal local leaders:

- They came from the villages they were to serve.
- They were identified by their peers.

- They came from poor to lower-middle-class parents.
- They had an altruistic commitment to serve people.
- They had a basic level of formal schooling, which put them close to their fellow villagers, but slightly above them in education.

These features made these individuals, as we will see later, ideally suited to influence their communities and optimally able to participate in the effort.

These "barefoot doctors," as they were called, were given just a few months of medical training. They were taught basic preventive practices that could quickly and significantly increase health in rural areas. They were taught to treat the most common maladies. And finally, they were taught to refer more difficult cases to commune hospitals. The results were immediate and dramatic. Since the majority of health complaints are easily diagnosed and easily treated, these "doctors" were incredibly effective. Health-related habits in rural villages improved rapidly. Practices such as basic hygiene and boiling water were adopted faster than in most any similar kind of effort—and in a country larger than most and more populous than any other in the world! This wasn't heavy-handed policy setting—Mao couldn't have pulled *that* off. This was—and still is— leadership at its best. This was strong leadership at the top supporting local work by barefoot doctors. Exactly the combination all would-be change agents need.

What Mao was able to do was to get rapid adoption by engaging the combined talents of almost two million carefully selected partners. By targeting his efforts on those with characteristics most suited to innovation *and* leadership, he vastly accelerated his change strategy.

All available research on change suggests you will need to do the same. To succeed you will need to know (1) how to identify the most potentially powerful change agents and (2) how to work with them effectively in diffusing change.

WORKING WITH YOUR BAREFOOT DOCTORS

This section is all good news. Working with barefoot doctors is far easier than working with most of the population. These people are more easily influenced through direct appeals. Early adopters are more open to logical arguments, less cynical, and quicker to adopt new practices.

So here we go. We'll look next at how to find your barefoot doctors and then at strategies to help them succeed.

How Do I Find My Barefoot Doctors?

Sometimes the Painfully Obvious Is Obvious

Let's start with some good news. Finding your organization's opinion leaders is *not* like finding Waldo. In fact, it's quite easy. It turns out that those who fit in the early adopter category also tend to be those who are most respected and most connected to others in the organization. So you look for those who are the more respected members of the organization. It just so happens people know who they respect. Also, since you work in this place as well, you'll know the names of quite a few of them.

Beyond coming up with names off the top of your head (a good place to start), you can use a number of techniques to generate candidates. Researchers have successfully used structured observations, sociometric rating methods, self-designating techniques, or informant ratings. We recommend the last. Since all of these methods are about equally effective, why not use the easiest?[9]

Informant ratings is just a process of asking people throughout the organization to designate the two or three people they most respect. This creates a large list, which is whittled down by selecting:

- A representative sample
- totaling about 5 percent
- of those who got the most designations

The representative slice should draw from all functions (horizontal), levels (vertical), and other important demographic categories (gender, tenure, race, and classification).

Don't Forget to Include Managers

Unlike Chairman Mao, you have people in positions of authority who wield great power in the situations you're trying to influence. Well, some do. Formal power and social influence can go hand in hand. People in most organizations tend to look to their direct supervisor and higher-ups for cues of acceptability. Include all leaders from the start. In the next chapter, we'll explore steps leaders can take to enhance their credibility. For now, we'll simply suggest that, although all leaders may not be natural and credible barefoot doctors, to leave them out of your strategy would lead to disaster.

> Although including leaders in every step of the change process will never guarantee success, leaving them out will guarantee failure.

How Do I Engage Barefoot Doctors?

What is destructive is impatience, haste, expecting too much too fast.
                                                            MAY SARTON

It's time to apply everything we've talked about so far. Barefoot doctors, like all humans, are driven by their mental maps. Your job is to help them understand why your vision or plan is reasonable, possible, and fair. But we're getting ahead of ourselves. First, you have to find forums in which you can spend time talking with your early adopters, opinion leaders, or barefoot doctors.

Spend Time with Your Opinion Leaders

Once you've identified those who serve as key links in the diffusion of a more vital culture, your job is to spend time with them talking about your dreams. This is done formally by inviting them to participate on committees and cross-functional teams. As you start change projects, go to pains to ensure that those on steering committees and cross-functional teams are heavily peppered with early adopters. Informally, you can spend time talking with your barefoot doctors by stopping by their workstations and chatting, sitting with them at lunch, or joining in their activities. Whatever the mechanism, good leaders find ways to spend time with key people. They don't wait to be approached; instead, they approach and spend time talking with those who are likely to give a change strategy its biggest boost. And they don't just talk about sports and immediate production problems. They share the vision.

Look at your schedule over the past few weeks. What percent of the time did you spend in contact with handpicked opinion leaders? You may not have thought of them as such, but think about who the influential people are in your organization and calculate how much time you've spent with them in productive dialogue. For many leaders, this mental exercise is quite revealing. Opinion leaders are treated like mysterious forces "out there," or possibly even the enemy. They act on the organization but are not acted upon. This has to change. Well-balanced leaders balance their time between traditional management activities and spending "quality time" with their barefoot doctors. They get up from their desks, wander around, and casually meet one on one and in groups with those who spend more time sharing the vision with the workforce than the leaders will ever have.

Involve Opinion Leaders Early in the Process

It's a mistake to formulate your ideas, allow them to incubate, tweak them, run them around the entire leadership team, put them in print, and then seek the advice of your barefoot doctors. You don't involve opinion leaders simply because they're good and credible conduits. They also have strong and reasonable opinions of their own. Talk to them during your formative stages of any change process. This takes discipline.

Leaders typically ascend to their positions because they're able to analyze data logically and make quick, effective decisions. They don't get to where they are by waffling or having weak opinions in the first place. Consequently, when in the middle of problem solving, visioning, or otherwise brainstorming, it's common for leaders to play through a whole variety of scenarios, come up with recommendations, and then make them.

This propensity to take quick, decisive action can get leaders into trouble. Well-balanced leaders continually seek input from people outside their group. This requires them to stop the locomotive of leadership enthusiasm and take an occasional walk around the countryside. As they walk, they continually seek the reactions of key people. "Are we missing something here?" "This sounds too good to be true—is it?" "How do you think this idea will be received?"

Savvy leaders have been known to stop an energetic leadership team discussion with, "It sounds like we have a lot of energy and ideas around this, yet I think it might make more sense to touch base with some other folks before we move on." Or "Why don't we put off this discussion until we can bring the other members of our action committee onboard?" By bringing your potential early adopters into the visioning and design process, you gain the benefit of their practical ideas early on—where an ounce of prevention can be worth a pound of cure.

One of the side benefits of involving opinion leaders early in the process is that you'll never create a "thirteenth fairy." If you remember from your childhood stories, a queen invited 12 of the 13 fairies in her kingdom to attend her newborn daughter's christening. Each of the 12 in turn gave the child a lovely gift, until the thirteenth fairy stormed into the room. She was furious for not having been invited. Instead of bestowing a blessing, she cursed the child to one day prick her finger on a needle and fall into a deep sleep for 100 years. It was the thirteenth fairy, upset for not having been included, that created "Sleeping

Beauty." She taught us the lesson that if you don't involve key people early on, in addition to missing out on their ideas, you can incur their wrath. It takes patience, more than some executives have, but if you don't involve opinion leaders from the beginning, your change effort may have to endure years of slumber.

Listen to Their Opinions

As with any influence strategy, during the early stages of the change process, don't just share your dream with your barefoot doctors, ask for their input as well. What can be done to make it more reasonable and attainable? What changes, if any, need to be made? Open the vision up to true dialogue. Your job isn't to convince, but to share your view, hear theirs, and jointly hammer out a vision everyone supports.

As much as you believe in your ideas, you must be tentative in explaining them. If not, you'll look like you're trying to ramrod your plan down the chain of command—mostly because that's what you're doing. This doesn't mean leaders should spend weeks coming up with plans only to throw them out the window at the whim of someone they run into in the hallway. Fortunately, opinion leaders rarely ask leaders to chuck out their ideas and start over from scratch. They aren't respected informal wielders of influence because of their inability to listen to and embrace good ideas. If your opinion leaders have concerns, they're very likely to be circumspect and legitimate. Our experience in launching ideas with key people has been exceptionally positive. Generally they provide helpful "tweaking." They understand the big picture, buy into the vision, and then help with some of the details of the implementation.

When opinion leaders do have major objections, it's good to get them out during the early stages when you can still make changes with relative ease. Rarely do opinion leaders bullheadedly resist new ideas or offer silly suggestions. Once again, the barefoot doctors you're working with are logical, less cynical than your average employee, and are more ready to adopt new ideas. That's why they're so influential.

Don't Move Faster Than Your Barefoot Doctors

In a sense, this is a stupid statement. It's akin to saying, "Don't move faster than your large intestine." You can't. The fact is, try as you might, it's impossible to outrun your opinion leaders. You can make policies or demand changes at the drop of the hat. You *can't* bring about lasting and meaningful change without the complete support of your barefootdoctors.

We're constantly amazed at how often leaders lose patience with the map-sharing process and try to move on without the support of their key people. They act as if involving others were nothing more than a courtesy gesture. After chatting, then arguing, about an upcoming project or change, they give up on open dialogue, simply announce the change, and watch to see what happens. Guess what happens?

For many leaders, the fact that they can't start with the honest desire to share a vision and then, if necessary, mandate change is a bitter pill to swallow. Only a handful of visionaries, secure in themselves, have embraced the concept that organizations move only as people completely understand and share in the vision. Most leaders read about the evils of handing down mandates and nod in agreement, then stray from the formula when faced with the enormous inconvenience of not being able to simply give orders. In addition, having been on the receiving end of orders for most of a career, most leaders aren't exactly thrilled with the idea that they can't model their careers after their former bosses. It hardly seems fair.

Leadership, despite the flamboyant imagery portrayed in books and movies, is not an act of supreme will or unique insight. It does not start out as a revolutionary vision, turn into a pep talk, digress to an argument, and end with a veiled threat. Do this in the schoolyard, and you'd be a bully. Leadership is the art of creating an environment in which all people can come to a common understanding. If you can't come to an understanding with your opinion leaders, you don't stand a chance with the remaining 86.5 percent of the organization. Not a chance.

And remember, working with opinion leaders is a two-edged sword. If you twist their arms, not only will they not be convinced, they'll likely bolt from the discussion, announcing to others how forceful and controlling the leaders are. You lose twice. And since these are opinion leaders, you lose big.

Provide Them with Direct Experience

Where possible, give your opinion leaders direct experience and then, if they're skilled, they can create a vicarious experience for others. For example, in one project where new manufacturing techniques were necessary to keep a plant from closing down, we used barefoot doctors right out of the chute. When diagnosing barriers to supporting the new behavior, we learned that many people believed they:

- Might not be smart enough to do it the new way
- Might have to work much harder

Since neither of these was true, we started a campaign through barefoot doctors to debunk the myths and reduce resistance to adoption. We sent the barefoot doctors to see and work in a place where the new behavior was already being practiced.

The effect? Enormous. According to pre- and post-tests, this direct experience with the behavior completely convinced this influential group of barefoot doctors that (1) the behavior was possible, (2) the behavior was reasonable, and (3) the behavior was necessary.

All that was left was to create strategies to leverage their influence. We codesigned a process that allowed them to tell their story throughout the organization. They began with their skepticism, articulated their fears (which were the same fears as their fellow employees), then shared their experience. They told personal stories and shared salient statistics. By telling their stories, these barefoot doctors created a vicarious experience for everyone. This social influence went far in helping to build support for the new behavior.

How to Help Barefoot Doctors Succeed

Opinion is itself one of the greatest active social forces. One person with a belief, is a social power equal to ninety-nine who have only interests.

JOHN STUART MILL

Why Do They Succeed in the First Place?

Leaders need to do more than develop a relationship with their opinion leaders. They need to take steps to ensure their opinion leaders' success. After all, a great deal of a leader's success rides on the success of his or her barefoot doctors. To provide a supporting hand, it's helpful to understand why opinion leaders often succeed, even without your help.

In section 1 we examined how people make choices. After describing how net value is calculated, we suggested that when examining the unknown probabilities associated with ability and outcome, people often look to others to see what happens. When so doing, they consider *outcome* relevance ("What if the same thing happened to me?"), *value* relevance ("Would I feel the same way?"), and *ability* relevance ("Am I similar in ability and consequently able to do what's required?").

Here's where opinion leaders play an important role. When serving as models, they are viewed as similar in ability and circumstances. They're like us. In fact, they're one of us. Stories about other locations, no matter how enticing, deal with different people and times, but these folks are just like us. What *they* can do, *we* can do. What *they* get in return, *we* get. How *they* feel about the results, *we* feel. In short, their actions, outcomes, and values are relevant. That's why we give them freer rein to modify our mental maps.

Probably even more importantly, when opinion leaders use verbal persuasion, they're seen as both knowledgeable and motivated to help. During the early stages of a change process, when people largely talk about what is being asked (i.e., what's in it for them, what will happen as a result, what the bosses are really after and why), opinion leaders are priceless. When they talk, even before they're able to continually practice what's been asked, people listen. For them, verbal persuasion works. In contrast, when leaders attempt to persuade others verbally, they usually meet with a great deal of resistance. They have to find a way to come up with actual and vicarious experience before they can expect to be believed. With opinion leaders, on the other hand, words alone suffice. But why?

They Share Our Interests

Scepticism is the beginning of faith.

Oscar Wilde

Accompanying every act of verbal persuasion is the question of motive. What is this person trying to get? Can I accept his or her arguments as simply food for thought that is free of political interests, or must I peer beneath the actual words and look for an underlying form of manipulation? By the time people have watched a million advertisements, been tricked by siblings, duped by salespeople, and manipulated by loved ones, they develop a protective armor of skepticism.

Fortunately, with time and experience, opinion leaders are able to break through this protective coating and engage in simple dialogue in which arguments are taken at face value and questions of motive are no longer asked. Ideas flow freely in an atmosphere of scientific inquiry. Leaders gain a deep trust through months, even years, of tireless inquiry and by continually looking for ways to share common values.

Maintain Your Distance.   To the degree that leaders are seen as narrow, supporting their own agenda rather than the workforce's, excessively driven by profit motives, and imbalanced in general, it's important that opinion leaders not be drawn too closely into the leadership family. Better to be a next-door neighbor than a cousin. Skilled opinion leaders protect their distance. Make sure that you do the same. Defer to their opinion regarding how frequently you should be seen in public forums together. Avoid the temptation to be continually singling them out for their contributions. Assign them to cross-functional teams and other public tasks sparingly.

Leaders, anxious to make good use of their barefoot doctors' insights and impact, can kill the goose that laid the golden egg. Opinion leaders usually have a good feeling for how much is too much contact, but if they don't particularly care for their jobs, they can be enticed away from the flock until they become one of "you" and not one of "them"—undercutting their credibility.

Most leaders, particularly frontline supervisors, are promoted out of the opinion leader ranks. Many are able to maintain their credibility with the workforce. However, few ever have the same level of contact. Naturally, you don't want to punish opinion leaders by keeping them in their current jobs where they have wide-ranging impact. By the same token, be aware of your level of contact. Nurture the delicate relationship. Too much exposure turns informal opinion leaders into management cronies.

Share the Whole Truth and Nothing But the Truth. Leaders continually face the challenge of deciding how much information they should share with the workforce. Controversial choices, political footballs, and complex decisions are often encased in shiny wrappings of partial truths. Leaders don't have the time to share the whole picture, work through the differences of opinion, and jointly come to a shared conclusion, so they only explain part of the facts—usually the more positive ones. They explain the benefits, leaving cost discussions to the imagination. They take the lead from politicians who find a way to say what they want, no matter the question. They avoid controversy like the plague.

What a mistake.

Take the time to discuss all sides of an issue with your opinion leaders. Obviously you don't have time to meet one on one with every employee. That's where your barefoot doctors work their magic. They *do* have the time. They're going to do it at the watercooler whether you like it or not. However, if you send them off with only part of the picture, not only will your opinion leaders not be able to discuss the entire issue, they'll end up looking like idiots when the whole truth comes out in the open. Do this once, and you've lost a golden resource.

Take the time to bring out all the objections, warts, and potential problems of a decision with your opinion leaders. Let them know why the benefits of a particular choice outweigh the costs. You can't do this without honestly discussing the costs and the steps you can take to lessen them. Count on the fact that the workforce is conjuring up every potential problem. That's why they're resisting in the first place. Until opinion leaders understand your entire mental map, with both positive and negative outcomes, they're not prepared to share the vision.

Trust in the workforce's ability to weigh the pros and cons associated with any decision. Count on your barefoot doctors to tell the whole story. Provide them with all the information they need to paint a complete picture. If your decisions won't stand up to the light of reason and public opinion, they're wrong anyway. Arm your barefoot doctors with their most important medicine—complete and accurate data.

Deliver on Your Promises. People often resist ideas, no matter how promising they may sound, because they fear a negative, but unlikely, result. Snake phobics have an unrealistic assumption that they'll be consumed if they so much as touch a boa constrictor. Employees worry that if they make very many cost-cutting suggestions, they'll eventually lose their jobs. Work teams fear that if they take risks, they'll get their heads chopped off. Suggestion committees believe that none of their ideas will ever be used.

As you become aware of common concerns and assure the workforce that their worst nightmares will never be realized, deliver on your promises. If you say, "Trust us, this won't happen," it had better not. Opinion leaders are going to be out there calming fears and clarifying realities—don't make liars of them. Don't put them in a position where the facts you're providing can't be trusted. Explain the odds associated with potential outcomes, avoiding terms such as *never* and *always*. If the odds are slim that something lousy will happen, state them as slim. Don't make promises you can't keep. If you *do* make promises, go to extraordinary means to see they're met. Fight as hard to maintain the integrity and credibility of your opinion leaders as you would your own. In fact, fight harder.

They Make Convincing Arguments

Those disputing, contradicting, and confuting people are generally unfortunate in their affairs. They get victory, sometimes, but they never get good will, which would be of more use to them.

BENJAMIN FRANKLIN

Opinion leaders are more than credible. Most employees enjoy a certain amount of credibility with their peers. Opinion leaders stand out from the crowd because, not only can they be trusted, they can be convincing. It's this one-two punch that makes them so powerful.

This is not to suggest that barefoot doctors are silver-tongued devils or orators by trade. They don't generally take courses from Dale Carnegie, nor do they see themselves as speakers. Instead, they quietly but effectively share their mental maps with their peers. They don't often argue, rarely end up in tiffs, and continually balance advocating their views with listening to others. They believe, but don't pontificate; are eager to express their views, but don't preach; and although they live with passion, they don't harangue. At least that's how your average barefoot doctor operates in your healthier organizations.

As a leader, your job is to provide these credible folks with a forum in which they can be heard and believed.

Create Forums. It's a rare leader who worries about finding ways for key people to be heard. Instead, most executives fight their way to the podium. Many protest that it's not their bag, but they step to the front of the room every chance they get. Leaders would do well to find podiums for the 13.5 percent of the workforce whom employees readily believe.

In a number of change projects we've done just that. In one case, a couple of highly believable employees were given new jobs. They were removed from a task that anchored them to a workbench and were given jobs that moved them around the entire work area. Before the transfer, these jobs had been filled by bitter employees who wandered around in a funk and peddled venom. This one move alone probably did more to help cascade and clarify the vision than all the other efforts combined.

On the same project, another couple of barefoot doctors were asked to cotrain once a week for a half day. As trainers they weren't as skilled as either the professional staff or many of the leaders. However, as opinion leaders, they were far more effective. Much of the training material (it dealt with customer service) was changed from a hard sell to a humorous, sometimes soul-searching, and always honest discussion of real issues. This in turn helped the training designers repackage the material for other classes.

Occasionally you'll run across an opinion leader who enjoys either writing an article for the company paper or appearing on a weekly video news show (the type produced onsite and shown on monitors placed throughout the company). Such people can provide a wonderful forum for discussing new policies, ideas, and challenges. If you give them enough slack to paint complete pictures, develop their own style, and frankly discuss serious issues, they'll continue to be opinion leaders. If you give in to the temptation to write their material, edit it to death, or coach them into an intellectual straitjacket, they'll look like management puppets.

A fairly large number of organizations are currently giving their opinion leaders a formal position. They've done away with traditional frontline supervisors and replaced them with team leaders who are selected from the hourly workforce. This strategy works best when the individuals placed in this delicate position are respected opinion leaders who are allowed to remain part of the workforce. Dress them in new clothes, put them in their own offices, and all you've done is create new frontline supervisors from your old opinion leaders.

Provide Training. As we suggested earlier, most opinion leaders aren't professional orators. Some are only moderately effective problem solvers. Others, in spite of their energy and good intentions, are a bit rough around the edges when it comes to interpersonal issues. How can moderately or even poorly skilled people still be opinion leaders? Actually it depends on the pool they're drawn from. In organizations where most people are fairly tough on each other, it's only natural that opinion leaders would be similarly inclined. But this doesn't mean they can't improve.

In one major intervention, we carefully trained opinion leaders in one-on-one, group, and formal presentation skills. It wasn't called opinion-leader training, but it was. Every time we brought together a cross-functional team, the group was trained in both group process and analytical problem-solving skills. Opinion leaders filled the ranks of these teams. On two separate occasions we asked leaders and a handful of opinion leaders to take part in a formal presentation to outside vendors and suppliers. We took the opportunity to train presentation skills, including one-on-one coaching. Opinion leaders benefited immensely. Finally, when dialogue training was offered to all employees, opinion leaders were trained in advance and then asked to cotrain the remaining sessions. Quite naturally, they learned the most.

Restrict Other Conduits. Opinions are like TVs; everyone has one. We've been talking about how to make the best use of opinion leaders without so much as mentioning that every organization is full of people who have dozens of opinions but aren't opinion leaders. Many are highly cynical and constantly upset and are bitter adversaries to anything that looks like change. Although they may not exactly lead the masses in any particular direction, they do tend to make a lot of noise, lead a handful of like-minded people off in their own direction, and generally disrupt the change process. To the extent there is a vacuum of much-needed information, these folks are encouraged, even rewarded. They feed on ambiguity. As long as people are unsure of what's going to happen, employees who have honed imagining the worst-case scenario to an art form are more than willing to throw in their two bits' worth, and they do.

Opinion leaders can be helped out a great deal if they and others are constantly updated on important decisions. Providing the workforce with a constant stream of what's happening and why tends to take the bite out of those who are feeding off ambiguity. This sounds easy, but it isn't. For example, a team meets and struggles through a tough choice. After several hours of lively debate, the group breaks up, and the decision is handed to the bosses whose job it is to spread the word. What happens? Unless the organization is filled with saints, the word of what took place starts seeping throughout the organization. Of course, only snippets make the rounds, and rarely are they given a positive spin. By the time the official word is released, a great deal of damage has been done.

Even when the decision is made by the top-level team, a similar process occurs. Some of the leaders rush off to other meetings, some get caught up in daily problems, and only a few go straight to their direct reports and share the message. Who knows what happens to the story as it chugs down the chain of command? Research has shown that whole sectors of the organization receive the word through informal sources—where leaders are at the whim of the messenger. Some never hear anything, and a vast majority receive different stories as the word is distorted down the chain. The most common problem is predictable. As the message is shared through normal channels, it typically shrinks. What starts out as a detailed report of what happened, why, and how it fits into the broader vision ends up being reported as "Here's the decision. Now let's get back to work."

Continually stirring the pot of misinformation does bosses and opinion leaders a great deal of harm. Instead of helping people interpret the meaning and implications of accurate information, opinion leaders end up spending their time seeking correct interpretations and fighting fires. This is hardly the best use of one of your most valued resources.

One organization we work with has made tremendous strides in this horrendous battle against misinformation. To assist barefoot doctors and leaders alike, one member of the leadership team is given the responsibility to update the computer bulletin board. At the end of every morning meeting, she logs into the software, then describes what the team discussed, any decisions that affect the workforce, and the reasons behind them. No tough decisions are communicated without an explanation of what the options were, why the choice fell out the way it did, and how it fits in with the overall mission. This bulletin board is checked every morning by all leaders. As soon as frontline supervisors receive the latest update (usually within a half hour of the morning meeting), they are asked to meet with their team and discuss the information, expanding, not reducing, the content. Then, as the workgroup breaks up and begins to discuss what the message *really* means, barefoot doctors start from a base of accurate data.

SOME PRACTICAL ADVICE FROM THIS CHAPTER

In this chapter we've asked leaders to be masters of social influence. You'd think, given the rich field of social psychology, that one could find a great deal of information about how to make the best use of social networks. Strangely enough, beyond the message that peers exert a great deal of influence and a handful of marketing models that tell us what to guard against when introducing new products, there hasn't been much written on what this all means to the leader. Our goal has been to move from describing the idiosyncrasies and horrors of social influence to prescribing actions leaders can take. Here are some of the recommendations we've made.

- *Identify barefoot doctors.* If you want opinion leaders to help carry the vision throughout the company, you ought to know who they are. Do you have a good idea of whom people listen to and believe? If you don't, ask around. It doesn't take long to find your barefoot doctors.
- *Spend time with them.* Since opinion leaders can be found in any position or location, it's not likely that your normal travels will routinely bring you in contact with them. Do you go out of your way to create informal meetings? Have you wandered down the hall to chat with a key person in the last couple of weeks? Do you have people you routinely bounce ideas off, just to see what they're thinking—people who don't fit into your normal leadership slots? If you don't, start.
- *Bring them in the loop early.* Have you created a "thirteenth fairy" over the past couple of months by forgetting to include a key person in an important decision? Have you been known to stop a team that's about to rush off half-cocked and suggest that they think about touching base with key people before moving on?
- *Listen to their opinion.* As you meet with key people, do you really listen? How often do you change a plan based on their reaction or advice? Do you touch base with opinion leaders as a token gesture but fail to heed their advice? Don't even bother to touch base with opinion leaders if you have no desire to learn from them.

- ***Don't move faster than they do.*** Have you ever gotten into a heated discussion with key people and found yourself thinking, "They don't agree now, but I'm going to go ahead anyway."? Have the patience to move at the pace of your key people. You can't outrun them anyway.

- ***Provide them with direct experience.*** Since not everyone can make that key field trip or try out the new process, make sure your barefoot doctors get a chance to personally experience whatever you're recommending. Then they'll be able to create a believable, vicarious experience for others through their vivid stories. Go out of your way to give your key people hands-on experience with whatever you're suggesting.

- ***Maintain your distance.*** Despite the temptation to co-opt key people at every turn, make careful use of their time. If you spend too much time with your opinion leaders, some of them will lose their credibility.

- ***Share the whole truth.*** Have you ever been so caught up with the potential benefits of a new idea that, when sharing the concept with your key people, you forget to openly discuss the potential downsides? If you send your barefoot doctors into the field with placebos, it's only a matter of time until you destroy your relationship.

- ***Deliver on your promises.*** Never put one of your key people out on a limb and then saw it off. If you send someone out with a story and a promise, deliver on the promise. Make sacrifices. Do what it takes, but don't ever make a liar out of an opinion leader. You'll only do it once.

- ***Create forums.*** Appoint opinion leaders to cross-functional teams. Put them in jobs where they can have a great deal of contact with other people.

- ***Provide training.*** Help the good get even better. As you schedule interpersonal skills training, bring your opinion leaders in early. Have them cotrain. Give them one-on-one coaching.

- ***Restrict other conduits.*** Cut off rumors at the source. Put systems in place to get accurate information to every employee. If you don't, opinion leaders will spend most of their time correcting misunderstandings and debunking rumors instead of sharing and translating the vision.

Managing Symbolic Action

All the world's a stage, and all the men and women merely players.

WILLIAM SHAKESPEARE

In our last chapter we looked at ways to use Cell 3 (social influence) to help bring about change. Our premise was that leaders are not always in a position to deliver a credible message. Consequently, we suggested that they use opinion leaders and other barefoot doctors to help spread the word. A substantial portion of Cell 3's strength is drawn from the social influence of local opinion leaders. Effective leaders tap into this vital power source to foster new behavior.

But leaders must not rely exclusively on others. They are an irreplaceable part of everyone's

	Motivation	Ability
Individual	1	2
Social	**3**	4
Organizational	5	6

277

social environment. They can and do act in ways that lead to change. *Everything* they say isn't discounted or held in disdain. Skilled leaders wield their own social influence through critically timed and carefully enacted actions. They behave in ways that are visible, believable, and correctly interpreted.

To do so requires a sense of drama. In fact, a couple of decades ago one of the authors wrote an article entitled "Managing Is a Performing Art." It was rejected by a reviewer who suggested that if the silly premise contained in the title were true, one day Ronald Reagan would be president of the United States! Oh, that we had kept the review.

The point is that most people don't eagerly embrace the notion that leadership and acting have a lot in common. If acting means behaving in ways that are inconsistent with one's beliefs, then we agree. If acting means finding creative and effective methods of being seen and believed, then we buy into this notion. Shakespeare was right. The world is a stage, and leaders play a rather large part.

Your Audience: Every Stakeholder

Leaders, whether they like it or not, are constantly being watched. How they behave under critical circumstances has an enormous impact on the credibility of their espoused values and culture vision. Talk all they might, it's how they perform "onstage" that determines whether people believe them or not. When a value has been previously given only lip service, the need for credible action is just that much more important. For instance, you've talked about quality but done only whatever it takes to ship your product on time. You've extolled the value of teams but relied so heavily on individual contributions that group performance has been given no attention. You've openly heralded the importance of creating a learning environment and then chopped the head off the first person who took a risk and failed.

Worse yet, you didn't do all of these things, but a long line of leaders before you had the nasty habit of espousing one set of values while living another. It's not as if they were raging hypocrites; they just weren't always viewed in the most positive way. The values they preached sit before you now as lifeless forms. Unfortunately, these are the values that you embrace. Your job is to find a way to breathe life into values that are nearly dead. Like Christ stepping up to Lazarus' cave or Elisha facing a faithful widow's dead son, your job is to create the powerful force that transforms values that were once dead into active, breathing, motivating forces.

How's that for a challenge?

Actually, it *can* be done. Leaders can imbue nearly dead values with the vital life-giving force of credibility, but not without a great deal of thought and an appreciation for symbolic action—*your* personal Cell 3 influence on people in your organization—and *not* without giving up a couple of commonly held fantasies.

- **Fantasy Number One.** A good mass-media campaign will do it.
- **Fantasy Number Two.** You can do this *and* your "regular job."

Leaders have to do more than give a talk, design banners, appear on video, write a pithy memo or two, and otherwise count on "mediated" events to get their word across. Dead values require more credible actions. In addition, leaders can't expect to do what it will take only by coming up with an idea or two on their way to work. Their desire to imbue questionable values with life isn't a part-time job that can fit in the cracks. It isn't a hobby, it isn't a project, and it most certainly isn't a program (complete with a beginning, middle, and end). A leader's drive to imbue nearly dead values with life has to approach a near-maniacal passion. And then for this effort to really succeed, this all-consuming drive must be coupled with a flair for drama if it's ever going to be seen, believed, and correctly interpreted. To see how passion and drama work in concert to breathe life into values, let's look in on Patrick McDuffy again.

These Really Are Our New Values. Honest!

(Any resemblance between any character in the following story and real characters is purely intentional.)

Patrick McDuffy felt exhausted. It was Saturday evening, and he was driving home after three long days at a Vermont retreat. Some retreat. Into the wee hours of the morning he had argued, listened, and philosophized with the other members of the management team. It had taken them three long days, but eventually they had hammered out a shared vision of the organization's future. It was hard to believe that 36 hours of noodling had been boiled down to a one-page statement of their company's mission, values, and guiding principles.

Now, as he sat comfortably behind the wheel of his 1965 Mustang, he wondered how he and the other executives could engage 2,700 other employees in the vision captured on the single page. How could they communicate their hopes and dreams in a way that was understood?

Better still, what could they do to ensure that their message was not only understood, but believed?

To date, the management team's track record hadn't been so great. Last year, only two months after returning from a similar retreat, McDuffy had found sarcastic parodies of their newly articulated values scratched into the walls of the rest room. The lofty terms *integrity, loyalty,* and *service* had been replaced with *gullibility, duplicity,* and *servitude.* McDuffy had been quite certain that the mistakes weren't spelling errors.

Sending out a memo announcing their vision and giving speeches apparently hadn't had the desired effect. New values had to be communicated in a different way. But how?

Another Catch-22

Perhaps they shouldn't have made speeches about the new values. Getting product out the door on schedule had been the most important value before the retreat. Nobody had exactly needlepointed a sampler with the words "Get It out the Door," but everyone knew it just the same.

When it came right down to it, people probably would have been suspicious if they had made a public issue about the schedule. Important values simply weren't discussed. People acted in ways that made the values obvious, but they never talked about them. *Public* discussions were reserved for values that were espoused by people who wrote books or who sat in spacious offices. "Wannabe values" belonged on large banners or in annual speeches. There was no place for them in the trenches where people knew what really mattered.

So, here we are, thought McDuffy, *smack dab in the middle of a catch-22.* The existing values and behaviors had yielded the existing results, and they simply weren't good enough. The values the executive team had come up with at the retreat might yield new results, but people wouldn't learn about them unless someone made them the subject of a public discussion. Of course, if you talked about your new values, people probably wouldn't believe you. On the other hand, if you didn't talk about your new values, how would people know what's important?

It was an interesting challenge, McDuffy thought, *to breathe life into languishing values without giving energetic speeches, writing sincere memos, and producing forceful, catchy banners.* And then he remembered an experience he had had earlier in the year with his son. It had taught him about the power of sacrifice.

It Takes Sacrifice

After Patrick had been traveling five days a week on a new product rollout, his son Josh had asked him to attend a fathers-and-sons outing together. Patrick couldn't go, so he promised Josh he'd make it up to him. He was tired of having his home life pass by while he memorized the gates of the country's airports. He'd find a way to change his life around, even if it meant switching jobs. McDuffy still remembered the look on Josh's face when he promised to make it up to him—as well as his son's feigned enthusiasm when Josh replied, "Sure you will."

McDuffy decided then and there to do something to earn his son's trust. Three days later when Josh asked to go out for a pizza, McDuffy had looked longingly at his 105-inch wrap-around stereo TV. It was the first day of NFL action, and he'd been looking forward to it for six months. He had just watched two hours of pregame and now sat with the remote control melted into his hand. His son looked at him, then the TV, and smirked.

That's all it took. McDuffy bolted to his feet, and off they went to one of those pizza places that use motorized cartoon characters to drive kids into a frenzy and parents into therapy. Nobody had actually said anything to McDuffy, but as he went out the door with Josh in hand, his wife and other two children had looked at him with newfound respect. He was going to miss the 49ers/Redskins game! Maybe he was serious about changing after all.

How different this experience had been from the one he'd recently had at work. The chairman of the board had just announced an empowerment program—power to the people and all that. There had been a lot of hoopla about reducing the differences in the hierarchy. In addition, the *customer* was now supposed to be "boss" (above the *bosses*). Yeah, right. In any case, treating the bosses with reverential awe was supposed to be a thing of the past. It had been a nice speech.

Two days later, while flying to an outpost in Chicago, McDuffy had used a bonus coupon to upgrade to first class. Seated two rows in front of him had been the chairman. They had nodded politely to each other and then turned with relish to their respective Tom Clancy novels.

The next day, McDuffy's boss, eyes bulging with stress, had called him on the carpet. "What in the heck were you doing seated in first class?" probed his boss as the veins in his forehead curiously transformed into pulsating ropes. The chairman—that's right, the king himself—had called down and asked how a guy at McDuffy's level justified flying up front. The chairman had never called before in his whole life, and now this!

The upgrade explanation was sufficient to placate his boss, but McDuffy never forgot. *Right, we're supposed to reduce differences in the hierarchy,* McDuffy had fumed, *and the chairman wants to know why some lowlife like me is permitted to sit next to him.*

Sacrifice, not rhetoric, breathes life into values. In fact, McDuffy began to realize that it was futile to try to push for new values "out there" in the organization. He had to begin by fostering *his own dedication* to them. Values live in individuals, not in organizations. Speeches just raise questions. This sacrifice thing was worth exploring in more detail.

A Taxonomy of Sacrifices

As McDuffy examined the two contrasting experiences, he began to draw some conclusions. First, speeches by themselves simply threw down the gauntlet. They more or less dared people to catch you acting in ways that are inconsistent with the new vision.

Second, actions without some kind of up-front announcement could easily go unnoticed. Had he not talked about changing his life, the trip to the pizza parlor might have been logged as nothing more than a trip to the pizza parlor. And finally, even if a sacrifice is believable *and* visible, it might not be correctly interpreted. This he had learned from a quip contained in his latest edition of *Management Bromides:*

Patterson's Warnings

Warning Number One: *In an environment of mistrust (i.e., the known universe), all ambiguous behaviors will be interpreted negatively.*

Warning Number Two: *All behaviors are ambiguous.*

McDuffy had taken these warnings to mean that if you don't help people interpret what you're doing, they aren't very likely to give you the benefit of the doubt. In fact, they're likely to interpret your actions through a lens of cynicism.

Breathing life into a new vision (assuming you have one), McDuffy concluded, would require more than a sincere speech. The leaders would have to find ways to sacrifice for their newly articulated values. And these sacrifices would have to be Believable, Visible, and Correctly Interpreted.

It was to these topics that McDuffy threw his efforts. First, he tackled the believability challenge.

Making Actions Believable

"One can't *believe impossible things," said Alice. "I daresay you haven't had much practice," said the Queen. "When I was your age, I always did it for half-an-hour a day. Why, sometimes I've believed as many as six impossible things before breakfast."*

LEWIS CARROLL

McDuffy quickly learned that some "sacrifices" appeared more credible than others. For example, consider the chairman of the board who had given a speech on empowerment. Did giving the speech constitute a sacrifice?

It depended. Sacrifice isn't in the doing; it's in the circumstances. McDuffy recalled the story of Thomas Jefferson, who tearfully left his ill wife in Virginia to work in Philadelphia with those discussing American independence. Twice he had refused the request of his colleagues until it became clear they desperately needed his support. What a sacrifice. Jefferson truly believed in the importance of the Colonies' cause.[1] But what about the chairman's speech? Had the circumstances been such that giving a speech had required sacrifice? No. He hadn't even written it. Some speechwriter from headquarters concocted the document.

McDuffy recalled the time when he first learned that the president of the United States had not actually written a speech McDuffy had really enjoyed. Sure, the president may have outlined the speech and agreed on the concepts, but he hadn't taken the time to write it. Lincoln wrote his own Gettysburg Address. It was from the heart. He had taken time from his grueling schedule to write a number of drafts to be sure every word would carry his meaning. It was *that* important to him.[2] If it's important, McDuffy concluded, you sacrifice time for it. This became McDuffy's first guideline for making sacrifices believable: *If it's really important, spend time on it.*

When that same empowerment program had been rolled out, the senior executives refused to fund any training. No matter how many arguments were made, nobody seemed to be willing to spend a buck on the newly espoused value. This seemed fishy at the time. From the experience, McDuffy drew up guideline number two: *If you care about something, you should be willing to spend money on it.*

Guideline number three came from a positive example. One of his most respected bosses had done something McDuffy had never forgotten. After violating an espoused value, his boss had made a public apology. He had swallowed his pride (which was akin to swallowing arsenic in the minds of every other leader McDuffy had ever seen) and admitted his error. The principle had been more important than his ego—now *there* was a sacrifice. McDuffy drew up guideline number three: *If a value is important, you'll even sacrifice your personal pride.*

The fourth type of sacrifice came as a real shock. The same boss who had made a public apology did something nobody had ever done before— he sacrificed a previous priority. For 30 years the company had shipped on time. They may have shipped junk once in awhile, but they shipped. And when the quality movement arrived? They still shipped on time.

Then one day his boss had faced a "moment of truth." Either the product was going to have to be reworked to meet quality standards and thus miss the deadline, or the deadline would have to be met by shipping a substandard product. His boss had opted for quality. People were still talking about the day when quality was infused with credibility. McDuffy concluded with guideline number four: *If you really care about a new value, you'll be willing to sacrifice a previous priority.*

So there they were—McDuffy's four guidelines. For a sacrifice to be believable, it must involve some combination of:

- Time
- Money
- Ego
- Reordering of Priorities

STRATEGIES FOR MAKING SACRIFICES *BELIEVABLE*

McDuffy found dozens of examples of how these four values were sacrificed in some rather prominent settings. Each case helped executives make a newly promoted value more believable. He began assembling notes to be sure his learning would be cumulative rather than repetitive.

How You Use Your Time Reflects Your Values

Time is the most valuable thing a man can spend.

THEOPHRASTUS

Time is one resource for which no substitute exists. Children know that there's no such thing as "quality time." There's only quantity time. If you ever want a dose of reality, track how you spend your time over a month. Then ask yourself, "If I were someone else, what would I conclude about my values?"

What values would members of your organization say you hold by the kinds of activities that consume your time? Is your time spent in operations, budgeting, and micromanagement? Is the time you have to interact with others spent telling, cajoling, and politicking? What values are manifest in how you spend your time? What do you feel worried about? What do you spend idle time thinking about? What do you do with discretionary moments? Answers to these questions provide insight into your actual (versus your espoused) values.

If your answers to these questions are not the ones you prefer, change is possible. New values—preferred values—can replace the present lesser ones, just by spending time on them. Sacrifice breathes life into the values of both those who are watching the sacrifice and the person who is making it. As renowned social psychologist Leon Festinger once said, "Rats and people come to love things for which they have suffered."

Consider examples of some insightful people who know the importance of sacrificing time to breathe life into values.

Jack Welch at General Electric has expressed frustration at the slowness of change in his large organization. But with tireless determination, he continues to manifest his commitment to the values he espoused years ago. He spends 70 percent of his time talking about, arguing for, and demonstrating these values—even when he would rather have made a pronouncement or changed a policy.

John Young, the former president of Hewlett-Packard, spent 50 percent of his time working to perpetuate and develop the culture of that company.

Parents who want to foster the shared value of learning will spend time visiting museums, reading, and studying with their children. They don't have to tell their children to value learning. Their offspring "inherit" the value because they daily experience their parents' love of it. Children learn more from what their parents spend time on than from what they say (their "espoused" values).

Of course, spending time doesn't mean just large blocks of time. People judge what's important to you by what you give brain time to, that is, by what you attend to and get excited about. For example, the story is told about how President Reagan would sometimes doze in meetings while domestic issues were discussed. As soon as international issues emerged, he would physically and noticeably lean forward. Everyone knew what he cared about.

One way to demonstrate commitment through sacrificing time is to begin noticing and changing what you lean forward for. When issues of customer service, integrity, or employee development emerge, do you take note, probe for detail, and pay attention? Sometimes it's simply a matter of discipline to channel our automatic interests in new directions.

Time and Endurance

Leaders who are trying to promote new values often lament that it takes so long. "How many times," they ask, "will I have to repeat this message before it gets across?" It can be frustrating to talk and talk and not see others buying into the values. The honest answer to this question is, "It will never get completely across."

Positive values will never become self-sustaining in a culture, a relationship, or in ourselves. Over time, they become easier to sustain as we internalize them, but they must be fought for vigilantly or they wane. In times of peace and ease, the value of freedom declines. And as it declines, we begin to lose it. Any value worth fighting for must be fought for forever.

How many times do you have to repeat the message before you and others finally get it? Maybe a good rule of thumb is once or twice for every person in your organization. If you have 500 people in your organization, maybe when you've repeated it 1,000 times some will finally believe you're sincere. Or maybe somewhere along the way you'll just lose count and realize that if these really are *our* values, then just the very acts of talking about them, walking with them, and sacrificing for them are their own reward.

How You Spend Your Money Reflects Your Values

The three most important things a man has are, briefly, his private parts, his money, and his religious opinions.

Samuel Butler

Let's talk about something you value *and* that you might be willing to sacrifice—money. When leaders sacrifice real coin of the realm, people tend to believe that they care. For example, when executives at Universal Card Services spend precious capital dollars purchasing ergonomically designed workstations, posture-correct chairs, and other comfort-enhancing devices for customer-service employees, they confirm their commitment to their espoused value for "Employee Delight."

When Motorola continues training, even in soft economic times, to the tune of 3 percent of their payroll costs, they breathe life into their espoused value for developing human potential. When Ben & Jerry's Ice Cream brings a massage therapist in to work on employees who are doing all-nighters to get a machine back on line, they show they're serious about their commitment to quality of work life.

Are You Nuts?

John Drewes, president of a midsize intermodal carrier company in Sacramento, California, demonstrated undeniable congruence with its espoused value of serving the customer. In 1985, almond growers in the Sacramento Valley had a tough year. Consequently, Drewes's company expected volume from this important customer to drop significantly.

Standard pricing policy would have called for shipping prices to rise substantially for the suffering almond farmers. Drewes recognized their plight and made personal visits to each of the principals involved. He explained that he understood their situation and was prepared to help out by keeping his pricing at the previous year's levels. He wasn't sure, he continued, whether he could maintain those prices indefinitely, but at least for the present year they could count on no increase.

John expected nothing more than goodwill from the gesture. His drivers, mechanics, and other employees were moved by his sacrifice. His espoused value for service became a real value to many former skeptics.

Sacrificing Ego Reflects Your Values

The only wisdom we can hope to acquire
Is the wisdom of humility: humility is endless.

T. S. ELIOT

One day Bill Hewlett, cofounder of Hewlett-Packard, was leaving his office after a long day. In leaving, he inadvertently left the copy machine turned on. He hadn't quite rounded the corner when a lady on the janitorial crew shouted after him, "Hey, you! You left the copier on!" Hewlett immediately reversed his course, retraced his steps, turned off the machine, and thanked the lady. She reminded him of how Bill Hewlett had said how important reducing wasted costs was to the company's ongoing vitality. He listened patiently, apologized again, and promised that it wouldn't happen in the future.

The next week at a company picnic, the lady saw this same Mr. Hewlett giving a speech and realized whom she had confronted. From that day forward there was no question to her, or to the many others to whom she recounted the story, that Bill Hewlett truly valued conservation. She knew because he was willing to sacrifice ego for conservation.

Perhaps the largest sacrifice executives make occurs when they willingly place ego on the altar of their espoused values. When individuals are willing to demonstrate vulnerability or risk embarrassment on behalf of a value, the value takes on a deeper meaning for all those who recognize the sacrifice. More importantly, it grows in significance to the person making the sacrifice as well. Again, examples might help.

An executive at AT&T determined that his value for "being right" and "appearing competent" had to give way to a higher value for honest communication. He noticed a tendency among members of his organization to defer to him and realized that he had actually encouraged the deference. He was quick to shoot down opposing views and used his keen judgment to shred weaker arguments.

To communicate his belief in candid dialogue, he decided to make a sacrifice. He met with his staff and talked openly about his past shortcomings, expressing his desire for a change. He asked for people to "push back" on him when they disagreed. His invitation was met with external nods and internal cynicism.

The meeting then moved to routine business. On one particular issue he stated his thoughts, then invited others to "push back." An uncomfortable silence lingered. Finally, a newer member of the team spoke up. He expressed an opposing view and shared his reasons. No one looked directly at the executive. Using their politically safe peripheral vision, they were intensely aware of his every gesture. They watched as his typical reaction to opposition emerged—his jaw tightened and his ears turned pink. Then they watched him relax, compose himself, and say, "Those are sensible arguments. Tell me more."

Everyone present heaved a sigh of relief. He had passed the first test. It looked like he was serious.

Every person at that meeting walked out having felt the sacrifice of ego this leader made. In the following months, they watched him hold employee meetings in which he met harshly critical comments with probing questions and genuine openness. Little by little, his value for honest communication became more widely shared, and a new level of dialogue emerged.

These examples point out two specific ways leaders sacrifice ego for higher values:

- Publicly acknowledge personal violations of the value.
- Subordinate personal comfort to the value.

Sacrificing Other Key Priorities Reflects Your Values

We mentioned earlier the fantasy that you can foster significant change while still doing your *regular job*. Give it up. If you're trying to enthrone a new value, you often have to demote or depose an old one. If you want a strong family, some of your career ambition may need to bite the dust. If you want a culture of creativity, you'll have to sack some ceremony and deference. If you want to invite innovation, some predictability and control will have to go.

Perhaps the most powerful tool for lending credence to values lies in one's perceptual filters or lenses. They drive your most routine behavior, and through these behaviors people assess what's really important to you.

Monomania

The passions are the only orators which always persuade.

FRANÇOIS, DUC DE LA ROCHEFOUCAULD

When you passionately care about something (that is, when you care about it more than almost anything else in the world), this something becomes the center of your existence—and if not the center, then somewhere close. Oh yes, and just about anything can become an object of passion. For example, while taking her retired grandfather, Waldo, through a major university, a young woman was puzzled to note that all the elderly gentleman really cared to visit was the boiler room. Never mind the artwork on display in the fine-arts building or the repository of dinosaur bones stored under the seats at the football stadium. Waldo couldn't wait to muck around in the boiler room.

On the way to the boiler room (something the granddaughter had to ask directions to—in spite of the fact that she had walked by it nearly every day for four years), they walked through the bookstore. Waldo commented vigorously about the floor tiles. Apparently they were "real buggers to clean." As they meandered through the science building, passing a crowd that was fascinated with a molecular exhibit, Waldo commented on the number of unsightly nose prints on the exhibit's glass—and what it would take to remove the offending grease marks.

As the young woman thought about it, her grandfather's interest came as no surprise. He had worked for 30 years as a custodian for a midsize junior high school. Cleaning materials lay at the center of his universe. Schools were not temples of learning—at least not to this retired janitor. To him they were grease, dirt, and graffiti magnets. Nobody ever doubted what was important to him. He viewed the world through freshly cleaned glasses and continually focused on the number, length, shape, size, and quality of any streaks thereon.

Many exceptionally bright and creative people are similarly fixated, viewing the world through a single-value lens. "Single-minded monomaniacs," as Tom Peters referred to them, care so deeply about one issue that they find a way to work it into their every conversation. They interpret events through their single lens, and they're wonderful teachers and agents of change.

Professor J. Bonner Ritchie of Brigham Young University tells of a time when he and his teenage daughter were cruising along an autobahn in Germany. Bonner misjudged the road conditions and ended up with the vehicle's wheels pointing skyward. As the car settled into a ditch, shrouded in dust and debris, he turned to his daughter and exclaimed, "What a wonderful learning opportunity!" For him, it was no gag line. He was as serious as a heart attack. Despite the monumental inconvenience and expense that lay ahead, Bonner saw the calamity as a learning opportunity. Why? Because, as anyone who knows him will tell you, learning lies at the center of his universe.

Leaders, caught in the throes of change, are essentially being asked to expand the center of their universe. They must either put something else in the center or at least make room for an additional occupant. In either case, the newly elevated value had better become part of the new interpretive lens, or it'll never be believed. Like Dr. Ritchie with learning and the custodian with cleaning, leaders have to find a way to interpret the world through their new passion. If not, they can count on the amount of cynicism expanding.

Consider the expressions of a "monomaniac": *"Oh yes, we're facing a downturn in the economy. What a wonderful opportunity for us to implement our new quality system."* or *"Oh yes, we're experiencing an upturn in the economy. What a wonderful opportunity for us to implement our new quality system."* or *"Yes, it is a good morning, isn't it? It's particularly good for working on our new quality system."* or *"Hit by a truck, was he? Perhaps the engorged subdural hematoma will help rearrange his thinking to be more supportive of our new quality system."* (Okay, so the last example is over the edge, but you get the picture.)

The ultimate form of sacrificing a previous priority is giving up its place at the center of your interpretive lens. As you view circumstances through a new lens, you ask new questions, attend to new issues, and interpret events in new ways. And people believe your commitment to the new value.

STRATEGIES FOR MAKING SACRIFICES *VISIBLE*

Make visible what, without you, might perhaps never have been seen.
                                                    ROBERT BRESSON

It's time for leaders to learn from another group of specialists. In the quote above, Mr. Bresson was suggesting that the task of a cinematographer was to make the invisible visible. And so leaders have one more job. Like the cinematographer, they must find ways to help people see what they might not have otherwise seen. But how?

Sacrificing time, money, ego, or a previous priority helps make newly espoused values believable. But what does it take to make values visible? Closet sacrifices, no matter how sincere, don't help foster a new vision. While Mother Teresa's private works do a great deal of good, they also serve to influence the behavior of others when they're made public.

To make new values more salient, to turn them from invisible forces to visible behaviors, leaders must be found constantly:

- *"Talking the Talk"* (speaking about their vision)
- *"Walking the Talk"* (acting in ways that are consistent with the vision)
- *"Stalking the Walk"* (finding and rewarding others who act in ways to support the vision)

Simply talking about values isn't enough. Talk has to be backed up by action. Likewise, action without talk is equally insufficient. Action, talk; talk, action—they have to be a team.

Talk the Talk

Let's shoot a hole in a common leadership myth. For years, people have been arguing that platform skills (such as the ability to speak in public or charismatically make presentations) are not necessary to effective leadership. To support this assertion, scholars point to leaders who have achieved noteworthy results but who have been genuine "snoozers" when put in front of an audience.

Such logic is akin to saying that you don't need ropes to climb the Eiger. Perhaps not, but they sure help. Our experience is that leaders who succeed without strong "talking" skills (be it in large groups or one on one) do it *in spite of* this deficit. If you need to engage people in your quest, you need to communicate with them. Leaders who are incessantly and *skillfully talking the talk* are far more effective (all other things being constant) than those who don't. In two change projects the authors worked on, the human resources manager went so far as to bring in a speech coach to help executives improve their ability to talk the talk in front of large audiences.

Listed below are some other methods savvy executives have used to "talk the talk" as a way to make their sacrifices visible. Notice that all of them involve a sacrifice of time and personal vulnerability. Later we'll look at skills and principles of talking the talk well.

- **Brown-Bag Lunches.** Invite a handful of employees to come to an informal dialogue where the values are discussed in relation to day-to-day concerns. Talk about recent, true-to-life examples.
- **"Speak Up" Forums.** In newsletters, in employee meetings, or in structured interviews, encourage employees to "speak up" about ways they see values being actualized or compromised in the organization. Take responsibility for researching and responding to every comment.
- **Video Messages.** Create video speeches that reinforce the values. Link speeches to interviews with people who have experienced actual sacrifices.
- **Single-Point Lessons.** Develop "lessonettes" (five to ten minutes long) that dramatize ways values can and should be expressed in the workplace. Go out and meet with employees in their regular staff meetings and teach these points.
- **MBWA (Management by Walking Around).** Wander around and hold informal chats with employees regarding their feelings about the values. Ask for examples of ways leaders and others could be more consistent with them.
- **Newsletter Articles.** Write regular articles in company publications about the values, ways they're being practiced, or recent decisions made in support of the values.

A Matter of Timing

Talking alone doesn't make something visible. There's an art to timing your comments. Those with a real sense of drama understand how timing and ordering their comments can have a big impact on their visibility. For example, consider a poignant scene from the movie *Twelve O'Clock High*. The vignette captures the drama possible in sacrificing key values.

The scene we're referring to involved a group of pilots who were debriefing after their first successful bombing run. One of the pilots had pulled away from the group (breaking the integrity of their formation) to help out the pilot of another plane. Gregory Peck, playing the role of Colonel Savage (the squadron's leader), queried the errant pilot. Rather than launch into a lecture on the importance of holding their position in the formation, Peck took a different route. He asked the pilot if he knew the colleague who had been in trouble.

The aviator explained that the pilot at risk had been his roommate. Peck stuck with that thought for awhile. The pilot continued to talk about how he respected and admired his roommate. Peck allowed the group time to think about the loyalty they had developed for their own roommates.

As the emotion grew to a crescendo, Peck turned to the battalion adjutant and told him to draw up a new billet structure. Nobody was to keep the same roommate. At first, no one could believe that their leader would intentionally slash one of their only luxuries—deep and abiding friendships. Peck pounced on the teaching moment. He pointed out that the flight integrity of the battalion was even more important than friendship. Eventually, they would have no friends if they sacrificed their position in the air.

Colonel Savage, the movie character, had been drawn with a deep sense of drama. He understood that a questionable value could be elevated to new heights by placing it above what had previously been inviolate. More importantly, he appreciated the importance of highlighting the significance of an old value (one that had been long understood and cherished) *immediately before* sacrificing it to a new one. He waited until all eyes were on him, he created a sense of drama, and then he sprung his message. Peck knew how to make his talk visible. He understood that visibility, like humor, is often a matter of timing.

Walk the Talk

Only moments after you've taken the time to "talk the talk," people will look to see if you're sincere. They'll watch to see if you "walk it." As we suggested earlier, many are looking to prove that, at your core, you're basically a hypocrite. When you espouse a value, you put a target on your back. You dare people to find you behaving in ways that are inconsistent with your public word. And some can't wait to see you fall flat.

Others try to protect themselves. They want to believe your magic story, but dare they? Dare they make themselves vulnerable by embracing a new hope? They don't do this easily. They need proof. So they watch.

They watch to see if you're going to turn the dream into a reality. They turn to you for proof. Consequently, as soon as you take a stand for a value, 1,000 eyes are trained on you to see if you're going to stray from the formula—some hoping for you to fall, others praying for you to succeed.

Isn't leadership fun?

Fortunately, people won't be watching everything you do. Whether you scratch your ear or arch your eyebrow in the rest room is probably unimportant. But a scratch or an arch during an important plant tour can lead to wild interpretations. We once watched a group of senior managers "debrief" an executive vice-president's tour. A full 30 minutes of the discussion focused on whether he shook his head or just twitched at a certain proposal.

These critical moments are called "symbolic." The actions taken in these instances will be interpreted by members of the organization as evidence of whether you're "walking the talk" or "stomping the talk." The monomaniacs discussed earlier would never miss an opportunity to give evidence of sincerity to their value because they own it to the bone. For us mortals who constantly struggle with the depth of our commitment, a more conscious effort is required. We must both recognize and seize symbolic moments. Symbolic moments occur when:

- Two or more values are perceived to be at odds.
- At least one person who will blab is watching.

Unfortunately, a staggering number of situations fit these two criteria. As one person put it, "The higher you climb up the flagpole, the more others can see your rear end." The larger your stewardship, the greater attention will be paid to even your smallest actions. Here's an abbreviated list of actions that invite misinterpretation: policy decisions, written communications, budget announcements, systems and structures design, perks, dress, titles, promotions, meetings (what's on and off the agenda; what's first, second, third, and so on; who's invited and who's not; where they're held; where they aren't held), and just about everything you do with the performance-review cycle.

Recognizing and seizing all these moments requires greater awareness than any one person possesses. The ultimate goal, then, is to come to own the values so deeply that such competence becomes natural and automatic. In the meantime, you must learn to seize the moment.

Seize the Moment

Here are three steps you can take to help you in your efforts to be seen as an honest leader who can be counted on to not only talk the talk, but walk the talk.

Invite Open Feedback about Violations of Values. One of the best ways to identify where you're vulnerable is to ask others which of your actions are currently being viewed as inconsistent with what you're espousing. Once you know which values are seen as most vulnerable, you know where to focus your attention. One company we referred to earlier used a "Speak Up" column in an internal publication to invite this kind of feedback. Focus interviews and one-on-one discussions are two other excellent ways for leaders to identify their most visible conflicts. Remember, your goal is to identify which values are seen to be questionable so you'll know where to focus your attention.

Identify the Situations in Which You Are Most Likely to Trespass. Once you're aware of which values are seen to be at risk, assemble a list of the situations people seem most concerned about. If, for instance, issues relative to compensation and reward draw the most criticism, this can become a cue to leaders that any time this kind of decision is being made they must slow down and assess congruence with the espoused values. After assembling the categories of situations to which you must be better attuned, determine which ones are spontaneous (they happen to you) and which ones are planned (you can see them coming).

Plan How You Will Respond in These Situations. Next, decide how you'll respond in the planned situations. These are the easy ones. Come up with some ideas on your own, and then ask your insightful and honest colleagues how to "walk" and "talk" the ideas appropriately. In addition, draw heavily from your opinion leaders when seeking advice on how you should respond to "moments of truth." For spontaneous situations, practice answering tough questions in congruent ways.

Publicly Acknowledge Your Fallibility

We have all had the experience of finding that our reactions and perhaps even our deeds have denied beliefs we thought were ours.

JAMES BALDWIN

Finally, since you most certainly will act in ways that make it look like you don't really believe in certain values, get good at sacrificing your ego. If you mess up, don't be afraid to apologize. Explain the circumstances, and restate your commitment.

> Of all the ironies of leadership, perhaps the greatest is that leaders most convincingly show their strength by publicly admitting to a mistake. It takes confidence to be able to say "I was wrong."

For example, consider the humble pie consumed by the president of a large health-care firm. At the time, he was holding a video conference with virtually every employee in the company spread across a dozen states. During the early stages of the two-day session, he explained that the company would be hiring two more vice-presidents to help reestablish control over a growing problem. Within moments, people from all over the country cried "foul." Everyone from a phlebotomist in Fargo to a housekeeper in Chicago complained that putting in new people at the top violated their core value of employee involvement. They suggested that control came through a capable and committed workforce, not through more bosses at the top. Others vehemently spoke about the sacrifices they had been making to cut costs and couldn't imagine how adding two top-salaried bosses who would be far removed from any real customers would do anything other than add to their expenses.

The consultant working with the president called for a break. "We're facing a moment of truth," he suggested. "If they're right and you're wrong, it's time to back off." Of course, it wasn't simply a matter of who was right and who was wrong. There were pluses and minuses to the decision. However, as the president thought about the reaction and the arguments people were making, he had to agree with most of them. So he decided to back off. This, of course, meant withdrawing two jobs that had been offered to senior executives—and all of the negative consequences associated with reneging on a contract. Nevertheless, the value for employee involvement warranted swallowing the bitter pill.

The leader came back from the break, stood in front of the camera, and announced to 35,000 employees that they were right. He wouldn't be bringing on two more people. He apologized for missing the implications of his decision and went on from there. That moment, according to the consultant, was the turning point of the conference, and 35,000 potential cynics believed that the head honcho wasn't a hypocrite after all. "Had he not admitted to the mistake," explained the consultant, "nobody would have placed any credence on what he said from that moment forward. By admitting it, he let everyone know he really was committed to their value of involvement. He never looked stronger."

We hope leaders won't have to make public apologies very often. Nevertheless, should the occasion arise, seize the moment. Show your strength by being able to say "I was wrong."

Response to a Crisis

If people are still curious about whether you're really "walking the talk," any doubt they may have will disappear during a moment of crisis. When you're caught between a rock and a hard place, people will draw their most intractable conclusions about the "real" motives of their leaders.

A crisis, by definition, is a time when a key value is at risk. At this moment, all eyes are on the leaders. If they scuttle the newly espoused value in favor of the old, you can bet they've just fueled the fires of cynicism. On the other hand, if they choose to reaffirm the new value over the old, they've gone a long way toward enhancing the credibility of the new value.

For example, while conducting a two-day off-site meeting for senior executives, the vice-president in charge received an emergency phone call. Due to a human error, several million customers had been denied their service—one that was essential to the running of hospitals, airports, and other vital industries. The VP checked to see that the problem was being resolved and then returned to the off-site meeting.

As word of the emergency spread, everyone expected the VP to announce that due to circumstances beyond his control he'd be leaving. He didn't. He explained the crisis, what was being done to resolve it, and then asked the facilitator to continue with the discussion.

Before the off-site meeting began, the VP had spoken of the importance of the meeting. He'd carefully crafted a memo outlining the proposed agenda and how each item linked to the overall corporate mission. He'd explained how the meeting would be used to develop a three-year strategy and had asked that everyone clear his or her calendar to attend. If necessary, vacations were to be rescheduled. The off-site location was selected for its strategic advantage rather than its recreational appeal. Every detail of the agenda had been carefully orchestrated to communicate, "This is important!"

None of the elaborate preparations matched the impact of the VP staying for the meeting, in spite of the fact that the organization faced a crisis. The VP couldn't have orchestrated a better way to communicate his support. He, like most skilled leaders, looked on a crisis as a teaching opportunity. He practically leaped at the chance to show his commitment. Where else could he count on the undivided attention of every executive? Where else would his actions be viewed as the "real" interpretation of his value system?

If you're having trouble convincing people you're serious about a newly espoused value; if the value is one that historically has been given lip service, but has not really been seen as all that important; and if you're really serious about elevating its importance, wait for a crisis. Then leap on the learning opportunity. Sacrifice the old value. Affirm the new value.

Stalk the Walk

The fame of heroes owes little to the extent of their conquests and all to the success of the tributes paid to them.

JEAN GENET

McDuffy realized that as others begin to make sacrifices, an executive's job is to make these sacrifices visible as well. Leaders have to find a way to make new heroes and heroines—ones who have taken the risk associated with walking the new talk. Employees need to know leaders are doing more than just talking about the importance of new behaviors—they're watching for them and are rewarding those who are willing to try something new.

The most common attempt to find and reward new heroes is to create an "employee of the month" program. Although these are generally well-intended attempts to foster excellence, they typically fall short of what it takes—unless accompanied by myriad other practices.

When we hold someone up as a hero, we must consider who, where, and how. If trust between managers and nonmanagers is low, then a manager (the who) recognizing someone in a corporate banquet (the where) by awarding them a plaque (the how) may hold little value. In contrast, a teammate who pats a co-worker on the back in front of his buddies may make a tremendous difference. The setting, the method, and the delivery of recognition and praise are crucial elements to consider as you attempt to find and reward new heroes and heroines.

Following are some effective ways to watch for, identify, and reward those brave souls who embrace the new vision.

Tell Stories

In newsletters, single-point lessons, and speeches, telling a vivid story of someone heroically enacting a company value has a tremendous impact. An internal customer, for instance, who writes an article about her supplier who stayed up late to complete a project can draw the attention of many to a heroic sacrifice on behalf of a value. Good leaders are often good storytellers.

Recognize Heroism

In local publications and in public forums, recognize heroism. When Jan Carlzon of Scandinavian Airlines wrote the book *Moments of Truth*,[3] his primary audience was not the general public. He claims he wrote it to his employees. The book had a lot more credibility and was more likely to be read by them if they bought it off a book rack at their local bookstore.

Recognizing heroic behavior in an article in a local newspaper, or even in paid advertising space, can be very potent in reinforcing values. Saturn Corporation has done a wonderful job of creating new heroes by sharing hero stories with America in its television commercials.

Reevaluate Reward Systems

Formal rewards (compensation and promotion) speak loudly for or against values. Redesigning human resources systems to be more consistent with values is often very important in recognizing and rewarding the right people.

We caution executives not to place too much hope in the effect an overhauled human resources system will have on behavior. This is kind of a "darned if you do, darned if you don't" activity. People tire of changed human resources systems, and if they gamed the old one, they'll figure out how to game the new one. If you don't remove obvious hypocrisies, you'll give evidence to support continued cynicism. The most you can hope for is a removal of the disincentives to behaviors that support the values. Attempting to create incentives for every positive behavior is like trying to pay people for kindness. Extrinsic rewards shouldn't be allowed to overwhelm what should be intrinsically motivating actions.

Management by Walking Around

As you wander around, ask for examples of people who are "doing it right." Give pats on the back generously, and take those people with you whose "pats" others would value receiving.

"Give a World of Thanks"

At the Universal Card Services unit of AT&T, employees can give each other "A World of Thanks." These are nothing more than kind notes on special note paper acknowledging "noteworthy" efforts. Receiving a handwritten note from a busy leader thanking you for a job well done can be as welcome as a fresh, cool breeze in a stuffy room.

STRATEGIES FOR ENSURING THAT SACRIFICES ARE CORRECTLY INTERPRETED

All meanings, we know, depend on the key of interpretation.

GEORGE ELIOT

By this point, McDuffy was becoming a real expert on breathing life into values. He had learned that values need to be believable, visible, and correctly interpreted. Believability depended on sacrificing something that really was a sacrifice. Next, he'd discovered that to make values visible, they had to be talked about, hunted down, and rewarded (stalked). Now he faced the final challenge: Ensuring that values were correctly interpreted. He had saved this challenge for last because he knew it would be the most difficult.

It Takes Some Convincing

People seem to be born with built-in duplicity sensors. McDuffy himself had been quite a cynic. Worse yet, even when duplicity shouldn't have been an issue with a newly espoused value, it had been. Examples were plentiful.

In one organization, an expensive coffee mug with a fancy depiction of the new mission statement was distributed to each employee. Some employees observed that the new mugs were a full ounce smaller than the older ones. They decided that the new mugs were an underhanded attempt to get people to drink less coffee. To them it had been a thinly veiled cost-cutting device. A decision in another organization to eliminate time cards was interpreted as an attempt to cut jobs (four full-time clerks were employed filing the time cards).

What were the words of warning McDuffy had read? Oh yes, in an environment of mistrust, all ambiguous behaviors will be interpreted negatively. And, of course, all behaviors are ambiguous.

Talk the Walk

McDuffy learned that people often look behind the actions for the motive that *most confirms* their current worst perception of the company's leaders. Because of this unfortunate dynamic, it's essential that leaders not only scrupulously walk the talk (make decisions consistent with the values), but that they help interpret the walk as well. To do so, they must "talk the walk." With each action, they must go to great pains to reveal their thought processes and motives. They must clearly tie the decision to their values. Once again, McDuffy found examples helpful.

He learned of one executive who had been trying to make it legitimate for people in his organization to balance professional with personal needs. The executive had realized that people were being ground up by the corporate machine. Many (maybe most) were sacrificing precious family relationships and long-held personal goals. He could relate. He had made the same sacrifices. So he scheduled his first vacation in 10 years. He decided to take a month off and travel with his 19-year-old son (who was soon to leave the nest forever) to China.

Word of the vacation hit the grapevine instantly. Several people hinted that this executive was looking for other jobs. Some said he was distancing himself from problems that would hit while he was gone. In a dozen "creative" ways, they began interpreting the action in the worst way possible.

The executive responded brilliantly. Rather than simply allow rumors to grow, he "talked the walk." He took a significant chunk of time at the next all-employee meeting to teach about the value of balance they'd been pushing. Then he paused and spoke personally about his relationship with his son. He told of their 10-year dream of going to China. He described what he was about to do to demonstrate his support for balance. Employee perception changed noticeably in a matter of minutes. By walking the talk and then talking the walk, this talented leader took giant strides in reinforcing a new value.

Of course, this single event didn't turn the tide of workaholism. Over the next few months, he continued to support people who left meetings early in order to be with their kids at a soccer game or attend a family reunion. He asked every leader to sit down and look at his or her workload and personal balance. All of these, and similar actions to put balance back into people's lives, were reinforced as employees remembered the top executive's trip to China with his son.

BREATHING LIFE INTO LANGUISHING VALUES: McDUFFY'S SUMMARY

McDuffy had come a long way. He had taken the concept of sacrifice and found ways to apply it to his own troubled situation. First, McDuffy had learned to think of organizational culture as a slow but inexhaustible inertia driving people in a certain direction. He found that the behaviors expressed by a certain culture endure until new forces begin to turn them in another direction. Since the existing culture clings to deeply held values and assumptions, changing its direction will be like turning back the Missouri River. It can be done, but only with incredible effort.

Next, through careful analysis he had learned that sacrifices, no matter how sincere, can breathe life into languishing values—but only if they're believable, visible, and correctly interpreted.

Believability, McDuffy discovered, requires honest sacrifice. Giving a speech, writing a memo, or paying someone to make a banner rarely qualifies. On the other hand, giving up precious time, scarce money, delicate egos, or previous priorities helps ensure believability.

Visibility, McDuffy learned, requires talking the talk. Leaders need to follow their actions with ongoing discussions of their values. Talking, walking; walking, talking—they have to be a team.

In a similar vein, once the talk is walked, the walk must be stalked. People who are beginning to incorporate the new values into their daily work lives should be made the company's new heroes and heroines. Executives need to break away from mahogany-lined offices, stalk those who are doing the right thing (in spite of years of contrary history), and then celebrate their actions.

McDuffy learned about the importance of talking the walk. Once believable sacrifices have been made and put before the public, leaders need to ensure that their actions are interpreted correctly. If not, in an environment of mistrust, all ambiguous behaviors are interpreted negatively.

As McDuffy reviewed his recommendations, it sounded like a lot of work. Making sacrifices believable, visible, and correctly interpreted wasn't going to be a piece of cake. And the job would probably never end. But then again, who ever said change would be easy? Besides, McDuffy had set his standard for success high. Two years from now he was counting on reading a healthier brand of graffiti on the rest room walls.

Finally, McDuffy found a book by a popular culture theorist who stated that the stories told in organizations were representations of its values. If most of the stories were cynical in nature, you could bet you had a culture of mistrust. Over the following months, McDuffy found that stories that had begun as cynical moved gradually toward cautious scorn (a mix of hope and fear) and finally grew into bald-faced praise. Passing through these phases took months (and even years in some places), but they happened.

IN SUMMARY

Cell 3 wields a great deal of influence. Most of what we do is affected by our trust in the opinions of others and our desire to fit in socially. Effective leaders master Cell 3. They understand two critical principles. When it comes to turning a dream into reality:

1. You can't delegate it.
2. You have to delegate it.

You can't delegate it. Patrick McDuffy discovered that unless leaders take personal ownership in, and even sacrifice for, the new values and behaviors, they won't happen. Less effective leaders forget this over time. You can't delegate the leadership of change. It will require a huge chunk of your time. Make sure you're serious about your intended changes, because the road is always long, occasionally tedious, and often personally threatening. You will have to resist the urge to be sidetracked at any point. You will need the grim determination to repeat your message for the millionth time in a tone of voice that sounds like you just received the present you've always wanted. You will have to confront how your own behavior perpetuates the current culture. You must be willing to sacrifice time, money, ego, and previous priorities on behalf of the new values. This isn't a hobby; it is your primary job as a leader.

You have to delegate it. Most people will make the final decision to try a new behavior for reasons other than because you asked them to, or even because it might be beneficial. They will do so because a respected colleague is already doing it. You have the ability to build awareness of need. You have the ability to let people know this is expected of them. You can even show your sincerity by doing it. These actions are necessary but insufficient to encourage widespread adoption of the new way. What will make or break it is the presence of other agents of change more proximate to the workforce. You'll need *barefoot doctors*. Much of your influence should be directed toward them. You must give them what they need to succeed.

CHAPTER 12

Putting the Punch in Praise

The deepest principle of human nature is the craving to be appreciated.

WILLIAM JAMES

Praise is a powerful Cell 3 tool. Wise leaders use it to make heroes and heroines out of people who are moving the organization toward vitality. They scour the organization regularly, looking for opportunities to commend, compliment, and congratulate. They never underestimate the power of praise in helping shape a new culture.

A few years ago, one of the authors saw the need for a focused essay on praise. He compiled the following dozen principles as a way of helping

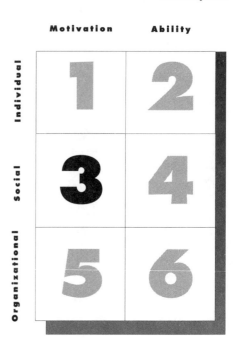

leaders who were missing out on or overlooking this tremendous Cell 3 lever.

He started with a word of caution. After all, in spite of the fact that praise is cherished by employees, touted by leaders, and lauded by researchers, it has great potential for abuse. He discovered this obscure fact some 40 years ago while collecting bugs. Here's his story.

The Roi-Tan Cemetery

When I was a little tyke, I loved insects. Sometimes I'd watch ants for hours as they hauled Lilliputian bundles down footprint valleys and up tennis-shoe mountains. On listless summer days, I'd crumble a Necco wafer over our front-porch deck and then lie back and watch as hundreds of tiny stevedores struggled to carry pastel sugar boulders across the mottled surface.

My dad, seeing that I liked insects, helped me move from casual observer to hunter. He encouraged me to start a full-fledged collection by scrounging a discarded Roi-Tan cigar box and pouring melted paraffin in the bottom. After the wax hardened, he presented me with a covered pinboard to be used for mounting dead bugs.

I delighted in the gift. For a week I scurried around with a Kerr quart jar, gleefully capturing anything that had the temerity to crawl or fly within my reach. Within a few days, my homemade display case was packed with spiders, dragonflies, and beetles—all neatly pierced with a pin and exhibited in rows, carefully arranged by species and size.

Surprisingly, despite my original enthusiasm, I quickly became bored with the hobby. My parents chided me for not having "stick-to-itiveness," but I felt little guilt. I knew that I hadn't quickly lost interest like a mindless twit who would never amount to anything (my older brother's words). I hadn't loved insects in the first place. What I had loved was insect *life*. The job of managing a bug cemetery didn't hold much appeal. I preferred watching two armies of ants battle feverishly over a decaying bird. Catching a glimpse of a dung beetle taking flight (not unlike a garbage truck going airborne) was equally fascinating. On the other hand, gawking at one trapped in a box with a pin stuck through its neck held no appeal. To me, insect carcasses just weren't insects.

Praise Carcasses

Praise, like the insects I captured as a boy, also has a soul. And, like any living creature, if you dissect praise into its parts, you're left with a hollow carcass. Praise, stuck to a wax board with a pin through its neck, despite its toothy smile and fancy language, takes on an aseptic, clinical sheen and becomes a cold tool wielded by hucksters, flim-flam artists, and charlatans.

The prize for stripping praise of any vestiges of life has to be given to an MBA student I once taught. He wrote a haunting paper about how he had employed "positive reinforcement" to entice his roommate's significant other to sleep with him. Day by day he plotted new ways to "reward" his unsuspecting target until he achieved his goal. It was enough to make your skin crawl. Praise, used as a club, is an ugly tool.

A DOZEN PRINCIPLES

Some people pay a compliment as if they expected a receipt.

"KIN" HUBBARD

This chapter is intended to aid the well intentioned. We hope to capture what is decent in all of us and nurture it. Those who seek a deeper understanding of the fragile act of communicating admiration may benefit from a dozen principles we've learned from the best. The principles include:

- Praise often.
- Praise with panache.
- Celebrate small successes.
- Praise in perpetuity.
- Praise with feeling.
- Praise with clarity.
- Praise efforts, not just results.
- Praise accomplishments of which the other person is proud.
- Know what the other person values.
- Praise individuals in private.
- Praise honestly, and then stick to it.
- Allow others the delight of giving praise.

PRAISE OFTEN

Praise can have a remarkable impact on the human spirit. I learned this lesson over 25 years ago while laboring in the beautiful city of Rio de Janeiro. Here's what happened.

The Professional Poker Chipper

One day while rummaging through a specialty bookstore, I stumbled onto a copy of Dale Carnegie's extraordinary book *How to Win Friends and Influence People*.[1] I was immediately impressed with his intriguing suggestion to praise someone every day. He argued that praise was extremely underutilized and that just about everybody needs to sip from the river of adulation more deeply. Start with strangers, he recommended.

Within an hour of reading Mr. Carnegie's invitation, I boarded a rickety bus that passed through a seedy barrio just outside Rio. Jammed in the claptrap vehicle were people from all walks of life— and some of their pigs, snakes, and chickens. As the decaying vehicle precariously plowed through the crowded streets, slowing only to allow passengers to board and exit, I was reminded of a carnival ride from my youth—only on a carnival ride you never *really* think you're going to die.

In the center of this pulsating miasma of commuters struggled a 16-year-old boy. His miserable job was to collect money for the ride (a whopping three-fourths of a penny). His task was to sell a poker chip to passengers who boarded through the rear door. Customers then used the chip as a pass to exit through the front. The driver had no time for taking money. He was consumed with careening through the street at a speed that would throw Ralph Nader into a seizure. The task of extracting the fare from a reluctant populace fell on teenage boys, who were paid 75 cents a day. The job was smelly, uncomfortable, and thankless.

And yet the spirited young man I watched that morning was the picture of professionalism. Slithering his way through a tangled mass of flesh, fur, and feathers, he smiled infectiously as he made change. When he finally clicked his poker chips at me, I decided to give Mr. Carnegie's advice a test. "I've been watching you," I began. *"É verdade?* [Really?]" he responded with a hint of suspicion. "Yes," I continued. "For over a year I've been riding buses in this neighborhood, and I've never seen anyone as effective at his job as you are."

The 300-Watt Reaction

And then it happened. The young man absolutely oozed with pleasure. It turns out that this boy, trapped in a man's job, had worked on that dilapidated bus for over three years, starting full-time when he was 13.

During that period of unrelenting jostling, gibing, and jabbing, not once had anyone mentioned his professional demeanor—not his supervisor, not the driver, and certainly not a passenger. I was the first. So when I praised him for his work, he was stunned, then moved. As the compliment sunk in, his easy smile surged from 50 to 300 watts. I had made a friend.

From that moment on, the poker chipper wouldn't take my money. In fact, whenever he spotted me walking near his route, he'd ask the driver to pull over and let me on. Then he'd introduce me as his *amigo Americano* to an annoyed mass of passengers. Once he asked me where I was going, and when he learned that my destination was two miles off his route, he didn't falter. He briskly announced that the bus would be taking an unscheduled side trip and advised the driver of our new destination.

I've never forgotten the lesson taught me in that rickety bus a quarter century ago. I'd seen praise work its magic. Although I'm far from perfect in expressing appreciation, I'm different for having had the experience. I know that praise can heal the wounded psyche and is as near at hand as your best intentions. It should surprise no one to learn that well-balanced leaders praise whenever they get a chance. They don't just wander around looking for problems. They're equally desirous to find "things gone right." They understand that the number one complaint expressed by employees (one that has remained at the top of the list for over 25 years, despite the fact that it is published more often than any other leadership fact) is that their bosses don't recognize them when they do a good job. Well-balanced leaders are doing their best to turn this statistic around. It is they who taught us that praise is nature's most valued interpersonal gift. And from that observation we develop our first principle: Praise often.

PRAISE WITH PANACHE

I can live for two months on a good compliment.

MARK TWAIN

Skilled individuals, in addition to the fact that they praise more frequently than your average bloke, also praise with more verve. They express admiration with energy and flair. Unlike many of us who hesitantly express our admiration (as if we have a governor or brake on our creative expression), they praise unfalteringly and with real panache. Consider one of the world's best.

Marden's Miracle

When it comes to praise, it was Marden Abodi who taught me the difference between frequency and quality. He not only praised often, he praised with a genuine flair.

Mr. Abodi taught my daughters piano during their midteens. He followed a long line of strict traditionalists who had shamed, harangued, and otherwise shackled my children to the ivories. Mr. Abodi brought the storm-trooper tactics to a screeching halt. He had been a protégé of Arthur Rubinstein and was himself world renowned for his animated interpretation of Scott Joplin. But would he be a competent teacher? Knowing how to play is not the same as knowing how to teach.

We had no reason to worry. Mr. Abodi had studied with two creative masters, not one—Rubinstein, the master performer, and Suzuki, the master teacher. After Rubinstein taught Mr. Abodi to play like an angel, Suzuki taught him to teach like a saint. Suzuki, the Japanese master, avoided the traditional "three R's": rebuke, reprimand, and reproach. Instead, he praised with panache, and Mr. Abodi learned well.

Our daughters returned "born again" from their first lesson with their new teacher. The flamboyant Mr. Abodi, who looked more like Hollywood's stereotype of an eccentric artist than a dowdy piano teacher, had been a veritable cheerleader. As he listened to his new students perform, he paced back and forth—punctuating his rapid strides with an occasional, "Wonderful!" It was clear that he reveled in their success.

A Gift for Flair

As the months unfolded, Mr. Abodi (who became Marden to me) did more than provide verbal rewards to his students. He cared enough to learn about their other interests. When he discovered they cared about fashion, he gave them French fashion magazines he'd picked up in Paris. He also found dozens of ways to say, "Good job, I'm proud of you." During lessons, when new students wandered in, Marden had my daughters perform for the novices and then gloated over their prowess. He took particular pride in having them perform for adults.

Marden had a passion for praise. He gave it with his own special brand of verve. He was demanding, but when things went well (and something always did), he meted out praise in heaping, creative spoonfuls. While other teachers had felt constrained in their expressions of admiration, Marden turned each word of praise into a celebration. It is to him we dedicate our second principle: Praise with panache. His message, in essence, was, *"Don't just pick up the frequency, pick up the energy."*

CELEBRATE SMALL SUCCESSES

The human tendency to regard little things as important has produced very many great things.

G. C. LICHTENBERG

To praise often, you continually have to find something worth praising. And this isn't easy, particularly when you're looking to praise with panache. In fact, there are days when it's wearisome to find something you'd feel good about "damning with faint praise." Peak performance isn't always easy to detect.

Therein lies the challenge. Most of us reserve our expressions of admiration for "knock-your-socks-off" performances. We shouldn't be so stingy. There really isn't a quota. Praise has hardly been overdone and will never be out of fashion. We don't have to wait for an Olympic-class performance to open our mouths. In fact, we should be comfortable praising quite normal improvements. This too I learned the hard way. Here's what happened.

Waiting for a Blue Moon

I can take any amount of criticism, so long as it is unqualified praise.

ATTRIBUTED TO NOËL COWARD

One day while consulting with a sprawling manufacturing plant in the Midwest, I stumbled on an important principle of praise. I had just expounded on the need to praise often and with passion. After relating the stories of the poker chipper and Mr. Abodi to the attentive executives, the president asked what they could do. In response, I asked what had gone well that day.

"Gone well?" the president asked with a look of shock. He couldn't think of anything. He had spent the entire morning working with problems—things that had gone wrong, not right. When he asked his direct reports for examples of positive performance, they too came up empty-handed. And so did the superintendents and frontline supervisors.

So I gave this group of leaders an assignment: Look for "things gone right." Look for people who are acting in ways that are consistent with your vision of the future.

When I returned two weeks later, the group was still struggling to ferret out a performance worth celebrating. They were searching for an accomplishment that occurred once in a blue moon. Of course, a blue moon had not yet broached the horizon. After further reflection, we changed our expectations. The managers agreed to look for a less world-shaking accomplishment—until someone asked the pregnant question: "Why celebrate easily achieved performances? Isn't it dangerous to reward mediocrity?"

This question, of course, raised a critical issue. Most of us fear rewarding mediocrity. Praise remains in our holster—just waiting to be drawn when the first world-class performance ambles by. We're not about to get excited over trivial accomplishments. Consequently, we're stuck waiting for greatness to come our way.

But are we justified in our restraint?

To answer this question, let's turn to those who routinely reward modest performance—animal trainers. They've been looking at the pros and cons of rewarding small improvements for decades.

Lessons from Shamu®

Courage is only an accumulation of small steps.

GEORGE KONRÁD

Imagine that your job is to train a whale to perform at Sea World. Not just any whale, but a killer whale, and not just any killer whale, but Shamu®—one of the first killer whales ever trained.[2] Suppose that your assignment is to teach Shamu to leap out of the water and over a stick that you hold 10 feet above the surface.

Question: Where do you hold the stick the first day of training? A long way from your body, right?

After a moment's thought, you might suggest that you'd hold the stick only slightly above the surface. You certainly can't expect the whale to vault to record heights on the maiden leap. After further reflection, you might conclude that you would place the stick slightly under the surface. It's senseless to wait for the whale to track down the stick. If you really put your mind to it, you're likely to conclude that it makes sense to place the stick at the bottom of the pool. This is a whale you're dealing with, remember, and you can't expect her to pass over the target by any means other than luck. It's not as if you can start the training session with a goal-setting discussion.

Once the stick sits squarely on the bottom of the pool, you wait for Shamu to pass over it. Then you give her a juicy fish. After she does this a few thousand times, she finally "understands" that when she swims over the stick, she gets a fish. Now, you can start moving the stick off the bottom. You've almost completed the training.

Let's return to our question. Can similar "techniques" be used with people? And if so, wouldn't it seem manipulative? Before we answer this burning question, let's examine a more rigorous and time-tested line of research. Let's turn to a creature with whom we share a more intimate bond. Let's turn to rats.

Several Steps down the Food Chain

As strange as it may sound, the idea of rewarding in small increments was developed decades ago when scientists experimented with ways to teach rats to navigate a maze. Researchers learned that you could "shape" a rodent's behavior by rewarding minute accomplishments. Of course the answer didn't come easily. The discovery came after scientists had used a variety of unsuccessful methodologies. At first, researchers hooked rodents up to electrical wires. Then they zapped the rats for making wrong turns. Although this technique was moderately successful in the short run, with repeated trials the rats ended up being the rodent version of Barney Fife—twitching, nervous, and unpredictable.

In a desperate attempt to motivate the rat to succeed, one group of scientists placed the rat at the end of the maze and then rewarded it over and over. Now the rat knew *why* to make the trip; it just didn't know *how* to make it. Newly motivated, it ran faster and more frenzied as it banged its way frantically through the maze—highly energized, but singularly unsuccessful.

Eventually it occurred to the researchers to break the task up into hundreds of small steps, teach each one, reward it, and then link the pieces together. Scientists placed the rodent at the beginning of a complex maze and then gave it a pellet for turning its head in the right direction. After a few trials, the rat would consistently turn its head in the correct direction. Next, the scientists rewarded the rat for moving its paw in the right direction until this step was learned. Eventually (trivial movement by trivial movement, pellet by pellet), the rat would learn to run the entire maze. Scientists called this process of providing rewards for incremental achievements "shaping." It works wonderfully with rats, guinea pigs, and an occasional killer whale. But, returning to our original question, would shaping work with people?

Back up the Food Chain

To most of us the idea of shaping human behavior is repugnant. It might work with rats, but who wants to encourage people down a maze with pellets? Humans, unlike other animals, can communicate freely. You don't have to say "correct turn" with a ham sandwich. Words will do just fine. In fact, with humans you can actually sit down beforehand and talk about desired and undesired behaviors. You can come to an agreement without having to hand out M&Ms or crank on a few volts.

But before we throw out years of research with a single, self-righteous toss, let's see how the principle might apply to people who don't communicate well—children. Maybe they're ripe for the use of shaping techniques. Consider a study I conducted over 15 years ago with my own kids.

Sharing Can Be Fun

I conducted the following study at a time when I had been having trouble encouraging my toddlers to share their toys. They were far more interested in owning toys than in spreading the wealth. I'd heard of the idea of rewarding children for doing the right thing (what a concept); unfortunately, I'd never been able to catch them in the actual act of sharing. They'd mastered grabbing, hoarding, and fending off intruders, but sharing still remained out of their reach. My plan was to encourage sharing by making a big deal about something that looked like, but wasn't exactly, sharing.

Since I was conducting my experiment as part of a class project, I actually sat down in a small roomful of kids and watched them play. After about half an hour of cavorting, fighting, drooling, and general chaos, I noticed my daughter Rebecca put down a toy that a little boy immediately picked up and hauled out of harm's way across the room. I jumped into action. Shouting to get the mob's attention, I exclaimed, "Do you know what Rebecca just did?" Everyone, including Rebecca, glanced at me with a look of "No. What?" I continued, "She just shared a toy with Timmy. She had been playing with it and let Timmy have a turn. Isn't sharing nice? Now, both of them get to play with the toy."

I couldn't believe the crowd's reaction. My first thought was that Rebecca would charge across the room and reclaim her toy. I couldn't have been more wrong. She basked in the praise as if her actual plan had been to share (rather than to snag) the Mr. Potato Head from the kid next to her.

And then it happened. Everyone else started sharing. The kids gleefully ran around the room giving their toys to each other. I was stunned.

Now, as effective as shaping was with my toddlers (returning to our recurring question), wouldn't it be insulting to shape adults' behavior? What kind of adult wants a path of pellets spread across the work floor? What thinking husband asks for a wife who is hell-bent on using shaping techniques as a means to get him to take out the garbage? ("Gee, sugar lips, I noticed you gazed toward the garbage. That makes me feel warm all over. Thanks a lot.")

Obviously, nobody wants to be treated like a rat in a maze. People deserve more respect. After all, they're people. And yet the research is so elegant, the impact on children so powerful. It would be a shame if the experimental findings couldn't be applied to adults. Aren't there some principles we can extract from the endless list of shaping studies and apply them to adults?

Actually there are, but they're only allowable if you have the right attitude.

Celebrate, Don't Manipulate

Usually we praise only to be praised.

FRANÇOIS, DUC DE LA ROCHEFOUCAULD

First, let's summarize our dilemma. If you don't reward performance until it's "perfect," you'll have a long wait. Honest expressions of admiration will continue to be as rare as wing tips in Wyoming. If you don't wait for perfection but reward small achievements instead, you might be viewed as someone who is "shaping" behavior and is therefore manipulative and insincere. People will still yearn for honest praise; only now they won't trust you.

What's a person to do?

The solution lies in your attitude. If you embrace praise solely as a way to shape behavior, you risk creating the praise carcass we talked about earlier. At the moment you express your appreciation for a small improvement, if you're thinking of the day you'll be able to get what you *really* want, you're in immediate danger. You'll be using praise to pry—as you'd use a crowbar. It will be a cold and hard tool. Worse yet, it will be dishonest.

In contrast, if at the moment of giving praise for a small improvement you're thinking *only* of the improvement, you're on the right track. For example, when a loving parent thrills at a child's first step, honest appreciation is given for the step itself—simply because the step thrills the parent. *Before* there was only crawling—and now this! Praise isn't given because the parent believes that one day in the distant future the child will win a marathon.

Small increments, like small steps, can and should be rewarded with the step itself in mind. This doesn't mean that the celebrator has no view of the future. Individuals surely realize that the first step can and will lead to the second. Yes, and someday there may be a marathon victory. Nevertheless, the purpose and emotion of the moment should be to focus on the first step and not to contrast it with the fourteenth step. ("Wonderful, Abe! You returned a book in a snowstorm. Now, maybe someday you'll be president!")

A laboratory study of sensitive individuals would reveal them rewarding incremental performance, but a study of their hearts would reveal that they genuinely celebrate small successes. Balanced leaders praise often, with passion, and with an eye for jointly celebrating the tiniest of improvements.

PRAISE IN PERPETUITY

Donald Petersen, former Ford chairman, sent short, sincere, positive messages to people he worked with every day. He suggested: "The most important ten minutes of your day are those you spend doing something to boost the people you work with."

The examples we've given of sincere recognition up to this point have been mostly verbal. We'll now turn our attention to something more solid than vocal vibrations. We'll explore a form of recognition that can last a lifetime. As with our first three principles, I learned much about the fourth by accident. Ironically, the insight came when I was making fun of someone (a fact that doesn't exactly make me bristle with pride).

The Golden Doorstop

While I was serving as a young coast guard officer at a small shore station near San Francisco, my tiny office was refinished, save for the installation of a tiny doorstop. This job took another year to complete. (Actually it took a year to start and three minutes to finish.)

I was singularly unimpressed with the construction crew's efficiency, so I decided to tease the construction manager. Years of honing my cynicism to an art form simply couldn't go unused. After all, this was a silly doorstop, and it took a *year* to install.

To capture just the right amount of sarcasm, a fellow officer and I created a bogus "letter of appreciation." First, we typed a few paragraphs of biting cynicism on elegant paper. Then we made a mock medal from a piece of used typewriter ribbon and a brass button off a discarded pea coat. Finally, we glued the medal to the award and hand-carried it to the construction manager's office. To give the ceremony the appropriate tone, we played a recording of "Semper Paratus" (the coast guard song) as we read the sarcastic letter. Finally, to finish off the phony award, we took a Polaroid photo of the event and gave it to the surprised manager.

In spite of the satirical tone surrounding the event, the manager was touched. He could see that we had put thought into the ceremony—never mind the mocking undertone. He was honored to have someone thinking of him at all. Even though the letter was for a trivial achievement, it came with a handmade medal, and his colleagues had delivered it with fanfare and a hearty laugh. We had no idea he would be moved by our sophomoric prank.

This story reaffirms our earlier point that praise should be given often. Here was a guy who was so hungry for recognition that even insincere appreciation was accepted with enthusiasm. He saw what was good in an act that was mostly sarcastic and cynical. But this isn't where the story ends. What follows taught us an additional principle.

The Gift That Keeps on Giving

About four years after we delivered the bogus certificate of achievement, I returned to the scene of the crime. I had long since left the coast guard and was now studying 30 miles down the road at Stanford University. A research project took me a stone's throw from the gracious manager who'd been able to discern the good in our mostly farcical praise. As I nonchalantly walked down the street a half block from the manager's office, he caught a glimpse of me out his window. He immediately ran into the street and invited me in for a chat. I'd forgotten about our prank. In fact, I'd forgotten about the manager.

He hadn't forgotten me *or* the questionable gift. As I entered his tattered, cramped office, several young members of his staff asked if I was the one who'd given him his now-famous award. He'd obviously told others about the peculiar certificate and dog-eared photo conspicuously displayed on the wall next to his gray desk.

What had started as a joke resulted in more than a moment of pride for the honoree. Since we made a personalized gift that the manager put on display, the honor continued over the years. Whenever a new employee would ask about the curious-looking certificate and photo, the manager would tell the story of its origin. He'd energetically explain how these crazy guys had surprised him with this imaginative ceremony. And in retelling the story, he relived the moment.

We learned a pleasantly surprising principle from this experience. When praise is accompanied by a physical reminder, it can give and give again. Like parents who emotionally turn to an aging plaster of Paris handprint years after their baby has left, the manager often glanced at his piece of memorabilia and relived fond memories. We could have thanked the manager over the phone. We might have even sent him a letter. Instead, we turned the praise into a unique gift that remained out in the open. And since passersby frequently asked about the curious award, he enjoyed praise given in perpetuity.

Worldwide Appeal

An automobile executive spent several months studying manufacturing procedures in Japan. When he left Japan, his host presented him with an expensive wristwatch. When the Japanese executive visited the next year, his American host gave him a collection of U.S. silver dollars.

Now, whenever either of the two visits the other, they make a show of their presents. The American executive makes sure he wears the special watch. In turn, the Japanese executive always reaches into his pocket and pulls out one of the silver coins.

PRAISE WITH FEELING

The young man who has not wept is a savage, and the old man who will not laugh is a fool.

GEORGE SANTAYANA

So far we've assumed that praise is a natural extension of our heartfelt feelings of admiration and pride. And yet, when taken into organizations, praise is often stripped of its emotional genesis. This should never happen. It took an earthquake to teach me this principle.

Shaken to My Senses

Our family was awakened one morning by a mild tremor. The shaking caused no damage to our home, but shook a small shelf *I* had installed above my teenage daughter's bed. We were wolfing down breakfast when the sound of something like tinkling glass alerted us. My daughter bolted up the stairs and then returned from her room in tears. I was surprised by her reaction. The combined value of the porcelain figurines on the shelf couldn't have been more than 20 dollars.

"I was saving them to give to my own daughter someday," she explained through her tears (unknowingly twisting the knife in my heart). Her childhood friends had given her the delicate trinkets. Each had special meaning, in spite of its unimpressive price tag. The tiny deer had been a gift of a friend from Japan whom she'd met in kindergarten. The frilly porcelain basket had been a gift from her first piano teacher.

Since I had inadvertently destroyed all of her knickknacks by not securing the shelf well, I decided to help rebuild her collection by giving her an exquisite collectible. I was feeling *particularly* guilty, so I bought a piece of blown glass at Saks Fifth Avenue. I had no reason for buying the gift other than I had been thinking of her and her lost memories. She was touched by my efforts, and I'll always remember that day.

Our figurine collector is away at college now, and the glasswork sits on her shelf in the space once occupied by porcelain memorabilia. Whenever I see the blown-glass figurine, I think of that day, the gift of love, and what it once was like to have a little girl around the house.

A Kinder, Gentler Organization

Organizations typically stifle individuals who have the gall to display their feelings. Consequently, efforts to rejuvenate praise in the workplace often result in cold and calculated programs. Despite their original intentions, leaders systematize, homogenize, and eventually leach praise of any remnants of feeling. Praise becomes "positive reinforcement," which, in turn, becomes an "employee-of-the-month" program. *A surefire method to destroy sincere admiration is to institutionalize it.*

In the shuffle to provide formal, companywide recognition, the tender part of giving is lost. And with the loss of the emotional core, praise transmutates from a warm expression of admiration to a calculated attempt to alter behavior. Nobody has a "child of the month" or a "best friend of the week."

True moments of appreciation are never systematized. They consist of glances, special thoughts, reflective (not expensive) gifts, and considerate expressions.

The "F Word"

Lou Tice calls *feelings* the "F word" of organizations. He's right. Organizations haven't allowed employees to express their feelings. I once sat in a meeting where a senior executive summarized a discussion by stating, "In a way, what we're talking about here is *love*." The ensuing silence was frightening. People began to look at the floor or elsewhere to avoid eye contact. The guy had flipped out. He had said "love" in a boardroom. What was the world coming to? Would Phil Donahue soon become the CEO?

Leaders aren't likely to talk about love if they can't express feelings in general. This is not to say that leaders don't have deep feelings and emotions. They do. For example, I once gave presentations to several groups of hard-nosed, ex-marine-type executives from Ross Perot's organization, EDS. As we talked about their most memorable experiences at work, they often teared up. To become balanced individuals at work, leaders will have to learn to open up.

Organizations will become healthier as leaders learn to express their softer, gentler side at work. Certainly leaders can find a way to include sincere emotion in their expressions of appreciation. Although every business accomplishment need not be accompanied by a shower of tears, there are times when honest feelings have a place.

Skilled individuals allow their own tender emotions to be an integral part of the gift of praise.

PRAISE WITH CLARITY

There is no greater impediment to the advancement of knowledge than the ambiguity of words.

THOMAS REID

Praise, no matter how frequently given or passionately felt, can still be misunderstood. This principle I also learned the hard way.

Looking for Love in All the Wrong Places

I once agreed to give a series of speeches to several divisions of an organization. The CEO wanted me to deliver the presentation on consecutive Saturdays at seven locations across the United States and Canada. At the time, I was holding season tickets to a nationally ranked college football team—on the 50-yard line, no less. The prospect of missing the gridiron battles just to face unknown audiences wasn't exactly alluring. But the persuasive CEO caught me at a weak moment, and I accepted the assignment.

What a bonehead move. I should have stuck with football. Even the humiliating defeat against the archrival would have been more fun than the beating I took over the next two months.

The Angry Oil Painting

Under normal circumstances a consultant can expect to be greeted by a fairly friendly audience—or at least one that's willing to tolerate you until you prove yourself. That is, under *normal* circumstances. To this day I don't know what was going on with this particular company, but when I showed up to give my first speech, I knew I was in trouble. The people staring at me from behind their crumpled cardboard name tents looked like images from a surrealistic painting. Had Salvador Dali painted a group of corporate executives, this would have been the bunch who posed.

This was going to be a hard room to work. To make matters worse, the audience next door—separated from us by a paper-thin accordion partition—was watching a Lou Holtz videotape and laughing uproariously. (Never follow Lou Holtz. People want to bundle him up and take him home.) My group, in contrast, was positively funereal. When my speech ended, the audience bolted out the door like school children at recess. I wondered what changes, short of coaching Notre Dame, I could make to improve my next performance with another new crowd.

I should have wondered harder. The next week's experience was no better. People weren't even attentive enough to be hostile. After only a few minutes, most fell into something that looked remarkably like a coma. At one point I tried to liven things up by shouting "fire!" Nobody budged. When people finally came to at the end of the appointed hour, most had wrinkle marks on their faces. As they languidly exited, I noticed that each table was spotted with embarrassing pools of drool. I hadn't been at my best.

By the third week I was desperate. Sure, I had bombed before and lived to tell about it, but I still had five performances in front of me. My contact person was beginning to lose faith in my ability to turn the audiences around. The skeptic was distressed about several dozen speech reviews he'd read. Participants had used words like *jerk, irrelevant, stuffy,* and *waste of time*. He took these as a bad sign.

Success, I Think

Finally my luck changed. My third experience was hardly even noxious. Several people actually seemed to pay attention to what I was saying, nodding their heads in approval. I was obviously doing something that worked. But what? At the end of the speech, a member of the audience approached me and generously muttered, *"I really enjoyed your remarks."*

As he turned to walk away, I practically tackled him. "If you don't mind my asking," I queried, "just what about my speech did you like?" *"I thought you did a good job,"* he immediately responded, smiling as if he actually had said something of substance. (So, it's *good* stuff you're looking for. What could I have been thinking?) "Thank you," I continued, "but if you could be just a little more specific," I probed—crossing the line that separates a skilled inquiry for clarity from the endless prying of a desperate man. "What exactly did I do that you liked?" He paused and then, after a few moments of reflection, blurted, *"I just thought as far as good speeches go, yours was one of 'em."*

Obviously, someone had sent this guy to torture me.

The impact of the well-intended praise was, at best, mixed. Although I was encouraged to learn that I had pleased someone, I was discouraged because I didn't know what I'd done. I had no way to build on the experience. Still in front of me were four untried audiences. I wasn't even marginally confident that I could replicate this modest success. Not, at least, until I knew what I had done differently.

The Test of Clarity

The great enemy of clear language is insincerity. When there is a gap between one's real and one's declared aims, one turns as it were instinctively to long words and exhausted idioms, like a cuttlefish squirting out ink.

GEORGE ORWELL

Although I may have crashed and burned in this series of presentations, I did learn from the humbling experience. I discovered that when giving praise, it's helpful to be behaviorally specific, particularly when the person on the receiving end is uncertain about what's going well and could use some help focusing on the precise behavior that is valued. Your vision of Cultural Vitality has to be so clear that you and others will know it when you see it and can praise it when you do.

If, after you give praise, the other person is uncertain about what you liked, you have completed only half the job. The person knows how you feel but doesn't know what he or she's done. Praise, stated vaguely, captures what could be meant by the expression "warm fuzzies." You may feel warm about what you did but remain fuzzy about exactly what it was.

For example, when praising my speech, it would've been helpful if someone had mentioned behaviors I could repeat (e.g., "I enjoyed the stories about your children. They helped me relate to what you said.").

Skilled individuals provide clear, unambiguous messages of praise. They explain what they like *and* the result.

PRAISE EFFORTS, NOT JUST RESULTS

Wherefore have ye rewarded evil for good?

Genesis 44:4

As we rush to praise clearly, we can fall into a simple trap. We can focus on results rather than efforts.

But He Got the Trains to Run on Time!

Let's return to the manufacturing setting we referred to earlier—the site where the executives were looking for a once-in-a-blue-moon performance. After several weeks of straining to find diamonds, they finally stumbled onto a startling achievement. One of the manufacturing areas set a performance record. The crew had assembled more units in one day than ever before. The superintendent who first learned of the new record burst into an executive council meeting with the news.

The president immediately called for a celebration. For the next five minutes the team brainstormed ways to reward the performance. They settled on breakfast with the plant manager (as if hourly employees were dying to dine with the big cheese).

In addition to their self-centered analysis, I had another concern. *"What exactly did the crew do to set the record?"* I asked.

The executives looked at me as if I were a cockroach on a wedding cake. "Why do you ask?" defended the president. "This is a time to celebrate, not rain on their parade."

"When I interviewed groups of hourly employees last year," I explained, *"I was disturbed by their colorful stories. Several revealed that it was common practice to break corporate policy, even the law, to achieve short-term advances."*

"Are you suggesting that the afternoon shift did something shady to beat the production record?" asked the quality control manager with a look of terror.

"I don't know," I continued. *"It's just that when the only data point you have is a result, rather than a strategy, you're vulnerable. For all you know, the crew illegally held back production yesterday to inflate today's numbers. Or maybe they let quality slip. They could even be lying about the actual numbers. Without a clear understanding of what led to the alleged success, you can only wonder. You may be rewarding behaviors that are far from rewardable."*

"That's right," piped in the controller, "Mussolini got the trains to run on time, but look what he did to succeed."

The president, twitching nervously, put the celebration on hold until the leadership team was able to gather more information.

What I learned from this interaction is that, as annoying as it is to work in an organization where, as Gore Vidal said, "A good deed never goes unpunished," it may be worse to work in one where "no bad deed goes unrewarded."

Don't think about rewarding results until you clearly understand the strategies the workforce used to achieve them.

Focus on Process, Not Results

The book *Kaizen* by Masaaki Imai highlights the Japanese appreciation for the importance of rewarding effort and not outcome.[3] It tells the intriguing story of some waitresses whose job it was to serve tea during lunch at one of Matsushita's plants. They noted that the employees sat in predictable locations and drank a predictable amount of tea. Rather than put a full container at each place, they calculated the optimum amount of tea to be poured at each table, thus reducing tea-leaf consumption to half.

How much did the suggestion save? Probably only a small sum, yet the group was given the Presidential Gold Medal. Other suggestions saved more money (by an astronomical amount), but the more modest proposal was given the highest recognition because it captured what the judges thought was the best effort. They rewarded the process, knowing that if you reward process, results take care of themselves.

Telltale Signs

It's easy to tell when individuals are rewarding outcomes with little or no idea of how the results were achieved. During training sessions, leaders often ask us if it's okay to follow praise with problem-solving probes. For example, they suggest a person might say, *"You did a great job in getting the job out on time. Thanks. Now, what was it that led to our achieving the goals this time? What did we do differently?"* This strategy appears reasonable but fails on two counts. First, it feels like giving and taking away. *"Nice job, but . . ."* Second, it's clear that the praise is aimed at the result and not the strategy or action.

If you focus on strategies as well as results, you won't be tempted to go on a fishing expedition. You won't reward an achievement that rode in on the backs of employees or was attained through illegal or immoral means. Nor will you douse well-earned praise with a sobering discussion of past problems. The next time you're tempted to go fishing, ask about the cause before you reward the effect. Then, like the truly skilled, you'll reward efforts, not just results.

PRAISE ACCOMPLISHMENTS OF WHICH THE OTHER PERSON IS PROUD

Among the smaller duties of life I hardly know any one more important than that of not praising where praise is not due.

SYDNEY SMITH

The story is told of a performing artist who stormed offstage in the middle of a standing ovation. She'd been insulted. By her standards, her performance had been mediocre. She felt patronized by the audience's energetic applause. Whether the audience felt sorry for her or actually enjoyed the performance was irrelevant. What mattered was that the artist didn't want to be praised for what she judged to be a substandard accomplishment. She wanted it reserved for her finest work.

Perfect Attendance, Big Deal

Organizations make similar mistakes. As desperately as executives need to increase their efforts to recognize positive performance, they must be careful not to praise performance in which people take little pride. We watched this happen one day. It was an awkward, embarrassing experience for everyone involved.

The event in question had been scheduled to honor perfect attendance logged by midlevel union leaders. Not only was it embarrassing to discuss attendance with members of the leadership corps, but the standards for perfect attendance were so low, the whole ordeal was a sham. The rules for perfect attendance allowed sick days, *excused* days, and two unexcused absences. (Makes you proud, huh?)

To honor those who were being given the award, the division manager stopped by and mumbled a few words of appreciation. The honorees milled around, stared at the floor, and looked like kids who'd just been given a medal for calling the fire department—after having set the fire in the first place. The personnel manager stood next to me and, under his breath, made fun of the whole mess. When the speech was over, those honored made a hasty exit, while those who bestowed the honor stayed behind and bad-mouthed the meaningless celebration.

Take the time to discover how others feel about their accomplishment before scheduling a celebration. Don't give a standing ovation for a performance the other person sees as inadequate or even average. If you're not sure how the other person feels, ask around. Those close to the achiever are likely to know how he or she feels. Ask the person directly. Just don't jump in without testing the waters.

KNOW WHAT THE OTHER PERSON VALUES

In a clever article found on the cover of The Wall Street Journal, *the author discusses what she thinks are inappropriate holiday gifts. She argues that many men pay little heed to their loved one's wants when selecting presents. Among her favorite "insensitive" presents was a manhole cover. That's right, one of her friends was given an 80-pound steel disk by her husband. He found it on a beach, covered with tar. The impetuous lover thought it was a clever gift because it had his loved one's initials forged into the steel. And they say romance is dead![4]*

In each of the examples we've used to illustrate the first eight principles, we've assumed that whatever we've done to reward the other person would actually be rewarding. Such an assumption can be dangerous. When it comes to rewards, a rose is not always a rose. Consider the following sad, but true, story. This time I *really* messed up.

The Marshmallow Massacre

Most of us can recall our first date as if it were yesterday—some with fond memories, others with slightly tainted recollections, and still others with sheer horror. Mine fell into the horror category. Well, not the whole thing. It actually started out on course. I had a date with a nonrelative. This was a plus. She seemed amused with my nervous chatter. We even danced and talked, just like I knew what I was doing.

Then came the games. Some of the couples were starting to dance too close for the parents' taste. A few even began to seek out dark places. And then, as if on cue, Ward Cleaver jumped in and shouted, "Let's turn the lights on, the music off, and play some good old-fashioned games." I hardly knew the girl I was with, so the prospect of competing in a coeducational arena appealed to me. I liked to compete. I figured that my date would be impressed if I won an event or two. *I* would be. My friends would be. It only stood to reason that *she* would be. Now that's where I went wrong. I had been reared with no sisters, so what did I know about girls' predilections? Precious little.

The first competition was a game of the "bobbing for apples" genre. Only instead of apples, we used marshmallows, and instead of floating in water, they hung by string from the ceiling. Each boy was asked to put his hands behind his back and then eat, unassisted, six marshmallows that had been spaced a few inches apart on two feet of string.

A Chance for Victory

Here was an event tailored to my unique skills. It involved eating sugar. I had been in training since birth. When the gun fired, I chomped into the marshmallows with reckless abandon—well, as reckless as you can be with marshmallows. My competitors gingerly nibbled away. What a rout. I grazed straight up the string, swallowing all six marshmallows in about 30 seconds. The Little Lord Fauntleroys hadn't even finished one. They simply stood by, dabbing their cheeks with a corner of their napkin. This was going to be easier than I thought.

When I announced my victory, all eyes turned to me in shock. Nobody in the crowd could believe I had finished already. Then, within three ticks of the clock, looks turned from surprise, to admiration, to disgust. Not only had I eaten the marshmallows, I had swallowed the string as well. Hanging out of the corner of my mouth was six inches of unswallowed evidence.

As people looked on in revulsion, I was faced with a puzzling question. Do I swallow the rest of the string and run the risk of it getting tangled in my intestinal tract? Or do I pull back the two feet I had swallowed and chance whatever happens when you retrieve something from your stomach? (An activity I vaguely remembered from health class as being dangerous and not a lot of fun.)

In retrospect, swallowing may have been the more prudent tactic. Or perhaps retrieving the string in the privacy of the bathroom would have worked. Yanking back the string in the midst of the crowd was a definite mistake. But what did I know? This was my first date. To be truthful, in the heat of the moment I actually thought it might be "cool" to pull a string out of my stomach. It would never be an Olympic event, but it was sort of athletic. Maybe I hadn't started out to compete in the string pull, but throwing in a novel skill could be an added bonus. I could excel in two events.

The Marshmallow Turns

What I hadn't counted on was the marshmallows. They came back with the string—slimy and dripping with the orange soda I had swallowed as a precompetition pick-me-up—six candied corpses on the rebound. I also hadn't counted on the trapdoor at the end of my esophagus. As I awkwardly jerked the string out of my gullet, the fleshy appendage hung on to each marshmallow. In the end, not only did I pull back a disgusting mass of slime and goo, I retched as each marshmallow hung up on the trapdoor.

The overall effect was not good. I yanked on the string—choking, spitting, retching, and gagging. The crowd looked on in horror—choking, spitting, retching, and gagging. Well, not everybody. The guys cheered raucously, counting each marshmallow as it slithered out of my mouth—as if each were a touchdown or an extra point. The girls, on the other hand, enjoyed the show a whole lot less. They covered their eyes, backed off in horror, and raced to the bathroom—where competition for the toilet bowl was fast and furious.

I didn't get a good-night kiss when the party came to an end that evening. After all, this was the early 1960s, a first date, and my companion had been rushed home under heavy sedation. All things considered, things could have gone better.

My Eureka Experience

As I lay awake that night trying to figure out where I had gone wrong, it came to me in a flash of insight. The fact that I choked on the string was not the problem. Although gagging on the marshmallow residue probably detracted from my mystique, what really had gone wrong was my attitude. I had assumed my *date* cared about what *I* cared about. I actually believed that she would be impressed by my hard-earned victory. The guys were impressed. They still talk about my string-retrieval trick. My date, on the other hand, marched to the beat of a different drummer. She wanted a guy who, when faced with a fork in the road, took the road *more* traveled. She wanted the strong, silent, average type. At least I think that's what she wanted. Actually, she never spoke to me again.

The point is, I sought to give her a gift she didn't really want. I looked into her heart and saw my own wants and desires. Boy, was I wrong.

When It Comes to Rewards:

Rule of Thumb: Reward others with what *they* want,
                    not with what *you* want.
Corollary: When in doubt, find out what they want.
Addendum: When dead certain, check anyway.

Skilled individuals take the time to learn what others value. And because the gift is also seen as thoughtful, it is doubly powerful.

PRAISE INDIVIDUALS IN PRIVATE

He who praises everybody, praises nobody.

SAMUEL JOHNSON

To expand the use of praise, many organizations have installed public-recognition programs. Although the intent of such efforts is to encourage positive performance and raise overall morale, you can't always predict the impact. In several of the organizations the authors have consulted with, leaders have learned that recognition given in a public forum can actually reduce employee satisfaction.

Unnecessary Competition

Employee-recognition programs can be dangerous. Rather than allow for joint success, any "of-the-month" program elevates a single individual above the crowd. Those not selected (everyone else) may wonder, "Why not me?" In fact, more than one study has revealed that a great majority of employees believe they're deserving of special rewards. Rather than feeling proud of the lucky recipient, the majority of employees are upset because they believe they deserve the recognition instead.[5]

Perhaps such unintended results would be tolerable if the reward actually motivated or pleased the recipient. Unfortunately, most recipients of public recognition know that their peers resent them. They also recognize that any reward that has been systematized is suspect in the first place. Consequently, it's hard to find the winners of any employee-of-the-month program. Even the winners end up losing.

A Source of Cynicism

Singling out individuals in public has still another disturbing side effect. It encourages cynicism. Leaders often select individuals because they're "outstanding team players." The authors of the award use words such as *collaboration* and *cooperation*. It doesn't take a rocket scientist to conclude that the "of-the-month" award pits individuals against each other in order to single out the most collaborative "person-of-the-month." Employees, recognizing the convoluted logic of competing to see who can collaborate the best, tend to snicker at the leaders' lack of insight and possible insincerity.

No Collaboration Goes Unpunished

In one automobile facility, a senior manager learned a disturbing fact about the formal suggestion program. The top award for a suggestion made by one person was $6,000 and a sports car. The top award for a suggestion made by two people was $6,000 and no car.

When the executive called the person in charge of the program and asked why the discrepancy, the bureaucrat responded, "How do you expect us to divide a sports car in half?"

Risky Business

Honest criticism is hard to take, particularly from a relative, a friend, an acquaintance, or a stranger.

FRANKLIN P. JONES

Criticizing public praise programs can be hazardous to your health. On those few occasions I have openly questioned the value of group recognition for individual achievement, leaders have not always responded well—in the same way that starving jackals don't respond well to wounded zebras. Leaders remember their recognition programs for their perfect intent, rather than for their imperfect results. Consequently, they often become defensive when their brainchild falls under attack. *"You mean to tell me that employees are dissatisfied with our wood-carver-of-the-month banquet?"* question senior managers. *"Why those ungrateful . . . ."* Or worse still, they plunge their heads in the sand. *"You're wrong. Our people love the program. I just know they do."*

And they might. Unfortunately, attacking the recipients or denying the data is hardly the fitting response to criticism. Rather than assert the merits of their program and the reasons it's a smart idea after all, prudent leaders direct their efforts to more private forms of recognition. Simply canceling the public programs in anger or openly criticizing the "ingrates" is hardly the mature reaction. Finding fewer public forums to reward individuals in nonprogrammatic ways is a sensible approach.

Reward Groups for Group Accomplishment

While it may be risky to single out individuals in front of their peers, this doesn't mean there's no place for public commemorations. When joint efforts lead to joint success, joint celebrations are appropriate. In fact, as organizations attempt to shift to a more collaborative, team-driven approach, rewarding collaboration makes sense—as long as the entire group is recognized. Of course, rewarding one group in front of another can cause problems.

> In short: When passing out praise, make sure that everyone within earshot is a recipient.

PRAISE HONESTLY, AND THEN STICK TO IT

One afternoon my father-in-law stopped by with some peaches he had just picked from the trees in his yard. He asked me if I'd bake him a peach pie. I gladly said I would and the next day presented him with the finished product. My father-in-law is not exactly generous in giving compliments, but he told me how good the pie tasted. I beamed with pride, until he added, "Guess I picked those peaches at the perfect time."[6]

VIRGINIA FRANZEN

Fifteen years ago I taught the ins and outs of giving recognition in about 30 minutes. After all, what could go wrong? Nothing, or so I thought, until I had the following experience.

The Backhanded Commander

One day, after suggesting that praise needed to be delivered in a way that was specific, I threw in as an afterthought the idea that you also needed to be nonpunishing. I laughed over the prospect of delivering praise in a punishing fashion. "Who could possibly punish someone while delivering praise?" I mused aloud.

A young military officer sitting in the front row suggested that it was easy to punish someone when giving praise. In fact, he had a boss who did it all the time. *"He shakes my hand and then stabs me in the back,"* explained the young lieutenant. He went on to explain that his boss would say things like, *"Good job. Who would have thought?"* or *"Excellent work! Why aren't you always this good?"*

The lesson we learned from this ensign is simple. Once you've decided to travel the trail of recognition, don't stop halfway or take a detour down the path of rebuke. Make your praise unconditional. The receiver understands that an honest compliment does not imply an impending promotion, raise, or elevation to knighthood. You don't have to give and then take away just to play it safe. In fact, it's better not to give at all than to offer backhanded praise. Skilled individuals find a way to praise and then live with what they've just said or done.

In summary, decide what's worth praising, praise it, then move on.

ALLOW OTHERS THE DELIGHT OF GIVING PRAISE

Knowing how to give praise is only half the formula. If those receiving the reward don't appreciate it, all is lost.

Let Them Eat Cake

One day during my teenage years, I whipped up a double-chocolate cake for a church bake sale. Later, the person who bought the cake was surprised to learn that a teenage boy had baked it. After all, this was the early 1960s when the dominant male role model was still John Wayne. Most boys would've been ashamed to admit they so much as poured their own cereal, much less baked an entire cake from scratch—unless, of course, baking a cake involved firing a high-caliber weapon.

The man who purchased and sampled my cake came over to our table and told me how much he liked my creation. He pointed out that he was particularly impressed I had produced the masterpiece from scratch. I took the compliment with the grace of a teenage boy. I stammered, looked hangdog at my feet (as if I'd been caught picking my nose), and feebly argued that the cake really wasn't any good.

After the well-intentioned man left, my mother sidled up to me and suggested that I didn't know how to take a compliment. "You essentially told Mr. Jackson that he had no taste," she explained. "Next time, just smile graciously and say 'thank you.'"

Most of us would feel more comfortable expressing our sincere appreciation if those receiving it didn't give us such a bad time. So, we share the advice of a loving mother. Envelop yourself in praise by simply smiling and saying "thank you." Allow others the joy of giving.

SOME PRACTICAL
APPLICATIONS FROM THIS CHAPTER

We are not only gregarious animals, liking to be in sight of our fellows, but we have an innate propensity to get ourselves noticed, and noticed favorably, by our kind.

WILLIAM JAMES

The advantage of doing one's praising for oneself is that one can lay it on so thick and exactly in the right places.

SAMUEL BUTLER

As we mentioned earlier, this particular chapter has been in print in one form or another for several years. In a very real sense, it's been pre-tested. We've had a chance to share the message and watch for changes. The results haven't been very impressive. Leaders usually have enjoyed the material and often have talked extensively about what they plan to do to make praise part of their daily routine. Unfortunately, few have followed through. In most cases, employees still suggest they aren't recognized sufficiently for doing a good job.

As we've talked with leaders about the problem, even completed a Six-Cell analysis, the barrier to increasing praise has become clear. First, most people don't have a way of cueing themselves to see and talk about positive events. They are so caught up in "solving problems" that most go through life watching for negative exceptions and not positive actions. Second, most leaders don't have at their fingertips a variety of creative, heartfelt methods for sharing their appreciation. After saying "thank you" (something they could still do a lot more of), they don't know what else to do. Consequently, your assignment for this chapter is to pull your team together, share the principles taught herein, and then jointly brainstorm two lists of ideas.

Cueing Mechanisms

First, identify ways you can remind yourself and others to be constantly on the watch for positive performance. Ideas can range from simple calendaring, to placing notes in critical locations, to placing positive performance on the top of your standard agenda. Generate a list of 10 structured steps you can take to ensure you're on constant alert for "things gone right." Select at least three or four methods from the list, and put them in place. One method we highly recommend is memorizing the list of your selected vitality behaviors. (Putting the list of behaviors on a laminated card is helpful.) Once internalized, the behaviors should practically leap out when observed by leaders. For a more complete list of cueing techniques, see the last third of chapter 16.

Creative Methods

Second, generate a list of two dozen ways of expressing appreciation beyond a simple "thank you." Expressing your thanks should remain at the top of the list, but for those who would like to show a little more creativity, come up with an expanded list. The idea isn't to be wacky or to draw attention to yourselves, but to find honest and clever ways to let others know you value their contribution. After you've come up with and tried several new methods, meet and generate still more ways. Make this part of a quarterly agenda.

CHAPTER 13
Helping People Work Together

A team effort is a lot of people doing what I say.

MICHAEL WINNER, BRITISH FILM DIRECTOR

Motivation
Ability
Individual
Social
Organizational
1
2
3
4
5
6

One day two of the authors witnessed a pathetic scene. At the time, they were seated in the stands, watching a group of six-year-olds play their first game of organized soccer. In preparation for the big event, the young players had spent three weeks learning all about teamwork. The challenge had been to teach them to guard their own territory instead of running helter-skelter after the ball. The expression "There is no *I* in *team*," had been elevated to a mantra.

When the game finally got started, the kids did remarkably well. It was an adult who

strayed from the formula. In spite of all the talk about teamwork, the coach repeatedly encouraged individual achievement. His focus on the individual came to a peak when a rather aggressive kid hogged the ball and scored—knocking down our favorite tyke and turning parents and spectators into screaming idiots. Instead of being reprimanded for his selfish behavior (dream on), the pushy kid was practically enshrined on the spot. The exuberant coach literally lifted the ball hog onto his shoulders and ran around the field in a victory lap. Parents and friends joined in the frenzy.

From that moment on, it was every kid for himself or herself. Collaboration and mutual respect were replaced with flailing elbows and vicious kicks to the shin, as each child madly dashed to take control of the ball. "Teammates" spent as much energy trying to steal the ball from *each other* as they did challenging the opponent. After all, they needed the ball to score, and if they could score, well, who had ever seen such spectacular praise?

What makes this story so distressing is its universality. The coach had talked about helping one another out, but when it came down to the heat of the game, it was the kid who shot the ball into the net who got all the glory. It's the American way.

Sad But True

Americans talk about teamwork as if they owned the patent, and then treat individual achievers, even those who turn against their colleagues, to a hero's welcome.

CELL 4: TEAMWORK

In this chapter we'll deal with the pervasive and costly problems associated with poor teamwork. Instead of looking at individual action, we'll look at *inter*action. More specifically, we'll look at handoffs and assists—between individuals in the same workgroup, between departments, between divisions, between any entity that should behave as a team. (And that entity can be *big*. For example, the authors consider themselves an integral part of team Milky Way.) Just like a soccer team, any group of interdependent people is successful only if members "work and play well with their friends." For the game to proceed well, people must pass the ball to one another. Of course, instead of passing soccer balls, employees pass on resources.

That is, they provide:

- Valuable information
- Vital materials
- Necessary authority
- Indispensable help

Being able to diagnose why people are having problems sharing resources is vital to effective leadership. We realize that this topic could take up a book or two, so we've picked our targets with care. We'll explore typical situations. In a nutshell, we'll address this question: When Cell 4 is low, what can a leader do?

Some Typical Cell 4 Problems

Cell 4 problems deserve a special look. Their symptoms, causes, and appearances are exceptionally varied, often making their diagnoses confusing and their remedies less effective. For example, a process-improvement team we once consulted with tried to map how work was typically handled in a bank. The assignment was to look at possible savings in time and money. When we asked why a simple approval took an average of three days, team members offered a number of reasons. The executive VP traveled a lot. The form was complex and had to be returned for more information. The internal mail system was slow. Despite the many excuses, the answers seemed rather shallow, even phony.

At lunch, one of the team members came clean. "The real reason is hard to talk about," she offered. It turns out that the EVP was sleeping with his assistant, who was using the approval as a way to punctuate her power. What should have taken about four hours was taking three days. Naturally, nobody was willing to talk about the delay because it was the secretary's fault, and everyone was afraid to deal with someone who was "so close to the boss."

This awkward situation represents two different Cell 4 problems. Problem one: Team members weren't receiving the approval they needed because the secretary was intentionally withholding it. Problem two: The information on *why* the problem existed was kept from the boss. In both cases, the information or authority was available, but people chose not to relinquish it. Thus, Cell 4 was the problem, not Cell 6. Organizational ability (Cell 6) was working just fine. The systems were in place to generate the data. On the other hand, thinking, breathing human beings were standing in the way of progress. Such is the nature of Cell 4.

Similarly Distressing

You can't design a process well enough that one angry person can't screw it up—or structure an organization in such a way that it can't be gummed up with pettiness and revenge.

Of course, all Cell 4 problems don't grow out of ill will or sabotage. For example, a mechanic who worked for the company that was having trouble with approvals was constantly being prevented from fixing a pump because a colleague unknowingly kept putting the adjustment wrench in the wrong place. The person who wasn't completing the adjustment didn't have the necessary resource (Cell 4) because a co-worker simply didn't understand the job (Cell 2).

Listen to the following six complaints. Each came from an actual organization and is the result of people not sharing vital resources. Each is different in both cause and consequence.

- "About once a month I come to work and find all the work in progress has been 'stripped off the line.' The day-shift supervisor, behind in count, drained every part and left me and my shift high and dry."
- "It's hurry up and wait around here. I send in a request, but it doesn't get signed off till Martha studies it to death. I mean *every* request."
- "When we're up against deadlines that are almost impossible to meet, the group across the hall never even thinks of chipping in— even if they're ahead of schedule or at a lull. If we ask them for help, they find things to do that make them look busy."
- "I worked on a project for three months, thinking I was solving an incredibly important problem. Then I learned that a guy not three doors down from me had solved the problem months ago. He knew what I was working on, but said nothing. When I asked him why he had kept quiet, he explained that he didn't meddle in other people's business."
- "Over the past few months, it has been increasingly difficult to find new tools for our machines. The tools are being ordered, but they keep disappearing. One day when I was looking for a gauge, I opened up a locker in the next department and found five cases of new tools. The other department had been hoarding them."
- "When we recently were asked to cut our head count by 10 percent, the leadership team met and insisted they couldn't cut a single person. So instead of making a careful study and hard choices, we ended up cutting 10 percent across the board. It was stupid."

It Takes Six Cells to Understand Cell 4

In each of these social "ability" problems, people aren't giving others the help, authority, information, or materials they need. Of course, the question left hanging is "Why?" What's keeping these people from sharing? Are they simply selfish dolts who care only about their own lives? Is the organization structured in such a way that "helping behaviors" are made more difficult? Do people dislike each other and take joy in causing problems for others?

The answer is, "It depends." To comprehend why people aren't readily "passing the ball," we must rely on the same diagnostic technique we've been using to understand any behavior that's at risk. We have to look into each of the six potential sources of influence. For example, the shift supervisor in the first mini-case "stripped the line" because the reward structure (Cell 5) encouraged leaders to maximize their own numbers even at the expense of others. Martha studied requests to death because her boss never said anything good to her if she processed a request rapidly, but ripped her head off if she made a mistake in reading his priorities (Cell 3). The group that never lent a hand failed to help out because they didn't like doing the required work. They found it boring and repetitive (Cell 1).

You get the point. Cell 4 problems always involve other people who are not sharing vital resources. Why they don't share materials, information, authority, or help can be a function of any one of the six cells we've been studying, although Cell 4 problems are usually due to a combination of factors.

Now, having said that a complete and balanced diagnosis is necessary when facing a Cell 4 problem, we'll avoid rehashing what we've examined so far by looking at the factors that *most commonly* lead to Cell 4 problems. These include:

- An incomplete vision of teamwork
- The inability to communicate well
- The wrong reward structure
- The fear of empowering others

AN INCOMPLETE VISION

And if the blind lead the blind, both shall fall into the ditch.

Matthew 15:14

Let's start with a Cell 2 problem that can impact Cell 4—a lack of understanding. As we've suggested earlier, few people have a clear picture of teamwork. Worse still, what they *do* know about teams often raises suspicions. Your average employee has spent too many years learning about, and reveling in, individual achievement to readily embrace the notion of switching to teams. Besides, who wants to be absorbed into an amorphous mass known as a "team" where people continually chant "There is no *I* in *team*"? That expression alone is enough to make most people break into a sweat. In fact, when one of the authors once gave a speech entitled, "There may not be an *I* in T-E-A-M but there is an M-E," the idea was enormously well received. Audience members, tired of the current love affair with synergy, liked the idea of allowing room for individual achievement and recognition.

Pardon My Hypocrisy

It's not that most employees are self-serving dweebs who can be forced into a crowded elevator only at gunpoint. They can—and do—work in groups. It's just that most of us operate with a limited view of what a team really can be. We hear about teams, are impressed with parts of the picture, and then proceed to put only a few pieces of the puzzle into place. The unfortunate result of such limited vision is that we often end up looking like hypocrites or, worse yet, like idiots. One of the authors once gave a speech on teams to a group of corporate executives. A member of the audience came up to him afterwards and said, "I like what you recommended. It's exactly how I *ran* my teams." Another fellow ventured to the podium and suggested, "That team-involvement thing you talked about really works. It tricks people into thinking that your ideas are theirs, so they work harder!"

Our guess is that most team members don't like to think of themselves as rats being herded through a maze, nor do they warm up to the idea of being tricked into working harder. Now, you might argue that the expression "*ran* my teams" was an unfortunate choice of terms. It simply demonstrates how old language often spills into new visions. That happens. However, had you heard the rest of the conversation in which the fellow spoke in a patronizing, singsong tone; continually referred to women as girls; and talked about "what was good for them" (to name but a few of his inconsistencies), you'd have to agree that this guy publicly spoke of the importance of teams but sounded a great deal more like a traditional (and mostly autocratic) leader than anyone who works effectively with people.

To demonstrate what happens to a person who embraces the *trappings* of teams but understands little of the underlying philosophy, we've videotaped a variety of common statements and then showed them to audiences across the country. The hands-down favorite vignette depicts a man holding up a trophy and stating:

> *I can hardly believe that I've won this. I knew my accomplishments were as good as they've ever been, but to win an award of this nature, well, it's just too much. I'd like to start by thanking my teammates. You know, this award is really for them. Without them, I could never have made the incredible contributions I came up with. They were always on the sidelines, rooting me on, sending me help, doing their little jobs. Sure, my ideas led to a new product line. Sure, I was honored by the National Academy of Technicians. Sure, I stun myself with my own efforts. But without friends, without my teammates at my side to share in the glory, this award would just be a giant piece of metal announcing to the world how brilliant I've been over the past decade. My thanks to the little people. This is for you.*

People laugh at this character. Why? For the same reason they laugh at most things—the script is so true to life. Most of us have seen someone just like him. Most of us have done something just like it.

It was only a matter of time until this and other vignettes we captured on video were given the label "mis-spousing." Each was an example of a person openly *espousing* a view, but *contradicting* the content of the message in the process. For example, a frontline supervisor stands in front of a grungy-looking production line and exclaims, "I'm afraid he just isn't cut out to be a modern leader like you and me. He just isn't sensitive and compassionate—I say we bring him down." Or "We're going to have to find a way to talk to each other in a more professional way. I tell you what—*you* start. You're the one with all of the personality flaws and dumb ideas."

Each of these "mis-spoused" statements was actually uttered by a living, breathing human being who is a victim of an incomplete vision. When it comes to teams and teamwork, just about everyone understands only bits and pieces of the whole picture. Even the formal, academic definitions are severely limited.

What's a Team?

A team is a team is a team. Shakespeare said that many times.

DAN DEVINE, FOOTBALL COACH

Scholars typically consider teams to be two or more people who share a common objective. That's why teams can range in size from a two-person lemonade stand to a workgroup to a company to even a country. When faced with a common objective, maybe even a common enemy, people feel a sense of camaraderie and start acting as a team. But then again, facing a common objective doesn't automatically turn people into a true team. For example, people who climb onto a plane going to Sioux Falls share a common objective, but it's unusual for them to "pull together " into anything that looks like a team. In fact, given today's troubles with bags and baggage handling, if the flight is like most, the passengers will smile at each other pleasantly as they enter the plane and then elbow their way to the overhead compartments where there's a pitched battle over carry-on space. They don't become a team.

Other authors add the proviso that a team is made up of people who not only share a common objective but also are interdependent. This adds an important dimension. For instance, take a close look at a company that structured jobs in such a way that some employees were no longer dependent on one another, but were formed into a "team." The group even got their own team room. They soon became known as the group of people who were "all dressed up with nowhere to go." They met twice a week and had nothing to talk about. When you have no interdependence, you're not likely to build a very tight team.

But being interdependent and sharing a common goal still doesn't transform a group of people into a team. Most workgroups already share common goals and are highly interdependent. And yet, few are teams. The fact that they're interdependent only aggravates people. They hate having to rely on others, and, in many cases, scarcely tolerate one another.

You Gotta Have Heart

What people really want from teams is not the rubbing of elbows or the reliance on others. They crave something with more heart. When people speak of teams they've enjoyed being part of, they never talk about interdependence and common goals. Instead, they tell stories that include three important features. They remember what it was like when they could always count on each other for support. They recall how they respected each other—warts and all. They share vignettes of how each willingly sacrificed for the good of the whole. Support, respect, and sacrifice typically don't make it into team definitions, but they should.

An Important Addition

Without heartfelt support, mutual respect, and a willingness to sacrifice, teams are just groups of people pretending to be something they aren't.

Support

As we meet with groups that are forming into teams, we always conduct an exercise that asks people to express what they want from each other. It takes a while to get participants to open up and talk about what they really desire, but, with time, they almost always settle on an important characteristic. They want to know that the people they work with are "there for them." That is, should they have a bad day, they want to be able to count on their colleagues to help them out. They, in turn, offer the same deal.

The support healthy teammates ask for extends beyond pitching in and helping out with a job. It includes emotional support as well. People expect their colleagues to stand shoulder to shoulder against a common enemy by confronting anyone who has the audacity to attack a teammate. Healthy teams are made up of people who never join in when outsiders try to bash a colleague. When someone suggests a teammate has done something dumb or wrong, they respond with something like, "That surprises me. My guess is he had a very good reason for what he did. He's a sharp guy, and I'm sure he knew what he was doing. Let's go find out what he had in mind."

It's gratifying to watch a group transform into a team as members begin to realize their colleagues are good, decent people. They refuse to make the fundamental attribution error about people in general, and then go the extra mile by swearing to always impute good motive to their teammates. Exceptionally effective teams insist that imputing good motive be one of their ground rules and act true to their word, despite enormous outside pressures to feast on the mistakes of a fallen colleague.

When you can count on others for their support, the very nature of work changes. Knowing that people around you are thinking good thoughts about you and are willing to fight for you, should the occasion arise, adds a quality to work life that can't be purchased through increased wages or other benefits. Only *teammates* can give each other such a gift. Those who give and receive that gift *always remember* what it was like when they were part of a team of people who offered each other physical, intellectual, and emotional support. To quote a friend who looks back at a time when a group she worked with supported each other under trying times. "Those were the Camelot years."

Respect

Combining people with diverse backgrounds and interests into a cohesive team requires still another dimension. People don't have to love each other, they don't have to even like each other, but they do have to find a way to respect one another. It's important that people realize teams are not necessarily made up of individuals who are so much alike that they drink beer together, become the godparents of each other's children, or share vacation cabins in Aspen. In fact, this is rarely the case. However, effective teams *do* find a way to admire people for what they have to offer *without* forcing everyone into the same mold.

As you talk with teams that are obviously well adjusted, you'll almost always be regaled with heartwarming stories of how one member did something incredibly valiant, and yet stupid. People will talk about the more creative member with a sort of awe—and then end with a tale of how she parks her car at work and then walks home, forgetting that she drove to work. The clerk who "can keep better track of a quality process than any person on earth" is then kidded for being so well organized and disciplined that he irons his socks. The team leader is bragged about for his laid-back style that allows for maximum involvement and then is teased for falling asleep at the big corporate shindig.

Given that people are imperfect, respect can be earned only as individuals learn that strengths and weaknesses go hand in hand. Effective teammates understand that one of the reasons they've been pulled together into a team is to help round out each other's flat sides. Nobody should ask a person who is valued for his incredible organizational skills to suddenly become spontaneous. To quote one team member, "You don't criticize a hippopotamus for not being able to hover in the air like a hummingbird." You accept people's strengths, knowing that they'll have weaknesses in other areas. You can't be methodical *and* spontaneous. Of course, cutting each other slack doesn't grant people the right to excuse or revel in their idiosyncrasy. However, it does give them permission to bring their strengths to the team without being beat up for their weaknesses. The bottom line? When groups gel into teams, count on people bragging about each other and then, with a grin, telling stories of how their strengths occasionally turn into pretty silly behaviors.

Sacrifice

The ultimate measure of a team's cohesiveness—of a society's, for that matter—is the willingness of individuals to make sacrifices for one another. Never was this more obvious to us than one afternoon in Detroit when Mike DeIrala, quality manager of the Ford Sterling facility, burst into our consulting office with an announcement— "Today we became a team!"

We had been working with Mike and his colleagues for several months as they tried to move to a more team-driven approach, but only after something critical had occurred in a meeting did Mike truly believe they had pulled together as a team. For a period of several years before the pivotal meeting, there had been one area in the plant that had never been able to meet its production and financial goals. An area manager would be put on the job—selected for a stellar record and a willingness to take on the near impossible—and then would fail within a few months. It was always hard on the leadership team to see a colleague walk a tightrope and eventually plummet to the ground. The battered manager would always be transferred to another setting and told how "he really hadn't failed," but it always felt like failure to everyone involved.

Then it happened. Mike and his colleagues were sitting in a yearly planning meeting in which each had been asked to set a 10 percent cost-improvement goal and to develop a plan to achieve it. As each person shared his or her ideas, one member stopped the discussion and asked a question that forever changed the team. "Are we going to ask our new area manager to set a similar goal and then fail?" At the time of the meeting, the plant was between area managers. A new one had been selected but hadn't moved into town yet. The curious member of the operating committee wanted to know if the new person would be forced to walk the same precarious tightrope and eventually plunge into failure as they all stood and watched. "What do you have in mind?" asked the plant manager. "Why don't we all take up a little more of the 10 percent cost-cutting goal and lower the goal for the area we know will fail without our help?" "I more than met my goal last year," chimed in one of the other area managers. "What if I were to take on a couple of extra percentage points?"

From that point on the operating committee did two things. First, each person tried to determine what it would take to get the suffering area on its feet. Second, everyone sacrificed a resource. Some took on more rigorous cost-cutting goals, others transferred stronger frontline leaders to the area, and still others found ways they could provide much-needed support. All of this was done in the absence of the person they were pitching in to help. The team became a team when they realized if one of them failed, irrespective of how well they knew or liked him or her, they all failed. Not only did they come to recognize the importance of helping each other out if they were all to succeed, but they understood it called for sacrifice.

Empathy

Perhaps Mike was referring to the emotion of the moment when he said they had finally become a team. For years, team members had sympathized with colleagues who had struggled in the "tough area." Mike understood that feeling *sympathy* for the person in the killer assignment wasn't enough. Until people felt the same pain—until they *empathized*—they were merely observers and not true teammates. Once they felt *empathy*, they did more than sit at their desks and sign condolence cards. They helped shoulder the burden.

One Final Ingredient

Groups become teams when members don't just *sympathize* with their colleagues' problems, they *empathize*. They feel others' successes and failures as if they were their own.

It's hard to create a culture of empathy. Most people are so linked to their own goals and objectives that they're unable to shoulder the emotional burdens of distant co-workers. This changes only as people truly identify with the successes and failures of their colleagues. For example, we recently worked with a green-field facility that was having problems. The new facility was supposed to produce software products for a clamoring market, but one of the production processes was out of control. Everyone was ahead of schedule except one team of experts who just hadn't been able to figure out how to produce their piece of the product. As a result, nothing was coming out the far end of the building.

The production manager, quite naturally, was in a tizzy. What was amazing is what happened when one of the authors approached a technician who'd just been granted a prestigious patent. When asked how things were going, his response was touching. "Not good!" he responded. "We haven't been able to get all of the bugs out of the process. It's been real hard." He used the term *we* as if he were working right alongside the team that was under the gun. He and his team were on top of the world—if you looked at their goals and objectives—but as long as the *facility* was in trouble, he felt in trouble as well. He wasn't about to hold a celebration as long as his teammates down the hall were fighting for their lives.

Let's complete our definition of a team. A team consists of a group of people who:

- Are interdependent
- Share a common objective

- Offer heartfelt support
- Share mutual respect
- Willingly sacrifice for each other
- Feel genuine empathy for each other's successes and failures

The first two characteristics describe the circumstances that call for a team. The last four help transform interdependent individuals into a team. Groups often experience Cell 4 problems because they possess the first two characteristics but lack the last four. People are thrown together with a common objective and structured in a way that makes them interdependent, but they lack a true appreciation for one another. Two out of six leads to disastrous results.

THE INABILITY TO COMMUNICATE

If one does not understand a person, one tends to regard him as a fool.

CARL JUNG

Next, let's look at another Cell 2 problem that impacts Cell 4 performance. It's hard for a group of people to make deep commitments—especially the kind called for when you swear to support, respect, and sacrifice for one another—if teammates don't communicate well. In fact, if a group of people can't openly and honestly communicate with each other, it's only a matter of time until they're at each other's throat. Consider a common example.

"The Fundamental Four-Step"

The void created by the failure to communicate is soon filled with poison, drivel, and misrepresentation.

PARKINSON'S LAW

Kent and Rebecca work at the corporate offices of a midsize food services company. Like most white-collar professionals, they care a great deal about their careers, are looking to move up, and worry just a little about how they're viewed. Oh yes, and Kent has it in for Rebecca. What she did was unforgivable. Taking potshots at his big presentation three months ago—at the most vulnerable moment of his career—is more than he can overlook. Kent had observed Rebecca do something at a critical moment during his presentation to a group of 30 corporate executives. After seeing her in action, he drew a number of conclusions about what she was doing and why she was doing it. He concluded that her leaning toward a peer and laughing was in reaction to his mispronunciation of a word and putting up the wrong slide at that moment. It was obvious she was trying to attack his work. He concluded she was rude and vicious. He never shared his observations with her. He never inquired to find out what was really going on. He kept silent, and acted on his conclusions instead of checking them out.

We've seen a hundred Kents. In fact, his action began a process we see so often that we've given it a name: "The Fundamental Four-Step." As the title suggests, it's a dance. It takes two people mirroring each other's footwork to pull it off. Both have to agree to make the fundamental attribution error. Each must draw the worst possible conclusions about the other's behavior. Both must agree to never check with the other person to see whether these conclusions are accurate. And since they don't check out their conclusions, they automatically act them out. Here's how.

Kent began avoiding contact with Rebecca. Rebecca noticed the avoidance and drew a number of negative conclusions about it. He's a sexist pig. He's threatened by strong women, and, since I challenge his ideas, he sees me as one. Rebecca acted on her conclusions and began assembling data for a grievance against Kent. Kent got word of it from a friend in human resources and intentionally joined one of Rebecca's task forces to undermine her case. Rebecca discovered the breach in privacy and added it as evidence to her case. How did this *happen*?

Actually, Kent and Rebecca would never have been able to maintain their poor relationship without tacitly agreeing to dance a dance of four simple, yet destructive, steps.

"The Fundamental Four-Step"

1. Draw the worst possible conclusions. (That is, make the fundamental attribution error.)
2. Refuse to check out your conclusions.
3. Act on your conclusions as though they were true.
4. Interpret everything that follows as additional evidence your original conclusions were true.

Fortunately, the story of Kent and Rebecca has a happy ending. Rebecca noticed she was dancing "The Fundamental Four-Step" with Kent and decided to take action. She exited the dance floor by suspending her conclusions about Kent and forcing herself to assume that he might, in fact, be a reasonable, rational, and decent human being. It was a stretch at first, but she operated on blind faith in humanity. She approached him and expressed a willingness to talk. She asked a number of questions about what she was doing that irritated him. When she heard how she had offended Kent at the meeting, it all became clear to her. The laughing and side conversation in the meeting began when the person next to her had crossed his legs and hit her in the knee. Her knee flew up in reflex and kicked a briefcase that had a cup of coffee on it. Luckily, the cup was empty. The two of them laughed at the chain reaction, apologized, then turned back to the meeting.

"Embarrassed and ashamed" was an understatement of how Kent felt. A couple of minutes of dialogue would have saved three months of plotting Cell 4 moves and countermoves. Fortunately, even though the problem wasn't nipped in the bud, it was killed before it did real damage.

How was it resolved? With dialogue. Two people sat down and decided to approach an embarrassing and threatening subject through candid dialogue rather than through silence or eventually violence (confrontation, court battles, and yelling matches). Rather than draw negative conclusions and begin "The Fundamental Four-Step," skilled people approach each other in open conversation, share their conclusions, and check them out before they run off half-cocked and cause problems.

Interpersonal conflicts, age-old feuds between departments, and ineffective internal customer-supplier relationships can be resolved 99 times out of 100 if people will only exercise the modicum of faith required to assume that others are reasonable, rational, and decent—and then sit down with them to talk things out. Mutual purposes are quickly discovered, new information is shared that causes both to interpret past behavior in a different light, and Cell 4 becomes stronger than ever.

Savvy leaders pounce on differences of opinion and infighting as opportunities to build teamwork. They recognize if they can find common ground (the kind that resolves differences of opinion), not only are they reducing arguments, they're expanding people's team boundaries. As individuals share mental maps, they not only share facts and values, they also come to understand how much they have in common. With time and increased understanding, people move from "enemies," to "them," to "us."

Although we'll devote an entire book in *The Praxis Leadership Series* to the topic of fostering honest, open dialogue, we can give only a few helpful hints here.

Clarify Ground Rules

I know not anything more pleasant, or more instructive, than to compare experience with expectation. . . . It is by this kind of observation that we grow daily less liable to be disappointed.

SAMUEL JOHNSON

A good practice for any team (especially a new one) is to sit around a table, talk openly and honestly, and negotiate their ground rules—to discuss what they want and don't want in the relationship. To get to the skills and techniques of ground rules, let's back up a few paces and take a running start. Let's start with the question, "What is my team really about?" When individual team members can answer this question, there is more clarity of direction. To achieve this clarity, the leader must help develop a specific, detailed team mission, a definite charter, visible goals, a detailed schedule, and discrete roles and responsibilities. After these long-term and broad aspects are clear, there tend to be fewer false starts, fewer meanderings, and better measurements of results. (For more detail on how to create a vision, see chapter 3.)

Next, to get down to the nitty-gritty of daily action, leaders must help team members put meat on the bones of broad goals by helping to develop ground rules. Ground rules answer the question, "What do we have to do to work together to accomplish our goals?" These answers make the behaviors and actions needed for collaboration visible. Let's take a look at a typical ground-rules session.

From the Trenches of a Large Governmental Office

The authors were once hired to work with a team in a government agency in Washington, D.C., that was about to fall apart. After completing a quick diagnosis of the situation, we decided that the team needed to sit down and establish some ground rules. We gathered around a large conference table and asked members to tell (without mentioning names) what they liked and disliked in a teammate. After about 10 minutes of shallow discussion, it was evident this team wasn't going to talk about anything of significance. People talked pabulum and recommended placebos. They quoted books and spouted platitudes. "I like a teammate who is punctual, and I dislike tardiness." "I like a teammate with enthusiasm, a passion for excellence." "I have difficulty with teammates who think good is good enough."

These Pollyanna facades continued until we came to the secretary, who said, "Well, I think we should get honest here. I like teammates who treat me like a person, and not like a tool. Let me give an example. A lot of you come into the office and say to my boss, even when I'm sitting right there, 'Ruth, could I borrow Jane to do some typing?' You treat me like a monkey wrench. What I would prefer is, when you come in, say, 'Ruth and Jane, could I talk to the two of you about getting some typing done?' That would be better."

A half-dozen palms hit foreheads. It was a group V8 experience. Several apologies were expressed. Then the fellow sitting next to her spoke up. "Well, if we're going to speak the truth, I think teammates should call each other by the name they prefer, not some nickname. A lot of you call me 'Big Ed.' I call myself 'Ed.' I'm a little sensitive about my weight." There was a pause and some nodding heads. The team leader asked, "Should we go around again?" They did, and this time real issues were dealt with. Real ground rules came out—not textbook ground rules, but ones the team could commit to *and* that would help them work well together to accomplish a very important mission.

So what are some examples of ground rules, and how are they used?

- Treat team members with dignity and respect.
- Call people by their preferred names.
- When there's a problem, assume good intentions.
- Ask and listen, listen and ask.
- Deliver on your promises.

A half-dozen or so ground rules are reminders of what specific teams need to work on so they can avoid Cell 4 problems. This team posted the rules in their conference room and made copies on small cards to carry around. Oh yes, and similar agreements can be made within departments or even entire companies.

Rules Squared or Rules about Rules

The most important ground rules to clarify are the ones about how you'll deal with perceived violations of the ground rules. In any relationship someone will eventually think the other person is behaving in inappropriate ways. The ground rules that make or break a relationship are the ones in which you make commitments about the responsibilities of the offended party. Most people, as we described earlier, take offense, feel sorry, or get angry (and justify themselves for doing so) in the name of the other person's weaknesses. They don't like what's happening but at least it's not *their* fault. They have pain but no power. This is how "The Fundamental Four-Step" begins.

Good ground rules include commitments such as:

- Every time we get together, we'll begin by bringing up any unresolved issues.
- If I find myself drawing negative conclusions about a teammate, I will take responsibility to check out my conclusions with the person in question.

The utility of ground rules is increased when team members hold each other accountable. They point out when there are violations and work together to improve. Skilled teams pick a ground rule they're having trouble with and put it on the agenda. Then they discuss: "How are we doing?" and "What could we do better?" Ground-rules discussions take time and skill, but they usually net significant benefits. Checking progress regularly allows teams to solve problems rather than let them fester. It also provides time for praise.

Rules about the Soul of a Team

Over the years as the authors have met with various teams in ground-rules meetings, we've reserved the right to share our vision of what we look for in a teammate. As the discussion moves around the table, usually focusing on fairly mechanical aspects of teams, and it's our turn to say something, we always discuss one of four key elements—support, respect, sacrifice, and empathy. We don't add to the team's charter (since it's not our team) but we give food for thought.

Left to their own, few teammates ever bring up such emotional issues as imputing good motive or always being there for each other. However, as we tell stories of teams we've seen who have experienced empathy or fought for each other in the trenches, people invariably ask for the same type of support from one another. Our goal is to make it safe to talk about elements that really make a team work but, strangely enough, are rarely discussed. By bringing the characteristics into the open and discussing them, team members begin an important bonding process. Of course, no one can legislate empathy or respect, but you can set expectations. Teammates can jointly spin a dream and then can work on turning it into a reality.

Share Expectations Openly

Nothing sets a person up more than having something turn out just the way it's supposed to be, like falling into a Swiss snowdrift and seeing a big dog come up with a little cask of brandy round its neck.

CLAUD COCKBURN

Setting clear expectations doesn't just apply to intact workgroups. Leaders can use the same technique to help resolve conflicts between competing groups. Ground rules are helpful in solving Cell 4 problems because they make expectations clear and public. When competing groups are at odds, an expectation-setting session can help reduce the tension. For example, one of our most miraculous experiences with setting expectations followed a bitter strike that had been broken—but only after the union had been brought to its knees. Angry and bitter hourly employees reluctantly returned to their jobs rather than lose them, but venom was flowing in the aisles. And this was a machine shop for an arms manufacturer. Scary!

One of the authors was brought into the problem-solving loop to help improve union-management relations. His first effort involved getting union representatives together in a room for a day. Management was likewise assembled in a room by themselves. Each group was asked to spend the day writing on flip charts their answers to the question, "What do you want for each of the company's stakeholders?" Each wrote furiously for hours.

Early the next morning he assembled the combined group with the flip charts all lined up at the front of the room. He asked all present to spend an hour walking around and reading the flip charts. During the next 60 minutes, an amazing transformation occurred. No one could tell the flip charts of one group from those of the other. The aspirations were the same. The common ground was enormous. Dialogue began that day.

The open and honest communication resulted in a list of mutual expectations—*behaviors* (what they would do) and *outcomes* (what they would achieve). Each group better understood what the other wanted. Both came to see they were not at cross-purposes and that the other group of people was composed of reasonable, rational, and decent human beings. The clear expectations became a framework for revisiting their needs and for working on the relationship in the future. The plant and thousands of jobs were saved, and, better still, nobody exploded.

THE WRONG REWARD STRUCTURE

The folly of rewarding A, while hoping for B.

STEVEN KERR

Now, let's look at how Cell 3 can have an impact on how willing individuals are to share resources (Cell 4). We'll start by returning to the soccer coach we introduced at the beginning of this chapter. He, like many leaders, inadvertently focused on individual achievement at the expense of collaboration. It's not that there shouldn't be a place for individual accomplishment in a team, it's just when that's all that is ever praised, important parts of teamwork are undermined. This lack of balanced attention is a common mistake largely fed by leaders' inability to see the act of collaboration.

For example, the soccer coach and everyone in the stands saw the goal. Since the act of propelling the ball into the net is the ultimate measure of success, it's the one people look for and dwell on. It's a matter of attention. Just try taking your eye off the ball. Football is no different. It has taken nearly three decades for announcers to see two linemen working *in concert* to make a hole for the running back. For years, the quarterback would hand the ball to a running back who would run through a hole wide enough to easily accommodate a Buick and then be dropped by a linebacker five yards beyond the line of scrimmage. Announcers would applaud the run. Dom DeLuise could have made it through the hole carved out by the struggling, unrecognized linemen! But since the announcers were focusing on forward ball movement, the person closest to the ball got the credit. Why? It takes practice to take your eyes off the ball and look for the support activities.

Common Errors

Leaders face the same challenge. Rather than focus on acts of collaboration, they focus on the ball. Here are some common mistakes.

Modeling Aggressive Individuality

Before leaders so much as say a word to their direct reports about teamwork, they have already sent dozens of messages about the topic—through their own actions. Employees watch how bosses treat each other and wonder if the people who are preaching teamwork have a clue about what it is. They watch closely as their bosses do everything in their power to achieve their own goals and wonder if teamwork will ever be anything more than a catchphrase. They can't recall a time when one of their leaders said, "You know, the more I think about it, I believe we should set aside the project we've been killing ourselves on for the past two weeks, take a brief hiatus from our own goals, and throw all of our support to Hugo on his project. He's in a pinch, and we should all lend him a hand." Instead, leaders demonstrate that you get promoted by moving heaven and earth to complete your own personal assignments. Employees hear the rhetoric, but if leaders have consistently acted in ways at odds with the dream, nobody believes them. As the speeches roll down from the podium, employees are reminded of the day their father cautioned them against smoking cigarettes while lighting up a Camel.

Leaders, quite naturally, don't want to be seen as hypocrites, but if they've been acting in ways that are highly individualistic for years, they aren't going to change overnight. They face a problem. If they're serious about moving to a team approach, they must start by working on their own team skills. That's a given. In addition, they have to go public with the problem. They have to talk openly about how they haven't always been the most team-oriented people who came down the pike and that they're working on it. If not, they won't be able to change fast enough (in a way that is seen by large numbers of people) to avoid the "hypocrite" label.

In addition to the fact that leaders have been sending mixed messages about teamwork, they often reward self-serving behavior in one of the following four ways.

Crowning the Messenger

Leaders are typically cut off from daily actions, so they see only the results of a team effort. They then make the mistake of rewarding the person closest to the final outcome. Someone walks into the boss's office with a final report of a team effort and gets praised to high heavens. It's the flipside of shooting the messenger and leads to team members fighting over who gets to take the good news to the boss. Of course, they fight that much harder when the news is bad.

Heralding the Familiar

When groups of experts are brought together into a cross-functional team, it's common for the leader to know little about the various fields of expertise that have been summoned into the group. This results in an interesting challenge. The leader has a hard time knowing who's shining and who's dogging it. Should there be a couple of people from the leader's own functional specialty, they will be much more likely to be given attention and, if they rise to the occasion, to be praised for their exceptional accomplishment. Without some type of peer evaluation or advice from other experts who understand the unfamiliar specialties, leaders are left either to blanketly praise group accomplishment or herald the familiar.

Lauding the Loud

Leaders rarely spend a great deal of time working alongside their direct reports in routine activities. They work in so many other forums that they sample only how people behave in meetings and other social events. They don't sit in the corner and watch a team in the throes of a problem. Instead, they watch from the stage while they're leading a meeting or conducting a joint problem-solving discussion. The behavior they're most likely to see—and eventually praise—is more flamboyant than that required in daily teamwork. People who are comfortable speaking in front of their peers are seen as the real contributors. If they can show how others are wrong, they really shine in front of the boss.

Stroking the Salient

Actually, what we're talking about here is salience. If you do the right thing, you stand out from the crowd. You become the ball everyone is following with such rapt attention. Of course, there isn't an employee alive who doesn't know and play this game. It starts in kindergarten when you're ripped from your mother's protective arms, thrown in with a group of strangers, and asked to fend for yourself. You quickly learn that if your precious ego is to survive, you have to find a way to get yourself noticed by that all-important creature known as your teacher—and in a positive way to boot. It takes a while, but you eventually find techniques to differentiate yourself from the pack. For example, you discover that when every other kid has his or her hand raised in the air, if you hold off to the very last second and then thrust your arm up in a burst of energy, it catches the teacher's attention and you're singled out from the sea of wiggling arms. Salience at last.

Perhaps the most valued form of salience, one supported by 12 or more years of formal education, is the act of being correct when everyone else is wrong. This isn't just salience, it's unadulterated ambrosia. If you can be the only one who divines the solution to a tough problem, well, it's the best thing ever. That's why kids in school end up hoping for the failure of their compatriots. If another student is called on, everyone prays he's wrong so he or she can get a shot at glory. Students literally groan when a classmate gives a right answer. However, if you're lucky, *really* lucky, one student after another crumbles into ignominy by giving the wrong response until the spotlight eventually rests on you. And then, with every single eye focused on you, if you and only you come up with the correct answer—well, what could be better?

If you doubt that this informal, and yet unrelenting, process practically whips people into selfish individualists, try to imagine a 14-year-old student following up on a colleague's response by raising his hand and saying, "I just wanted to point out that I think Chris's answer was positively brilliant. It was not only insightful, but it took courage to veer from the beaten path and risk such a clever solution. Congratulations, Chris."

Not in our lifetime.

It's little wonder that when asked to make a list of collaborative acts, ones that could be identified and rewarded, most leaders come up with a blank. They've spent a lifetime conjuring ways to stand out from the crowd—and now they're supposed to actually see what's going on inside the mass of flailing arms? It's not going to happen. Leaders can't reward teamwork if they can't see it, and individual acts of collaboration and support will continue to remain invisible as long as leaders focus on the ball when they should be watching the team.

To help with this exceptionally difficult problem, we've identified several subtle, often invisible, acts of teamwork that should be noticed and rewarded. These are the handoffs, passes, blocks, and other acts of support that typically go unrecognized but that build Cell 4 collaboration.

Acts Worthy of Your Attention

Heartfelt Support

Watch for individuals who go out of their way to lend a needed hand to colleagues. This comes in many shapes. The most obvious form is simply pitching in on a project when help is needed. However, as we suggested earlier, support also covers emotional buttressing. Should an outsider take a shot at a colleague, supportive teammates step into the breach and deal with the fundamental attribution error by imputing good motive. They stand behind their colleagues.

Mutual Respect

Teammates who respect their colleagues never take shots at them. Instead, they take every opportunity to express their admiration through both word and deed. They also care enough to share their honest differences of opinion. Rather than watch a shipmate go down to defeat or experience unnecessary problems, they jump in when they see that a decision, opinion, or action is likely to yield bad results. Watch for individuals who provide helpful, honest feedback by sharing their opinions in a tactful way, avoiding attacks. Pay special attention to individuals who don't tear down existing ideas or opinions. Instead, they help others gain a new perspective by building on what's there.

Willing Sacrifice

When one member of a team needs assistance, healthy teammates put their own tasks on the back burner and pitch in where additional hands and minds will help avert a disaster. This doesn't mean they completely abandon their own priorities, but that they're able to see the big picture and know when helping out a colleague better serves the organization. Reward individuals who have the sense to step back from myopic stances and do what is right to serve competing stakeholder demands. This is a rare enough deed that you'll want to watch for it and make a big deal about it when it happens. It'll take repeated efforts to convince most people that the needs of the many are more important than the needs of the few—or the one.

Sacrifice also covers ego. Teammates don't constantly look to take credit for their personal contributions. Instead, they understand that a team effort takes everyone's input. Even when their own contributions are exceptional, they don't look for ways to draw attention to themselves. They prefer to keep the focus on the team and on team results. Don't insult these people by dragging them into the spotlight, but remember their healthy actions when writing up their private performance reviews.

Genuine Empathy

Finally, watch for team members who revel in the successes and feel the failures of their colleagues. Of course, these will be the same individuals who immediately jump in with both emotional and physical support. On the flip side, be wary of individuals who celebrate their own accomplishments while colleagues are suffering challenges or losses.

Now, once you've duly noted behaviors that exemplify healthy teamwork, it's up to you to decide how to respond. In the last chapter, we spent a great deal of time highlighting various methods of delivering honest recognition, along with a handful of caveats. Our point in this chapter is that if you don't know what you're looking for, you'll follow the flamboyant act of scoring and miss the assists. Until leaders recognize and reward assists, most American teams will be little more than a group of stifled individuals who tolerate their colleagues while they wait for every opportunity to kick the ball into the net.

THE FEAR OF EMPOWERING OTHERS

The man who has ceased to fear has ceased to care.

F. H. BRADLEY

Before we bring this chapter to an end, let's look at one final Cell 4 barrier. It deals with the fear of empowering others. Up to this point, we've looked at why teammates haven't always been eager to lend resources. Now we'll turn our attention to why leaders don't always share an important resource—the authority or permission to make certain decisions. This authority, of course, is at the heart of empowerment. To be sure we're all singing from the same sheet of music, let's quickly define *empowerment*. Empowered individuals have the (1) skills, (2) desire, and (3) permission to do what it takes to meet competing stakeholder demands. In previous chapters we explored what leaders can do to supply the first two-thirds of the necessary ingredients. We looked at what it takes to develop skills and influence wills. We'll now turn to that sticky issue of granting authority to others. In some ways it's the most difficult element.

Leaders often don't grant others the permission to make certain decisions because they fear what will happen if they do. They dread the day when an individual or team, now given permission to make key decisions, makes a bad one.

Every Leader's Nightmare

One day while conducting a leadership training session in Indiana, a leader approached one of the authors as the morning break came to an end. The fellow was distraught, disgusted, and disillusioned. "Do you want to know what just happened back at the office?" he queried. "One of our newly 'empowered' teams just took a vote and decided not to serve the customer." He went on to explain that when a computer network had gone down, rather than hand-carry the data in process to the next station (something that a traditional supervisor would have asked for), they decided it wasn't their job and sat down until the network was back on-line. In the meantime, no products were produced, and the team members played cards. This particular leader's worst nightmare had come to fruition. He and other members of the senior management team had argued that if they were too lax in their control, the day would come when they'd be held hostage by the workforce. They had been right.

Given these and similar problems, it's little wonder that most leaders are reluctant to relinquish their role in making decisions. Their mental maps contain undesirable outcomes. They fear bad things will happen if they're liberal with permission or careless with information. For example, a manager we once worked with refused to allow people to travel without his approval. As a result, few people called on customers when it wasn't clearly justified. They weren't building important relationships, resulting in lost accounts and reduced orders. This vital customer-support activity would not start again unless Cell 4 was dealt with. This manager needed to give his people more authority regarding travel decisions.

Why was the manager so tightfisted with travel money? Actually, his fear was built on good intentions. He wasn't some control freak who enjoyed holding people on a string. He simply wanted to be careful with company resources. He understood that the battle of the bottom line is won by watching costs. Nothing wrong there.

But that was only half of the story. Quite frankly, he was operating from an incomplete mental map. As team members courageously challenged the manager's assumptions, as they asked questions to understand his motives, and as they creatively explored solutions, they discovered he was willing to create an industry-standard budget for travel and let them use it as they saw fit. By pegging the amount in the budget to competitive data, he was able to feel assured that costs were under control. By allowing the sales staff to make customer-service decisions, customer satisfaction improved.

Responsibility: The Cornerstone of Empowerment

As we suggested in chapter 2, the way to cure phobias is to restructure mental maps. Fears are removed only after people understand how their worst nightmare won't actually occur and how their needs can be met through alternative strategies. For example, the manager needed to know that the empowerment strategy that allowed his direct reports to take part in the travel budget wouldn't result in excessive spending and would result in better customer service. The solution didn't call for rocket science, only a way of convincing himself that his needs would be met.

The overall solution to any empowerment phobia is simple. Just remember that the cornerstone of empowerment is responsibility. For every new decision an employee is allowed to make, the responsibility for that decision has to be placed squarely on the person making it. For years, people complained about having responsibility without authority. Don't reverse the tables by granting authority without passing on the responsibility. That is, don't give open-ended authority. You rarely have it to give. Create the boundaries of authority by using natural constraints. Follow the steps of the worried manager. Share your philosophy of what should be done and why, and then provide a budget. After all, when you give someone the authority to make a decision, you've released a constraint. You've given the individual authority to use precious resources. The newly empowered employee can take longer, spend more money, use up more material, or call on more people. Don't be enticed into a mindless form of empowerment that gives limitless authority to act. You face the constraints handed to you by market conditions, so pass them on to others as you grant them the authority to make choices. Continually remind yourself that *the cornerstone of empowerment is responsibility*.

Information Empowers

Finally, let's look at one more feature of Cell 4. To what extent should leaders share information with others? Is it helpful to constantly share information, even material that is typically reserved for senior leaders' ears and eyes only? One thing is for certain, most leaders currently don't expend massive amounts of energy to make information available.[1]

Our rule is simple—if information can be put in the open where people can use it to inform their daily decisions and if it can be done in a way that doesn't compromise a confidentiality or expose a trade or strategic secret, *do it*. People make choices on the basis of their mental maps. The more complete and accurate the maps, the better the choices.

IN SUMMARY

In this chapter, we've explored the questions, "What can a leader do to help people work together?" and "What can a leader do to encourage people to share help, authority, information, or resources?"

The leader's constant challenge is to find ways to:

- Expand the vision of teamwork to include the "soul of a team"—support, respect, sacrifice, and empathy. Don't be afraid to talk about those parts of teamwork that are emotional and that offer comfort.
- Improve communication by clarifying ground rules and setting output and culture expectations.
- Work on informal rewards. Stop rewarding selfish actions, and start watching for, and rewarding, the "soul of a team."
- Eliminate empowerment phobia by providing others the balanced package of authority *and* responsibility.
- Share any information that will help people make better decisions.

S E C T I O N   4   Q U I Z

Let's see how much of this section has sunk in.

1. What is meant by the term "The Hawthorne Effect"?
   A. Social norms often influence behavior more profoundly than incentive systems.
   B. Individuals, when treated as if they are special or unique, often go out of their way to live up to positive expectations.
   C. Individuals, when forced to wear *The Scarlet Letter* (A) on their forehead, tend to be treated poorly by other members of their village.

2. Healthy team members:
   A. Sacrifice for one another.
   B. Feel genuine empathy for each other's successes and failures.
   C. Gladly swap dentures should social circumstances demand it.

3. Which of the following is true about sacrifice?
   A. It breathes life into nearly dead values.
   B. It's one of the few ways you can convince people you're serious about a value.
   C. It's something you do in private, but only when you know somebody is sneaking a peek at you. That way you can look like you're humble, sincere, and modest—and get credit to boot.

4. Define the term "early adopters."
   A. The primary target of savvy change agents.
   B. Individuals, unlike innovators, who serve as opinion leaders, speeding along the wide adoption of an innovation.
   C. People who are able to take in a child through legal means before the age of 15.

5. How do people typically misunderstand the concept of peer pressure?
   A. They act as if it has no impact on adults.
   B. They confuse the value of peers as purveyors of information.
   C. They mistakenly assume their colleagues should carry between 23 and 30 pounds per square inch, even though there's no scientific evidence to support the practice.

6. What's the point of the story "The Marshmallow Massacre"?
   A. Accomplishments that impress *you* may not impress *others*.
   B. When choosing a reward, make sure the other person values it.
   C. One of the authors really messed up on his first date.

Taking Charge

of *Things*

As we move into Cells 5 and 6, we're making a stark transition. We're now out of the people realm and into the world of structures, systems, environment, and other *things*. There are no people in Cells 5 and 6. None. *Ninguno. Nessuno.*

In this penultimate section, we strip humans from our formula and wander around the lifeless shell most of us imagine when hearing the term *organization*. We'll step into the physical structure, thumb through policy manuals, hold a magnifying glass up to performance-appraisal forms, stroll about the information system, take a drive down the electronic highway, and otherwise explore those structural features that similarly inspire and enable human action. Sounds (uh . . . how does one put it?) lifeless and numbingly boring? Actually, we'll explore only the nonhuman elements insofar as they affect people. As always, humans spice up the stew. Humans may not reside in Cells 5 and 6, but they do respond to them.

Chapter 14 examines what it takes to bring the formal reward system into alignment with the dream. Chapter 15 takes a glance into those features of the organization that enable individuals to do what it takes to meet competing stakeholder demands. Our goal in this section is to select a few key features from the organizational structure literature and turn them into leadership advice.

CHAPTER 14

Aligning Rewards

A feast is made for laughter, and wine maketh merry: but money answereth all things.

ECCLESIASTES 10:19

I n Cell 5 we look at how people's mental maps of the pay and performance management systems influence their behavior. As we examine the impact of financial rewards, we'll depart from some rather peculiar arguments made by management theorists over the past few decades about how "money is not a motivator." Neither practical nor intuitive experience supports any such idea.

Actually, we don't hold to the notion of motivators per se. We prefer to use the phrase *valued outcomes*. Money, as we all know, helps people achieve

a rather large number of *valued outcomes*. For instance, any parent knows you can influence a child to do something he or she finds intrinsically repugnant by offering cash. What child would ever eat broccoli, take out the trash, or do homework without external motivation? If it weren't for Cells 3 and 5, we'd be a world of scurvy-ridden idiots drowning in rubbish. Okay, so it's an overstatement, but you get the point.

For most people, the financial incentives found in Cell 5 motivate only insofar as they attach to Cells 1 or 3. In other words, no one is motivated by money for its own sake. With the exception of Uncle Scrooge (who was often seen bathing in cash), most of us seek money because of what it means or what it can buy. It may mean achievement, acknowledgment, opportunity, or security. It can help us buy . . . well, money can buy almost anything. (Of course, the things we buy and the meanings we attach to them are linked to social and intrinsic motivators. But that's a technical distinction.) We care about net value, and money is a *big* player when it comes to influencing one's overall outcome map. The bottom line (a money metaphor) is that most people's behavior can indeed be affected by the anticipation of earning money and all that it offers.

You'll note that in our discussion so far we've collapsed Cell 5 into dollars. When analyzing organizational motive, we could speak about pay, profit sharing, benefits, bonuses, financial awards, and a variety of other methods of providing incentives to employees, but for the purposes of this chapter, we'll generally speak of money. Whether it's paid weekly or at the end of a shift, linked to output or based on the entrails of chickens, we're talking about *dinero* and how it affects the human decision maker.

Having already examined the other two elements that help make up net value—intrinsic value (Cell 1) and social influence (Cell 3)—we're now at a point where we can examine how all of the pieces fit into the complicated puzzle known as *motivation*. To gain a better feel of how intrinsic motive, social forces, and cold, hard cash combine into net value, let's take a look at a real-life case. We've changed the names of the actual players in this case for a variety of reasons—mostly because these circumstances come too close to home for many readers. This story captures one of the most common challenges facing leaders today.

MEET HYRUM DENTON

Why is it that the owners' and bosses' dream ends up being my nightmare?
HYRUM DENTON

The following tale is sad but true. It's about Hyrum Denton, a 30-year employee who works for a midsize small-parts manufacturer located in northern Ohio. For the last 20 years of his 30-year career, Hyrum has worked as an electrician. He still has seven years until he qualifies for the company's retirement program, but he's in no hurry. His job has always been interesting, all of his close friends work alongside him, and the work he does leaves him enough energy at the end of the day to still shoot a good game of pool.

Over the past year, Hyrum has found himself in a pickle. All his life he's preached the adage "An honest day's work for an honest day's pay." His four children have heard it dozens of times. For the most part he's been true to this credo, but as of late he'd have to say he's lived up to only half of the deal—the pay part. He still was paid good money, but he wasn't putting in his best work. In an interview with an outside consultant, he even told the young "white shirt" that he and his buddies were holding the company hostage. His exact words were, "If we did at a supermarket what we do here at work, we'd have to wear masks."

Hyrum's trip down the road to indolence started with an innocent boating trip some 15 years earlier. At the time, he had just earned journeyman status, and he and his family were "rolling in it." At least that's what his wife Melba had said. She was so financially conservative that she thought buying store-bought bread was a sin. Now he was making real bucks. Demand for his company's product was at an all-time high, skilled tradespeople were hard to find, and Hyrum had become an overtime junkie. He had been working 55, sometimes 60, hours a week. Melba was buying bread now, and (getting back to the boating trip) he had laid down money for a boat and trailer. He never could have afforded such a luxury on his regular salary, but with the overtime nest egg he had set aside, he had been able to follow his father's admonition to "always pay cash for anything that doesn't have a basement or a four-speed transmission." It had felt good to plunk down $5,000 in cash. He had arrived.

It was on that first boating trip that Hyrum had made an important decision. Based on his most recent workload, it was clear he wasn't going to have a lot of those "Father Knows Best" moments when you come home from work at 4:30, play games with the kids, and solve teenage conundrums such as, "What do you do when you've said yes to a fella, and then the guy you really like asks you to the same dance?" Old Robert Young had given that hackneyed bromide quite a tumble. It had taken two episodes to figure that one out, and Betty (known to fans everywhere as "Princess") was a far better person for the experience. No, Hyrum was at the plant at 4:30, and 5:30, and . . . well, sometimes he didn't get home until 12:30 a.m. Melba had been solving those kinds of problems since he had mostly taken up residence at the plant. Rebecca, his "Princess," was now taking most of her advice from Mom.

All that time away from the family just didn't seem right, so Hyrum did what most of his buddies did. As he drove back from their first fishing excursion, he decided to give his loved ones the next best thing to *real* time: "quality time." Over the next five years, Hyrum and his brood moved into a bigger home, bought a camper to park alongside the boat, started to send the kids to the real college in Akron, and bought a BarcaLounger that came with everything but backup lights—and he had had *them* installed. (Hyrum had been known to announce the part about the BarcaLounger to just about any stranger who happened to walk into the pool hall.) Hyrum had given his family a lot more than he figured a guy who barely made it through the trade tech would ever be able to accomplish.

Despite his wonderful achievements, Hyrum had stepped across the line. It might have been for the camper, or maybe for the shiny new Evinrude engine for his boat, but it happened the day he began to buy things "on time." Actually, it wasn't the line of credit that had served as a noose. It was the fact that he was making financial commitments based on earning a certain amount of overtime. He'd always have his job (heck, he had more tenure than almost all of the bosses combined). But could he count on all that money that came from effectively working two jobs? Well, he did. And now, for over a decade, he had made plans, spent money, incurred long-term debt, and designed his lifestyle around his pay plus overtime. After a couple of years, he'd come to equate "base pay plus overtime" with "pay."

What Do I Care about the World Economy?

It was a rainy Monday morning when the word first reached the power plant Hyrum had been working in for the past couple of days. Competitors had begun to take a real bite out of their market, and the glory days were now over. Some boss had actually said, "The glory days are now over." What a pencil-neck. He wasn't sure what the "white shirt" meant at first, but it didn't take long to learn that the blue-collar translation was "Overtime is now a thing of the past." The plant still had a lot of work to do, so the workforce didn't exactly go cold turkey, but when the owners eventually invested 50 million dollars in new equipment, they completely restructured the plant so there really weren't very many overtime opportunities. The new cost structure didn't allow for it. Whatever that meant.

What it meant to Hyrum and his colleagues was that they had to be more creative. Here's what he was facing. The bosses kept giving fire-

and-brimstone speeches about the threat of competition and the need to cut costs. But no overtime? Get real. He still had two kids at home, one in college, and aging parents who needed his help. He'd refinanced his house so it would be paid for the same year he retired, but that was seven years off. Every penny he brought home was accounted for. He could do away with a few of the frills and maybe save 10 percent, but overtime consisted of 40 percent of his wages and virtually all of his discretionary income. If they were going to get serious about prohibiting overtime, he'd have to sell his house, cut back on everything he actually enjoyed doing, quit helping his folks, put off college for his last son, and maybe send him to the local JC (OCC—affectionately referred to as "Outcast Community College"). He hated to even think about it.

That's where creativity came into play. It wasn't as if he worked a production line. The bosses didn't blow a whistle at the end of the day, stop the line, and send him home. He fixed and installed things. Nobody could estimate the work he did with a stopwatch. If it took longer than the bosses originally imagined, well, problems do come up. So without ever saying anything to each other, he and most of his immediate co-workers silently slipped into a pitched battle for their lifestyles. They fought with the only weapon they had. They expanded the work available to fit their needed overtime hours. Most of them had long since cut back from pulling as many as six 12-hour days and were now working around 55 hours, but no matter the new workload, no matter how much the demand fluctuated, no matter what their monthly costs were supposed to come to, it was going to take Hyrum and his friends 55 hours to get their jobs done. It took that many hours to keep them afloat.

When that young consultant had interviewed him and his best friends about the job, Hyrum was the one who said they should be wearing masks. At first he couldn't believe he'd actually said the words aloud. He thought Meg was going to leap across the table and run a screwdriver through his neck. The words sort of jumped out of his mouth. Maybe he was feeling guilty. But why? He hadn't done anything wrong. He wasn't holding up banks; he was holding up his family commitments. Besides, he wasn't the guy who'd changed the rules after 15 years.

Now some of the younger employees were wise to his game and were starting to look at him as if he were a T-bone steak that had been left in the trunk for a couple of hot summer days. It was almost more than he could stomach. In order to stretch his job into overtime, he was taking too long to complete routine tasks, and everyone knew it. For a while he had solved this problem by going into hiding. He'd lay low for a few hours and then, when he came out from behind the lockers, he would whistle feverishly, work like a beaver, and nobody was the wiser. Then came management's number one weapon in the battle for lifestyle—the beeper. He sure hated that thing. It had been made by a company named QuikComm, but as far as he was concerned it should have carried the name, *"You Can Run, But You Can't Hide."*

Today Hyrum had hit a new low. "Seven more years," he had mumbled to himself as he exited another all-hands meeting. It had been like a high-school pep rally. One of the consultants must have dreamed up this baby. The head cheeses had created a stuffed dummy, put a "high cost" sign on it, and then burned it in front of the whole crowd. The workforce hadn't actually broken into a chant, but they had come perilously close.

The trump card had been played when the controller flashed up a photograph that was taken at the annual company picnic. Several teenagers, all kids who belonged to the gang that worked the loading dock, stood next to each other in a typical pose—big smiles and arms raised in jubilation. As Rita, the chief financial officer, spoke of excessive costs and the potential loss of jobs, the slide of the teenagers came up on a huge screen, and the crowd cheered. Family photos always drew a big response.

And then the slide changed right before their eyes. Some computer whiz had taken the original picture and superimposed McDonald's hats on the teenagers. "That's right," Rita had exclaimed, "if we don't find a way to continually cut costs, if we don't work as hard and smart as we can, it's only a matter of time until every one of *our* kids, and eventually *their* kids, will be working in the fast-food industry. Why? Because after we've lost all of our manufacturing jobs—and we *will* lose our jobs if we don't cut costs—everyone in America will be working at McDonald's, driving a tour bus at Disneyland, or taking out the trash for those who do."

What a travesty. All that was lacking was a loud rendition of the national anthem and the crowd would have broken into a chant, "Cut costs! Cut costs! Cut costs!" Talk about emotional blackmail. So why did Hyrum feel like everyone was looking at him? Was he becoming paranoid? No, paranoia is when you *imagine* that people are after you. People *were* after him. All the bosses, some of his old buddies, and virtually everyone with less than 10 years of seniority were putting the squeeze on him to give up everything he'd fought for. Not a chance. He'd hold out. He didn't know how, but he'd manage. After all, as his daddy had always said, when it came to good old-fashioned ingenuity, Hyrum had more than his fair share. He'd find a way.

The Challenge

Okay, you've heard the story. Now imagine that it's your job to design an intervention to get Hyrum and his co-workers to "put in an honest day's work." You can do anything you want. You can give speeches, design training, coach, make threats, use peer pressure, hire and put into place 200 barefoot doctors, or do anything else you can dream up. Except one thing. You can't play with money. Anything related to pay and benefits has been negotiated by the contract and is out of your control.

How successful do you think you'll be with old Hyrum?

Yes, Cell 5 can present some challenges.

We've chosen to talk about Hyrum and his friends because they show the important role Cell 5 plays in many interventions. As we argued earlier, each cell plays a part in the decision-making process. Cells 1, 3, and 5 make up net value for motivation. Any one of these cells can lead to a positive net value—if it's large enough. If people absolutely, positively love their work, they may even come close to starving for it. If they receive enough pressure from their peers, they may starve again. We just about drove this point into the ground in our last four chapters. And now we add one final element—cold, hard cash—and people will starve for it too. Well, actually, it keeps them from starving.

An organization's ability to motivate through formal rewards is, at once, all powerful and nearly powerless. It's all-powerful in that money can be used to buy what most people are looking for in Cells 1 and 3. Money opens the door. On the other hand, Cell 5 can be of little use to many leaders because they can't really use it as a lever. Employees like Hyrum find a way to yank the lever, and bosses often learn that the formal reward structure (rather than being a lever that can be continually applied, leading to gradually more or less influence) is a switch. It's either off or on. The person either keeps the job with its attendant financial benefits, or the person loses everything. This is particularly true in large, untrusting organizations that have negotiated "guaranteed employment." In some of these companies, the loss of a job isn't even a threat. You'd have to kill a really popular person to get fired. Even in companies that have established bonuses, profit sharing, and other discretionary systems, most are intended to add a tweak here and there. Leaders have a percentage point or two to play with.

In the case of Hyrum, leaders have no Cell 5 levers. Actually, all they have is a Cell 5 club. They have to get Hyrum to put in a hard day's work, quit padding his jobs, reduce his work to around 40 hours where it belongs, and bring costs into containment. And what *incentive* do they offer? The loss of his lifestyle? Prepare for a battle.

GIMME A LEVER

Money couldn't buy friends, but you got a better class of enemy.

SPIKE MILLIGAN

In the vital world we've been discussing in this book, we've been making some fairly straightforward assumptions. Leaders start with a dream that consists of identifying what products and services they want to provide to a clamoring marketplace. They imagine what they'll do, how they'll do it, and how the workforce will act when they really care about meeting competing stakeholder demands. As part of the dream, leaders clarify exactly what each employee is supposed to do. They identify behaviors that can be replicated by the employee and then measured and rewarded by the leaders. We even looked at how to measure the behaviors and take action should there be a gap. When it came to dealing with gaps, we examined four cells, each dealing with a different component of the overall stimulus to act—perceived net value.

Now we've added our penultimate feature—the organization's reward system. To finish our tale and to wire the reward system with the rest of our plan for achieving vitality, we have to find a way to link formal rewards directly to each employee's behavior and then use these rewards to get more of what you want and less of what you don't want. This, of course, assumes that you can play with the amount of rewards that flow through the organization—that you, not somebody else, can throw the switch.

These last conditions, of course, were precisely opposite those faced by Hyrum's bosses. We started this chapter with Hyrum's tale because it shows how miserable it is when, not only do you *not* have Cell 5 available to motivate people in the right direction, you have to *fight it* every day of your life. It leads to our first recommendation:

> Put the ability to use Cell 5 in the hands of each leader.

I Work for Gorbachev

What monster have we here?
A great Deed at this hour of day?
A great just Deed—and not for pay?
Absurd,—or insincere.

ELIZABETH BARRETT BROWNING

Ask your average citizen why the Soviet Union collapsed, and you'll receive a common answer. It failed, not ideologically or even politically, but financially. A socialistic state has no individual incentives and eventually falls apart. The jury is no longer out on this issue. To be able to come to this conclusion confidently, the world actually conducted an immense project in experimental sociology. The Soviet bloc was the experimental group, and western capitalistic governments served as the control. To turn the research into a rather elegant little study, the designers took a country, divided it in half, and assigned each to one of the two conditions. In the end, it is West Germany that really sticks in the craw of the socialistic ideologists. West German citizens' astonishing success (in contrast to friends and relatives across the street who waited in long lines and suffered the malaise of a stagnant society) was the straw that broke the camel's back.

We cite this example for a rather compelling reason. Many of the organizations we work with continue to fight for financial packages that verge on socialism: You earn more the longer you hang around; poor performers receive the same benefits as their effective counterparts; and "no good deed goes unpunished." However, if you do an excellent job, guess what? You get even more work to do. If you do a lousy job, you'll probably be left to rot in your cubicle. And don't forget the compelling feature that keeps certain people fighting for quasi-socialistic reward structures. A handful of adept folks like Hyrum can take control of their own special benefits. Dishonest, strategically placed employees can reward themselves through their own devious actions.

And to what do we owe these frightening circumstances? A raging inability to trust others—certainly, our inability to trust *a lot of* others. When you can't trust the bosses to divide up the bounty fairly, you tie their hands. You insist that every citizen take, not according to his ability or actual accomplishment (heaven only knows how we would calculate this in the first place), but according to his needs—which we evidently calculate with ease.

Mistrust is at the center of all of this. Union employees, reeling from the abuse of robber barons, had good reasons not to trust those who held the marbles, so they worked feverishly to do away with physical abuse and financial misconduct. Today, many organizations find themselves living in the repressive and constricting shadow of past abusers. Nobody, but nobody, is allowed to be judged or rewarded according to his or her accomplishments. This would mean relying on the honest judgment of leaders, and *they* can't be trusted. Instead of leaders, despoiled by poor judgment and petty insecurities, we rely on the calendar to determine how much each person makes with each tick of the clock. We have replaced misjudgment with tenure. The marketplace sets the entering salary, but from that point on it's the clock that rules.

Every organization that has solved the problems attendant to favoritism and misjudgment by removing the ability to reward people according to their deeds has, you might say, hired the devil to throw a thief out of their kitchen—and now they're stuck with a houseguest nobody wants. To cure the disease of inequity, the ruling body has conducted a modified frontal lobotomy—removing that annoying little area that controls one's sense of hope and personal destiny. (Insert your own metaphor here, and rank on socialism at your leisure.)

Today, in spite of recent improvements and a variety of newly created incentive programs, most organizations have effectively taken Cell 5 out of the game. Leaders are left to Cells 1 and 3 if they want to get something done. Either organizations provide leaders with virtually no financial leverage whatsoever, or they place such a small percent of an individual's financial incentives in the hands of leaders that Cell 5 leverage is, de facto, nonexistent.

A Deadly Imbalance

It actually gets worse. Leaders haven't removed themselves from the incentive game. Many share a large part of the profit pool. Since they have no guarantees or separate organization to fight for their cause, leaders have made sure that they enjoy the topside benefits during good years. In fact, in Hyrum's organization, the leaders recently split over five million dollars in profits. Remember, the organization had been struggling, so they restructured it, reorganized it, and trained their people to cut costs. The customer-service program clicked into full gear, and the continuous-improvement system yielded a great deal of positive results. The company went from being the high-cost, medium-quality player to the low-cost, high-quality one. Customers poured in, and profits soared. Now the bosses are taking home a lot of money, and everyone knows it. This fact hasn't been lost on Hyrum, who over the next few months will start arguing that he actually deserves the overtime he works.

This has to change.

In Hyrum's organization, and ones like it, the next time senior executives and union leaders sit down at the bargaining table, their number one agenda item needs to be a profit-sharing plan. What form it takes doesn't really matter. Employees simply need to be included in the profits. Their efforts need to be linked directly to the bottom line. Workgroups need to be turned into profit centers where people are motivated to cut overtime hours and increase productivity because they know these improvements will translate into shared profits. If restructuring cuts overtime, as is the case with Hyrum, make sure that the profit sharing translates into some cash. If the pie is divided through a stock-option plan, the stocks need to be liquid. Hyrum can't defer all his profits until retirement. He needs money now.

Lincoln Electric put profit sharing in place decades ago, and employees still make 20 percent more than their counterparts in other organizations while the company itself turns a handsome profit. This idea isn't new. It's called capitalism. It's just that most companies have lost the vision. If Hyrum's company doesn't do something, count on the pendulum swinging back to higher costs (meaning more take-home pay for Hyrum) because nobody is going to believe the call that says, "If we don't cut costs, we'll all lose our jobs." What they're going to hear is, "If we don't cut costs, the bosses aren't going to continue taking home huge bonus checks." Which leads us to our next conclusion.

> Leaders will always be caught in a pitched battle as long as *they're* motivated by bottom-line profits and *hourly employees* are motivated by overtime.

Self-Esteem Plummets

It's a shame that in some companies employees can join in the good times only through deception. Instead of jointly celebrating the organization's effectiveness with a victory check, they skulk around finding ways to log more time at work—reducing efficiency, developing bad habits, and undermining self-esteem. Instead of spending time with their friends and family after a hard and efficient day at work, they hang around their job, manufacturing overtime because it's the only way they can get their piece of the pie. Those who stay true to the work ethic, counting on some form of unscheduled or nonnegotiated bonus or "gift," are reduced to beggars who are led to believe that the bosses, out of their good graces, have chosen to throw them a bone.

How different it is when organizations choose to share profits. When things go well, employees are elevated to the position of victors in the battle to meet stakeholder demands rather than being reduced to beggars and thieves.

Our initial point is a simple one: If you don't make effective use of Cell 5, you lose twice. First, employees are often lured into unproductive actions in order to take back what they think they deserve. Second, when leaders desperately need sources of influence to bring about important changes, they reach into their bag of motivators and, instead of finding three, come up with two.

Organizations that have removed any semblance of performance-based incentives must put them in place. Organizations only beginning to toy with systems that pay for performance need to put more teeth in their plans. But not without some changes.

GATHER RELIABLE, FAIR MEASURES

For at least another hundred years we must pretend to ourselves and to every one that fair is foul and foul is fair; for foul is useful and fair is not. Avarice and usury and precaution must be our gods for a little longer still.

JOHN MAYNARD KEYNES

Performance-based incentive systems, when they're finally put into place, often fail because nobody trusts the measures. Employees are told what to do, and then leaders are the ones who play judge. They decide whether people have done what they've been told, how well, and for how much. Come time to divide up the pie, and leaders are the ones who hold up a card with a 7 or an 8 or a 9.5. This causes problems. Even if the leaders are exceptionally competent at evaluating, they face the challenge that in every group of 100 employees, about 80 of them *think* they're in the top 20 percent. Uh-oh.

But let's deal with these problems one at a time.

Observe Behavior on the Floor

Half of the problem with being a poor judge of performance stems from the challenge we discussed in chapter 8—leaders are cut off from actual performance. They see only a handful of indicators, can be easily fooled, and become political animals rather than competent judges and coaches.

If leaders continue to cut themselves off from accurate performance data, performance is driven by "perception" rather than fact. This lack of reliable data often results in insufferable deference to authority. We've all worked with people who were miserable colleagues, only moderately effective at serving their customers, but who treated their boss like a king or queen. These people have been taught that the boss is their customer. If they're right, other stakeholders take a backseat to the person in the corner office, and they're eventually promoted for their efforts.

The solution to this problem still stands. Leaders have to find forums where they can continually and accurately observe behavior at work. They can't stare at the scoreboard or just listen to people who whisper in their ear and expect to be either a good judge or a helpful coach. They have to look at all the factors that go into a success formula. Does the person not only complete his or her task, but also get along well with teammates? Does the person consistently get the job done but cause so many problems with peers that he or she is more of a liability than an asset?

By the way, when leaders are really good at their job, they don't just evaluate performance as they watch people at work—they shape it as well. By catching problems early on, they aren't forced to conduct performance-evaluation sessions where the other person is completely taken by surprise. Besides, they'll have solved so many of the problems along the way, the session won't have to be filled with bad news.

Document Your Observations

When dealing with poor performers, leaders often make a fatal error. They work closely to help correct problems, but when their efforts fail and it comes time to take disciplinary action, they have nothing to support their efforts beyond their spoken word. In day-to-day life, a leader's word has to be taken as gold. Other leaders can't be put into a situation where they have to be continually wondering if one of their colleagues is lying to them. This is such a basic fact of business that a leader's word is generally taken as truth. However, when it comes to taking disciplinary action or (on the other side of the coin) being granted a bigger-than-average bonus, one's word must be supported by written documentation. This often catches leaders by surprise.

Keep a log. Call it a diary, a performance record, or whatever, but sit down once a month or so and jot down some notes about each of your direct reports. If you don't keep your notes current, you'll be forced to conjure up an entire quarter's worth of observations in a single sitting. (That's why most people put off semiannual or annual performance discussions: The last-minute documentation is a real killer.)

As you routinely update your notes, try to recall both salient and subtle factors. Don't write down just the big-hit accomplishments. Once again, think about all the factors that go into satisfying all stakeholders.

Place a summary sheet at the front of your log as a reminder. This will keep your focus on what you should be noticing and documenting. The executives the authors work with in one organization carry a small laminated card containing a list of their core values and target behaviors. This list cues them on what they should be observing, coaching, and recording.

Continually share your observations with your direct reports. Nothing in your logbook should come as news to the person you're evaluating. It's not a secret document. Granted, only you and the person you're evaluating should have access to it, but the information you're recording should be a summary of observations of the initial event or pattern you observed, along with the subsequent coaching you offered and the action plan you jointly developed. The log should not be filled with juicy tidbits you'll be using as ammunition during a performance-review discussion. The same is true for positive performance. It's a shame when exceptional actions are discussed only during a formal performance review. As we suggested in chapter 12, opportunities to enlist the power of praise are legion and should be used often and documented while the activity is still fresh in your mind.

Record both behaviors and outcomes. As you take notes, try to document both what happened (usually the outcome that drew your attention in the first place) and the specific action leading to the results. Most documentation is chock-full of results, with little or no defensible evidence of what the person *did* to help achieve them. Think of yourself as an author gathering observations for a carefully crafted story—the ending by itself won't be enough.

Bring Others into the Loop

What we're about to say is controversial. We're going to recommend that the immediate supervisor not be the only one providing performance data. The fact that others *need* to be brought into the loop isn't open to debate. Everyone knows that customers and other bosses have valuable data that should be brought to light. Their insights, observations, and recommendations should indeed be included. But we're also going to recommend that an individual's peers be brought into the discussion. Nobody has a more accurate and complete picture of performance than peers. Nobody spends more time with them; nobody else routinely gets to see them in their bosses' absence—and watch what they *really* do. Peer data is invaluable.

As teams continue to be used with greater frequency, many organizations are also bringing workgroup self-appraisals to the table. Teams are allowed to analyze and critique their own performance. The renowned organizational theorist Ed Lawler and his colleagues studied this issue quite thoroughly.[1] By conducting an in-depth analysis of a handful of organizations, Lawler and his team attempted to determine the practices that most related to high team performance. The emphasis was on "team." The organizations in question were staffed by people who worked in jobs that were complex and interdependent. They were not songwriters (who work well in isolation), but technicians, researchers, and skilled tradespeople who worked on projects that involved many others. Lawler asked the question, "What factors are consistently present in the teams that most frequently meet or beat their goals?" Some of the candidates were:

- Presence of a strong supervisor
- Clear performance standards and job specifications
- Individual incentives and special awards
- Workgroup self-appraisal

The research results stood common wisdom on its head. Rather than showing that strong supervision and clear standards drove effectiveness, the data showed *no connection between these variables and team effectiveness*. The strongest correlate of team-based performance was workgroup self-appraisal. And yet almost all performance-management systems, especially in the U.S., are designed around the exclusive control of the supervisor.

Another important finding was the irrelevance, and occasionally the impediment, of individual incentives. Not only did individual performance awards not help boost team effectiveness, at times they actually hurt it! We talked about this in chapter 8 when we examined the impact of extrinsic rewards on behaviors that should be intrinsically rewarding.

Unfortunately, the whole idea of gathering and using both peer data and self-reported team data generally leads to raised eyebrows and looks of concern. And why not? Given that most organizations are trying to shift to a collaborative team environment (the very thing Lawler was studying), asking people to rank each other could easily pit people against one another. Now, instead of kissing up to bosses, people start kissing up to co-workers whom they view as "swing voters."

Organizations need to experiment with both forms of data gathering. As of yet, we're not sure anyone really knows enough about the most effective uses (and common abuses) of self-reports and peer reviews to give practical recommendations. Some organizations insist that team members evaluate each person and that they must come to something close to consensus—all ratings must fall within a very small range. Other companies insist on a strong appeal process.

The point is, leaders have to find a way to continually gather complete and accurate data when assessing performance—particularly if the data are going to be used to help dispense financial incentives. The more data that can be brought into the loop, the better for all parties. Just because gathering peer data surfaces new problems is insufficient reason not to experiment with the process. Most problems we currently experience in the performance-management cycle stem from the fact that we haven't always been willing to try new, sometimes hard, procedures. So we end up taking the easy route—gather little data and don't allow it to impact how money is allocated—and end up being driven by whim, innuendo, and tenure.

LINK BEHAVIORS TO REWARDS

Many good compensation schemes fail to motivate, not because there's something wrong with the plan, but because employees never understand how it works.

For instance, one of the authors conducted interviews in a 300-person organization in which all full-time employees had participated in an ESOP (employee stock ownership plan) for over three years. In spite of the obvious incentive to look after the cost and revenue side of the business to boost stock participation and value, no discernible change of behavior had occurred in the three years. Why? Most people had no idea how their behavior would translate into increased stock prices.

Go Public

One of the most successful Cell 5 interventions ever reported had nothing to do with redesigning the compensation system. The leaders simply took time to explain the system they had in place. Members of the executive team circulated throughout the company, explaining to each of the frontline employees how his or her actions built or destroyed Outcome Vitality and, therefore, job security and bonus pools. Before the explanations, employees didn't understand the link between their own actions and the bonuses they received at the end of the year, or the layoffs that occurred with some frequency. When these thoughtful leaders took their story to the people, they helped employees update their mental maps, and behavior changed.

Think Small

Another strategy for tightening the link between performance and profits is to structure organizations into mini-business units, each with its own mini-mission and set of stakeholder outcome measures (customer, investor, people, other). The smaller the unit, the greater the sense of control.

A specialty insurance company with whom we worked took bold steps in this direction. The company was broken into "programs." Each program went after a unique customer group, was assigned capital and given profit-and-loss responsibility, and had personnel permanently assigned to it. Each person in the program (usually 15 to 50 in a program) had a real sense of how his or her work impacted the whole. Each began to see how incentive pay was based on natural market consequences instead of on arbitrary supervisory conclusions. The impact on the culture was marked. Innovation, customer responsiveness, and personal responsibility increased noticeably as people began to understand the new, more natural, rules.

Avoid a Lot of Moving Parts

No matter how thin you slice it, it's still baloney.

ALFRED E. SMITH

For people to see how their routine behavior links to financial outcomes, leaders must make the compensation system simple and easy to understand. Many incentive systems are so weighed down with clauses, formulas, and guidelines, they're almost impossible to comprehend. For example, we came across one recently that divided top managers' compensation into 20 chunks. Five percent came from community-satisfaction measures. Another five came from scores on a 360-degree profile. Yet another five was based on employee-satisfaction scores. And so on. It was as though the corporation was trying to single out every little behavior the managers were supposed to enact and pay them a nickel for each one. This system failed the simplicity test. Worse still, it in no way helped inform people how they should be spending their time.

How different this system is from the one designed for its store managers by the Outback Steakhouse restaurant chain. Their idea is simple. Managers make a fixed percentage of the profits of the firm. A substantial portion of the profits is rolled over for up to five years, so the emphasis is on long-term value, not on a single year. That's it.

Most organizations are unable to keep their incentive plans simple for one of two reasons. Either people don't trust each other, or leaders are using the incentive system in place of normal performance appraisals.

Mistrust

Every time a new formula is put into place, you can bet somebody somewhere is trying to make sure his or her interest is being protected. If you can't trust leaders to calculate and share profits honestly, you have to come up with dozens of ways to guard against their clever bookkeeping and selfish reshuffling. "There are no profits, because we plowed everything back into a secret project. Sorry." Or, "You thought we calculated profits before sending money to shareowners and calculating the bonus. What a shame. You see, we divide up the profits after leaders calculate their own bonuses. It's only fair."

> The degree of simplicity of an organization's financial incentive system is inversely proportional to the amount of trust between employees.

Misuse

Bloated, convoluted, and nearly incomprehensible incentive systems can also be a function of misuse. Instead of giving candid feedback and confronting unproductive behavior, leaders mistakenly rely on dollars *alone* to send the message. They hope decreased incentive pay, missed salary increases, or loss of advancement opportunities will say the words they can't bring themselves to express in routine performance-management discussions. Most people would rather have a root canal than conduct one-on-one performance-coaching sessions. We've already identified several reasons for this hesitancy, but mostly people loathe the idea of sitting down in a formal session to share bad news based exclusively on outcome measures, without even a hint of what the person is doing to cause the poor results. Until leaders find a way to continually and routinely observe people at work and give timely, sensitive coaching, organizations will persist in trying to link daily performance foibles to financial incentives. It's a poor marriage.

Compensation systems should never be used as the only tool for solving specific behavioral problems. They certainly *should* be used to reward overall performance, but can't replace skilled coaching. Using broad financial rewards as the only tool for solving specific behavioral problems is akin to using a chain saw to perform surgery.

BRING YOUR PAPERWORK INTO THIS CENTURY

It isn't necessary to imagine the world ending in fire or ice—there are two other possibilities: one is paperwork, and the other is nostalgia.
FRANK ZAPPA

Usually leaders don't attempt to bring about a long-term culture change by starting with the performance-appraisal paperwork. This is good news. Employees must first have a clear understanding of the corporate vision, how it translates into actions that support stakeholder groups, and what it means about their job, how they spend their time, and what they should care about. Until employees are familiar with the basics, the paperwork doesn't really matter.

However, after you're a year or so into a long-term change project, it's probably time to take a look at your performance-appraisal documents. If you're like most leaders, you don't pay much attention to the forms until somebody is pressuring you to complete your latest appraisals. That's when it would be nice to pull out a printed document and see a fair number of the actions you've been talking, walking, and stalking actually appear on the forms. Most forms are filled with words taken from the tables of contents of introductory organizational behavior texts. Designers go with old standbys such as initiative, integrity, and honesty. Now that we think about it, the words may have been taken from the Boy Scout oath.

Whatever the origin, the leadership categories most organizations use are not tailored to the mission statement. Put the two documents next to each other, and look for similarities. If they appear as if they came from different planets, you're a pretty typical company. Pick the top two or three items from your vision, and make sure they find a way onto your appraisal form. Leave room for each subunit to link its own mini-mission to the form. As much as it pains you, don't turn this job over to a clerk. Remember, the work you'll be doing eventually links to Hyrum's take-home pay.

TO FIRE OR NOT TO FIRE?

Discipline is a symbol of caring to a child. . . . If there is love, there is no such thing as being too tough with a child. . . . If you have never been hated by your child, you have never been a parent.

BETTE DAVIS

Before we conclude this discussion, let's take a look at one final and somewhat frightening dimension of Cell 5. The ultimate use of the formal rewards cell is to remove all rewards—which is HR-speak for firing someone. For most of us, terminating an employee runs against everything we stand for. We've seen people reach for this option when less intrusive steps would have been substantially more effective, if not humane. We've critiqued leaders for using a howitzer to hunt a sparrow. But before we get too smug, let's see when using formal sanctions might be necessary.

Vinnie's Last Gasp

Vinnie, a middle manager working for a public agency, was reluctant to participate in any of the "culture change garbage" his leaders were advocating. On more than one occasion he'd opened staff meetings with a vile attack on the new values and behaviors. One day he went so far as to publicly humiliate an employee who'd dared to talk about the newly posted vision statement. The message was clear—in order to survive in Vinnie's shop, you had better not support the "warm-and-fuzzy junk" certain people were pushing.

As leaders above Vinnie became aware of his hostile position, they decided to behave in ways consistent with the vision. They tried coaching, candid feedback, soliciting concerns and, finally, a healthy dose of patience. It didn't take. The leaders learned that, contrary to the popular adage, time doesn't heal all wounds. In some cases it just pours on salt. With each hostile attack, vindictive statement, or sarcastic reaction to the vision, Vinnie began to stick out like a sore thumb. Early on, if Vinnie had been pressed hard or even sanctioned for what he was doing, people would have criticized leaders for being "autocratic in the interest of force-feeding enlightenment." However, as time wore on and leaders continued to allow Vinnie to roam freely, spouting opposition, and ripping apart the vision, people began to wonder if the big bosses were really committed to the new values.

So the bosses found themselves facing two equally unattractive choices. Should they continue to model patience and mercy and run the risk of being viewed as hypocrites? After all, they were allowing Vinnie to walk all over many of the espoused values. Or should they take aggressive action and run the risk of being viewed as hypocrites? The bosses still come down on people if they don't fall into line. Tough choice.

What made this challenge particularly sticky was that Vinnie was also not hitting his performance targets. If he were to be fired, transferred, demoted, or otherwise sanctioned, there was the distinct possibility that people would conclude, "Oh sure, we're supposed to be quality driven, interpersonally sensitive, and customer centered, but if you miss your numbers, wham! They're on you like *E. coli* in an undercooked burger."

On the other hand, had Vinnie scored high on traditional measures like surprising and delighting his customers, the chance to take symbolic action would have been greatly enhanced. If you take action against someone who is hitting the usual home runs but who isn't aligning with other parts of the vision, you make a symbolic statement that will long be remembered.

The principle we advocate here is simple. Coach, coach, coach, and *then* move. Eventually Vinnie had to go. As is always the case, the needs of the many are greater than the needs of the few. You can't continue to allow someone to wreak havoc with struggling values without eventually hurting everyone. As tough as it was to let Vinnie go (a euphemism for firing him), it had to be done.

Vinnie serves as an example of a person who simply refused to buy into the vision, but leaders face similar problems when people simply aren't able to do their jobs. As demands increase, not everyone can step up to the new challenges. So what do you do with them? If you're like most leaders, you let them hide in the woodwork, placing even more pressures on those who can carry the load. You spend 80 percent of your time talking about the 3 percent of the people who really can't fit.

The principle here is the same. Allow every opportunity for people to learn new skills. Teach, teach, and teach again. But when it becomes clear that certain people just aren't going to be able to do what's required and you can't move them to a place where their skill-set fits, have the good sense and compassion to release them. Don't patronize them by assuming they'll never be able to get another job outside the firm. Don't continue to trap them in a job they can't do. Don't insult them by allowing them to work at a pace and skill level below what is required. Use "tough love." Draw on the final and ultimate source of Cell 5 power. Let people go.

SOME PRACTICAL ADVICE FROM THIS CHAPTER

Our discussion of Cell 5 has focused on a handful of key issues. We've tried to explore the big picture rather than get sucked into the idiosyncrasies of rating scales or the mechanics of how to actually divide the pie. Think about the following.

- **Share the pie.** Our first desire was to take on a challenge we've been facing for years. We're weary from slugging it out alongside leaders who've not only been prevented from using Cell 5 as a source of motivation, but who've had to fight it at every turn. We argued that until organizations find ways to legitimately include all employees in some form of honest profit sharing, leaders are cut off from a key source of influence, and employees are often forced into counterproductive actions. Serious imbalances in the distribution of wealth never spawn Cultural Vitality. Stand up for profit sharing. Voice your opinion. Share this chapter with people in a position to do something.
- **Clean up your performance-management system.** Next, we suggested that a great number of the problems currently associated with performance-management systems are related to mistrust in the evaluation process. Because bosses are viewed as poor judges, the link between performance and reward is suspect. To improve the evaluation process, we suggested that leaders (1) take more care in observing people at work, (2) carefully record what they observe, and (3) expand the number of people involved in the process. How do you stack up? If *you* started splitting up parts of the pie based on actual performance, would people trust your ability to make a fair evaluation?
- **Link incentives to behaviors.** From there we moved to the importance of making a clear link between financial incentives and daily behavior. We suggested that a great number of reasonable systems fail simply because people don't understand them. To rectify this problem, we recommended that leaders openly explain the relationships, keep the unit of analysis as small as possible, and use simple systems. Finally, we hinted that the formal paperwork eventually needs to be updated. Do the people who work for you act as if they have a clear understanding of how their performance level links to incentives? If not, what steps should you take?

CHAPTER 15

Making "Things" Work

We live in a world of things, and our only connection with them is that we know how to manipulate or to consume them.

ERICH FROMM

U p until this section we've treated an organization as a living culture—it's been all elbows and eyeballs, shared values and assumptions. If it didn't have a heartbeat, we weren't interested in it. To keep our focus, we set aside the bricks, paper, mortar, and other *things* found in and around organizations and acted as if they're nonexistent (or certainly of no concern).

In this chapter we'll repent of our excessively focused human ways and take a look at the features of an organization that, once we change

Motivation   **Ability**

Individual	1	2
Social	3	4
Organizational	5	6

them, actually stay changed—or at least stay changed until we tinker with them again. We'll look at Cell 6. This cell holds all of the non-human factors that either prevent people from doing what's required to meet stakeholder demands or enable them to do so. Cell 6 includes everything from tools and budgets to air-conditioning ducts.

These nonhuman features don't always come to mind when leaders look for either causal sources or influence levers. At least some of them don't come to mind. Actually, many leaders act as if their *only* levers were policies, procedures, and memos. These features are worn to a nub.

However, when trying to decide what it would take to encourage two "incompatible" but interdependent groups to collaborate more effectively, few people would think to move their offices next to each other or to rebuild their space to include common areas. When trying to encourage frontline supervisors to openly discuss vitality numbers more regularly, most leaders would hold a meeting and ask their supervisors to openly discuss vitality numbers more regularly. Few would follow the lead of the theme park we referred to in chapter 5 and post the numbers on giant placards every day.

When you think about it, if you could achieve what you're looking for by shifting a wall, changing a reporting structure, putting in a new system, posting numbers, or otherwise working with *things*, the job of leader wouldn't seem like such a death-defying feat. After all, these are *things*. They lie there quietly, never talking about their own assumptions or preaching their pet values. They never have foul breath because they don't breathe. They never have family problems because they can't reproduce. They have neither opinions nor the need for opinion leaders. And if this isn't enough to make you want to adopt them, they never resist change and stay put forever once you change them.

The reason we don't make good use of these lovely *things* as much as we ought to, or use them incorrectly when we do, is twofold. The first is the problem of visibility. We don't see systems very readily. Work practices don't walk up and whisper in our ear. When it comes to environmental factors, we actually go to pains to shut out the impact of our work environment. We are, in Fred Steele's words, "environmentally incompetent."[1] For example, if you're like most of us, when you're reading on a plane as the sun slowly sets, you find yourself squinting in the dark until the flight attendant comes by and turns on your light.

Second, even when we do think about Cell 6, we don't have many thoughts. More specifically, we don't always understand how *things* influence behavior. The trick of Cell 6 lies in understanding how changing physical feature X or system Y will lead to behavior Z. Cell 6 is all about linking *things* to desired behaviors. To the extent that we

(1) remember to think about Cell 6 and (2) are able to come up with theories of how changing *things* will readily and quickly change behavior, we'll have one more set of tools on hand.

The following pages will be devoted to just that job. Our goal is to prepare leaders to look at a problem, leap about as far away from the fundamental attribution error as possible, and land on a set of theories that explores how change can be facilitated through pulling a nonhuman, Cell 6 lever.

Hey, These Eggs Aren't Sunny-Side Up!

You can get anything you want at Alice's Restaurant.

ARLO GUTHRIE

To get a feel for the potential power of nonhuman elements in orchestrating change, let's look at a study conducted in the late 1940s by William Foote Whyte, a professor at the University of Chicago who was asked to consult with the National Restaurant Association.[2] (At that time you *couldn't* get anything you wanted at Alice's or anyone else's restaurant.) Your challenge is to see if you can come up with the same successful solution Whyte recommended.

The Problem

After World War II came to an end, the U.S. entered the Eisenhower era of peace, growth, and prosperity. Along with this growth, Americans began eating out in unprecedented numbers. The restaurant industry wasn't ready for the deluge of customers. As business accelerated, so did the conflict between servers (they were all waitresses) and cooks (all men). Strife often broke out in loud accusations and verbal attacks at the kitchen counter. Although these altercations were usually out of sight of customers, they were typically within earshot. The results were predictable. Not only were customers annoyed, the tiffs often resulted in late or incorrect orders. Both Customer Net Value (CNV) and People Net Value (PNV) were affected. Turnover was high; customer complaints were frequent.

Diagnosis

By observing a sample of the restaurants where conflict was reported, Whyte experienced the problem firsthand. He noted that the waitresses would rush to the counter, call an order to the cooks, then rush out. If the order was not ready when they returned, they would urge the cook to hurry—shouting expressions of encouragement such as, "Hey, hairball, where's the breaded veal? You got a broken arm or what?" The cooks usually responded in kind. Later, when the waitress received an incorrect order, recriminations would be exchanged. When frustrations were especially high and waitresses were yelling at the cooks to hurry up, the cooks intentionally slowed down. Whyte even observed cooks turning their backs on the servers and intentionally ignoring them until they left, sometimes in tears.

As Whyte studied the cooks, he noted that, in relation to the servers, they were almost always older, of greater seniority, more highly skilled, and much more highly paid. The cooks (read men) deeply resented being "bossed around" by younger, less-experienced, lower-paid women.

Six-Cell Analysis

This problem presents some very interesting challenges. A partial Six-Cell analysis would show the causes to be residing in several cells.

Cell 1: Neither cooks nor servers appeared to derive satisfaction from making the relationship work.

Cell 2: Neither group demonstrated adequate interpersonal skills—no one clarified orders; people used disrespectful language and tones of voice.

Cell 3: An attacking adversarial group norm had developed. Each group of co-workers saw the other group as adversaries.

Cell 4: Servers could not serve customers if cooks provided food that was prepared poorly, delivered late, or was not what was ordered; cooks could not deliver the correct order if they did not receive clear, accurate information.

Cell 5: Both got paid for punching a clock. Building PNV, CNV, or INV was irrelevant.

Whyte's Solution

Which of the problems should a leader work on? Send a memo urging cooperation? Improve the recruiting or selection process? Conduct a training session? Although there is merit in considering each of these potential solutions, Whyte dove to the heart of Cell 6. In his view, it would be easiest to simply restructure the relationship—that is, *physically* restructure it. He recommended a simple spindle. The servers were to place on the spindle a *written* order that clearly communicated the customers' requests. Cooks were then to pull orders off and fill them in whatever sequence seemed most efficient (though generally following a first-in, first-out policy).

Whyte's recommendation was tried at a "pilot" restaurant the next day. Training consisted of a 10-minute instruction session that was given to both cooks and servers. Managers reported an immediate decrease in both conflict and customer complaints. Both cooks and servers preferred the new structure, and each group reported being better treated by the other group. The Restaurant Association published the new system throughout their membership. Whyte's spindle (it later became an order wheel) did not deal directly with interpersonal relationships, status consciousness, or gender conflict. It did, however, simply and effectively solve a problem with a work process, thus boosting PNV, CNV, and INV.

Such is the potential leverage of Cell 6.

"THINGS" WORTH THINKING ABOUT

In spite of the fact that Whyte's solution seems obvious today, at the time the research was completed, his elegant remedy wasn't apparent to anyone who looked at the problem through traditional lenses. Whyte was able to see factors that psychologists, trainers, and leaders alike couldn't see because he looked in a different place. He looked at the relationship between *things* and people. More importantly, he knew where to look. Of the infinite number of *things* out there, he had a sense for those that were likely to cause problems.

For the past 45 years, scholars have followed in Whyte's footsteps, composing theories and writing books. There now exists a separate literature devoted to the relationships involving spindles, chairs, reporting structures, wall color, work flow, hat size, and productivity. If it has cast a shadow on a team, been touched by a leader, or fallen under the gaze of an executive, somebody somewhere has written a book or an article about it. In the next few pages, we'll discuss a scant handful of the issues that grace the libraries of these structuralists. From the hundreds of possible issues, we've chosen physical features that have given our clients fits. We've limited our selection to structural characteristics that leaders might actually think about and draw into their Six-Cell repertoire. We've included those that have an obvious impact on the human decision-maker's mental maps and on the net value of his or her behavior choices.

Since we care about *things* only insofar as they impact *people*, our analysis of Cell 6 will not be restricted to this cell alone. We'll explore Cell 6 as a *causal agent* or influence lever, knowing full well that it can affect all other cells. For example, the way employees physically lay out their work has an impact on individual ability (Cell 2). The sheer size of an organization often creates a sense of alienation (Cell 1). Propinquity (nearness) influences social interaction patterns, which, in turn, create peer pressure (Cell 3).

We've divided the nonhuman material we'll be covering into four bins. First, we'll take a look at how information flows into mental maps. Second, we'll look at the symbolic and functional impact of physical features. This will be followed by a short discussion of structure. Finally, we'll explore the impact the sheer size of an organization can have on decision making, morale, and accountability.

Manage the "Data Stream"

Among all the world's races, some obscure Bedouin tribes possibly apart, Americans are the most prone to misinformation.

John Kenneth Galbraith

As leaders struggle to determine why certain undesirable behaviors *are* occurring while other desirable ones *aren't* occurring, they'd do well to ask three questions:

- What information led to the behavior we're observing?
- Where did the information come from?
- What is it about the way we're structured that made this information available while other information wasn't?

It's this last question that leaders need to examine most closely if they expect to get to the structural roots of any problem. As the following example demonstrates, few do.

Why Don't They Care about What I Care about?

Jamal Jones, special services director for a medium-size financial services company, was fit to be tied. For six months he had been trying to come up with ways to reduce costs in his area. Nothing seemed to work. As he spoke with a consultant from the company's human resources staff, he lamented that none of the employees he worked with really cared about costs. "They care about their own working conditions, and they even seem to worry a fair amount about the customer. But talk about costs, and your words fall on deaf ears."

When encouraged to extend his analysis beyond "they don't care," Jamal came up with the following suggestions.

- They find no satisfaction in saving money (Cell 1).
- They aren't sure how to do it (Cell 2).
- Their supervisors don't encourage it (Cell 3).
- They aren't rewarded for it (Cell 5).

While broadening his analysis helped Jamal postpone his original solution of "firing all the lowlifes," he still couldn't come up with an understanding of what to him was the critical question. "How can well-intentioned, hard-working people (he wanted to avoid the fundamental attribution error) show so little concern for the lifeblood of the company—its profitability?"

It turned out that the human resources specialist was sensitive to structural issues. He asked Jamal, "What's going on in the environment that's making it difficult for staff members to focus on cost issues?" He primed the pump by asking, "Do employees have accurate and timely information about costs?"

When he thought about it, Jamal realized that employees:

- Have no information on unit costs
- Never see financials
- Don't come into contact with owner or shareholder concerns
- Are not involved in cost or revenue-related decisions
- Don't have the authority to influence significant economic issues

Without changing how information flows through the organization, Jamal is left to a limited set of influence tools. If the people working for Jamal don't routinely have information that informs correct behavior, and if Jamal doesn't see this void as an important problem, he ends up focusing on other areas—motivation, for example. He relies on speeches, memos, banners, and other techniques aimed at firing up people to take on costs. He tries to overcome the impact of a sea of *existing* data with an occasional burst of *hot* data: Here's what *I* (the boss) care about. When results don't measure up, he's left wondering, "How come I care about certain factors a great deal" (and, by definition, what *I* care about *is* what's important) "and the workforce doesn't care about them at all?" (Meaning they're shortsighted and wrong.)

The answer to Jamal's question lies in how a person's daily contacts affect his or her data stream. Jamal's workday differs remarkably from the average employee's workday. For example, he starts out every Monday morning with a weekly cost review where high-level executives sit around a table (one large enough to land a Harrier jet) and discuss numbers. Several tell stories of how they're about to get blindsided by a new competitor who's going to reduce prices. They all talk about capital deployment, cost containment, revenue building, and productivity. In short, every member of the executive team is bilingual, and their second language is accounting.

In addition to this weekly "kickoff for cost savings" meeting, Jamal receives a daily printout of profitability and cost numbers. If one area is low, it's circled in red by his boss (who has already looked at the figures). The red ink is no accident. It was carefully selected, his boss once explained, because it's "the color of blood," and he hadn't been smiling at the time. As one might guess, Jamal cares a great deal about reducing costs.

Frontline employees, in contrast, live in a very different world. They hear about cost issues from Jamal (who they think is marginally desperate and totally obsessive), but when it comes to their daily work, they mostly fret over material defects and resource shortages. They walk beneath cost banners on their way to handle customer complaints about quality problems and delayed schedules. They leave a cost lecture in order to meet with suppliers and to brainstorm solutions to compatibility problems. To nobody's surprise, they end up worrying about what their daily walk puts them in contact with—customer, supplier, and employee issues.

Each group has it own daily work pattern that puts it in contact with a stream of data. Jamal faces a stream that keeps him focused on profitability figures, while his employees' daily contacts keep them focused on solving customer and supplier problems. Consequently, Jamal is driven in the direction of cutting costs, while everyone else tries to figure out how to garner more resources (i.e., spend money) to solve customer problems. Jamal tries to mitigate the data flow by sharing his personal opinions, punctuating them with fiery speeches and clever phrases. Unfortunately, his short-term bursts don't make up for the overwhelming impact of a veritable deluge of other data. Neither Jamal nor his team has a complete view of what needs to be done to keep the balance and, given their very different stream of data, they're always at odds with one another.

What's a Leader to Do?

The most obvious solution to inadequate, imbalanced, or inaccurate information is to structure the information flow in a way that channels information where it needs to go. For instance, Jamal's team members need to be exposed to the same data that's driving Jamal. They need to be exposed to unit costs, financial results, owner opinions, and other cost factors that are currently leading Jamal to believe that cost cutting is a top priority. By the same token, Jamal needs to be confident that the customer and supplier data that the employees are exposed to finds a way onto his mental map. Without similar data flowing through similar streams, both sides end up raising their voices or otherwise drawing down on their power base to make their data sound more important. When this doesn't work, they rely on "trust me" strategies to win people over to their point of view. ("I know you haven't heard much about this issue, but trust me, it's important.")

Throughout this book we've talked about the power of data. Now we're simply adding the concept of structure. We're suggesting that leaders would do well to look at the conduits or structural forces that drive the flow of data. (Remember the spindle?) As leaders find themselves wondering why people just don't "get it" (why they don't seem to care about what's really important), they need to step back and look at the data stream. To ensure that the stream is rich, accurate, and continually flowing, leaders must pull their attention away from the messages floating along the stream and look at the stream itself.

To explore these data conduits, it's time to go back to some of the questions raised in chapter 2. With whom are employees coming into contact? How frequent and poignant is the interaction? Are hourly employees personally experiencing customer concerns and then trying to convince their bosses through verbal persuasion? Are leaders having personal contact with people or circumstances that communicate the imminent threat of a massive customer defection and then trying to share the data through a short speech given by a frontline supervisor whom no one respects?

Information, remember, is most powerful when personally experienced, has less impact when vicariously experienced, and is the least influential when received as verbal persuasion. Understanding this principle, Ray Kroc, founder of McDonald's, structured frequent contact between all executives and the hamburger-eating masses. Realizing that absence makes stakeholders grow irrelevant, he decided that everyone at headquarters would spend two weeks a year flipping burgers, packing Happy Meals, and making change. In similar fashion, Saturn Motor Company trains welders to read and understand financials and involves frontline workers in regular cost reviews.

Leaders need to explore the data exchanges that are *not* face to face or lip to ear. They need to examine their mediated messages. What data printouts do employees pore over? What charts do they examine? How do computers share information? How long does it take? What media transmit the data—TVs, newspapers, charts, computer printouts, memos, banners, radio shows, e-mail? How visually clear is the information? Is important data lost in a sea of numbers? Do employees need a degree in statistics to understand the meaning of the charts? Do people understand the implications of the charts? If a line goes up, what does it mean? Do employees know what it would take to get the line moving in the right direction?

Opening the Door to Structure

When people disagree, ask: What separate data streams have taken two groups of reasonable, rational, and decent people and put them at odds with each other? What can leaders do not only to change the messages floating in these streams, but to change the course, size, shape, and flow of the streams themselves?

Master the Use of Physical Features

We shape our buildings: thereafter they shape us.

SIR WINSTON CHURCHILL

Churchill was right. The physical environment has a *profound* impact on individuals. The buildings we build, the noises we create, and the smells we exude all influence our moods, our assumptions, and even our choices. However, as individuals are deluged with stimuli, they eventually become unaware of the impact the physical environment is having on them. When Fred Steele, the renowned sociotechnical theorist, accused managers of "environmental incompetence," he wasn't talking about an insensitivity to spotted owls. He was accusing people of not being able to see the effect of the immediate work environment on individual behavior.[3]

For example, the authors met one morning with the president of a large insurance company. To reach his office, we had to traverse six hallways the length of landing strips and pass four different secretarial stations. At each station we were visually frisked and vocally questioned. The president's first words as we sat down were, "I get the feeling people around here are scared to talk to me." Perhaps he had missed the fact that his office was laid out like Hitler's chancellery. (Hitler demanded more than a quarter mile of hallway so that visitors would "get a taste of the power and grandeur of the German Reich" on arriving.[4])

Later that day as we sat in a restaurant during the noon rush hour, we ate our meal much quicker than any of us had originally planned. Tired from a hectic schedule, we had agreed to "veg out" over a leisurely lunch. Forty-five minutes later we were back in our office wondering if we had forgotten the meaning of leisure. Perhaps we were unconsciously whisked along by the restaurant organist who had been instructed to play faster tunes as the lunch line grew. During off-hours we had heard her play slow love songs. Hadn't we wolfed down our entrée that day to the beat of "The 1812 Overture"? Maybe we picked up our pace because the restaurateur had purchased chairs from furniture designer Henning Larsen (who "developed a chair that exerts disagreeable pressure on the spine if occupied for over a few minutes").[5] Maybe the clouds spilling over from the smoking section irritated our sinuses and pushed us along. One thing for certain, none of us gave any of those physical features a second thought. We just ate faster and less comfortably than we had planned.

After lunch, as we sat in our meeting room brainstorming rough scripts for an upcoming video shoot, we found ourselves having trouble coming up with creative ideas. We began to beat ourselves up for not being very clever—as if cleverness simply sprung from creative minds, independent of the world around it. Perhaps the physical world was exacting its toll on our ability to do our job. Was our mental stupor affected by the walls? They were made of glass, and people kept walking by and waving. What impact was the room temperature having on our creative endeavors? You could have hung beef in the place. How about the color and texture of the walls and furniture? It was modern—somewhat stark. Would different visual stimuli have helped? Were we nearly brain-numb because most of our spare blood was now congregated in our stomach, digesting a slab of lasagna large enough to double as a lifeboat?

Toward the end of the day, when a couple of new employees walked in to ask a question, we were dressed in suits (left over from our morning meeting), and they were dressed in jeans and T-shirts. Did that add to the discomfort they obviously felt? Sure, they had interrupted us, but could the clothing differential actually have had an impact? Why were they sweating when it was 58 degrees in the room?

Now, be honest. Who thinks of this stuff? Actually, it's a matter of cognitive style. A segment of the population pays fairly close attention to their visual world, while others live mostly inside their thoughts—leaving their day planner wherever they set it down and walking around perpetually unzipped (the person, not the day planner). Of course, even those who are more visually sensitive rarely link the three-dimensional world they're experiencing to employees and their ability to meet competing stakeholder demands. That would be weird. Few people, when attempting to change behaviors, stop and ask to what degree the physical environment is encouraging today's behavior and what will have to be changed to encourage tomorrow's.

As inured to the environment as most of us are, we're not as bad as the oft-mentioned frog that can be put in a pot and brought slowly to a boil without even noticing. (What kind of person discovered this?) Sooner or later environmental features reach out and grab our attention. In some areas most of us are routinely aware of the effect of the ambience. We have a favorite place for reading, playing, romancing, and doing homework. We realize that if we want our kids to read, maybe we should take the TV off the central altar in our living room, put up some actual bookshelves, and lay some periodicals and magazines around. Ultimately we learn to manipulate physical settings to affect behavior and to influence experience. Nevertheless, we miss hundreds of opportunities each year to use physical factors to our benefit.

What's a Leader to Do?

When making decisions about the layout and feeling of the work environment, examine how *things* influence employees' ability to do their jobs. If nothing else, locate a copy of Fred Steele's *Physical Settings and Organization Development,*[6] or assemble a task force of opinion leaders and ask them to explore the individual and social impact of your physical surroundings on your culture.

When trying to figure out what it'll take to get something done, break away from the tendency to preach, and look at the physical features surrounding the people. Explore the effect of the sheer physicality of the place. Don't make the mistake a company down the road from the authors made. When building a new factory and office building, they put *white carpets* in the office portion of the building. The first time a front-line employee tracked greasy footprints across the office floor was the last time blue-collar production employees and white-collar support staff ever met face to face. One carpet killed tens of thousands of important conversations. It took an outside consultant to point out this simple fact to the leadership team. They weren't thinking physical features.

Ensure That the Physical World Is Congruent with Your Espoused Values

The whole visible universe is but a storehouse of images and signs to which the imagination will give a relative place and value; it is a sort of pasture which the imagination must digest and transform.

CHARLES BAUDELAIRE

Despite our discussion to this point, not everything about Cell 6 remains invisible. Certainly, inanimate structures and out-of-sight policies, procedures, and systems have a hard time competing for a leader's attention—given that human beings walk, breathe, shout, and constantly demand action. Nevertheless, certain physical features almost leap out at people and slap them up the side of the head. Once an environmental feature has our attention, our active imaginations transform the visible universe into all kinds of interesting meaning. But how? What makes an inanimate object stand out from its peers? And once it has our attention, what gives it meaning?

The inquiry into what makes something leap out at you as a "figure" while everything else stays behind as "ground" has been going on for decades. Without getting into the nitty-gritty of a field that would give most of us a brain embolism, let's suggest that the part leaders should care about deals with *incongruity*. It's akin to humor. Something is funny because it affronts our expectations. The class clown shouts, "Wow! What a funny-looking apple," as he reaches into his lunch bag and pulls out an orange. Physical features leap out at employees when they stand in contrast to what people expect or want.

For example, a top-level leader gives an impassioned speech about the need for common ground, teamwork, collaboration, and a more egalitarian approach to day-to-day work. He's wearing a $1,500 suit, is standing on a stage, is perched over a lectern, and actually uses the word *egalitarian* as part of his spoken vocabulary. Those who have been to his office (which is precious few, but they*all* talk about the experience) can't help but notice an entire wall devoted to his personal accomplishments. He's pictured with celebrities, captains of industry, and even a U.S. president. He sits behind a desk that was hand-carved by an entire South American village and is surrounded by paneling and cornices made of enough hardwood to require the deforestation of central Uganda.

Actually, the sheer beauty of the place was once appreciated by a workforce that took pride in being part of a company that could afford such opulence. However, now that everyone's talking about teams, de-emphasizing social differences, and fretting over every scrap of wasted paper, the sumptuous office leaps out at you. It stands as a testament to incongruity. Couple this with the fact that the company's latest fundraiser consisted of a "Save the Rain Forest" dance, and the hardwood office leaves a lot of people wondering how serious the leadership team is about their espoused values.

What's a Leader to Do?

Chapter 11 covered the ins and outs of managing symbolic action. We won't cover that turf again. Suffice it to say that leaders should be well attuned to what messages their physical environment is sending. What do physical features say about how leaders feel about frontline employees, tenure, diversity, openness, teamwork, honesty, quality of work life, customers, cost efficiency, and learning?

When people look at your rows and rows of assembly-line-looking cubicles, what do they conclude about what leaders value? Whose pictures adorn the front entry—executives' (past and present) or customers'? Who is given prime parking spaces? (If you're trying to emphasize function over status, the distance from the parking space to the work area should be inversely proportional to the frequency a person uses his or her car *during* the average workday.)

Take out your mission and values statement, and go on a walk around your offices and work area. Look at banners, posters, pictures, work spaces, shrines, and other physical indicators of value. Do they align with your value statement? Or better yet, ask opinion leaders to conduct a "hypocrisy study." Have them report on the mixed signals *things* in your organization are sending.

Since many leaders find themselves sitting in office spaces designed decades ago (when bosses sat at the top of the building in sumptuous surroundings), they're at risk of being seen as hypocrites with few options for change. This doesn't mean they need to "ugly up" their work space in the name of equality. However, they can take out the huge desk and replace it with a small work table. They can put in a conversation area consisting of a few chairs around a low circular table so they no longer have to sit behind a huge wooden barrier during every conversation. Leaders can also change what they have on their desks and walls. Do they really need a personal shrine? Lastly, they can make better use of their atriums and massive entryways. Some organizations are now using them as high-quality meeting areas with cafe-style tables.

Steps can and should be taken to align the symbolic messages quietly and convincingly uttered by your physical surroundings with the core values you've so carefully included in your mission statement.

Mitigate the Crippling Effects of Size

Man is small, and, therefore, small is beautiful. To go for giantism is to go for self-destruction.

E. F. SCHUMACHER

Anyone who has spent more than a few weeks in a large company is aware that size has a profound impact on the feeling and functionality of an organization. No one can leave the comfort and simplicity of a lemonade stand and enter the sterile caverns of a large company without asking, "What have I gotten myself into?" Scholars over the past two decades have been asking the same question. Schumacher, with his catch phrase "small is beautiful," captured the emotional and intellectual climate of his time. As organizations continued through the 1960s and 1970s to grow to the size of small countries, employees pined for the good old days when people enjoyed working for a cause, while leaders yearned for the near-extinct "mountain gorilla of management"—control.

The all-important data stream that we referred to earlier is enormously influenced by the sheer number of people in an organization. It doesn't take a Ph.D. in mathematics to realize that the number of possible interactions rises dramatically with each added person, function, department, or layer. "For instance, in a social system with 100 members, 4,950 links are possible (computed by the formula $N(N-1)/2$ where N is the number of individuals in the system). In a system of 200 members, 19,900 links are possible; with 1,000 members, almost a half-million links are possible."[7] Uh-oh. Of course, these numbers reflect only the *possible* links in an ideal world and say nothing about the potentially negative consequences lurking in a swollen data stream. Adding or decreasing the number of people, functions, departments, and so forth not only affects the *quantity* of the data but the *quality* of the data as well.

With time, and as employees are exposed to more people, technology, and information than they can handle, they begin to form into specialty teams where they can cut the world into pieces they can handle. The results of such specialization aren't all positive. In fact, it's usually only a matter of time until specialty teams are filled with structure-based conflict, stakeholder zealots, and organizational bigots. Nobody does it on purpose, but it happens.

Before we advocate tearing down large organizations and reassembling them into several hundred lemonade stands housed in tents, let's take a look at the unintended negative consequences of size and see if we can eliminate them. After all, few leaders have the authority to break their company into smaller units. Nevertheless, they *can* mitigate the impact that size has on the average employee. Once leaders realize that size reduces the number of interactions employees have with key stakeholders, stirs up conflict, creates a sense of alienation, and leads to a loss of accountability, they're in a better position to do something about it.

Watch for the Three Structural Ingredients of Conflict

Of all of the negative effects resulting from increasing size, perhaps the most predictable is conflict. The larger an organization grows, the more you can expect people to go at it hammer and tongs. However, when caught in the throes of conflict, few leaders attribute arguments, imbroglios, and tension to size. This source usually remains invisible. Instead, most leaders assume that conflict stems from differences in personality. They point to variations in ethnicity, gender, political orientation, age, and functional specialty. Almost none point to structure. Remember the waitresses and cooks? They went at it because of age and gender differences, right? Wrong. Their problem lay in the structure. What's interesting about the restaurant example is that they had the structural ingredients for conflict in spite of the fact they were quite small. After all, it's not size itself that causes conflict, it's the conditions size often creates. These ingredients are:

- Interdependence
- Conflicting goals
- Infrequent interaction

Put these three elements into an organizational soup, and you can practically taste the acrimony. Let's consider each in turn.

Interdependence. This element is easily understood. Parties rely on one another to achieve their goals. Alone, they're stuck. Combined, they have a chance. For example, in a medical center, a nurse depends on the doctor to be on time, fill out paperwork, and provide clear instructions. The doctor depends on technicians to complete the lab work correctly, provide supplies when needed, and properly schedule services. In an interdependent situation, the actions of one affect the results of others. If people are not interdependent, conflict is less likely. You may get on your spouse's nerves, but you rarely get on your neighbor's spouse's nerves. The larger an organization grows, the more people grow interdependent.

Nobody has time to do everything that's required, so people become specialists—all depending on each other.

Conflicting Goals. When people are interdependent but are given conflicting goals, trouble is near at hand. For instance, when a manager is held responsible for hitting production targets while her direct reports are paid by the hour, reach for the Bromo. When a plant manager wants to ship parts but the quality office is after zero defects, you've got a tinderbox just waiting for a match. In large organizations, stakeholder-driven goals are usually sliced into flat-sided subgoals to help people focus on something they can understand. The problem is that one group of specialists' focus becomes another group's frustration. In the arithmetic of large organizations, two half-goals rarely add up to a whole goal. They usually add up to an argument.

Infrequent Interaction. Now, imagine you have two groups that are interdependent, have conflicting goals, and rarely interact. You can pretty much count on a running battle. Infrequent interaction pumps air into the fuel and heat of conflict. Quite naturally, structure drives interaction frequency. It's mostly a function of physical distance. One researcher demonstrated that when people move closer together or farther apart by just 10 or 20 yards, the result is order-of-magnitude differences in frequency of contact.[8] When a sister of one of the authors moved five miles farther away, he noticed they got together about 80 percent less often. If you have people who are highly interdependent (cooks and waitresses), have conflicting goals (what's good for one didn't always help the other), and have low interaction (they rarely talked, other than yelling at one another), you can predict the possibility of venom, vilification, and vindictiveness!

What's a Leader to Do?

Informed leaders look first in Cell 6 when attempting to deal with rivalry and conflict. Before they throw training or speeches at the problem, they look for the three structural ingredients. The easiest to deal with is the interaction rate. Most leaders increase interactions by assembling cross-functional teams. Some, such as Coregis Insurance, break functions apart and have interdependent individuals actually sit next to each other. Others work on systems for making communication and interaction easier. Electronic networks, groupware, and teleconferencing help. Still, we have yet to see any of these take the place of just bumping into each other every morning.

The shared-goal problem is handled, as you might guess, by asking interdependent groups to share goals. Sounds simple. It's not. If people can't wrap their minds around the whole business process and don't interact enough with other critical groups, they begin to feel frustrated. They are responsible for achieving larger goals but feel powerless to really affect them. One solution is to break the organization into "mini-missions." Shoot for the smallest size that still adds value to all stakeholder groups. Set joint goals and develop shared metrics with interdependent departments. Have interdependent functions create their own shared metrics and meet regularly to reduce conflict and improve accountability and results.

The final structural solution we've seen work well is to eliminate interdependence. Many organizations are simply reducing the number of specialists they use and increasing the number of generalists. For example, many hospitals, rather than have a physical therapist, x-ray technician, hematologist, admissions clerk, and lab technician all working together, have eliminated them and put in a "Robo-nurse" who is trained to do 90 percent of what a typical patient needs. The nurse has no one to fight with over schedules, priorities, and the like, so conflict evaporates.

Clever solutions to structural conflict abound, and the possibilities for creative and fresh solutions are endless. Our critical point is simple. Leaders who operate in a Six-Cell context make sure they look at Cell 6 issues for a first crack at reducing conflict. When they stare into the face of conflict, they turn from personalities to shared goals, interaction rate, and interdependence.

Temper Single-Stakeholder Zealotry

A fanatic is one who can't change his mind and won't change the subject.

SIR WINSTON CHURCHILL

When a group of employees face only a fraction of their overall audience (usually customers) on a daily basis, and then deals with only one issue concerning that stakeholder (say quality), they often end up seeing themselves as ombudsmen or defenders of the faith. They become the gurus of quality, or the flag carriers of the schedule, or the cost-cutting specialists. Many organizations have gone so far as to *intentionally* create such positions.

The unintended negative consequences of such stakeholder specialization are obvious. Rather than a culture of balance, organizations begin to look like courtrooms. On one side of the hall you find the prosecution, and on the other side you find the equally vocal defense team. Specialists in and of themselves aren't a problem. However, when individuals begin to see themselves as the *only* defenders of a particular perspective and when others begin to buy into the notion, dialogue is replaced with zealotry, self-righteousness, and fanaticism. Instead of open, honest, and healthy mental-map sharing, advocates try to convince the "unwashed" masses of the importance of their pet cause. Consider the words of a machine operator who spoke out during a culture interview. When asked what his job was, he responded:

> *My job? I'll tell you what I do. I protect the customer from this company. Every time some pinhead from headquarters comes up with a cost-saving idea or some kiss-up engineer decides that it's okay to let a lower-quality product slide by, I stand up for the customer. You know why? Because if I didn't, nobody else would.*

The danger with this person's thinking lies in its self-righteous passion. Rather than staring at apathy (the mortal enemy of excellence), His leaders are faced with what appears to be something they've tried to foster—a passion for serving customers. That's two good things, right? Passion, and for customers, no less! Who could ask for anything more? Actually, such zealotry can be just as dangerous as apathy. When enthusiasm leads to either-or thinking, everyone's at risk.

Consider the language—*pinheads* and *kiss-ups*. This is not a good sign. Passion toward one stakeholder or issue doesn't have to lead to cruelty toward others. But it happens. When people start aligning themselves with their favorite cause, when their daily stream of work puts them in contact with but one stakeholder or one set of issues, it's usually only a matter of time until leaders face a workforce that's fanatical about one set of concerns while apathetic, or even blind, toward most others. That is, unless leaders are sensitive to the impact of a narrow flow of data and take steps to mitigate its blinding effects.

What's a Leader to Do? Whenever you find yourself watching two individuals or groups of people, each fighting vehemently for one stakeholder or cause as if it were the *only* thing that ever mattered, the hair should stand up on the back of your neck. Size and its stepchild, specialization, are beginning to turn your staff into single-issue employees.

Leaders who want their employees to consider the whole picture when analyzing the impact of their decisions will go to great lengths to avoid such parochial thinking. They insist that people take several sides of an issue rather than fight for their pet cause. They continually remind people to break out of their own specialty and think in terms of the entire stakeholder population.

The true test of a parochialism lies in *who* makes *what* arguments. For example, imagine that you've put a video camera on a cross-functional team made up of *nonparochial* specialists who have been asked to discuss a wide-reaching problem. These are people who, in spite of their specialties, maintain a multistakeholder perspective. If, after recording a two-hour meeting, you were to show the tape of their discussion to a group of strangers, they would be hard-pressed to tell you which one was the quality guru, which one was the human resources specialist, or which one was the financial wizard. Within a healthy team, the controller is just as likely to bring up a "people issue" as the employee relations manager is to fret about costs. Granted, specialists are the content experts and carry the latest and most accurate data, but they don't blindly fight for a cause.

Watch your own team in action. Do only the specialists talk about their specialty, or do other employees share their concerns?

This particular line of thinking brings us back to the thesis of *The Balancing Act*. Every employee needs to care more about stakeholder balance than about meeting the needs of any single stakeholder group. A vital culture is one in which employees are willing and able to meet competing stakeholder demands, not one in which people are willing to defend a lone stakeholder or pet issue—as if nothing else existed.

> The enemy of balance is not ignorance; it's the near-blinding belief in a just cause. When analyzing your own culture, remember:
>
> Well-balanced specialists carry *data*, not *torches*.

Eliminate Organizational Bigotry

In all matters of opinion our adversaries are insane.

MARK TWAIN

As face-to-face interaction with key people is made difficult by size, employees routinely demonstrate an "us-versus-them" mentality—where "us" is their small workgroup and "them" is anyone else, both inside and outside the organization. Such exclusionary language forms the foundation of organizational bigotry. People become strongly partial to their own workgroup, specialty, or department, yet intolerant of those who differ. Frankly, it's difficult for most people to think good thoughts about 100 or more strangers. As the number of "strangers out there" goes up (particularly strangers who are causing problems), the likelihood of imputing good motive goes down. When imputing bad motive becomes common, organizational bigotry lies just around the corner.

What's a Leader to Do? Leaders who worry about creating a larger sense of team than "you, me, and a couple of our good buddies" are sensitive to corporate jingoism and workgroup bigotry. They openly fight unhealthy characterizations and unflattering labels. They don't allow team members to bad-mouth anyone—not even "them" and "they." When an employee starts complaining about "them," savvy leaders ask "who?" and then encourage a Six-Cell causal analysis: "Who exactly are you talking about, and what do you suppose has led them to act that way?" They refuse to sit around and "trash" different professions, shifts, divisions, or even unidentified strangers. They realize that such self-serving bigotry rarely leads to solutions and invariably erodes the very foundation of teamwork.

Aware that organizational bigotry often stems from a lack of interaction, skilled leaders go to pains to increase social "mixing." Inspired by Muzafer Sherif's early work on interaction patterns and higher-level goals (Sherif learned that kids at camp rarely judge mates outside their cabins as friends—until they're forced to work jointly on a common problem),[9] proactive leaders work carefully to shift interaction patterns and to broaden goals. Some form cross-functional teams with the purpose of putting people who have been at odds with each other into a team that has to come up with a solution to a common problem. Similarly, they rotate individuals through a variety of tasks and positions in order to help employees "walk in others' moccasins."

To maximize daily interaction patterns, many leaders follow the lead established by Hewlett-Packard in the early 1970s. They require a midmorning and midafternoon break during which, short of a nuclear attack, everyone is asked to mingle over fruit and juices. Clean desks are ruled out of bounds. Everyone is encouraged to leave their current projects out on their desks where others can see what they're doing and ask questions. Where possible, office layouts are shifted or redesigned with social interaction in mind. More often than not, individuals who are dependent on one another are moved to adjacent or even shared work spaces. Groups that had been at each other's throats are shifted to spaces that share conference rooms, support staff, and common eating areas.

Many groups are starting to use high-tech tools to encourage inter-action. However, this can happen only if leaders are committed to frequent face-to-face contacts. If not, left to their natural impact, most high-tech tools isolate people, cutting them off from dialogue. To counteract the effects of technology, smart leaders establish the following norm: Voice mail and e-mail cannot be used to give unilateral complaints or commands, but instead must be used to invite dialogue. Rather than leave a terse note stating, "Have the Postal Code project to me by noon," employees are encouraged to state, "I need to talk to you about the Postal Code project. I'll be around all morning. Give me a call as soon as you can." Although voice mail and e-mail have made it easier to leave information with people who might otherwise have been left out of the loop, when used as information dumps, particularly when used to register complaints or to fire off unilateral commands, electronic messages simply add to conflict by fueling the fires of disrespect.

As the cost of video conferencing decreases, many organizations are using high-tech tools to lead to the second-best alternative to face-to-face dialogue—face-to-monitor dialogue. Interdependent groups that are separated by miles, even oceans, are routinely brought together for an electronic conversation. Some companies are beginning to use videotape as a way of leaving messages between shifts. Rather than write complex notes about quality concerns (ones that are frequently avoided because they're so hard to compose), people are encouraged to point a camera at the problem and discuss the implications to the next shift. Although videotape isn't as helpful as face-to-face contact, when people can't be brought together (shifts don't overlap), videos provide a great deal more data than can be left in a note and are enormously easier to make. Of course, many organizations (aware that different shifts are often at each other's throats) simply schedule a half-hour overlap where time is taken to pass the baton. When this is cost prohibitive, frontline leaders often work the times that overlap the schedule transitions.

As organizations continue to grow, causing people to become increasingly isolated from one another until they're eventually cut off from most of the people with whom they're interdependent, leaders must be sensitive to the telltale signs of insufficient face-to-face contact. Stakeholder zealotry and departmental bigotry are the litmus tests of workgroup jingoism. As intergroup conflict escalates, wise leaders ask, "What can we do to increase face-to-face contact?" They dive deep into Cell 6, look for the impact of size and space, and seek individual, social, and even structural fixes.

Refuse to Set Policy for the Lowest Common Denominator

So many signatures for such a small heart.

MOTHER TERESA, ON FILLING OUT FORMS IN A CALIFORNIA HOSPITAL

As their organizations grow and as leaders begin to lose contact with "all those strangers out there," many become nervous. After all, if each employee makes only one disastrous decision, then ... (The thought is mind-boggling.) The reaction of top leaders to the threat of so many poor decisions is predictable. Every time a freewheeling decision maker fouls up, a new rule is made, a new policy is passed, a new signature is called for, or a new procedure is demanded. In short, every thinking person is dragged down to the lowest common denominator. Each is treated as if he or she were the most incapable and unmotivated employee. And bureaucracy is born.

Given that most people choke at the very thought of bureaucracy, how do leaders invite it into their own offices? Consider an example the authors observed recently. A frontline leader nervously holds his first two-way discussion with a team of union employees. He's not real smooth with a group, doesn't know how to answer tough questions, and ends up in a heated argument. Within minutes of completing the meeting, senior union officials burst into the management team's office and complain. The top managers immediately react to the threat. They prohibit all two-way meetings. From now on, meetings will be used for information sharing only. There will be no dangerous question-and-answer period. Their rash response to an individual problem was to implement a structural solution. A policy was set. No routine meeting will ever end up in a heated argument again. Of course, effective leaders who, up until that moment, had used two-way meetings as an integral part of their leadership style, are now prevented from using an incredibly helpful tool.

Special Notice: It has come to our attention that a valued employee was recently injured while eating spaghetti with a fork. From this day forth, all employees will be required to eat pasta with their hands.

What's a Leader to Do? Fortunately, the solution to this problem isn't a tough one. Don't solve problems by immediately creating a policy that restricts the entire workforce or pits teams, leaders, or workgroups against each other. Use policies, procedures, forms, signatures, and other strictures sparingly. If one person messes up, don't make everyone pay by universally restricting behavior. If a whole bunch of people mess up, don't immediately reach for a policy. Cut off every problem-solving discussion that's starting to take the path to bureaucracy by completing a Six-Cell diagnosis. Look at every cell before you restrict behavior. Train to increase skills, share information, fix the flow of data—in essence, do what it takes to make people better decision makers before you decide to refuse them the right to make a choice.

A Working Definition: *Bureaucracy*—Responding to one person's perceived lunacy by forcing everyone else to wear a straitjacket.

If you're suspicious that your organization already suffers from constipation, hardening of the arteries, or has otherwise taken away decision-making authority at every turn, zero-base your policies and procedures. Pull together a team, and examine every form, approval process, policy, procedure, and anything else that structurally limits choices. Ask:

- Does this structural approach deal with symptoms or root causes?
- Are we choosing the quick, easy option instead of working through the real problem of mistrust or incompetence?
- Is there any other way to solve the problem short of denying people freedom of choice?
- If we're at risk, do we have to cut employees out of the loop completely, or can we take a more empowering step and set guidelines or boundaries?
- Can we deal with deviations by increasing accountability rather than by reducing freedom?

Bureaucracy's True Promise

The guarantee that a leader receives (as a result of limiting *everyone's* ability to make a decision whenever *one* employee makes a mistake) is not the assurance that the error will be avoided, but the absolute certainty that clever, motivated, and well-intentioned people will be frustrated, stifled, and eventually stripped of their dignity and initiative.

Fight Alienation

We have created an industrial order geared to automatism . . . where a
pervasive neurosis is the final gift of the meaningless life that issues
forth at the other end.

LEWIS MUMFORD

Size does more than separate individuals from one another—it creates
intergroup conflict, debilitating bigotry, and a stifling bureaucracy.
When taken to the extreme, size has a numbing effect on the human
psyche. The ultimate example of the neurosis created by sheer mass
was demonstrated in the Ford Rouge facility. Between 1918 and 1928,
Ford operated a gargantuan factory that totally integrated the automobile manufacturing process (starting with wood, ore, and latex at one
end and pumping out automobiles at the other).

> *It was a mile and a half long and three quarters of a mile wide. Its*
> *eleven hundred acres contained ninety-three buildings. . . . Some*
> *seventy-five thousand men worked there, five thousand of them*
> *doing nothing but keeping it clean, using eighty-six tons of soap*
> *and wearing out five thousand mops each month.*[10]

Bigger wasn't better, it turns out. The working conditions in the Rouge
became nearly unbearable. People who had labored their whole lives
as craftsmen in small shops entered a dark, dank, cavernous factory
where they often described themselves as "mere cogs in a massive
machine." Arguments, fistfights, thefts, and drunkenness were common. No small part of this unhealthy culture resulted from an incredibly repressive leadership style and working conditions that would keep
a dozen of today's safety and health specialists occupied for a century.
(All of this, by the way, has been changed.) Nevertheless, the sheer size
of the facility and the sense of being only one of thousands of people
exacted their toll as well. Interviews in today's Fortune 500 companies,
while clean and downright chipper by comparison, often reveal a similar sense of alienation that is born of size.

Fortunately, the problem of "feeling like a cog" doesn't have to be
the natural consequence of working for a large company. Granted,
shrinking the size of an organization can alleviate part of the problem;
however, even people working for companies of less than 30 employees have been known to complain about not feeling valued or not understanding how their work really matters. A sense of belonging is not
guaranteed by a small number of square feet per employee any more
than a sense of alienation is directly proportional to the size of an
organization's roll.

What's a Leader to Do? When culture assessments reveal that people "feel like cogs," work on (1) continually praising accomplishment (see chapter 12), (2) creating a sense of unity in the immediate workgroup (see chapter 13), (3) linking individuals' actions to the vision and the overall product and service mix, and (4) making sure your physical layout and internal structures aren't encouraging or adding to conflict. For example, the authors once consulted with a company whose work area covered over three million square feet, whose ceilings were 40 feet high, and where a walk around the place reminded one of Dante's inferno (flames actually shot out of orifices everywhere you looked). And yet, in two of the 17 workgroups, morale was high. People often spoke with pride about their own accomplishments and the team's latest production records. Nobody complained about the working conditions, nor did they suggest they felt like cogs.

As researchers studied the two frontline supervisors who had overcome enormously unpleasant physical surroundings, they learned how these two leaders differed from their colleagues. First, the effective leaders took members of the assessment team around their area and introduced them to each employee, explaining how great each was at his or her job. They bragged about each individual as if each were part of an Olympic relay team. Their respect for one another was obvious and sincere. Their less-successful colleagues took the assessors on a tour of the *machinery*, while their employees stood idly by.

Second, like barefoot doctors, the dynamic duo were drawn from the workforce. Their social interests were similar, they spoke a similar vernacular, and they obviously enjoyed being with the colleagues they worked with. Both did a great deal with their teams off-site, attending christenings and weddings, and generally fitting into the social structure. Their 15 less-successful colleagues were all college grads who were taking a short turn "out on the floor." They aspired to different jobs and circumstances, dressed in more upscale attire, read different magazines and periodicals, and acted as if bowling teams were a crime against society.

Third, the successful team members identified with their workgroup. Although the teams themselves were referred to as numbers (area 14 and area 22), team members continually used these monikers as if they were describing the Green Berets or the von Trapp family. Finally, the successful leaders paid no heed to corporate policies that prohibited personal items in the work area. They allowed, even encouraged, people to bring pictures of their families, trophies, flower arrangements, and other personal items to work. As the researchers walked around the area, observing an occasional plastic flower hanging out of a rusted conduit, these small attempts to "freshen up hell" appeared ridiculous. But then they began to realize that here were people who would be working in the same spot for years. Healthy team members had carefully brought pieces of their home to their work, and they were proud of the effect.

People don't become cogs simply as a result of size. It takes size and certain ineffective leadership actions to engender a sense of alienation. When leaders legitimately respect and admire individuals, when they care about them as people (working hard to foster a sense of personal worth and allowing people to create a sense of home), some of the dehumanizing effects of size disappear.

Stand Up for Personal Accountability

We are responsible for actions performed in response to circumstances for which we are not responsible.

ALLAN MASSIE

The natural sister of alienation (the sense of being a "cog") is the loss of individual responsibility. People begin to think, "Since there are so many of us here, what difference could any *one* of us make?" This diffusion of responsibility manifests itself in many ways. At the societal level, individuals feel free to do pretty much anything and become mobs. Criminals who fall into mob behavior are judged by juries who fall into the civilized version of the same behavior. They become victims of the "insurance company" syndrome. They award huge amounts to plaintiffs because they believe that doing so doesn't harm anyone. When a man spills hot coffee in his lap, why not force McDonald's to pay out hundreds of thousands of dollars? Not because the crime (if there was one) deserves the punishment, but because Ronald and his friends have deep pockets.

At the organizational level, this diffusion of responsibility plays itself out in similar ways. Individuals begin to believe that one person's actions don't really matter. Their extra efforts won't make things any better, nor will their mistakes cause any harm. Special efforts, risk taking, and embracing new ideas can be left to others while they hide safely in a sea of faces. On the other hand, they can cheat the company by manufacturing the need for overtime, putting in a mediocre effort, or even taking office materials and electronic equipment home (saying, "They won't miss it."). These losses will also be absorbed by the masses. (In several organizations the authors have worked with, it's *policy* to order two to three times what is required if the material being ordered is something people would like to take home—VCRs as opposed to coolant .)

Out of the Mouths of Babes

Years ago, when a young girl was interviewed on television by Art Linkletter, she explained that her dad worked at a factory that produced light bulbs and toilet paper. Art asked if she was sure that one place produced these obviously incompatible products. "Oh yes, I'm sure," she responded. "That's what daddy brings home in his lunch box every day!"

Employees aren't the only ones who shift responsibility from themselves to the masses. Leaders fall into similar traps. Many managers treat budgets like "funny money." They talk about internal transfers of funds as if the money grew on trees. They blow out their budgets at the end of the year, thinking only of their need to justify equal amounts next year. After all, what impact can *they* have on the bottom line?

This particular negative consequence of size should scare leaders to death. Not only is the loss of personal accountability incredibly costly, it's also fairly likely. In three change projects the authors worked on, several large pockets of employees in each organization admitted that they put in only a fraction of the effort they could provide and showed no interest whatsoever in cutting costs or increasing productivity. As cultural assessors talked with these employees, it became clear that most of them worked hard in other realms of their lives. Several had businesses on the side, one was a city councilperson, many worked for volunteer groups, and yet at work all were only partially engaged because "our efforts don't really matter."

Connecting Personal Performance to Organizational Vitality

These inaccurate mental maps are hard to change because they're true, if taken at the individual level. That is, if only one person in a large company fails to measure up, others *will* carry the weight. Of course, when virtually everyone believes the same thing, the assumption ceases to be true. The best way to handle a disconnect between personal performance and Organizational Vitality is through a three-pronged approach.

First, don't make the mistake of saying, "If employees don't person-ally measure up, the company will be overrun by the competition." Threats rarely work. As we suggested in chapter 7, it's far better to fo-cus on the intrinsic satisfaction of doing one's best than it is to talk about generic long-term consequences that may not come to pass. Appeal to personal pride rather than to fear.

Second, divide workgroups into accountable profit centers, or at least continually publish and explore team effectiveness. Publish team num-bers, make team costs visible, and celebrate team productivity. Focus on what people can control. For instance, Courtney Smith, president of Chicago-based Coregis Group, broke his specialty insurance com-pany into "programs." Each has a distinct market, balance sheet, and P&L. The result has been an increased sense of control, accountabil-ity, and focus for hundreds of employees.

Other companies, such as W. L. Gore, attend to size like a catechism. At 200 employees, the company divides—building a new facility and creating a new unit—rather than suffer the cultural impediments of size.

Link personal rewards, praise, and (eventually) gain sharing to individual and small-group contribution. And *never* model the attitude of, "It's only a couple of pennies." Let people know that you, the leader, take personal responsibility for every piece of paper you save.

Third, make the company your own. Several leaders the authors have worked with use the expression, "If I owned this pop shop . . ." They mentally reduce the size of their large organizations by publicly asking, "If I were the owner of the company, would I spend the money this way, employ this resource, or squander that effort?" It's astound-ing how many decisions are reversed after people ask, "If I owned this place, would I do this?" When leaders continually shrink the organi-zation by taking on the view of personal ownership, many employees follow suit. People can feel personally responsible, even when they don't own the pop shop.

Separate Necessities from Niceties

Unlike other forms of life, man's greatest exertions are made in the pursuit not of necessities but of superfluities.

ERIC HOFFER

As leaders and employees alike wrap themselves in the comforter of "the organization will take care of me" and begin to lose a personal sense of responsibility for the vitality of a company, many forget what they really need to complete their jobs. They begin to confuse niceties with necessities. They don't openly oppose productivity gains or cost-cutting efforts. They wouldn't dream of stealing. They might even be willing to step up to the plate and give their best effort. However, they see no reason why they and their department can't buy whatever suits their needs. Since they aren't purchasing personal items, what could be wrong with getting the best tools, or a larger computer screen, or a new desk? After all, each of these items will make them either more productive or better suited to serve their customers. They come to view money as if it flowed out of a never-ending corporate stream. "It's only $500," they mutter. (This insensitivity to large amounts of money should throw a responsible leader into shock.)

Nip such thinking in the bud. Divide up the "infinite pool" of corporate funds into small pools or workgroup budgets. Tie the budget to the profit-sharing pool. If you don't share profits, at least treat the budget as if it were both real and generous. Talk about ways to save money in each account. Explore each request for better equipment or materials to improve working conditions by asking, "If I owned this pop shop, would I make this purchase?"

End the Proliferation of Non-Value-Added Work

As organizations grow in complexity, so does the need to create support systems. Layers of management, meetings, reports, support teams, coordinating systems, and other appendages proliferate as complexity increases. All can be necessary appendages. However, if a diffusion of responsibility has slowly taken over the culture, then workgroups and support areas are added with the same lack of concern for accountability that individuals demonstrate when carelessly buying new tools—only now, leaders are buying whole workgroups, functions, and divisions without regard to costs or purpose. Of course, once you've created a superfluous appendage, it may take an act of congress to do away with it. On the other hand, it may take just one person asking if the emperor really is wearing clothes.

> Bureaucracies are like police forces turned on end; they exist to protect and serve—themselves.

To avoid the dangerous proliferation of non-value-added activities and functions, periodically zero-base your organization. Stand the emperor up to scrutiny. Question the need for every activity or function. Start with the assumption that all activities that are not part of your core competency need to be dumped, outsourced, or cut back. Don't look at people. You can deal with people later. If you look at people, you'll grow soft. Look at functions as they relate to your mission. Obviously, you'll end up keeping many of your support efforts. You might even expand some. However, if you don't periodically ask hard questions about each area, you'll end up with a fair number of functions that are outdated, unnecessary, and very expensive. If you're serious about your zero-basing, you'll occasionally make some fairly significant changes. You'll decide to eliminate whole divisions or product lines that are neither profitable nor core to your business. You'll cut back on support groups that add more costs than provide real benefits. You'll outsource activities that specialty companies can provide with greater efficiency.

Once you've decided where you need to snip, *then* worry about people, lifestyles, and the most efficient and humane way to implement the plan. Remember, every time you worry about the loss of one person (something any caring person would do), think about what you're doing to make everyone else more vital. As terrible as the metaphor may sound, organizations that are continually growing eventually become like overloaded lifeboats. If leaders don't occasionally trim the weight, everyone goes down. In truth, anytime you structure around the needs of the one, all of the silent stakeholders suffer. Star Trek's Mr. Spock was right: The needs of the many are greater than the needs of the few.

You're Not in This Alone

We're all of us sentenced to solitary confinement inside our own skins, for life!

TENNESSEE WILLIAMS

By now, you may wonder if you're really going to be able to think about and make good use of Cell 6 strategies. The good news is that you don't have to solve Cell 6 problems all by yourself. In fact, you'd better not. One of the authors learned this principle while working with his highly inventive son. Here's his story.

> *I once had an interesting discussion with my six-year-old son. He had committed the unspeakable crime of calling his sister a "dummy." As a consequence, I sent him to bed early. As I sat on his bed to wish him good night, he protested that I was mean, hated*

him, and was enjoying his punishment. I took a couple of minutes to explain what I had done and why. As an afterthought I asked, "What would you suggest I do to help you stop saying things that hurt your sister's feelings?" He became silent. His piercing blue eyes showed deep thought, then he said, "I think I should go to bed early for a week, and I should put up a sign on my door so I'll remember not to say mean things." I used the second suggestion to great benefit.

Cell 6 Decisions: Standing Targets for Misinterpretation, Abuse, and Gaming

Let's be very clear about this point. When you work *on* other people (trying to change them without involving them), you practically dare them to resist you. For example, if the six-year-old in the story hadn't helped his dad come up with the behavior-change plan, he probably would have held his tongue—but only when Dad was around.

When you quietly (even secretly) set up systems, structures, and policies in an attempt to influence others' behavior, they rarely respond to these structural changes by acting like rats in a maze, dutifully following the structure to the prize at the end. Quite the opposite, they typically see these "walls" as challenges to be overcome. They climb over them, dig under them, or blast their way through them. You can count on the fact that structural changes are standing targets for misinterpretation, abuse, and gaming. No structural design is immune.

People fight systems or policies because, without being involved, they often misinterpret the intent, not because they are inherently malicious or stupid. For example, a manager moves furniture and offices around in an attempt to bring various functions together. The people who are affected decide that the purpose was to tear them away from their dear friends or turn them into "generalists" who earn less. When you ask people to get approval for purchases over $1,000, you may be trying to ensure wise decisions in the use of precious resources. The people seeking the purchase order, however, may see the requirement as a slap in the face or as an accusation of incompetence or dishonesty.

Is it possible that people will interpret structural changes in a positive light? Maybe. But you have to remember that every Cell 6 decision involves trade-offs. You try to put two people closer together and unintentionally put two others farther apart. You try to encourage collaboration by giving team incentives and you diminish individual incentive. There's always the chance that people will only see the downside and assume leaders are dimwits. This freezes many managers into inactivity.

The solution to misinterpretation and misunderstanding is simple. Involve others in the restructuring process. If you do, you'll enjoy two benefits. First, structures can be looked at from a variety of perspectives. Second, and more importantly, when people face the trade-offs of Cell 6 decisions together, they begin to respond to the *intent* of the structure instead of its form. Rather than rats trying to beat someone else's maze, they become partners in shaping their own behaviors to help balance the needs of all the competing stakeholders.

The first step, then, when a Cell 6 problem is identified, is to ask for help. Invite those most affected by the problem (as well as those who have helpful expertise) to join a cross-functional task force. Ask the task-force members to diagnose the nature of the problem, define the desired results or behaviors, and work together to design possible solutions. Implement their suggestions as a pilot, and then fine-tune the strategy before you implement a systemwide change.

For example, consider a banking organization with which the authors worked. The senior leaders were committed to reducing bureaucracy. More specifically, they had decided to reduce the vast array of forms that had proliferated like bacteria in a petri dish. To take on this formidable task, they convened a team made up of employees from various levels and parts of the organization. The team was asked to study the forms-approval process and make recommendations for streamlining it—without losing accountability.

The team soon discovered that the average form required six signatures. One actually required 14. These signatures obviously didn't appear overnight. Adding 6 to 14 steps to every key decision yielded the following consequences:

- It took forever to get anything done.
- People felt disempowered. There was nothing that could be done to speed things up.
- Many of the people who signed the form admitted to collusion. They didn't study the issue, but instead looked at the previous person's signature and then signed.
- Accountability was diminished. With six or more signatures, no one person was responsible.

The team went to work on busting the structural bureaucracy. They interviewed experts, tracked the forms, mapped processes, and came up with several recommendations. First, they explained that a distinction needed to be made between requesting, giving approval, inspecting, and being informed. Someone requests, someone approves, one or two others audit or inspect—everyone else is simply informed. The team also realized that 80 percent of the forms were "low risk." The amounts of money involved were not large, the impact was not great, and there had been few problems in the past. To accommodate the need for efficiency and speed (a customer demand), careful use of resources (an investor demand), and a less frustrating process (an employee demand), they decided the low-risk forms needed just two signatures—the requester and the approver. They dropped the other four. When it was necessary to inform others, they sent copies to affected parties. About 15 percent of the forms were "medium risk." There was greater financial or technical impact for these. For these, the team recommended three signatures—requester, approver, and reviewer (usually an accountant or administrator). The final 5 percent were "high risk." For these, the team recommended four signatures—requester, approver, and two reviewers (often including legal or environmental experts).

By differentiating the various roles of previous signatories and by identifying the risk, response time decreased, while accountability and efficiency increased.

After finishing the task, the team was given a new responsibility. They were asked to look at the low-risk forms and determine what it would take to give authority to individuals to do what they needed to do without having to seek permission from anyone. What would it take to do away with those forms altogether *and* still ensure that the organization wasn't at risk? What skill, information, or other tool would be needed to eliminate a full step?

This example teaches an important lesson. When leaders made use of a cross-functional team, they were able to deal with Cell 6 issues in a way that was far more sophisticated and less time consuming than what they could have done on their own. Not only did they eliminate the inherent problem of misunderstanding, abuse, or gaming by different stakeholder groups, they learned that they weren't alone.

SOME PRACTICAL ADVICE FROM THIS CHAPTER

We started this chapter by suggesting that Cell 6 isn't often used as a leadership tool. Most leaders don't think in terms of physical features, data streams, structure, and the like. To help make at least some of the tools more visible and usable, we focused on six areas in which Cell 6 can be particularly helpful. Here is some of the advice we offered.

- **Manage the data stream.** Since people make choices based on mental maps, it only makes sense to take a long, hard look at what streams of data are pointed at those maps. When people seem to be continually at odds, look at the stream of data and not just the material floating in it. Where necessary, adjust the stream itself.
- **Master the use of physical features.** The physical features surrounding people at work often play an important role in their ability to complete their required tasks. For example, the visual field of a room has an impact on people's creativity. Or it least it can. Temperature, lighting, furniture layout, and all other physical items play a role in daily productivity. Take a look at Fred Steele's *Physical Settings and Organization Development*.[11] Talk with your human resources specialist. Start to work on your environmental competence.
- **Ensure that the physical world is congruent with your espoused values.** Take a walk around your buildings. With your mission in mind, look at the sheer physicality of the place. Are the messages communicated by the physical choices you've made also in line with your written mission and values statement? Does the structure of today reflect the values of, say, 20 years ago? Start with your own office. If you want to be stakeholder driven, what evidence is there in your office itself that suggests you care about stakeholders? Was it designed two decades ago when offices were places to hide you from people and to serve as a shrine?
- **Mitigate the crippling effects of size.** As people make less and less contact with key stakeholders (as their organizations grow), watch out for single-stakeholder zealotry, departmental bigotry, creeping bureaucracy, alienation, and the loss of personal accountability. Temper zealotry by increasing the contact. Mix people around. Assign competing groups to cross-functional teams. Encourage daily informal chats. Eliminate bigotry by refusing to allow bad-mouthing and "they" bashing. Ask people to complete a Six-Cell analysis rather than simply assume that others are "bad" and "wrong." Refuse to reduce people to the lowest common denominator by avoiding the one-size-fits-all "policy trap." Don't restrict behavior across the board without first working on every other cell. Fight a sense of alienation by mentally shrinking the organization. Value individuals, measure small-group accomplishments, and allow people to personalize their work space. Stand up for personal accountability by creating a "pop shop" mentality. Don't let people confuse niceties with necessities. Annually evaluate the need for each support group.

- **Stand up for personal accountability.** Many organizations suffer from a loss of personal accountability. Size never improves this problem. The more people there are to pick up the slack, the easier it is for employees to assume that their efforts really don't matter. New change efforts are avoided. Why take a risk when others can do what's necessary? Personal integrity is often compromised. "I can take a little here, snip a little there, and nobody will care. This place can afford it." The solution here is clear. Cut the organization down to size. At least mentally reduce it to a small company or group. Focus on individual performance. Link performance to small-group goals. Ask the question, "If I owned this popshop...?" Never make the mistake of modeling, "It's only a couple of pennies."
- **You're not in this alone.** Finally, we suggested that Cell 6 changes are like throwing a firecracker into a bus. You're sure the change will influence behavior, but you can't predict exactly how (or even how the results will be interpreted). To ensure your people understand and are committed to the intent of your structures (rather than searching for ways around them), partner with your people in all changes. A "B grade" plan that has the backing of all stakeholders will probably outperform an "A grade" plan imposed by someone seen as an outsider by any of your stakeholder groups.

A WORD OF CAUTION

You don't need to be an expert to avoid being a victim.

The tools and insights that reside in Cell 6 offer no more of a complete solution to organizational ailments than any one of the other five cells—taken in isolation. Unfortunately, hundreds of gurus have convinced themselves that if you change structure, people will fall into place (like so many peas rolling through a straw). Such simplistic true-believerism serves none of us well.

We suggest a less fanatical approach. We call for balance. We hope leaders will now take the time to analyze Cell 6 forces that typically go unnoticed. However, they need not become experts or, worse still, structural zealots. Instead, we encourage leaders to add an understanding of the impact of nonhuman forces to their growing Six-Cell toolkit and to use this more balanced and complete knowledge for both analyzing problems and for designing remedies.

We've taken the time in this book to explore each of six separate sources of influence. Our goal has been to help leaders break the habit of responding to problems by looking at them through a single lens and then, to no one's surprise, always coming up with the same old strategy. Possessing a knowledge that cuts across individual, social, and organizational domains, and having an appreciation of the difference between "can't do" and "don't want to do," puts leaders in a position to bring virtually hundreds of theories and practices to bear. We hope this more complex, and yet more balanced, approach serves leaders well. It represents the best thinking and actions of the scholars and leaders we've learned from over the past two decades and is the most likely route to Organizational Vitality.

A PRACTICAL ASSIGNMENT

Record your core company values on a 3 x 5 card. Walk all over your facility with the card in hand. Examine its nonhuman features. Look at banners, posters, pictures, work spaces, shrines, and other physical indicators of value. To what extent do they reflect your espoused values? Look for incongruities. Search for ways to involve all stakeholder groups in making improvements.

S E C T I O N   5   Q U I Z

It's time for one final test.

1. Why worry about linking incentives to behavior?
   A. Without a tight linkage, incentives will fail to reinforce desired behaviors.
   B. Without a tight linkage, incentives lose both their instructive and motivational qualities.
   C. Without a tight linkage, incentives eventually decouple from targeted behaviors, float into space, and destroy the ozone layer.

2. When it comes to making the best use of the formal reward system, savvy leaders always:
   A. Gather reliable, fair measures
   B. Observe behavior on the floor
   C. Deal only in small, unmarked bills

3. Since Cell 6 is largely invisible, what do effective leaders do to make it more salient?
   A. They step out of the data stream, set aside the items floating in it, and look at the stream itself.
   B. They purposefully walk around their buildings, looking for incongruities between their espoused values and the symbolic messages inherent in the physical surroundings.
   C. They add salt.

4. What's meant by the expression "reducing people to the lowest common denominator"?
   A. Designing policies to restrict behavior every time one person makes a mistake
   B. Treating every person as if he or she were the most ignorant and unmotivated employee
   C. Forcing all employees to major in math

5. What did Fred Steele mean by the expression "environmental competence"?
   A. Being aware of the effect the physical environment is having on you
   B. Refusing to be a victim of structure, physical features, systems, and other nonhuman factors
   C. Refusing, despite peer pressure and local customs, to order peregrine falcon à la king or to sign up for a weekend whale-hunting junket

Conclusion

We'll bring this book to a close with three kinds of advice. Each is intended to help the reader take the concepts we've discussed and reduce them to the "small change of daily experience." We'll start by examining how to use this text as a guidebook or blueprint for change. This should be easy, since we wrote it with this purpose in mind.

Next we'll examine how key principles and theories can become part of a leader's daily leadership repertoire. Although not everything a leader does is aimed at changing people's values and assumptions, everything eventually does touch people and affects human interaction.

Finally, we'll explore why most books that call for leaders to actually *do something* are hard to translate from print to action. Under normal circumstances, the reader, no matter how well intentioned, sets a book down, walks out into that pulsating miasma called an organization, and is quietly enticed by friendly, nearly invisible, stimuli onto the treadmill of habit. With this in mind, we'll finish our work by exploring ways to help the reader step off the treadmill of habit and step onto the road of change.

C H A P T E R   1 6

Moving from Print to Action

A conception not reducible to the small change of daily experience is like a currency not exchangeable for articles of consumption; it is not a symbol, but a fraud.

GEORGE SANTAYANA

A GUIDE TO ORGANIZATIONAL CHANGE

Section 1 laid down a challenge—work toward vitality or slip toward death. To move in the right direction, leaders were encouraged to break from single-variable thinking and work toward striking a balance between competing stakeholder demands. This important and precarious balance, in turn, called for three skill-sets. First, the ability to create a balanced, clear vision of detailed actions that lead to both Outcome Vitality and Cultural Vitality. Second, the capacity to continually and accurately measure how well your organization is achieving this balance. Third, the knowledge of what steps to take should your organization lose its balance and start to drop a chain saw or two.

Section 2 created a theory base for all of our subsequent recommendations. We refused to pretend that organizations "behave." Rather, we suggested that a leader's challenge is to influence individuals. To get a handle on these cognitive creatures, we created a model of individual behavior selection by answering the question, "Why do people do what they do?" It was at this point that we introduced the pivotal concept of net value. People, we suggested, when faced with a choice, stare into the pool of anticipated consequences, expected abilities, and values and come up with a net value, or overall feeling for whether an action is worth the effort.

Without an understanding of this net value, no one can predict behavior very well. Of course, if you can't predict behavior, you're left to the buffetings of chance. The good news is that the model we introduced predicts behavior quite well. Unlike personality "color codes" or simple labels, social cognitive theory forecasts a great deal of what will happen. The bad news is that the model calls for continuous monitoring of ever-changing values and assumptions. This need for constant updating is exacerbated by the fact that the number of values and assumptions a person carries at one time (one's personality) is astoundingly large.

To help leaders organize this enormous array of mental forces in a useful way, we created the Six-Cell Balancing Tool. The purpose of this unique tool was to take the nearly infinite assortment of values and assumptions that act on the human decision maker and to place them in six helpful bins. Our goal was to separate these sources of influence into handy intellectual receptacles to ensure that individual, social, and organizational factors receive equal attention. The tool helps leaders complete a balanced diagnosis so they can also develop a complete action plan. By examining individual mental maps, social forces, and organizational factors, leaders were encouraged to continually draw from a wide, balanced range of influence strategies.

Section 3 provided methods for taking stock. It helped leaders answer the questions "What do you have?" and "What do you want?" This, we suggested, is where any long-term, systemwide change starts. Leaders, whether they're corporate executives or frontline team advisors, were encouraged to dream a dream. Knowing that one day they'll face the Cheshire Cat, they were asked to identify, up front, which road they want to travel and why. Leaders were cautioned against coming up with warm-and-fuzzy (yet vague) ideas or clever-sounding catchphrases. Instead, they were asked to paint a detailed and clear picture of their relationship with each of their stakeholders. In particular, leaders were urged to create a fine-tuned vision of their most immediate stakeholder group—their employees. In their "ideal world," how would employees behave on a daily basis? What would be their relationship with each stakeholder group?

Next, leaders were advised to take two distinct and different steps to continually and accurately measure their ongoing efforts. First, they were instructed how to conduct a culture assessment. The goal was to help leaders see beneath espoused values and common problems to the mental maps that drive daily behavior. Armed with an understanding of deeply shared and widely held values and assumptions (culture), leaders would be in a strong position to deal with causes rather than be stuck hacking away at effects.

Having completed our review of a culture assessment, we walked boldly into the middle of an area seldom explored by practical-minded leaders. We studied what it would take to transform surveys, questionnaires, and other "soft" measures from guilt-inducing, noxious probes into helpful, informative, and timely tools—ones that assist in measuring an organization's pulse *before* having to usher in an autopsy. Our goal was twofold. First, to help leaders become informed consumers so they could make sound choices when selecting from competing measurement tools. Second, to arm leaders with frequent, accurate, pulselike measures of Cultural Vitality—including Six-Cell analysis, which helps leaders know what levers to pull to influence change.

The remaining two sections of the book examined methods for taking actions, cell by cell. Leaders (having dreamed their dreams, tested their realities, identified gaps, and picked a handful of targets) were now in a position to take action. So we provided plenty of pages of advice. Unfortunately, since we didn't write a book that came with either training wheels or a truss, we weren't able to include detailed advice for each cell or to dive deep into specific problems. We'll do that in the sequel to this work, *Son of Balance*. Actually, it'll be called *Juggling Chain Saws*. This sequel (the second book in the *Praxis Leadership Series*) will delve into specific problems such as raging mistrust, stifling bureaucracy, and frightening deference to authority. Having created the theoretical underpinnings in this, our first book, our next offering will have the space to explore a wide range of potential actions.

Which returns us to our point. How can *The Balancing Act* be used as a guidebook?

On Becoming a Leader-as-Change Agent

You can call a wharf rat a pony, but I wouldn't put a saddle on it.

If you'd like to use this text as a guide to orchestrating long-term change, start by reading (or at least selectively sampling) this entire work. We assume that if you've found your way to this particular paragraph, you've done more than scan the headings. Once you have a solid understanding of the change process we're recommending, return to chapter 3 and review what it takes to create a detailed, compelling vision. You may already have one. If you do, jump ahead to chapter 4 on culture assessment. If you don't, it's time to dream. You should have a clear vision of what you want, even if you have only a file clerk and a part-time potato peeler reporting to you. The rule here is simple: If you're a leader, you should have a vision.

Actually, the lower you are in the hierarchy, the more likely it is that you've been thinking about what you'd like to see happen once you're in charge. You've probably been thinking about the title of Dr. Seuss's wonderful book *If I Ran the Zoo*. Every time something goes wrong, looks crazy, or makes no sense to you, you think to yourself, "If I ran this place . . ." Okay, so maybe you don't exactly *run* the zoo. Perhaps the reptiles and monkeys fall into someone else's domain. But it's never too early to dream—even if you're only in charge of the two guys who clean out the rhinoceros's cage. Whether you're the CEO or the newest team leader, give chapter 3 a thorough going-over.

Once you have a fairly clear picture of your "ideal" organization, division, department, area, or workgroup in mind, it's time to pull your team of direct reports together and sculpt your shared dream. Use this book as a culture-change driver's manual. Encourage everyone to read chapters 1 through 3. You may be tempted to make copies of key pages and share them with your team, but this would be in direct violation of U.S. copyright law. Should we learn about this vile act, we'd have to notify the copy-cops, who would gleefully throw you into the slammer where you'd be forced to mingle with villainous people of a similar ilk (i.e., thugs who tear the tags off mattresses or maybe even brutes who illegally tap into their neighbor's HBO). Don't make us turn ugly. Pass the book around, buy multiple copies, or read passages aloud (this can be a real treat). Whatever your preference, do what it takes to get everyone on board with the recommended theories, principles, and practices. For your convenience, there's an order form at the back of this book.

From this point on, you should alternate between reading, discussing the topics as a team, and then going out and *doing* something. The visioning chapter should be followed by the culture-assessment section, which, in turn, should be followed by creating a pulse survey. Once you've surfaced your key issues, selected targets for change, and completed a Six-Cell diagnosis, the remaining chapters provide a detailed reference both for understanding what you're seeing and for taking action. Remember to keep your actions focused and to use your pulsing and culture-assessment process as a way of measuring your progress. Some of the steps will take a month or more to complete. Don't lose focus. Tenaciously keep at it, and you'll start the ball rolling in the right direction. That's all you can expect. In the change game, slope is everything.

Don't look for an organizationwide epiphany or sudden, dramatic changes in output. It takes three to five years for widely shared and deeply held values and assumptions to change in a large, complex system—weeks or months in a small team or department. You're not pointing a gun at people and demanding that they hand over their old attitudes; you're taking steps to encourage people to come to new understanding, develop new perspectives, and reorder their values. These silent sources of influence don't exactly jump out at you. In fact, you'll have to go out of your way to surface them during the culture-assessment process, and you'll have to go out of your way to see them as they slowly change as well.

The good news is that outsiders will notice differences. Like an uncle returning after a three-year absence and patting a six-year-old on the head, they'll announce, "You've changed." You'll know that *something* has been going on because your vital indicators will have been slowly improving. However, when outsiders take one look around and announce there's something "different going on," you'll be certain that your efforts are starting to yield lasting dividends.

Of course, none of this will be easy. If you decide to step up to the plate and take a swing at creating lasting changes in Cultural Vitality, you'll be joining a rather exclusive club. As you continually work on your balancing act, doing everything in your power to improve stakeholder satisfaction, not only will your organization benefit immensely, you'll be one of those rare leaders who can go home at night and honestly state, "I'm doing more than putting out fires and making widgets—I'm orchestrating lasting change." Having said and done this, you'll be among a select group of people who can call themselves "leaders" without using the term incorrectly.

HOW ABOUT A LEADER'S DAILY REPERTOIRE?

The concepts we've written about extend their tendrils beyond the change process. They apply to everything a leader does. This should come as no surprise, given that most of the authors' research has consisted of watching people as they labor at everyday tasks. Our goal in studying people at work has been to surface shibboleths—distinguishing characteristics that guide *daily* action. In the next few pages, we'll share five features that color most of what an effective leader does. All were described, in part, in earlier chapters, but are of greater importance than has been discussed thus far. These distinguishing characteristics include (1) an acute self-awareness, (2) a complex self-image, (3) a healthy view of people, (4) a comprehensive toolkit of theories and tactics, and (5) a focused passion for change.

An Acute Self-Awareness

Know thyself.

INSCRIPTION ON THE ORACLE OF APOLLO AT DELPHI, GREECE

Balanced leaders are sensitive self-monitors. They live life at two levels. At one level they analyze problems and take action, like everyone else. At another they don't comb their hair in front of another person without asking what message this could be sending. They realize that, as a boss, they no longer have the luxury of taking action without thinking about how these actions affect others' mental maps. They know that others will draw conclusions, both positive and negative, both correct and incorrect, about the meaning behind their actions. Of course, being self-aware doesn't mean being self-absorbed. On the contrary, effective leaders turn outward, continually keeping their eyes on stakeholder demands.

Also, don't confuse self-aware with meek or mousy. Effective leaders aren't afraid of being in the spotlight. They blend the keen self-monitoring skills of a sensitive facilitator with the flamboyant flair of an actor. This doesn't mean that they're loud, bigger than life, or socially aggressive, but, like any good actor, they know when a raised eyebrow sends the right message and when it doesn't. This self-aware actor, as he or she gathers an increasing number of theories about how people respond to a certain action, eventually grows into the effective leader of symbolic action we discussed in chapter 11.

A Complex Self-Image

Public opinion is a weak tyrant compared with our own private opinion. What a man thinks of himself, that it is which determines, or rather indicates, his fate.

HENRY DAVID THOREAU

Among the millions of mental maps that make up one's personality, perhaps the most important to the leader is his or her sense of self. As young people mature, watching leaders on TV (usually portrayed as the buffoon, such as Mr. Carlson on *WKRP in Cincinnati*; or the vile enemy, such as Roy Biggins on *Wings*), they start to develop an image of a leader. Later, as they observe real bosses at work and eventually start acting as a leader on their own, they draw broad conclusions about what leaders actually do. Eventually these mini-maps of assumptions combine into a global image of who leaders *are*. This global sense of self is often expressed as a metaphor. For example, if you talk with leaders who have labored long in traditional organizations, they'll often describe themselves as a *coach* whose job it is to inspire the team, or a *military general* who inspires the troops, or a *cowboy* who rides the range. (You don't want to work for the last guy.)

Effective leaders view themselves in a very different way—particularly leaders who work in *team* or *empowered* environments. When asked to describe how they see themselves, they don't talk about John Wayne, George S. Patton, or Margaret Thatcher. In fact, they rarely come up with a single role model or clever metaphor. Instead, they talk of how their job is to *create an atmosphere in which others can thrive*. They often use terms such as *catalyst* or *facilitator*. Actually, they have a whole range of terms for describing their various roles as they move from creative visionary to cultural anthropologist to cognitive psychologist. When effective leaders talk about their jobs, the traditional language of power and control is conspicuous by its absence.

Color Me Complex

One day we overheard two executives talking about a personality test they had just completed. It was one of those 30-item surveys that puts you in a box. "I'm red," explained the first executive. "What color are you?" Without missing a beat, the second executive responded, "I'm plaid."

Arriving at a complex self-image doesn't come easily for most leaders. Moving from the role of highly driven individual contributor to that of a leader calls for gut-wrenching changes. Once you're a leader, no longer is it appropriate to leap forth with a stream of energy and a never-ending flow of ideas—only now in front of a group of direct reports. It doesn't work that way. After years of hard work and self-development, leaders now can carry forth their plans only through *others*. A position of authority or expertise (being the brightest engineer, most skilled financier, or cleverest marketer in the room) can actually work against a leader. If not careful, wielding this scepter of influence can stifle others, frighten direct reports, and unwittingly encourage deference.

To survive the transition to leadership, leaders must put their functional expertise on the back burner and become the concerned scientist we described in chapter 2. They don't have to abandon their expertise; they just shouldn't employ it as a club or as their primary tool. Instead, they must hone their skills as a visionary, as an observer of underlying values, as a dramatist, and as a social scientist. Without the skills and theories we've described in earlier chapters, leaders are left performing their old job (while looking over someone else's shoulder), or end up futzing around their office searching for something to do.

Obviously, many leaders do develop these insights. However, those who aggressively seek the skills of the well-balanced leader learn them much faster than those who stumble on them by chance—or gather them slowly and painfully through the school of hard knocks. We hope the theories and skills contained in this book will accelerate a leader's ability to break away from past practices and take on the complex roles required of true leadership.

A Healthy View of People

Each time an actor acts he does not hide; he exposes himself.

JEANNE MOREAU

Effective leaders not only see *themselves* as complex creatures who are not easily pigeonholed, they view *others* the same way. As concerned scientists, they realize that only a detailed and careful analysis will help them understand others. They work hard at avoiding the fundamental attribution error. Rather than assume that people who are behaving in ways inconsistent with the organization's vision are *willfully defying* leadership, they seek more information. They typically start their analysis with the question, "I wonder what led to that response?" They'll even begin their inquiry with an admission that they might have a role in the problem—"I wonder what we've done to create the conditions leading to that reaction?"

How different it is to work with leaders who assume people are interesting, decent, and a delight to be with—even when doing things that are hard to understand. Effective leaders are a great deal like Charles Kuralt, the wonderful American reporter who used to travel across the country and chat with people he thought were interesting. As you watched Mr. Kuralt interview a man in Magoffin County, Kentucky, who sings all the while he's delivering mail on a mule, or as he talks with a fellow in Darwin, Minnesota, who saves twine on what is now the largest ball of twine in the world, you could tell he thought these rather eccentric folks were okay by him. He obviously liked people. You could see it in his eyes and feel it in his questions.[1]

Contrast his treatment of people to similar TV shows with less heart. We're reminded of a relatively mean-spirited one that aired weekly, scanning the globe for what the moderators called "amazing" people. Only the moderators didn't treat their guests as if they were the least bit amazing. They talked to them in ways that let the audience know they thought the guests were loony (e.g., the lady who was knitting a sweater for the president's dog). As they chatted with the "amazing" victim, they'd roll their eyes at just the right moment, and the camera would cut to a live audience pointing and laughing at the poor guest. It was demeaning for guest and moderator alike.

When you think people who are not like you (who don't share your opinions, who care about things you don't find the least bit important, and who seem indifferent to your sacred cows) are inferior or wrong, you will treat them accordingly. They, and everyone within eyeshot, will be aware of what you're thinking. You can't disguise your view of humanity, try as you might. The harder you try to wear a mask of tolerance, the more you reveal yourself. On the other hand, if you think of people as partners, soul mates, colleagues, fascinating creatures, noble by birthright, and rational by nature, you'll employ the language and methods of the concerned scientist.

Developing a positive view of people isn't easy if, like many of us, you've spent a great deal of your life criticizing or constantly being upset by others. This is particularly true of people who've been near the top of their class for most of their life. Moving from "what's wrong with *them?*" to "what's going on here?" calls for constant self-monitoring. You have to catch yourself as you're thinking and saying, "Can you believe what those numskulls did?!" Take a deep breath, and ask instead, "Hmm, what do you suppose led to that?" This simple shift in thought and language slams the door on self-righteousness while opening the gates to understanding. It also puts you in the rather exclusive group of leaders who quickly, readily, and expertly identify and solve problems.

Now, if you think we're describing a pushover or a nice person who's going to finish last, remember, we're summarizing the characteristics of top-performing leaders we've observed in places ranging from coal mines to college campuses. A positive view of people is not an entrance requirement for the Gandhi school of leadership. It's a distinguishing feature of those who master the balancing act.

A Comprehensive Toolkit of Theories and Tactics

Man is a tool-using animal. . . . Without tools he is nothing, with tools he is all.

THOMAS CARLYLE

Self-aware people who come into leadership jobs with a complex and positive view of themselves and others need more than this healthy perspective and honed sensitivity. They need the conceptual and behavioral tools of leadership. A mathematician wouldn't *think* of showing up to work without a protective "phalanx" of theories, formulas, and principles. Leaders should be equally armed. It's always thrilling to watch marketing specialists, nurses, programmers, and other individual contributors who, the moment they're promoted to a leadership position, make an aggressive, active search for leadership theories, models, and practices. As thrilling as it is to watch, it's also rare.

Strangely enough, precious few people assume the same level of thought that has gone into math, physics, finance, law, and other "professional" fields has gone into the field of leadership. They assume that law, medicine, and other professions are entered through the portal of schooling. Leadership, in contrast, comes with an appointment. You're *shaped* through years of formal socialization into a doctor, lawyer, or engineer. You're *dubbed* a leader. It gets worse. Many believe in the widely shared myth that only those who have been dubbed a leader *and* who have been born to the position are going to be effective. The rest will just be managers or individual contributors traveling under a borrowed passport. Consequently, many people, when they first move into a leadership position, don't think for a moment that they need to go to school—formal or otherwise. After all, they've already been "born and dubbed." What else could they need?

It's easy to see how these assumptions are formed. People *do* observe "leadership." It's not as if they're being thrown buck naked into an operating room with a patient, a job description, and a scalpel. Before most people are promoted to a leadership position, they've had a chance to watch good and bad examples and develop a long list of ideas of what they'll do once *they* "run the zoo." They've been schooled on the job. In addition, leadership assignments often come years after formal schooling has been completed. People aren't about to take a couple of years out of the shank of their career just to bone up on a job they've already been given. Their lifestyle won't permit it. And then there's always the nagging suspicion that the material served up by behavioral scientists, applied or otherwise, isn't that easy to turn into practice.

Who wants to take the time to study something that isn't going to help anyway? Combined, these forces lead most people to treat leadership as an appointment, and not as a set of hard-earned theory and skills.

Skilled leaders aren't born to the job any more than skilled surgeons are. Genetics may play a role, but so do the 12 or more years of schooling required before your average citizen is allowed to cut open a heart and repair it. Most countries would do well to put leaders through a similar education process before they allow them to cut open organizations and repair them. Okay, so nobody is going to demand 12 years of formal schooling as a prerequisite to taking the helm, but there's a lot of room between the over 4,000 days of education it takes to be a surgeon and the zero days it takes to be dubbed a leader.

We're not going to change this curious inequity, but *you* can. You can set your own standard for education and personal development. The fact that you're reading these words suggests that you're already proactive. Keep up your quest for knowledge. Don't leap out of one profession, steeped in its own language, theory, and philosophy, only to land on the barren ground of intuition, bad examples, and faith in your ability to apply "common sense." Leadership deserves the same care as any other discipline. You don't have to find yourself on barren ground, given the vast opportunity for learning. For one thing, there's a veritable wellspring of leadership theories available.

The Written Word

There are worse crimes than burning books. One of them is not reading them.

JOSEPH BRODSKY

Over the past 20 years, several authors have provided leadership material that is theory based, practical, *and* accessible to the leader. We've tried to write our own blend of theory and practice in this book. Stephen R. Covey, Tom Peters, Harold J. Leavitt, William G. Ouchi, Peter M. Senge, James A. Belasco, Michael Hammer, John Champy, Kenneth H. Blanchard, Elliot Aronson, Robert B. Cialdini, and others have all provided insights that are well researched, theoretically sound, and fairly easy to read. Check the *Recommended Reading* section at the end of this book for a short list of books that we've found to be good reads for the aggressive leader looking to expand his or her toolkit of theories and practices.

Now, in order to find the time to open a book or two, you might have to change a work norm. You'll have to make it acceptable, even laudable, to read at work. Another one of this country's pathetic little tragedies is the fact that executives who pride themselves on the intellectual prowess of the workforce do everything but burn books when it comes to leadership education. Most leaders wouldn't dare be caught reading at work. There's an unspoken rule that says leaders should be busy *doing* something, something important that doesn't involve sitting at a desk and, *gulp*, reading. Of course, no one will actually come out and say that it's bad to read. It's sort of like clipping your toenails—you won't find a policy against it, but it's not the kind of thing you do at your desk either.

Follow the lead of Elaine, a midlevel manager working for, of all places, a cookie manufacturer. She shows up to work each day with a newspaper article, pamphlet, book, or some other form of written material. During open times and casual moments, she takes a few minutes to read. If she has trouble finding an open time, she schedules a half hour on her calendar for a meeting—and meets with a book. (This little intervention alone, structuring learning time into her weekly calendar, is worth more than its weight in gold.) She obviously views herself as a student of human interaction. She's constantly studying new ideas and methods. She's also enormously practical. She doesn't wait until she's digested a tome before taking action. As soon as she stumbles onto passages she's found particularly insightful or interesting, she shares them with her colleagues over lunch, in a meeting, or at the watercooler.

Single-handedly, this enthusiastic leader-scholar has created a passion for learning within her own circle of leaders. How unique is she? Consider the following statistic: The average person, after graduating from college, reads from his or her field (*rounded* to the nearest whole number) zero books a year (a round number if ever we've heard one).[2] Call us pessimistic, but we're betting that this is not a good sign.

If people watched you and your colleagues at work, would they describe you as "energetic, even passionate, *learners*"?

OJL (On-the-Job Learning)

There are three principal means of acquiring knowledge available to us: observation of nature, reflection, and experimentation. Observation collects facts; reflection combines them; experimentation verifies the result of that combination.

DENIS DIDEROT

To be honest, one of the best schools of leadership is found on the job— that is, if you know how to move from actor to learner. In chapter 4 we suggested several methods for surfacing values and assumptions. All required the ability to see beyond the immediacy of the moment to the underlying values and assumptions driving behavior. This ability to put on a different lens can help you learn leadership and other interpersonal skills as well. As you sit in meetings, follow the advice of the eighteenth-century French philosopher Denis Diderot: Collect facts through observation. Watch for actions that work and ones that don't. Look for shibboleths. You know who your opinion leaders are. What do they *do* that makes them opinion leaders? Watch them in action. You know the leaders with a reputation for both fairness and achievement. Watch them as they talk with their direct reports. What do *they* do? Look for identifiable behaviors you can adopt.

For example, when observing presentations, you'll notice that those who step away from the overhead projector and walk out into the audience make better emotional contact than those who act as if they're chained to the audiovisual equipment. Those who tell engaging stories to support their facts and figures keep the audience's attention. Individuals who vary their verbal pace, moving rapidly over certain phrases and slowing down to punctuate others, are more enjoyable to listen to. Those who engage the audience by asking questions, breaking them into small groups, or using other activities that turn the audience from passive observers into participants keep the energy higher and make involvement more widespread.

Every one of these presentation skills can be found in an introductory communications text. None were identified by dressing rats in tuxedos and placing them at podiums. They're shibboleths, duly recorded and taught by people who watch other people in front of audiences. They're recommended by scholars and authors who observe facts, combine them into mini-theories, and conduct experiments by trying certain actions and watching the results. It's not rocket science. Leaders do it all the time. Besides, most of us have so much intellectual capacity that sits idle during meetings and presentations that focusing on the *how* of what's going on gives us something to do—beyond counting the holes in the ceiling tiles or memorizing our fingerprint swirl patterns.

Actually, even though most of us have the intellectual capacity to focus on multiple targets, it isn't easy to get ourselves to do it. It takes discipline to pull yourself out of the "tractor beam" of content and into the field of process. However, as it becomes second nature for leaders to observe interactions at two levels, their insights grow geometrically. From one level they learn the content of the job; from the other, the touchstones of effective human interaction.

> A leader who is a perpetual student of behavior at work continually takes part in one of life's little pleasures—the thrill of peeling back the onion of human interaction and discovering the shibboleths of success.

A Focused Passion for Change

Without passion man is a mere latent force . . . like the flint which awaits the shock of the iron before it can give forth its spark.

HENRI-FRÉDÉRIC AMIEL

There's a danger in what we've recommended so far. We've covered more than enough theories and practices to last a lifetime. A leader could easily become overwhelmed by chasing too many rabbits. Our goal has been to help lighten the load through understanding, not to add to it by creating one more to-do list that goes unheeded. This is where focus is so important. Leaders (following contemporary bumper-sticker advice) should *think globally* by putting in systems that continually keep track of all stakeholders, but then *act locally* by focusing on improvements, one action at a time. Actually, juggling provides a good example. If you've ever read one of those "juggling for idiots" books, you know that after you've figured out how to keep two beanbags in the air, you next learn what it takes to get the third one started. Then you just continue doing everything else you mastered before. You focus on one action, and then return to the routine. The same is true for the fourth, fifth, and sixth beanbags. One new action, then back to the routine. (Of course, physical limitations soon come into play or we'd all be wearing fake red noses and riding unicycles.)

Self

Let's look at a leadership example. When the authors work with leaders one on one, we rarely focus on more than one skill at a time. For example, when coaching a leader who was trying to involve direct reports in more decisions as part of a "global" plan to move decisions closer to the customer, we looked at what he was doing to both encourage and discourage involvement. It turns out he mercilessly dominated meetings with his own ideas and suggestions. In order for him to "act locally," we encouraged him to listen more and to increase the number of questions he asked. To punctuate the point, we drew a large question mark on a 3 x 5 card and suggested he put it in front of him during the next three meetings and restrict his entire vocal activity to asking questions—as an experiment. This experience alone changed his perspective on what his immediate direct reports were able to do, left to their own creative devices. Several of them, given some air time and the permission to speak, were (and we quote), "practically brilliant."

Next, we looked at *when* it made sense to chip in with his opinions and *why*. Our goal wasn't to cut off all his ideas. We simply wanted to come up with a theory of when it made sense to speak his mind and when to hold back. Remember, we were working with a highly creative and energetic person whose working assumption was, "No idea of mine should ever go unexpressed." Behavior by behavior, theory by theory, this willing student made the transition from a dominating, moderately despised manager to what his direct reports eventually described as a leader who was "positively presidential."

Apply the same technique to yourself. As you read about, observe, are coached in, or otherwise become aware of leadership skills, try them one at a time. Based on your ongoing diagnosis, pick a skill-set from one of the chapters found in this book, and work on it—and it alone. Master one domain, then move on.

Others

Now, when working with*others*, leaders maintain focus by continually talking about, asking about, getting excited about, and otherwise spending time on the one area the leadership team has targeted for change. For instance, let's return to the group that was trying to improve their "openness" or willingness to admit they were falling behind schedule. The leaders of this organization kept focus. They brought up the problem in every meeting. They thanked people who talked about barriers they were facing. They worked on their scheduling process. Cell by cell they surfaced and removed barriers. They started with a stakeholder-based diagnosis, looked at what was going on in their own culture that was leading to the core problems, picked a target for change, focused their energy on it, measured it to see what was happening, and stuck with it until the problem was resolved. Then another problem bubbled to the surface, and the leadership team took it on with the same focused passion.

As a practicing change agent, if you're an omnivore who craves more than a bubbling pot of cooked vegetables for dinner, chase rabbits one at a time. (Please write us if you have a similarly helpful vegetarian metaphor.)

STEPPING OFF THE TREADMILL OF HABIT

No one would remember the Good Samaritan if he'd only had good intentions—he had money as well.

Margaret Thatcher

We now turn to our final challenge. What does it take to remember, on the fly, new leadership theories and actions? Of all the problems we've dealt with to date, this may be the most difficult. When you think about it, how many of us know, *really* know, that, if we provided more praise and recognition to friends, family, strangers, employees, and anyone else we come in contact with, we'd all be a lot better off? Who *doesn't* know that? You could ask any person at random what ingredient is missing from today's leadership formula, and he or she would respond, "Bosses need to be lavish in their approbation," or words to that effect. The need for more praise is the modern maxim of management. In spite of this painfully obvious knowledge, we don't do much. We, like the Good Samaritan, have good intentions, but, unlike him, we don't always spend the cash and actually *do* something. Why?

I'm So Embarrassed!

To answer this question, let's tune in to the "Oprah Winfrey Show" of August 4, 1995. She opened the program with the following statement:

> *I really don't like to beg, but I would beg you to watch this show today. I think it's going to be so important for so many people, particularly if you have children or you know somebody who has children. Serial killer Ted Bundy charmed and convinced young girls to get in his car by making up stories. His trusting victims believed his lies and they wound up dead. He killed 27 women.*

> *Using a hidden camera, we conducted an experiment to see how hard it would be to lure kids into dangerous situations. The results were terrifying. This stranger was easily able to lure teenage girls, young boys, college-age women, and even moms outside to his van.*

The show was riveting. Ken Wooden, a child safety expert, and J. J. Bittenbinder, a Chicago police detective, shared with Oprah and the viewing audience just how easy it is to lure people—adults and children alike—into a van. Wooden would approach mall patrons and ask for help, offer $20 for a job, promise $100 for a short "just say no to drugs" video shot, or pose as a law officer who suspected someone had been tampering with their car.

After the people walked up to the van, the van door opened, revealing the camera. Only then would Wooden tell the subject what was going on. How did they respond? Nobody said, "How funny," or "That's interesting," or "What a surprise." Nobody. To a person they lamented, "I'm embarrassed!" Why? Because every one of them *knew better.* They had seen similar shows, been to lectures, and watched announcements on TV. They *knew better,* but they still fell for the trap. So they were embarrassed.

It's wonderful that experts are working hard to help people make themselves more prepared for this dangerous world. Unfortunately, little of it seems to be taking. As you watch the experts practically plead with the audience not to follow strangers out to a van, you're left with the haunting feeling, "This isn't working." You showed us people who already knew better, and they all fell for the lure. Why would one more similar attempt to teach people, no matter how sincere, make a whit of difference? As people from the audience asked questions, the advice offered by the experts included, "Be careful," "Trust your instincts," "Don't overreact," and "Talk to your children." Nothing new there. So why expect it to make a difference?

This correct advice isn't good enough. There's no way current strategies will ever overcome the overwhelming power of social forces. They obviously have done little to protect people from the pull of routine interaction. People don't want to offend others. They don't want to be cold to every person they ever see outside of their close circle of friends. Besides, they can't tell where safety *stops* and danger *starts.* They don't recognize the telltale signs. So they lend a hand, look for ways to make money, and worry about their car—not because they've forgotten about the dangers of life, but because they can't see these dangers when they come wrapped in the package of familiarity.

Just when it looked as if the show would end on one more reminder to be careful, Wooden offered a piece of advice that could make a difference. When asked how parents could teach their kids that "this can happen to them," Wooden explained: "Teach the lures like we teach the alphabet."

He was right. It's all about lures.

Invisible Lures

Leaders who are trying to break the bonds of current culture are lured onto the treadmill of habit just as easily as people are enticed into a van. Comfortable, familiar surroundings certainly don't invite *new* habits. They invite *old* behaviors—in some cases, behaviors that have been linked to the same stimulus for decades. For example, a direct report approaches you with a problem, asking for advice. What do you do? You give advice, of course. Who wouldn't? But what if you've decided that people should be coming up with their own recommendations instead of running to you with a simple question of what to do? You decide that when the next person asks for help, you're not going to give a suggestion. Instead, you're going to come back with, "You're close to the problem. What do you think it'll take?"

If you're anything like the leaders we've worked with, you'll fail to live up to your promise 85 percent of the time. You'll spit out your recommendation, almost without thinking. If you're like 700 students we tested, you'll spout your answer 95 percent of the time. These, by the way, were students who were specifically warned against offering a suggestion less than 30 minutes before the test. Given that people are rewarded from birth to spit out answers to questions, this particular form of employee involvement scarcely stands a chance.

As a leader, you'll be lured onto similar treadmills of habit unless you can find ways to say, "Uh-oh. I'm being invited down the old path." Without recognizing the cue, lure, or "entry condition" that says it's time to try out something new, you're very likely to follow your traditional ways much like a rat running a maze.

We first learned of the danger of knee-jerk reactions while conducting research with a group of frontline supervisors in Columbus, Ohio. As they finished the final day of a weeklong problem-solving course, they exited the training room to return to work not 20 feet away. Before they could take a couple of paces, they were met by a group of employees who had run into problems while their bosses had been busy in training. The supervisors immediately started solving the problems. We watched in horror as none of them employed the problem-solving skills they had studied and practiced for four days. The frightening part of this observation was that many of the supervisors had scored high marks on tests that measured both motivation and ability to employ the skills they had just learned. In fact, the ink on the tests was still wet. The subjects had the skills and the desire to employ them, but, given the opportunity, they didn't. Why?

We immediately called the supervisors back into the training room and asked them why they hadn't used the skills they'd just learned. After a moment of puzzled reflection, one sheepishly responded, "I never thought of it." Others chimed in with similar explanations. When we suggested they probably weren't motivated, they argued they really *did* want to try new behaviors, but fell victim to old habits. Like racehorses champing at the bit, when the gate sprung open, they were off and running without so much as a moment's thought. The supervisors faced a stimulus (a familiar problem), and they reacted with a familiar response (their normal way of handling problems)—before "thinking."

The people in the mall and the leaders in the employee-involvement experiment followed the same pattern. After responding to a stimulus in the same way thousands of times, they respond to it again without "thinking." Leaders instantaneously gave an answer like the shopper who walked out to the van, carrying on the "friendly neighbor" script, almost as if they were actors in a play.

Remembering Where and When

The true art of memory is the art of attention.

SAMUEL JOHNSON

Changing old habits is never easy. When the habits are stimulated into action almost unconsciously, they're particularly difficult to shake. Listen to one of the authors as he tells of his personal battle with a disgusting "noncognitive" reaction.

I Feel Like a Salmon

About 15 years ago we bought our first house. We hadn't been in the home more than an hour when I walked onto the deck to take a look at the view. As I stood at the edge of the deck, my eyes drank in the expansive panorama until I eventually cast a glance downward. Six feet below me lay our backyard.

And then it happened. Before I had time to think about what I was doing, I spat off the deck onto the grass below. I had been married for 11 years when this took place, and during all those years, my wife had never seen me spit. That is until that fateful day on the deck.

It's never pleasant to be on the receiving end of a look of disgust from your mate, but to have legitimately earned a loathsome glance made it that much worse. I hadn't exactly picked my teeth with the salad fork, but by my wife's calculation, spitting came in a close second. She expressed her disappointment in me for the next 10 minutes or so while my two daughters sat nearby taking notes.

The part that bothered me about the incident was that I hadn't really spat out of choice. It had just sort of happened—not unlike swallows returning to San Juan Capistrano or salmon swimming upstream (an argument, by the way, that nobody bought). I had spent a good share of my youth on the docks of Puget Sound and, as part of a childhood ritual, had leaned over the edge and spit into the water a few thousand times. Consequently, when I leaned over the deck some 20 years later, I was seemingly stripped of all semblance of choice and propelled back to my youthful habit. Ptooey. It wasn't exactly genetic, but it was close.

I say this because, in spite of my family's revulsion, I continued to spit off the deck every time I wandered near the edge. I never actually *chose* to spit—not in any way that would hold up in court. In fact, had I actually thought about it, I'm sure I *wouldn't* have spit. But I *didn't* think about it. Like one of Pavlov's dogs that automatically salivated at the sound of a bell, I spat at the sight of a ledge. In fact, it got to the point where I knew I was in trouble before the spit hit the ground. But I kept on spitting.

I became interested in overcoming the habit because, not only did it affect my social skills, it also had direct relevance to our work with leaders. Virtually everyone we had taught new leadership skills faced a similar problem. They didn't spit, but they did react to old stimuli in ways that looked suspiciously noncognitive. They walked out of the training room and stepped into the enticing, comfortable culture that had elicited all of their old behaviors.

Stepping onto the Treadmill

Discovering that humans can respond very much like laboratory animals facing levers and mazes is not a particularly popular or heart-warming revelation. In fact, battles raged for over a decade between Berkeley and Harvard over that very subject. Clark L. Hull at Harvard argued for a stimulus-response model of behavior enactment, while Edward C. Tolman at Berkeley fought for a cognitive-based one. Tolman eventually won. It was he and his colleagues who took some of the first steps down the long road that eventually led to the social cognitive model we've drawn so heavily on throughout this book.

But what about the supervisors who fell back into their old habits without "thinking," the people lured to the van, or that nasty habit of spitting off the deck? None of the people involved in these circumstances looked much like careful decision makers. They weren't exactly examining potential consequences and coming up with a net value. Far from it. It turns out that Hull's stimulus-response theory captures a side of human behavior that can't be easily explained with a decision-making model. There are times when humans act out routines without much forethought or obvious attention. When the routine consists of a predictable conversation (as was the case with the supervisors), the semirigid behavior string (behaviors linked together one after the other) is referred to as a "script."

For example, you walk into a fast-food restaurant and order a chicken sandwich. You know the person taking the order will ask you if you want fries. If you say yes, you'll be asked if you want large. The same holds for a drink. This particular fast-food routine is so familiar you might even make your order while carrying on a side conversation. You know both sides of the conversation so well that the routine script doesn't require your "full attention."

Contrast this fast-food experience with a not-so-routine encounter such as ordering from a gourmet menu in Paris. You don't know the language very well, so you have to choose each word carefully. And then there's the annoying problem of combining the words into coherent French sentences. You also aren't very familiar with the local cooking, so you don't know exactly how the food will be prepared. In fact, you're worried you'll end up with french-fried brains or sweat socks à la king. You don't carry on a side conversation when ordering in Paris.

Now, imagine that before you walked into the restaurant, you decided you wanted to ask for extra napkins. In which location do you suppose you would be more likely to remember the napkins—at the fast-food restaurant in the U.S. or at the gourmet restaurant in France? If our research holds true, you'd do better in France. Ordering napkins in France would be part of a larger interaction that would require careful thinking and your undivided attention. The fast-food restaurant, on the other hand, might be such a comfortable sanctuary that you unthinkingly step onto the treadmill of habit and entirely forget about the deviation (extra napkins).

Breaking away from what is comfortable or routine remains an enormous barrier to adopting new behaviors. If we don't find cues or reminders that tell us to act differently, we're likely to be stimulated into old scripts that reap old results. To this day, only a fraction of what is learned in skill-based leadership classes finds its way onto the work floor because most participants walk out the training room door and step right onto the treadmill of habit. Books fare even less well. Unless something changes fairly drastically, people will continue to climb into vans, spit off decks, and fall into old leadership routines. Even if Oprah *begs* people to listen and even if the safety experts tell stories that make the hair stand up on the back of your neck, by themselves these tactics aren't enough. Ten years from now the same people will be making the same pleas with the same results. These energetic change-agents need to take the focus off their audience and look at why their tactics aren't working. They need to take their focus off how bad the outcomes are and shift to what the cues, lures, and "entry conditions" look like.

Curves Ahead

What can we do to "cue" (remind) ourselves to break away from old habits and try new skills? Perhaps we can learn from the highway department.

If ever there were a series of behaviors linked together into a comfortable routine, driving a car has to rank close to the top of the list. Most of us are so at ease behind the wheel that we devote only a fraction of our attention to controlling the vehicle. We carry on conversations, listen to music, talk on the phone, and in some cases (much to others' dismay) even do our taxes—all while driving.

Knowing that people fall into a comfortable stupor behind the wheel, highway experts post signs that warn of possible disruptions. When a road makes a sudden turn, experts don't erect a placard *after* the turn to explain why people are lucky to have survived the dangerous curve. They erect a sign that says "Curve Ahead." The intent is to pull drivers out of their routines, focus them on what they're about to do, and change their current behavior—*before* they get into trouble.

You'll note that with highways we have the luxury of posting signs just before a change in behavior is required. If signs were posted, say, five miles before a curve, people would tend to forget them. In fact, knowing exactly where to place the sign is a bit of a science. When it comes to cues, timing is everything. For example, there probably isn't an adult in the Western world who doesn't know that if a nuclear bomb were to be detonated 10 miles away, you shouldn't look at the blast. Only a fool would, right? But what if you and 59,999 other fans were sitting in Jack Murphy stadium watching the Chargers, and (heaven forbid) a terrorist ignited a nuclear device in La Jolla? Sixty thousand of you would turn your heads in unison and look at the flash of light. You wouldn't "think" about it; you'd just do it. Within seconds you'd all realize what was happening and cover your eyes. Of course, every last one of you would be thinking, *"Uh-oh, I stared at the flash."*

On the other hand, if a warning were sounded 30 seconds before the blast, not one of you would fry your retinas. Big deal.

An Ounce of Cues is Worth More Than a Pound of Harangue

When it comes to stopping knee-jerk responses:

- Cues or reminders are helpful.
- Timing is everything.

For example, guess what the "spitter" did to cue himself not to spit? He posted a sticky note on the door leading to the deck that stated, "Ledge Ahead." Then, every time he opened the door, he was reminded (moments before the impending stimulus) that, if he wasn't careful, he'd fall into his childhood habit. The sign helped him put *decision making* back into what had become a *stimulus-response chain*. In fact, after two weeks he was able to take the sign down. Perhaps the unrelenting disgust from his family eventually would have motivated him to think about the edge (although several months of haranguing hadn't worked yet), but a simple sign did the trick.

By the way, this "unrelenting disgust strategy" is quite popular. It's a subset of the fundamental attribution error. People *could* do what's required if they really, really, really cared, so we harangue, plead, beg, and then act disgusted when people don't do what they should. (Dang them, they just didn't *care* enough.) It's certainly what most safety experts are doing as a way of keeping people away from the van. Drawing from the same school, if you want to catch people before they mess up, you can use fear. One day a little neighbor boy of one of the authors kept asking him what time it was every 10 minutes or so. He was supposed to come home "before dark," but he never knew how late he could stay because *before dark* looked exactly like *way before dark*, and he ended up waiting too long and got a spanking. Fear kept him from forgetting, but it didn't help him.

Fear is, indeed, one way of keeping people focused. Unfortunately, when you have to be frightened of something that could come out of the blue at any moment and with little or no notice, the fear has to be unrelenting. For example, one of the few children that Ken Wooden was unable to coax out of the mall had just such an unrelenting sense of anxiety. His mother explained, "I really scared him. I scare him all the time.... And I just tell him *every day*, 'Never go with anybody.'" Every day, whoa.

We'll return to the child-safety issue later. For now, we'll suggest that in most leadership instances there are simpler, less tiring, and more humane solutions than creating a generic, unrelenting, often haunting sense of anxiety. For example, one of the neighbors eventually gave the fearful little neighbor boy a watch for his birthday. It was his "Curve Ahead" sign. The spitter put up a sticky note. Many leaders are currently putting up "Curve Ahead" signs all around them as they fight to break from tradition.

In short, when it comes to breaking away from the treadmill of habit, you can threaten and harangue, but we hold to the belief that an ounce of cues is worth more than a pound of harangue.

Signposts, Cues, Lures, Entry Conditions, and Other Aids

The palest ink is better than the best memory.

CHINESE PROVERB

How can leaders and others put up warning signs and cues? Let's look at several successful strategies.

Red Dots. For several years, consultants and therapists taught people how to reduce stress. The skills themselves were fairly easy, mostly breathing techniques that could be taught in a few hours. Unfortunately, the training didn't help much. It turns out that by the time your average stress graduate thought to apply the three-step technique, it was too late. They were already pumping adrenaline and bile. The "things out there" that led to stress were still leading them to stress. It was those nasty old stimuli leading to the same old response.

So, here's what the instructors began to do. They asked participants to identify the situations that normally led to stress. For some it was bumper-to-bumper traffic. For others it was arriving late. Others broke into a sweat over presentations or speeches. Each was instructed to put a small red dot on or near a physical object that would serve as a danger sign. Some put a dot on their watch, others on the steering wheel, others on the door frame above the door to the meeting room. The idea was to have participants tailor their own warning signs, ones that would cue them into their techniques *before* they were upset. To the extent people could predict locations and circumstances that led to stress, the dots helped out immensely.

As the authors have worked with leaders, we've asked them to use the same technique. Some have put dots on the printer that spits out bad results, traditionally leading to a headhunt. Others have put them on their phone where they used to get hooked into arguments with vendors and suppliers. Others have put them on the entrance to a meeting room where they had been sucked into arguments rather than use dialogue. In every case, the leaders look at the dot, stop, remember what they're *trying* to do instead of what they *used* to do, and are far better prepared to avoid the sucking effect of the black hole of tradition.

The Walking Accident. More than a handful of the leaders we've worked with over the years suggest that they can't put up a sign or place a red dot where it needs to go because the stimulus that takes them down the road of habit is a person. It could be anyone, ranging from bosses to customers. They can't exactly put a dot on the person's forehead, although most would like to. If the person in question drops out of the clouds and drags them into the mire, it's hard to do anything. However, if there's even a moment before the conversation starts, leaders can cue themselves to watch out for curves ahead. Place a "mental red dot" on the forehead of people who bring out the worst in you. As you first come in contact with them, cue yourself to be on your best behavior. Refuse to be dragged into the mire of your worst habits.

Notes. A variation on the dot theme is the use of notes, memos, signs, banners, and slogans. As motivators, these devices don't help a lot. Not many people join a cause as the result of a clever bumper sticker. However, as reminders, notes can be quite helpful. To the extent that the cues are timely, they can make a big difference. Perhaps the most useful written cue is the built-in agenda item. Leaders who want to focus attention on a core value or topic build it into their daily agenda as a standing item. That way, every meeting starts with the hot item. Nobody has to remember to bring it up.

A senior vice president of a bank that was trying to take the focus*off* how many loans were being made and put it *on* the profitability of the loans put the following question on the back of a picture that sat on his desk, "Tell me about our loans. How profitable are they?" The note was placed so he could see it every time someone walked into his office, and every time someone did, he asked the question.

Manufacturing managers who are trying to reduce costs often post displays of component parts and their respective prices at the point the parts are used—keeping costs visible. The theme park we referred to in chapter 4 posted its three key indicators in the open for everyone to see, every day. One client the authors work with posts stakeholder outcome numbers everywhere. The purpose is to regularly remind everyone of the need for balance. Nobody holds a party when one stakeholder indicator improves if another stakeholder measure takes a nose dive.

Calendars. Since most leaders are practically driven by their day planners, it's wise to use them to bolster Cultural Vitality. In addition to using the handy forms to schedule meetings, sit down at the beginning of the week, look at your meetings, and then write in a reminder of what you want to achieve in each. In one meeting, focus on what you should be doing differently as a leader. In another, decide what you want to reward. In another, focus on what it'll take to bring an opinion leader on board. Don't go into a single calendared event without at least two goals—the ostensible purpose and the cultural one. Oh yes, and remember the strategy of Elaine, the cookie manager. She scheduled time for what she thought was important, even if it didn't involve anyone else.

The Random Reminder. As many people log into the computer each morning, they're greeted by a vocabulary word, a clever expression, or a joke of the day. We think most leaders would benefit a great deal more from daily reminders of their key cultural focus than they'll ever gain from knowing the meaning of *quercitron*. Ask your specialists to build something into your software that pops a paragraph up to the screen each time you log in. Then, as you develop gaps and strategies, write a handful of cues and do's—things that remind you what you're trying to do differently and advice on actions you might take. Put your computer to work on cultural issues.

The Confederate. Select a colleague who sees you in action, and share your plans for personal and team improvement. Contract with each other to provide helpful feedback in core areas. Pick a single behavior, and coach each other. Schedule your feedback sessions. Bring more eyes into the game.

The Hunt. Set aside a time of day when you'll devote all of your attention and emotional energy to support the mission or change initiative. Take a half hour to hunt for opportunities to praise people who are going the extra mile. Make a big deal about teams that have embraced a new concept that aligns them more closely with your mission. Leap on opportunities to teach, espouse, symbolically act, and otherwise let people know *what* you believe and *why*. Try out a new concept you've recently learned in training. In short, act like an FBI agent going through weapons training in one of those mock-up villages where thugs, mothers, gangsters, and other plywood characters pop up and demand action. Stare at every interaction and ask, "What cultural weapon can I draw from my behavioral repertoire?" Don't shoot at every passerby. Most are innocent bystanders. Nevertheless, bring to bear the same focused energy of the federal agent who's really worried about acting appropriately (shooting at a child or waving innocently at an Uzi-toting gang member both lead to disastrous results). Nobody will pull you onto the treadmill of habit if you're completely focused on modeling correct behavior.

The "Uh-oh." The most common sign of straying from one's vision comes in the form of disappointment, stress, tension, anger, and other strong, negative emotions. For example, your dream is to influence people through a gentle sharing of mental maps, yet you find yourself caught up in the passion of winning an argument, forcing your ideas, pressing your points, and wielding the map-maker's pen like a sword. Uh-oh. You're trying to encourage people to own up when they're starting to fall behind a deadline, and the first time somebody takes a risk by admitting that they're slipping behind, you hand him his head on a platter. Uh-oh, again.

In both cases, you're halfway down the wrong path when you catch yourself. Don't make the mistake of assuming you have to complete the journey. Also, don't let disappointment lead to self-flagellation. Let it guide your corrective action. When you find yourself embarrassed by what you've just done (or are working up a head of steam), stop and suggest that there's probably a better way to handle the situation, and then simply start over.

The narrow (and often unforgiving) path toward mastering the complexities of change and leadership is rarely traveled in straight lines. Instead, it's traveled by leaders who occasionally step off the edge or bump up against a wall. Successful ones find their way back on course by using their reactions of frustration, embarrassment, and anger as cues to change rather than as fuel to propel them further into the abyss. Airplanes are off-course the majority of the time, yet they make it to their destinations. Keep self-correcting, and you will get back on track.

The Entry Condition. We can't finish this section without getting back to the van. None of what we've suggested helps deal with the toughest of all circumstances—a situation in which almost every cue moves you toward the abyss and you don't know it until it's too late. To avoid having to walk around in a constant state of heightened awareness, the question becomes, "What are the *telltale signs* or *entry conditions* that can serve as reminders, and how can you make use of them?"

First, let's suggest that the intuition or gut that experts encourage people to rely on is fed, not by mystical forces, but by subtle mini-theories. For example, you're walking in New York City at night, looking for an off-off-Broadway show. You make a wrong turn. As you continue down a dark street, you notice that you're the only person around. You take five steps and then turn around and head back into the crowded area. You rely on a mental map of safety tips. It cries out to you—you're in a big city, it's dark, it's shabby, and you should never, ever, be in a place where there aren't lots of people who can come running to your aid. Nothing can entice you to walk down that street. *Nothing?* Your "gut" isn't what's telling you what to do. It's your brain.

How about the van? If safety experts can't come up with specific, identifiable cues, people will continue to be lured away. Telling kids to watch out for strangers doesn't work. They think that strangers, given how you're describing them as potential kidnappers, are ugly, wear a Jason mask, and wield a knife. You have to teach them what strangers look like. You have to describe what you *mean* and what you *don't mean* by using contrasts. Pictures would help. By the time you're through, every kid should be able to explain that strangers are people they don't know. They can look like grandmas, clowns, police officers, or even moms and dads. They can be smiling, whistling, singing, tap dancing, or roller skating. The first warning sign comes when they walk up close to you and you're alone. The second warning sign comes when they talk to you.

We won't continue this discussion here (because it belongs in a kit for teaching kids how to avoid danger—which isn't the focus of this book). We *will* say, however, that until safety experts become cueing experts, they'll continue to fall woefully short. To become cueing experts, they'll have to identify specific warning signs that people can recognize. They'll have to conduct classes, and then, just as they did for Oprah, test the kids a few days later as they come home from school or walk in the mall. Until they know exactly what it takes to teach kids in a way that actually works, they'll end up like every other motivational speaker who thinks he or she is helping out with useful hints but who, in fact, does little more than focus on how awful present circumstances are and how we all ought to try harder.

What does this have to do with leadership? A great deal. Leaders, as they walk down the path of culture change, need to be aware of the danger signs as well. Without knowing the traps that lurk in the dark corners of tradition, they, and the people around them, will be lured into their old ways. They too must be aware of entry conditions and teach them to others. For instance, you've decided to form teams. The second day into the process, an employee approaches a newly appointed team leader and complains, "Jan isn't doing her fair share of the work. You need to go talk to her." Sounds innocent enough. Leaders have done this a thousand times before. Wrong. An alarm should go off. In the vision of the future, employees talk to *each other* about problems before they ever dream of bringing the leader into the picture. Being invited to help out is a lure. It never was before.

Try another one. A workgroup has been invited to take part in more decisions. The team leader started the process with a meeting devoted to empowerment. A couple of days later, you (the team leader's boss) are stopped in the hallway by a disgruntled employee. She explains, "You've got to do something about Scott. He met with us last week and told us that we get to make all the decisions from now on. Yesterday he burst into our area, screaming about a customer order that none of us wanted to do, and he told us we had to do it anyway. He threatened two of us with our jobs, swore at Maria [you'll be hearing about that I'm sure], and started tossing stuff around like a kid throwing a tantrum. Oh yeah, and when I told him I was going to talk to you about this whole mess, he said, 'Big deal. That windbag won't do a thing.' This empowerment stuff is all a bunch of hooey."

This little interaction is filled with fairly serious problems. In addition to the fact that Scott may have behaved incredibly unprofessionally (we have only one side of the story), the employee suggested that team members were told they would now get to make *all the decisions*. Red flag. However, as you might imagine, being told that one of your direct reports, a leader no less, called you a "windbag" may lure you away to the other topic. Your emotions might whisk you down the path of righteous indignation and away from a terribly inaccurate assumption and common misinterpretation. This, by the way, is not an either-or situation. Both problems need to be handled. However, half of the problem may be missed if you're lured into the van of vengeance.

To avoid cultural lures, anticipate how your vision will be turned into a nightmare through misinterpretation. What are the likely mistakes? What are the unhealthy habits that aren't going to go down without a fight? Talk to others who've gone through a similar process. Identify telltale signs of problems or "moments of truth." Being on the lookout for these common misunderstandings (and all the other cues) will help leaders step off the treadmill of habit and onto the road of change.

CLOSING REMARKS

There is no such thing as a perfect leader. . . . If there is one, he is only pretending, like a pig inserting scallions into its nose in an effort to look like an elephant.

Liu Shao-ch'i

Our search for leadership shibboleths has taken us on a long, and some-times intimidating, journey. One might quickly conclude that the balancing act is achieved only through monumental acts of talent accomplished by only a handful of leader-savants, imaginary charac-ters, or pathological liars. The truth is, none of the leaders we studied did *all* of what we've written about, nor did any of them focus on more than one or two strategies at a time. None were perfect. Nevertheless, all of the strategies we've discussed did come from a blend of theory and *actual* practice. Oh yes, and many leaders, over a period of several years, attempted virtually dozens of the tactics we've covered. All of the top performers held the broad theories and philosophies we've shared.

Our goal in *The Balancing Act* has been to provide a comprehensive guide that can be returned to again and again. We chose not to describe the world as out of control (a type of "chaos" that means you never have to say you're sorry), nor to suggest that a clever aphorism, fortune-cookie adage, or single focus will win the brass ring. Instead, we took the road less traveled. We wrestled with a theory that helps ex-plain why people do what they do and then built from there. We settled on that rocky ground somewhere between chaos and cookies and ar-gued for careful analysis and constant learning.

Despite the not-too-popular message that there are no easy answers, there *is* a delightful ending to all of this. Leadership skills and theo-ries *can* be learned. The amazing top performers we've worked with over the past two decades have been an inspiration to all of us. Not because they've been faultless, but because they've been willing to take on the elephant of leadership perfection—one bite at a time.

That's all anyone can ask—and all anyone can do.

Notes

Introduction

1. Albert Bandura, *Social Learning Theory* (Englewood Cliffs, NJ: Prentice-Hall, 1977); Albert Bandura, *Social Foundations of Thought and Action: A Social Cognitive Theory* (Englewood Cliffs, NJ: Prentice-Hall, 1986); for a list of most of Albert Bandura's writings, see Richard I. Evans, *Albert Bandura: The Man and His Ideas—A Dialogue* (New York: Praeger, 1989), 91–108. Everett M. Rogers, *Diffusion of Innovations*, 3d ed. (New York: Free Press, 1983). For a list of most of Solomon E. Asch's writings, see Irvin Rock, ed., *The Legacy of Solomon Asch: Essays in Cognition and Social Psychology* (Hillsdale, NJ: Lawrence Erlbaum Associates, Publishers, 1990), 293–95.

Chapter 1

1. John P. Kotter and James L. Heskett, *Corporate Culture and Performance* (New York: Free Press, 1992).
2. John A. Byrne, "The horizontal corporation," *Business Week* (December 20, 1993): 76–81, quote on 78.
3. Colin M. Turnbull, *The Forest People* (London: Chatto and Windus, 1961), 44. Among the BaMbuti (a tribe of pygmies), "various degrees of illness are expressed by saying that someone is hot, with fever, ill, dead, completely or absolutely dead and, finally, dead forever. "
4. See Mason Haire, "The Concept of Power and the Concept of Man," in J. Steven Ott, ed., *Classic Readings in Organizational Behavior* (Pacific Grove, CA: Brooks/ Cole Publishing, 1989), 454–69.
5. Daniel Yankelovich and John Immerwahr, *Putting the Work Ethic to Work: A Public Agenda's Report on Restoring America's Competitive Vitality* (New York: Public Agenda Foundation, 1983).

Chapter 2

1. The theory is referred to as Social Learning Theory or as Social Cognitive Theory (see also the sources by Bandura in note 1 of the introduction). Albert Bandura comments on the wider implications in a person's life of getting rid of snake phobia: "For most people this was a dramatic personal change. Here they were plagued with this problem for 10, 15, 20, or 30 years and they were able to overcome it in a few hours. Many of them described their experience as follows: Their life had been distressed, handicapped and constrained by the phobia for a long period. They originally believed that personality patterns were so fixed that it would be very difficult to change them. As they mastered their phobia they began to think, 'If I can change this area of my life, surely there must be other areas in which I can be more venturesome.' They were then coming in and reporting that they had been putting themselves to the test and improving their public speaking, social behavior and the

like. There would be no reason to expect such generalized benefits if only behavior was being altered. It became evident that we were doing something much more fundamental than just removing a phobia. We were altering people's beliefs about their coping efficacy which they were then putting to the test, succeeding and initiating positive changes in other areas of their lives." Richard I. Evans, *Albert Bandura: The Man and His Ideas—A Dialogue* (New York: Praeger, 1989), 12–17, quote on 13.

On the snake phobics, see, for example, Albert Bandura and Nancy E. Adams, "Analysis of self-efficacy theory of behavioral change," *Cognitive Therapy and Research* 1 (1977): 287–310; Albert Bandura, Nancy E. Adams, and Janice Beyer, "Cognitive processes mediating behavioral change," *Journal of Personality and Social Psychology* 35 (1977): 125–39; and Albert Bandura, Robert W. Jeffery, and Carolyn L. Wright, "Efficacy of participant modeling as a function of response induction aids," *Journal of Abnormal Psychology* 83 (1974): 56–64. Fear of snakes is called *ophidiophobia*.

Chapter 4

1. William G. Ouchi, *Theory Z: How American Business Can Meet the Japanese Challenge* (New York: Avon, 1982).
2. Thomas J. Peters and Robert H. Waterman, Jr., *In Search of Excellence: Lessons from America's Best-Run Companies* (New York: Harper & Row, 1982).

Chapter 6

1. Approximately 20 percent of the inmates serving time in state prisons in 1991 (over 700,000) had no prior sentence (page 13). "Violent offenders made up 65% of inmates with no prior record" (page 13; "violent offenses" include homicide, sexual assault, robbery, assault, and some others). "Almost a quarter [23%] of inmates without a prior record were serving time for homicide," which includes murder and negligent manslaughter (page 13). Nearly half (49%) of the total number of inmates were serving time for a violent crime. Approximately 65% of these inmates had not been previously "convicted in the past of a violent crime," and about 27% of them had never been "sentenced in the past to probation or incarceration, as a juvenile or adult" (page 11). Of the total number of inmates, 12.4 percent were serving time for homicide (10.6 percent for murder and 1.8 percent for negligent manslaughter; pages 45). "Almost 75,000 inmates were serving a sentence for murder" (page 6).

   "Among inmates sentenced for a violent offense, women (48%) were nearly twice as likely as men (28%) to have committed a homicide. Nearly half of these women had murdered a relative or intimate" (page 16). The survey uses the categories "intimate," "relative," "well known," "acquaintance," "known by sight only," and "stranger." Of all inmates who had committed a violent crime, 32 percent had committed it against someone in the first three categories (intimate, relative, or well known). "Among violent inmates, women (36%) were more likely than men (16%) to have victimized a relative or intimate" (page 16). Note, however, that women make up only 5 percent of the inmate population (page 3). Allen Beck et al., *Survey of State Prison Inmates, 1991* (Washington, DC: U.S. Department of Justice, 1993), 3–5, 6, 11, 13, 16. On "victim-offender relationships," see also Homicide: Behavioral Aspects, in Sanford H. Kadish, *Encyclopedia of Crime and Justice*, 4 vols. (New York: Free Press, 1983), 2:852–53.
2. Robert B. Cialdini, *Influence: The Psychology of Persuasion*, rev. ed. (New York: William Morrow, 1993), 119.

3. Velcro is a registered trademark of Velcro USA. Teflon is a registered trademark of Du Pont.
4. One of the authors heard this story at Stanford from Al Hastorf, Benjamin Scott Professor of Human Biology and Professor Psychology Emeritus there.
5. Joanne Martin and Melanie E. Powers, "Organizational Stories: More Vivid and Persuasive Than Quantitative Data," in Barry M. Staw, ed., *Psychological Foundations of Organizational Behavior*, 2d ed. (Glenview, IL: Scott, Foresman and Company, 1983), 161–68. See also Ron Zemke, "Storytelling: Back to a basic," *Training* 27 (March 1990): 44–50.

Chapter 7

1. William Foote Whyte et al., *Money and Motivation: An Analysis of Incentives in Industry* (New York: Harper & Brothers, 1955), 90–96.
2. Frederick Herzberg, "One More Time: How Do You Motivate Employees?" in J. Steven Ott, ed., *Classic Readings in Organizational Behavior* (Pacific Grove, CA: Brooks/Cole Publishing, 1989), 93–107.
3. Mark R. Lepper, David Greene, and Richard E. Nisbett, "Undermining children's intrinsic interest with extrinsic reward: A test of the 'overjustification' hypothesis," *Journal of Personality and Social Psychology* 28 (1973): 129–37.
4. Alfie Kohn, *Punished by Rewards: The Trouble with Gold Stars, Incentive Plans, A's, Praise, and Other Bribes* (New York: Houghton Mifflin Company, 1993). The Frederick Herzberg quotes on pages 173 and 184 are in Kohn, 189.

Chapter 9

1. Solomon E. Asch, "Effects of Group Pressure upon the Modification and Distortion of Judgments," in Harold S. Guetzkow, ed., *Groups, Leadership, and Men* (Pittsburgh, PA: Carnegie Press, 1951), 177–90. This article is conveniently reprinted in J. Steven Ott, ed., *Classic Readings in Organizational Behavior* (Pacific Grove, CA: Brooks/Cole Publishing, 1989), 152–62. These experiments are briefly discussed in Elliot Aronson, *The Social Animal*, 7th ed. (New York: W. H. Freeman and Company, 1995), 20–24; and Solomon E. Asch, "Opinions and social pressure," *Scientific American* 193 (November 1955): 31–35. Asch's series of studies is in Solomon E. Asch, "Studies of independence and conformity: A minority of one against a unanimous majority," *Psychological Monographs* 70 (1956).
2. Stanley Milgram, *Obedience to Authority: An Experimental View* (New York: Harper & Row, 1974). These experiments are briefly discussed in Aronson, *The Social Animal*, 40–46.
3. Martin T. Orne and Frederick J. Evans, "Social control in the psychological experiment: Antisocial behavior and hypnosis," *Journal of Personality and Social Psychology* 1 (1965): 189–200.
4. John M. Darley and C. Daniel Batson, " 'From Jerusalem to Jericho': A study of situational and dispositional variables in helping behavior," *Journal of Personality and Social Psychology* 27 (1973): 100–108.
5. A. M. Rosenthal, *Thirty-Eight Witnesses* (New York: McGraw-Hill, 1964). See also Robert B. Cialdini, *Influence: The Psychology of Persuasion*, rev. ed. (New York: William Morrow, 1993), 129–32; and Aronson, *The Social Animal*, 46–54.
6. Bibb Latané and Judith Rodin, "A lady in distress: Inhibiting effects of friends and strangers on bystander intervention," *Journal of Experimental Social Psychology* 5 (1969): 189–202.

7. Asch, "Effects of Group Pressure upon the Modification and Distortion of Judgments," 177–90. (See note 1.)
8. Milgram, *Obedience to Authority*. (See note 2.)
9. Frederick J. Roethlisberger, "The Hawthorne Experiments," in J. Steven Ott, ed., *Classic Readings in Organizational Behavior* (Pacific Grove, CA: Brooks/ Cole Publishing, 1989), 36–47, quote on 44. See also F. J. Roethlisberger, William J. Dickson, and Harold A. Wright, *Management and the Worker* (Cambridge, MA: Harvard University Press, 1964), 522.
10. Lester Coch and John R. P. French, Jr., "Overcoming resistance to change," *Human Relations* 1 (1948): 512–32. Also conveniently reprinted in J. Steven Ott, ed., *Classic Readings in Organizational Behavior* (Pacific Grove, CA: Brooks/Cole Publishing, 1989), 522–42, especially 530.

Chapter 10

1. Everett M. Rogers, *Diffusion of Innovations*, 3d ed. (New York: Free Press, 1983).
2. Ibid., xv, 15, 32–34, 54–56, 258, 266, 271. The story about the "Guy in Bermudas" is a somewhat fictionalized account.
3. Ibid., 11, 41, 243–45.
4. Ibid., 66, 187, 195–97, 289–93; figure on page 245.
5. Ibid., 241–70; figure on page 247.
6. The Yir Yoront (an isolated nomadic tribe of Australian aborigines) had used stone axes for centuries. Missionaries introduced steel axes "as gifts and as payment for work performed" to the Yir Yoront, hoping that a rapid improvement in living conditions would result. However, the consequences were unanticipated, far-reaching, and disruptive, and the religious system and social organization of the tribe became disorganized as a result of the tribe's inability to adjust to the innovation. Ibid., 32, 84, 389–90.
7. Ibid., 163–209, 271–370; figure on page 260 herein is taken from ibid., 165.
8. Ibid., 326–28.
9. Ibid., 277–81.

Chapter 11

1. Dumas Malone, *Jefferson the Virginian* (Boston: Little, Brown, 1948), 214, 241, 245–46.
2. Abraham Lincoln received an invitation on 2 November 1863 to speak at Gettysburg on 19 November 1863, 17 days later. He made at least two written drafts (perhaps more) of his Gettysburg Address and had made numerous revisions on those drafts, although his final speech differed somewhat from his last written draft (according to newspaper reporters and stenographers). See Carl Sandburg, *Abraham Lincoln: The Prairie Years and The War Years*, one-volume ed. (New York: Harcourt Brace Jovanovich, 1954), 439–47; Roy P. Basler, *The Collected Works of Abraham Lincoln*, 9 vols. (New Brunswick, NJ: Rutgers University Press, 1953), 7:17–23.
3. Jan Carlzon, *Moments of Truth* (Cambridge, MA: Ballinger, 1987).

Chapter 12

1. Dale Carnegie, *How to Win Friends and Influence People*, rev. ed. (New York: Simon and Schuster, 1981).
2. Shamu is a registered trademark of Sea World.

3. Masaaki Imai, Kaizen: *The Key to Japans Competitive Success* (New York: McGraw-Hill Publishing Company, 1986), 19–20, 107.

4. Ellen Graham, "A holiday hint: Dustbusters aren't forever, Jewels are," *Wall Street Journal* (December 11, 1990): A-1.

5. Alfie Kohn, *Punished by Rewards: The Trouble with Gold Stars, Incentive Plans, A's, Praise, and Other Bribes* (New York: Houghton Mifflin Company, 1993), 54–59, 136–38.

6. Virginia Franzen, *Reader's Digest* 139 (September 1991): 80.

Chapter 13

1. Although the "World Leadership Survey" indicates that a disparity exists regarding "access to information about company strategy" between those with the most responsibility and authority in a company and those with the least, the survey results are not specific enough to be very useful. See "World Leadership Survey," *Harvard Business Review* 68 (November-December 1990): between pages numbered 176 and 184. The results to this survey were reported in Rosabeth Moss Kanter, "Transcending business boundaries: 12,000 world managers view change," *Harvard Business Review* 69 (May-June 1991): 151–64.

   Here are some other questions in the survey related to sharing information. The totals are always (7%), often (26%), sometimes (44%), and never (23%) for the question, "Does your organization share strategic information with customers?" Ibid., 162. The totals are always (8%), often (29%), sometimes (46%), and never (17%) for the question, "Does your organization work with suppliers to design a product?" Ibid., 163.

Chapter 14

1. Allan M. Mohrman, Jr., Susan Albers Mohrman, and Edward E. Lawler III, "The Performance Management of Teams," in William J. Bruns, Jr., ed., *Performance Measurement, Evaluation, and Incentives* (Boston: Harvard Business School Press, 1992), 217–41.

Chapter 15

1. Fred I. Steele, *Physical Settings and Organization Development* (Reading, MA: Addison-Wesley Publishing Company, 1973), 8-9, 11, 111–45.

2. William F. Whyte, *Human Relations in the Restaurant Industry* (New York: McGraw-Hill, 1948).

   Whyte credits Edith Lentz, his research assistant, as the originator of the idea to use a spindle. See William Foote Whyte, *Participant Observer: An Autobiography* (Ithaca, NY: ILR Press, 1994), 150–54.

   Whyte also mentions that the waitresses put their written orders on spindles that were placed on a "warming compartment" that "was so high that only the taller waitresses could see over its top," thus eliminating the possibility of "friction" between waitresses and cooks. See William Foote Whyte, "The social structure of the restaurant," *American Journal of Sociology* 54 (1949): 302–10; and William Foote Whyte, *Men at Work* (Homewood, IL: Dorsey Press, 1961), 125–35.

3. Steele, *Physical Settings and Organization Development*, 8-9, 11, 111–45.

4. Ibid., 51–52.

5. Ibid., 41.

6. See note 1.
7. Everett M. Rogers, *Diffusion of Innovations*, 3d ed. (New York: Free Press, 1983), 294–95. This idea is also discussed in Tom Peters, *Liberation Management: Necessary Disorganization for the Nanosecond Nineties* (New York: Alfred A. Knopf, 1992), 257–92, especially 261. (Using Rogers's formula, the number 1,255 on page 261 in Peters should be 1,225.)
8. Peters, *Liberation Management*, 423–24.
9. Muzafer Sherif, *Intergroup Conflict and Cooperation: The Robbers Cave Experiment* (Norman, OK: University of Oklahoma Book Exchange, 1961).
10. David Halberstam, *The Reckoning* (New York: William Morrow and Company, 1986), 87.
11. See note 1.

Chapter 16

1. Charles Kuralt, *On the Road with Charles Kuralt* (New York: G. P. Putnam's Sons, 1985), 59–61, 153–54.
2. The first person who sends us a letter (ATTENTION: READING STATISTIC) with the correct source for this information will be sent a free copy of this book. For those interested in other statistics on reading, see "Signs encouraging for an upsurge in reading in America," *Gallup Poll Monthly* (February 1991): 43–53.

Recommended Reading

Aronson, Elliot, *The Social Animal*, 7th ed. (New York: W. H. Freeman, 1995).

Bandura, Albert, *Social Foundations of Thought and Action: A Social Cognitive Theory* (Englewood Cliffs, NJ: Prentice-Hall, 1986).

Bandura, Albert, *Social Learning Theory* (Englewood Cliffs, NJ: Prentice-Hall, 1977).

Beer, Michael, Russell A. Eisenstat, and Bert Spector, *The Critical Path to Corporate Renewal* (Boston, MA: Harvard Business School Press, 1990).

Belasco, James A., *Teaching the Elephant to Dance: Empowering Change in Your Organization* (New York: Crown Publishers, 1990).

Bennis, Warren, and Burt Nanus, *Leaders: The Strategies for Taking Charge* (New York: Harper & Row, 1985).

Bruns, William J., Jr., ed., *Performance Measurement, Evaluation, and Incentives* (Boston: Harvard Business School Press, 1992).

Cialdini, Robert B., *Influence: The Psychology of Persuasion*, rev. ed. (New York: William Morrow, 1993).

Collins, James C., and Jerry I. Porras, *Built to Last: Successful Habits of Visionary Companies* (New York: HarperBusiness, 1994).

Covey, Stephen R., *The Seven Habits of Highly Effective People: Restoring the Character Ethic* (New York: Simon and Schuster, 1989).

Hammer, Michael, and John Champy, *Reengineering the Corporation: A Manifesto for Business Revolution* (New York: HarperBusiness, 1993).

Imai, Masaaki, *Kaizen: The Key to Japan's Competitive Success* (New York: McGraw-Hill Publishing Company, 1986).

Katz, Daniel, and Robert L. Kahn, *The Social Psychology of Organizations*, 2d ed. (New York: John Wiley & Sons, 1978).

Kotter, John P., and James L. Heskett, *Corporate Culture and Performance* (New York: Free Press, 1992).

Leavitt, Harold J., *Managerial Psychology: An Introduction to Individuals, Pairs, and Groups in Organizations* (Chicago: University of Chicago Press, 1958).
Leavitt, Harold J., Louis R. Pondy, and David M. Boje, eds., *Readings in Managerial Psychology*, 4th ed. (Chicago: University of Chicago Press, 1989).

Milgram, Stanley, *Obedience to Authority: An Experimental View* (New York: Harper & Row, 1974).

Ouchi, William G., *Theory Z: How American Business Can Meet the Japanese Challenge* (New York: Avon, 1982).

Peters, Tom, *Thriving on Chaos: Handbook for a Management Revolution* (New York: Alfred A. Knopf, 1987).

Peters, Thomas J., and Robert H. Waterman, Jr., *In Search of Excellence: Lessons from America's Best-Run Companies* (New York: Harper & Row, 1982).

Rogers, Carl, *On Becoming a Person: A Therapist's View of Psychotherapy* (Boston: Houghton Mifflin, 1961).

Rogers, Everett M., *Diffusion of Innovations*, 3d ed. (New York: Free Press, 1983).

Seligman, Martin E. P., *Learned Optimism: How to Change Your Mind and Your Life* (New York: Pocket Books, 1990).

Senge, Peter M., *The Fifth Discipline: The Art and Practice of the Learning Organization* (New York: Doubleday, 1990).

Staw, Barry M., ed., *Psychological Foundations of Organizational Behavior*, 2d ed. (Glenview, IL: Scott, Foresman, 1983).

Von Oech, Roger, *A Whack on the Side of the Head: How You Can Be More Creative*, rev. ed. (New York: Warner Books, 1990).

Wilkins, Alan L., *Developing Corporate Character: How to Successfully Change an Organization without Destroying It* (San Francisco: Jossey-Bass Publishers, 1990).

Zimbardo, Philip, "Involvement and communication discrepancy as determinants of opinion conformity," *Journal of Abnormal and Social Psychology* 60 (1960): 86–94.

Zimbardo, Philip G., Ebbe B. Ebbesen, and Christina Maslach, *Influencing Attitudes and Changing Behavior: An Introduction to Method, Theory, and Applications of Social Control and Personal Power*, 2d ed. (Reading, MA: Addison-Wesley Publishing Company, 1977).

Index

A

Ability
  and behavior selection, 46–50
  organizational, 55
  relative, 148–149
  social, 54
Ability, individual, 53–54
  ferreting out, 204–207
Ability relevance, defined, 268
Acceptance data, 242–243
Accomplishments
  gauging how people feel about,
    324–325
  of group, rewarding, 330
Accountability, personal, 413–417
Adoption, of change, 255–261
Airline price wars, 9
Alienation, fighting, 411–413
Allen, Robert, vision of, 74–75
Analysis, Six-Cell, 130–131
Anthropology
  in leadership, 91–92
  as way to understanding culture,
    105–106
Appraisal form, updating, 383
Appraisals. *See* Self-appraisal, team
Asch, Solomon, 233–234, 238–240
Assumptions, defined, 96
AT&T, vision of, 74–75
Attention, acts worthy of, 356–358
Authority, deference to, 110, 232
Automobile industry, using CNV to
    predict changes in, 15

B

Balance, 29
  in Cell 6 issues, 422
  creating and maintaining, 2
"Barefoot doctors," 261–275
Behavior
  describing, getting good at, 137
  direct feedback on, 213–214
  influenced by tangibles, 388–389
  linking rewards to, 380–383

  linking vitality to, 129–130
  modeling, 206–207
  new, difficulty in implementing,
    444–445
  observing, on floor, 376–377
  See also Performance
Behavior enactment, models of,
    446–447
Behavior selection
  and ability, 46–50
  net-value, 57–58
  searching for useful theory of,
    33–38
Behavioral measures, creating,
    126–128
Behaviorism, 34–35
Believability, of sacrifice, 283–290
Books
  on leadership, 437
  recommended, 465–466
Brown-bag lunches, 292
Bureaucracy, 409–410
  reducing, 419–420
Bystander apathy, 232
  research into, 236–243

C

Calendars, as reminders, 452
Carnegie, Dale, 307
Change, 254–259
  focused passion for, 440–441
  organizational, guide to, 427–431
Choice
  individual, 183–184
  and involvement, 177–184
Clan, defined, 93
Clarity
  praising with, 319–322
  in rules for team, 349–352
CNV, 14
  at Kidney View Hospital, 26
  incomplete picture of, 17
Coach. See *Trainer*
Collaboration, 329–330
Command decisions, 179–180

465

New Releases from Thomson Executive Press

MANAGING DIVERSITY: PEOPLE SKILLS FOR A MULTICULTURAL WORKPLACE
by Norma Carr-Ruffino

Managing Diversity provides an inside look at meeting the challenges of cultural diversity in the workplace and profiting from its opportunities. Ideal for any manager or future manager—from the newest team leader to the accomplished head of the organization—this book will help you develop the people skills necessary to succeed in today's ever-changing, diverse work environment.

In addition to the main text, the *Managing Diversity Skill Builder* provides real-world cases and skill building exercises to help strengthen problem identification skills and solution strategies in the workplace.

WHY STOCKS GO UP (AND DOWN)
by Bill Pike

Why Stocks Go Up (and Down) provides a sound understanding of the fundamentals of investing in stocks and bonds—perfect for readers with little or no experience in the stock market, accounting, or finance. It details the basics of financial statements, public offerings, price/earnings ratios, and more—all with unusual clarity. *Why Stocks Go Up (and Down)* is the book you need to understand all the other investment books.

THE BUCK STARTS HERE: PROFIT-BASED SALES AND MARKETING MADE EASY
by Mary Molloy and Mike Molloy

A "must have" for anyone who needs to sell or market a product or service profitably. *The Buck Starts Here* focuses on how to stop spending money on sales and marketing activities that cannot be evaluated and start investing money in programs that accomplish specific, quantified, measurable business objectives.

Includes perforated workbook section containing all the blank forms discussed in the book—ready for use in your own business enterprise.

RULES OF THE GAME: GLOBAL BUSINESS PROTOCOL
by Nan Leaptrott

An essential tool for any businessperson in today's global business environment. Nan Leaptrott has applied her years of global business experience to present a simple, practical methodology for understanding cultural interaction today. *Rules of the Game* takes you beyond the "dos" and "don'ts" of international business customs to the rationale and reasoning behind these actions. With this thorough understanding of protocol and etiquette, you'll have the confidence to approach any culture and act consistently and effectively in all areas of business transactions.

Thomson Executive Press
A Division of South-Western College Publishing
5101 Madison Road
Cincinnati, Ohio 45227

To order, call the ITP Business, Industry and Government Group at 1-800-347-7707, or contact your local ITP sales representative.

To order additional copies of *The Balancing Act*, choose one of our

3 EASY WAYS TO ORDER

1) **By Phone:** Call 1-800-347-7707.
2) **By Fax:** Complete the order form below and fax it to 1-518-464-0342.
3) **By Mail:** Complete the order form; fold, staple, stamp, and mail.

- -

ORDER FORM

Shipping Address

Name _____

Organization _____

Address _____

City _____ State _____ Zip _____

Phone (_____)_____ Fax (_____) _____

Quantity	Title	ISBN	Unit Price	Total Price
1	*The Balancing Act*	0-538-86139-8	$27.95	$27.95
	Each additional copy sold at a 20% discount		$22.36	
Check Shipping Preference: ☐ Standard UPS ☐ 2-Day Delivery ☐ Overnight Express		Add sales tax if applicable		
		Shipping/handling		
		TOTAL AMOUNT		

Sales Tax

Residents of the following states should add appropriate sales tax:

Arkansas	Louisiana
Arizona	Missouri
California	North Carolina
Florida	Ohio
Georgia	Tennessee
Hawaii	Texas
Kentucky	Washington

Shipping

Calculate 8% of purchase price for regular UPS shipments. Add 10% for 2-day delivery; 12% for overnight.

Handling

$3.25 for orders under $50
$3.95 for orders totaling $50-$100
$4.25 for orders over $100

Payment

_____ Check enclosed. (Make check payable to: International Thomson Publishing.)

_____ Charge my credit card: ☐ Visa ☐ American Express ☐ MasterCard

Card Number: _____ Expiration Date: _____

Authorized Signature: _____

International Thomson Publishing
Business, Industry & Government Group
3 Columbia Circle
Box 15015
Albany, New York 12212-5015

(fold card here and staple loose ends together)